Abstracts
of the
Inventories
of the
PREROGATIVE COURT
of MARYLAND

Libers 110–118

1772–1774

Vernon L. Skinner, Jr.

Heritage Books
2024

HERITAGE BOOKS

AN IMPRINT OF HERITAGE BOOKS, INC.

Books, CDs, and more—Worldwide

For our listing of thousands of titles see our website
at
www.HeritageBooks.com

Published 2024 by
HERITAGE BOOKS, INC.
Publishing Division
5810 Ruatan Street
Berwyn Heights, MD 20740

Published 1988
Family Line Publications

International Standard Book Number
Paperbound: 978-1-58549-174-2

PREFACE

The probate records of the Prerogative Court of Maryland contain several types of records: testamentary proceedings, wills, administration accounts, inventories, accounts and inventories, and distributions. Each kind of record has value for the genealogist. Prior to 1777, all probate records were required to be filed with the Prerogative Court of Maryland.

An inventory was performed if the estate had moveable goods. The inventory included a listing of such things as clothes, household items, negroes, occupational tools. (A particular type of inventory cited debts due to the estate.) Items in the inventory reveal a great deal about the decedent and the family, especially his wealth, occupation, and manner of living. As part of the inventory, names of several other persons might be cited: appraiser(s) of the estate, creditors, next of kin (or relations), legatees, and administrators or executors.

The abstracts of the inventories herein cite the following:

Information about the inventory.
    Name of the decedent.
    Liber and folio reference.
    County.

Anne Arundel	AA	(1650)
Baltimore	BA	(1659)
Calvert	CA	(1654)
Caroline	CR	(1773)
Cecil	CE	(1674)
Charles	CH	(1658)
Dorchester	DO	(1668)
Frederick	FR	(1748)
Harford	HA	(1773)
Kent	KE	(1642)
Montgomery	MO	(1776)
Prince George's	PG	(1695)
Queen Anne	QA	(1706)
St. Mary's	SM	(1637)
Somerset	SO	(1666)
Talbot	TA	(1661)
Washington	WA	(1776)
Worcester	WO	(1742)

    Amount cited in the inventory. The amount is cited in pounds, shillings, and pence--the then currency. In some cases, the amount cited included part of a pence; this part has been dropped, for printing purposes.
    Date of the inventory.
    Date of the approval by the executor/administrator.

Name(s) of the appraiser(s).

Name(s) of the creditor(s).

Name(s) of the next of kin.

Name(s) of the executor/administrator.

Name(s) of other persons mentioned, except the persons cited in the list of debts.

All names are cited in the index; however, a name may appear more than once on a particular page. All efforts have been made to correctly interpret the names. However, sometimes the handwriting was difficult or impossible to read. The reader should refer to the original liber or photo-copy thereof when possible. No attempt has been made to coordinate differences in the spelling of names.

V. L. Skinner, Jr.
Brookeville, Maryland 20833
July 1988

Josiah Stamper (Quaker)   110.1   DO   £170.4.17   Jan 14 1772   Jun 17 1772
    Appraisers: Thomas Firmin Eccleston, Henry Dickinson.
    Creditors: William Wheland, James Gordon.
    Administrator: William Edmondson.

Josiah Stamper   110.6   DO   £147.6.10   Jun 17 1772
    List of debts.
    Administrator: William Edmondson.

Thomas Faulkner   110.8   DO   £13.1.12   Jul 27 1772
    List of debts.
    Mentions: Risdon Moore & Co., Anderton Eaton.
    Administrator: Nathan Faulkner.

Joseph Todd   110.9   DO   £1.0.4   May 5 1772
    List of debts.
    Administrator: Benjamin Todd.

Thomas Faulkner   110.9   DO   £25.18.6   Jul 27 1772
    List of debts.
    Administrator: Nathan Faulkner.

William Hatfield   110.10   DO   £54.12.3   Jun 23 1772
    List of debts.
    Administrator: Elijah Hatfield.

William Hitch   110.12   DO   £4.0.1   Jun 25 1772
    List of debts.
    Executor: Mary Hitch.

William Wright, Jr.   110.13   DO   £149.12.10   Mar 13 1772   Jun 17 1772
    Appraisers: G. Waters, John True.
    Creditors: Daniel Nicolls, James Wright.
    Next of kin: Roger Wright, Daniel Sulivane, Jr.
    Administratrix: Sarah Wright.

Joseph Bowdle   110.16   DO   £72.14.3   Jun 15 1772   Jul 20 1772
    Appraisers: Peter Edmondson, John Valliant.
    Creditors: Thomas Noele, Charles Blear.
    Next of kin: John Bowdle, Henry Bowdle.
    Executrix: Elisabeth Bowdle.

Thomas Faulkner   110.18   DO   £67.4.0   May 27 1772   Jul 27 1772
    Appraisers: Risdon Moore, Anderton Eaton.
    Creditors: William Richardson, Jr.
    Next of kin: William Douglass, Salathiel Faulkner, Asa Faulkner.
    Administrator: Nathan Faulkner.

George North   110.21   DO   £51.17.0   Apr 3 1772   Jun 9 1772
    Appraisers: Edmund Mace, Roger Jones.
    Creditors: Joseph Baron, Levin Dossey.
    Next of kin: Solomon Smith, Solomon Busick.
    Executrix: Rebecca North.

William Green, Jr.   110.23   Do   £18.3.6   Mar 18 1772   Jun 17 1772
    Appraisers: John Trice, James Hooper.
    Creditors: Joseph Richardson, Airey & Gilmor.
    Administratrix/Executrix: Elisabeth Green.

William Hatfield   110.25   DO   £75.1.8   Jun 25 1772
    Appraisers: Robert Clarkson, David Nutters.
    Creditors: Daniel Polk, John Richard.
    Next of kin: John Hatfield, Jonathon Hatfield.
    Administratrix: Elisabeth Hatfield.

Thomas Simmonds/Simmons   110.28   DO   £110.17.6   Apr 6 1772   Jun 21 1772
    Appraisers: William Jones, Thomas Vickars, Jr.
    Creditors: Archibald Pattison for Speirs & French & Co., Harrison & Sprigg.
    Next of kin: Peggay Simmons, Roseannah Simmons.
    Administratrix: Bridget Simmons.

William Hitch   110.31   DO   £93.5.7   Jun 5 1772   Jun 25 1772
    Appraisers: Robert Clarkson, David Nutter.
    Creditors: Daniel Polk, Manuel Manlove.
    Next of kin: Spence Hitch, Whitington Hitch.
    Executrix: Mary Hitch.

Samuel McClayland   110.34   TA   £6.18.2   1772   Aug 11 1772
    Appraisers: Charles Bullen, John Mulliken.
    Creditors: William Arrington, Daniel Maynadier, Jr.
    Next of kin: Fenley McClayland, Thomas McClayland.
    Administrator: William Stevens.

Cornelius Dailey   110.36   TA   £182.8.8   Mar 8 1769   Jul 14 1772
    Appraisers: William Kemp, John Gibson.
    Creditors: James Nichols (executor of George Lamberton), William Gibson.
    Administrator: Giles Hicks.

John Dobson   110.39   TA   £112.4.9   Sep 14 1762   May 5 1772
    Appraisers: James Baker, Thomas Robertson.
    Creditors: James Seth, Deborah Nicols
    Next of kin: James Dobson, Isaac Dobson.
    Administratrix: Jeane Scot.

Thomas Jenkins   110.41   TA   £103.3.1   1772   Jun 30 1772
    Appraisers: Charles Bullen, William Harrison.
    Creditors: William Stevens, William Hayward.
    Next of kin: Matthew Lewis Jenkins, Henry Jenkins.
    Administratrix: Lurana Jenkins.

John Harrison   110.42B   TA   £96.1.4   Oct 8 1769   Aug 12 1772
    Appraisers: William Sharp, Birkhead Sharp (dec'd by Aug 12 1772).
    Creditors: Prisilah Norriss, James Lloyd Chamberlaine, William Hanson.
    Next of kin: Mary Holmes.
    Administrator: William Harrison.

Solomon Perkins   110.45   TA   £69.16.0   Jun 6 1772   Aug 4 1772
    Appraisers: Samuel Cockayne, Aron Parratt.
    Creditors: Edward Trippe, John Martin.
    Next of kin: Philip Perkins.
    Administratrix: Mary Perkins.

George Laurence   110.49   TA   £102.1.11   Mar 10 1772   Aug 4 1772
    Appraisers: Solomon Neall, John Catogs.
    Creditors: Stevens Martins & Goldsborough, Richard Denny.
    Next of kin: Mary Hunt, George Hunt.
    Administratrix: Elisabeth Laurence.

Robert Brumwell   110.51   TA   £208.8.4   Nov 2 1771   Aug 4 1772
    Appraisers: Charles Pickarring, John Markland.
    Creditors: Charles Crookshanks, T. Sherwood.
    Next of kin: Edward Brumwell, Sarah Delahay.
    Administratrix: Mary Brumwell.

Thomas Powell   110.53   TA   £782.18.1   Mar 30 1772   Aug 4 1772
    Appraisers: George Dudley, Daniel Wilson.
    Creditors: Howell Powell, Matthais Gale.
    Next of kin: Howell Powell, Lydia Dickinson.
    Executrix: Elisabeth Powell.

George Eubanks   110.58   TA   £43.12.5   May 20 1772   Aug 5 1772
    Appraisers: Benjamin Parratt, George Dudley.
    Creditors: William Nicols, Robert Harwood.
    Next of kin: John Eubanks, Rebeca Eubanks.
    Administratrix: Rebecca Eubanks.

Rachel Willoughby   110.61   TA   £11.8.4   Jun 10 1772
    Appraisers: Samuel Hopkins, Richard Eaton.
    Creditors: Charles Crookshanks, Harrison & Sprigg.
    Next of kin: William Lee, Mary Mills.
    Administrator: John Willoughby.

John Faulkner/Falconer   110.62   TA   £161.11.0   Aug 7 1771   Aug 11 1772
    Appraisers: Abner Turner, James Kemp.
    Creditors: Tilghman & Nicols, Nicols & Chamberlaine.
    Next of kin: Jonathon Faulkner, James Plummer.
    Administratrix: Hannah Falconer.

Rachel Willoughby   110.65   TA   £153.17.2   May 27 1772   Jun 10 1772
    Appraisers: Samuel Hopkins, Richard Eaton.
    Creditors: Charles Crookshanks, Harrison & Sprigg.
    Next of kin: William Lee, Mary Mills.
    Administrator: John Willoughby.

Francis Register   110.68   TA   £51.1.7   Mar 28 1772   Jun 2 1772
    Appraisers: Henry Clark, Richard Johns.
    Creditors: Matthais Gale, Nicols & Chamberlaine.
    Next of kin: James Register, Hannah Register.
    Executor: William Nicols.

Macklin Elbert   110.70   TA   £180.17.4   Jan 24 1770
    Appraisers: Robert Pickering, Joseph Bewley.
    Creditors: Lodman Elbert, John Martin.
    Mentions: Mary Downes (late Elbert).
    Mentions: Jacob Seth, Charles Clayton.
    Mentions: William Bordley.
    Administrator/Executor: Mary Elbert (wife).

Thomas McCleland   110.73   TA   £19.18.2   Jun 1 1771   May 12 1772
    List of debts.
    Mentions: Joseph Bewley, Robert Pickering.
    Administrator: William Lavell.

John Price   110.74   TA   £3.6.2   Aug 24 1772
    List of debts.
    Administratrix: Rebecca Young.

Stephen Ratcliff   110.74   TA   £35.19.10   May 12 1772
    List of debts.
    Administratrix: Hannah Ratcliff.

John Martin   110.75   CH   £33.8.2   Nov 28 1771   Aug 19 1772
    Appraisers: William McConchie, Richard Barnes.
    Creditors: James Craik, Zaccheus Davis.
    Next of kin: Gillon Addams, George Adams, Levinia Martin.
    Administrator/Administratrix: Etheldar Martin.

Edward Ford   110.77   CH   £42.1.6   Sep 12 1772
    Appraisers: Stephen Compton, John Wilder.
    Next of kin: Richard Ford, Constrany Ford.
    Administrator: Charles Allison Ford.

Elisabeth Ford   110.78   CH   £164.3.10   Jul 10 1772   Sep 12 1772
    Appraisers: George Clk. Smoot, T. Harris.
    Creditors: George Gray.
    Next of kin: Allanson Ford, Charles Brandt.
    Administrator: Charles Allison Ford.

Humphrey Berry   110.80   CH   £298.4.9   May 14 1772   Oct 2 1772
    Appraisers: Thomas Smallwood, Jr., Richard Tubman.
    Creditors: Peter Campbell for John Glassford & Co.
    Next of kin: Joseph Berry, Hezekiah Berry.
    Executrix: Ann Berry.

Boles Bolthrop   110.82   CH   £483.7.6   Jun 10 1772   Aug 15 1772
    Appraisers: T. Harrison, Charles Brandt.
    Creditors: James Craik.
    Executors: Edward Smoot, Ann Bolthrop.

Miles McDonald/McDaniel   110.84   CH   £330.17.0   Jun 5 1772   Aug 15 1772
    Appraisers: Peter Dent, George Tubman.
    Creditors: Robert Mundell for John Glassford & Co., Joseph Aderton.
    Next of kin: Alexander McDonald, Zachariah McDonald.
    Administratrix: Ann McDaniel (widow).

Jacob Forry   110.86   CH   £17.0.3   Jul 24 1772   Aug 24 1772
    Appraisers: Thomas Semmes, Raphaele Neale.
    Creditors: Robert Mundell for John Glassford & Co., Zephaniah Turner for Barnes &
       Redgate.
    Administratrix: Rachel Leman (formerly Rachel Forey).

James Gray   110.87   CH   £409.3.6   Jul 20 1772   Sep 2 1772
    Appraisers: Richard Barnes, William McConchie.
    Creditors: Zephaniah Turner for Barnes & Redgate.
    Next of kin: John Gray, Benjamin Gray.
    Executors: Sophiah Gray, Jeremiah Gray.

Charles Ashcomp   110.91   SM   £268.19.0   Apr 9 1772   May 14 1772
    Appraisers: Richard Boarman,. William Bruce.
    Creditors: Robert Young for James Gordon & Co., Thomas Reider.
    Next of kin: Samuel Ashcom, Nathaniel Achcom.
    Administratrix: Margaret Ashcomp.

Teresa Stratford   110.93   SM   £137.0.0   Oct 9 1771   Mar 1 1772
    Appraisers: John Roberts, William Frazier.
    Creditors: William Hamenley.
    Next of kin: Ann Walker, William Rapour.
    Executor: Richard James Rapour.

John Baptie Lucas   110.95   SM   £48.15.7   Jun 12 1772   Sep 13 1772
     Appraisers: Enoch Fenwick, Ignatius Fenwick of E.
     Creditors: Athanasius Ford, Thomas Forrest.
     Next of kin: Elisabeth Lucas, Eleanor Lucas.
     Administratrix/Executrix: Ann Lucas.

Richard Barnhouse   110.97   SM   £446.6.5   Jul 1 1771   Aug 27 1771
     Appraisers: Kenelm Harison, Joseph Leigh.
     Creditors: Elisabeth Barnshouse, Robert Armstrong for James Buchanan & Co.
     Next of kin: Ann Barnhouse, Elisabeth Barnhouse.
     Executor: James Barnhouse.

George Fenwick   110.99   SM   £379.2.3   Aug 10 1772
     Appraisers: John Smith, Sr., Zachariah Forrest.
     Creditors: Archibald Campbell for James Gordon & Co., Athanasius Ford.
     Next of kin: Benjamin Fenwick, Robert Fenwick.
     Administrator/Executor: James Fenwick.

Mary Smith   110.102   SM   £202.5.2   Feb 19 1772   Sep 1772
     Appraisers: Thomas Richardson, Daniel Jenifer.
     Next of kin: Elisabeth Parrot Loker.
     Administrator/Executor: Michael Parker Jenifer.

Ignatius French   110.103   SM   £37.11.5   May 22 1772   Jul 21 1772
     Appraisers: Enoch Fenwick, Francis Borman.
     Mentions: John French, Ignatius French.
     Executor: James French.

Mr. Robert Cole   110.105   SM   £444.9.8   Aug 24 1772
     Appraisers: Clement Hayden, James Roach.
     Creditors: James Jordan & Co.
     Administrator/Executor: Robert Mattingly, Richard Melton, Bazil Hayden.

William Frasier   110.108   SM   £119.18.3   May 7 1772   Aug 29 1772
     Appraisers: Seneca Nelson, Joshua Graves.
     Creditors: James Jordan, John Ireland.
     Next of kin: Ann Simpson.
     Administratrix: Elisabeth Frasier.

John Francis Taney   110.110   SM   £879.18.0   Jun 16 1772   Jul 28 1772
     Appraisers: John Reeder, Jr., Ignatius Fenwick, Jr.
     Creditors: Archibald Campbell for James Gordon & Co., John Mussin for Alexander
          Cunningham & Co.
     Administrator/Executor: Elisabeth Taney, Nicholas Lewis Sewall.

John Glass   110.113   QA   £57.10.4   Jan 15 1772   Jun 25 1772
     Appraisers: John Fisher, Anthony Harrington.
     Creditors: James Nicols, Tilghman & Nicols.
     Next of kin: Margaret Glass (mother), Rebecca Glass (sister).
     Administratrix: Gartruge Glass.

Mathew Collins   110.115   QA   £58.12.7   Nov 17 1772   Aug 6 1772
     Appraisers: Basil Warfield, James O'Bryon.
     Creditors: Thomas Ringgold, James Hinson.
     Next of kin: William Collings, Mary Newton.
     Administratrix: Elisabeth Collins.

Richard Gafford   110.117   QA   £226.10.11   Mar 18 1772   Jun 24 1772
     Appraisers: B. Gould, Henry Elliott.
     Creditors: George Temple, John Sutton.
     Next of kin: Joseph Gafford, Richard Gafford.
     Executrix: Sarah Gafford.

Edgar Webb   110.120   QA   £103.15.8   Aug 6 1772
     Appraisers: Giles Hicks, Solomon Ranton.
     Creditors: Joshua Clark, Henry Casson.
     Next of kin: Mary Webb, Nancy Dwiggens.
     Administratrix: Ann Webb.

William Wyatt   110.122   WO   £77.2.2   Jun 6 1772   Aug 5 1772
     Appraisers: John Gibbins, Sr., John Cod.
     Creditors: Jehu Wyatt, William Holland.
     Next of kin: Jehu Wyatt, Dinah Latcham.
     Administrator: Caleb Wyatt.

William Pinder   110.124   QA   £282.16.8   Mar 2 1772   Jun 24 1772
     Appraisers: James Hackett, Richard Gould.
     Creditors: Edward Scott, Thomas Barratt.
     Next of kin: William Pinder, Sarah Comegys.
     Administrator: Edward Pinder.

Mr. Solomon Clayton   110.126   QA   £994.6.7   1768   Aug 3 1772
    Appraisers: John Willson, John Hammond.
    Creditors: Francis Hall, Edward Tilghmand.
    Next of kin: Edward Clayton, Charles Clayton.
    Executrix: Mary Clayton.

Hester Thompson   110.131   QA   £714.19.5   Oct 5 1771   Jul 2 1772
    Appraisers: John Brown, James Hackett.
    Creditors: Thomas Ringgold, Bishop & Walters.
    Next of kin: John Thompson, Catharine Thompson.
    Executor: Samuel Thompson, Sr.

Richard Smyth/Smith   110.136   QA   £104.19.10   Sep 18 1771   Aug 20 1772
    Appraisers: John Seeders, Charles Clayton.
    Creditors: Phil. Downes for William & James Anderson, Richard Willson for Robert
        Brown.
    Next of kin: Jonathon Green Smith, William Smith, Jr.
    Administratrix: Susanna Smith.

Thomas Meredith   110.138   QA   £307.13.10   May 21 1772   Aug 6 1772
    Appraisers: Basil Warfield, James Kent.
    Creditors: John Crawford, Charles Goldsborough.
    Next of kin: Sarah Meredith, John Meredith.
    Executors: Margaret Meredith, Thomas Meredith.

Rachel Chance   110.140   QA   £5.9.0   May 20 1772   Jul 2 1772
    Appraisers: Richard Mason, John Casson.
    Creditors: Thomas Young, Nicholas Price.
    Next of kin: Henry Oldfield, Elender Young.
    Executor: William Boon.

Boon Chance   110.141   QA   £69.14.2   Jan 20 1772   Jul 2 1772
    Appraisers: Richard Mason, John Casson.
    Creditors: Richard Chance, Absolom Chance.
    Next of kin: Richard Chance, Batchelder Chance.
    Executor: William Boon.

Matthew Bryon   110.143   QA   £519.19.9   May 21 1767   Jul 25 1772
    Appraisers: Samuel Waters, Jacob Seth.
    Creditors: Robert Campbell, William Hopper.
    Next of kin: Arthur Bryon, John Bryon.
    Executor: John Sayer Blake (surviving executor).

Isaac Turner   110.147   QA   £555.17.7   Apr 23 1772   Jun 24 1772
    Appraisers: Richard Mason, James Chetham.
    Creditors: William Moleston, Henry Casson.
    Next of kin: James Turner, Sarah Turner.
    Administratrix: Hannah Turner.

John Sherwood   110.150   QA   £0.18.9   Aug 20 1772
    Appraisers: John Downes, C. Downes, Jr.
    Next of kin: William Cowper Sherwood, Jonathon Sherwood.
    Administratrix: Catharine Sherwood.

John Pratt   110.150   QA   £35.15.10   Jan 13 1772   Oct 21 1772
    List of debts.
    Executor: Elisabeth Pratt.

Samuel Hodges   110.151   KE   £26.16.0   Oct 6 1772
    List of debts.
    Administrator: William Hodges.

William Williams   110.152   FR   £528.2.5   1772   Dec 10 1772
    Cash received.
    Executor/Executrix: Towen Williams.

William Williams   110.156   FR   £282.11.9   Sep 16 1769
    Appraisers: Zadok Magruder, Andrew Heugh.
    Mentions: Elisabeth Owen Williams, Elisha Owen Williams.
    Executor/Executrix: Towen Williams.

Lawrence Owen   110.156   FR   £334.3.5   Dec 12 1772
    Cash received.
    Administratrix/Executrix: Sarah Owen.

Thomas Harriss   110.160   FR   £212.1.2   Apr 29 1772   Sep 2 1772
    Appraisers: Allen Bowie, Edward Wheeler.
    Creditors: Robert Dirk, John Higdon.
    Next of kin: Nathan Harriss, Zachariah Harriss.
    Administrator: Nathaniel Harriss.

Samuel Howell   110.162   BA   £412.3.7   Nov 24 1772
    List of debts.
    Executrix: Sarah, wife of William Wirckworth.

Francis Neale   110.162   AA   £35.4.2   Aug 10 1772   Aug 20 1772
    Appraisers: John Campbell, Philip Hammond, Jr.
    Creditors: John Shuttleworth, Thomas Harwood.
    Administrator: Charles Oneale.

Nathaniel Adams   110.164   AA   £373.2.3   Sep 19 1772
    List of debts.
    Administratrix: Grace Adams, who married William Hutchings.

David Porter   110.164   BA   £8.15.9   Aug 13 1772
    Appraisers: Thomas Archer, John Hayes.
    Administrators: William McClare, David Dixon.

Winefred Lanham   110.165   PG   £10.10.0   Feb 26 1772   Mar 25 1772
    Appraisers: Henry Humfrey, Samuel Lusby.
    Creditors: Zachariah Jenkins.
    Next of kin: Edward Blackdock, Charity Blackdock.
    Executor: Edward Lanham.

Philip Pindell   110.166   AA   £1462.10.5   Jun 20 1770   Dec 15 1772
    Appraisers: Thomas Sprigg, Joseph Cowman.
    Creditors: John Thomas, Stephen Steward.
    Next of kin: Elisabeth Pindell, John Pindell.
    Executrix: Ann Pindell.

Samuel Daviss   110.170   AA   £53.14.3   Dec 1 1772   Dec 8 1772
    Appraisers: Gerrard Hopkins, Benjamin Gaither.
    Creditors: Joseph Johnson by John Davidson (attorney), Thomas Harwood, Jr.
    Next of kin: Richard Elliott, Robert Tongue.
    Administratrix: Catharine Daviss.

John Ashpaw   110.171   AA   £13.10.8   Nov 23 1772
    Appraisers: Daniel Smith, William Ridgely, Sr.
    Creditors: Charles Wiesenthal.
    Next of kin: George Ashpaw, Elisabeth Joyse.
    Administrator: Henry Ashpaw.

Isaac Hall   110.172   AA   £65.14.6   May 7 1772   Oct 24 1772
    Appraisers: Nehemiah Miller, Joseph Dorsey, Jr.
    Creditors: Samuel Duvall, Joseph Dorsey.
    Next of kin: son John Hall, son Joseph Hall.
    Administrator: James French.

Mrs. Meriam Richardson   110.174   FR   £1434.10.10 Mar 4 1767   Sep 23 1772
    Appraisers: David Lynn, Andrew Heugh.
    Next of kin: Meriam Haye, Jenny Waller.
    Executor: Samuel Chew.

Basil Wheeler   110.180   KE   £232.13.5   Nov 21 1771   Nov 9 1772
    Appraisers: John Williamson, Nathaniel Rogers.
    Creditors: Thomas Ringgold.
    Administratrix: Rebecca Wheeler.

Mary Scrivener   110.184   QA   £390.19.0   Nov 20 1772   Nov 20 1772
    Appraisers: John Birkhead, Samuel Birkhead.
    Creditors: Henry Darnall, Portland Manner, James Dick (attorney) for John
        Buchanan.
    Next of kin: Francis Scrivener, WIlliam Scrivener.
    Administrator: Francis Scrivener.

Benjamin Bowen   110.185   BA   £723.11.6   Mar 20 1772   Sep 14 1772
    Appraisers: George Ristead, Bale Owings.
    Creditors: William Lux & Bowley.
    Next of kin: Josias Bowen, Solomon Bowen.
    Executrix: Mary Bowen.

Mr. William Guyther   110.192   SM   £2833.19.3   Nov 10 1772
    Appraisers: Hugh Hopewell, Robert Watts.
    Creditors: J. Barnes, John McKay.
    Administrator: George Guyther.

Richard Chew   110.198   AA   £76.15.0   Apr 15 1771   Sep 22 1772
    Appraisers: Jacob Franklin, Isaac Hall.
    Executor: Richard Chew.

James Hollyday   110.198   AA   £14.11.11   Nov 1 1771   Dec 1 1772
    Appraisers: Thomas Deale, Samuel Lane.
    Administratrix: Sarah Hollyday.

Anthony Musgrove   110.199   AA   £74.17.4   Sep 7 1772   Dec 4 1772
    Appraisers: Anthony Holland, John Brown.
    Creditors: Edward Gaither & Mr. Raphael West, Thomas Gassaway (son of Michael).
    Next of kin: Samuel Musgrove, Sr., Samuel Musgrove (son of Anthony).
    Administrator: Anthony Musgrove.

Mr. John Worthington, Sr.   110.200   AA   £524.6.9   Aug 19 1766   Nov 12 1772
    Appraisers: Alexander Warfield, William Woodward.
    Next of kin: Samuel Worthington, Vachel Worthington.
    Executors: John Worthington, Charles Worthington.

Hezekiah Linthicum   110.202   AA   £153.16.8   1772   Dec 14 1772
    Appraisers: Gerrard Hopkins, Elijah Green.
    Creditors: Thomas Henry Hall, Jemima Sebby.
    Next of kin: Mary Towler, Richard Orruck.
    Administrator: John Linthicum.

George Ogg   110.204   BA   £501.17.17   Jan 1 1771   Aug 6 1772
    Appraisers: Nicholas Orrick, Christopher Owings.
    Creditors: Randall Hulse, William Lyon & Walker.
    Next of kin: Benjamin Ogg, William Ogg.
    Executrix: Hellen Ogg.

Ralph Smith   110.207   BA   £304.7.3   Sep 3 1772
    Appraisers: William Husband, Edward Morgan.
    Creditors: Francis Neill, James Armstrong.
    Next of kin: John Smith (son of Ralph), Jean Smith.
    Executors: Huldah Smith, Buckanna Smith.

Thomas Hutten   110.210   BA   £128.9.10   1772   Sep 22 1772
    Appraisers: Joseph Crock, Benjamin Mead.
    Next of kin: Choney Hutten, Aquilla Hutten.
    Administratrix: Catharine Hutten.

William Debruler   110.212   BA   £373.6.6   Sep 30 1772
    Appraisers: William Robinson Presbury, Henry Weatherall.
    Creditors: Buchanan & Cowan.
    Next of kin: William Presbury (mason), Cordelia Presbury.
    Executor: William Debruler.

William Wells   110.216   PG   ----   Nov 6 1772
    List of debts.
    Administrator: Thomas Smith.

John Cox   110.217   PG   £113.19.4   ----
    List of debts.
    Administratrix/Executrix: Sarah Cox.

Charles Robinson   110.217   BA   £47.8.2   Mar 27 1772   Sep 21 1772
    Appraisers: William Amoss, William Bull.
    Mentions: Richard Robinson.
    Executor: William Robinson.

Mary Beck   110.219   BA   £137.3.2   Nov 2 1772
(widow of Samuel Beck)
    Appraisers: John Day (son of Edward), John Waters.
    Creditors: James Maxwell, J. Beale Howard.
    Next of kin: Elijah Beck, Mathew Beck.
    Administratrix: Sarah, wife of Joseph Butten.

John Cox   110.222   PG   £697.18.8   1772   Aug 16 1772
    Appraisers: Thomas Morten, Thomas Freeman.
    Creditors: John Campbell for John Glassford & Co., Thomas Hamilton.
    Next of kin: Ann Cox, Walter B. Cox.
    Administratrix: Sarah Cox.

William Ramsey   110.225   BA   £26.16.5   May 6 1772   Oct 5 1772
    Appraisers: James Ellet, Benjamin Guyton.
    Creditors: Mordecai Durham, Jessey Bussey.
    Next of kin: Elisabeth Ramsey.
    Administratrix: Sarah Ramsey.

Smith Cornell   110.227   FR   £56.10.8   Jun 26 1772   Sep 24 1772
    Appraisers: Samuel McFerson, John McKorkle.
    Creditors: John McAllister, Samuel Wilson.
    Next of kin: Jacob Cornell, Benjamin Cornell
    Executors: Richard Cornell, William Cornell

Thomas Stonestreet, Sr.   110.230   PG   £565.5.6   Dec 18 1771   Mar 26 1772
    Appraisers: Robert Wade, Sr., Edward Clarkson.
    Next of kin: Basil W. Stonestreet, Edward Stonestreet.
    Executor: John Stonestreet.

Dobner Buckler Patridge   110.233   BA   £17.12.0   Jul 19 1772   Jul 20 1772
    Appraisers: William Wilkinson, William Lynch.
    Administrators/Executors: Ann Patridge, William Patridge.

Edward Stonestreet   110.234   PG   £240.15.11   Dec 16 1771   Mar 20 1772
    Appraisers: Robert Wade, Sr., Edward Clarkson.
    Creditors: Peter Campbell.
    Next of kin: John Stonestreet, Edward Stonestreet.
    Executrix: Eleanor Stonestreet.

John Cox   110.235   PG   £37.0.0
    List of debts.
    Administratrix: Sarah Cox.

William Wells   110.236   PG   £153.10.6   Mar 3 1772   Nov 10 1772
    Appraisers: Moses Orme, Jr., William Bright.
    Creditors: Charles Grahame for self and James Russell.
    Next of kin: Mary Marshall, Thomas Wells.
    Administratrix: Mary Wells (alias Mary Smith).

Mr. Francis Green   110.238   PG   £620.0.3   Apr 22 1772   Aug 28 1772
    Appraisers: Ignatius Wheeler, Robert Wade.
    Creditors: Peter Campbell for John Glassford & Co., William Beans.
    Next of kin: Benedict Green, Samuel Green.
    Administratrix: Elisabeth Green.

Henrietta Thompson   110.241   CH   £624.18.8   May 11 1772   Jul 13 1772
    Appraisers: William Leigh, George Keech.
    Creditors: Joseph Aderton, John Craigh for John and James Jemmison.
    Next of kin: Richard Borman, Joseph Thomas.
    Executrix: Rachel Brook.

Jane Jenkins   110.242   CH   £30.7.4   May 17 1772   Jul 11 1772
    Appraisers: Theophilus Yates, John Marshall.
    Creditors: Joseph Marbury for John Hanson, Jr., Dority Owens.
    Next of kin: John Jenkins, Philip Jenkins.
    Administrator: Thomas Jenkins.

William Nelson, Jr.   110.244   CH   £15.3.1   May 20 1772   Jul 9 1772
    Appraisers: William Braner, John Maddox.
    Creditors: John Craigh for John & James Jemmison, David Flint.
    Next of kin: William Nelson, Joseph Nelson.
    Administratrix: Elisabeth Nelson.

John Morningdoler   110.245   CH   £33.5.8   Dec 16 1771   Nov 13 1772
(also John Mourningdoler)
    Appraisers: Thomas Semmes, Raphael Neale.
    Creditors: James Craik, Anthony Bitting.
    Administrators: James Anderson, James Vineyard.

John Taylor   110.246   SM   £6.17.10   Oct 26 1772
    List of debts.
    Administratrix: Christian Taylor.

Basil Hamersley   110.247   CH   £311.9.8   Dec 10 1771   Feb 24 1772
    Appraisers: Stephen Compton, T. Harris.
    Creditors: Richard Leer, Ignatius Middleton.
    Next of kin: William Hamersley, Francis Hamersley.
    Administratrix/Executrix: Henrietta Hamersley.

Richard Brice   110.249   KE   £530.18.6   Oct 20 1772   Nov 4 1772
    Appraisers: Thomas Slipper, Hezekiah Dunn.
    Creditors: John Page, James Anderson.
    Executrix: Judah Brice.

Henry Glassford   110.253   KE   £124.10.3   Nov 18 1772
    List of debts.
    Executor: James Black.

John Younger   110.254   KE   £2.13.6   Aug 17 1772
    List of debts.
    Executor: Joseph Younger.

Isaac Boots   110.254   KE   £12.12.2   Nov 24 1772
    List of debts.
    Administratrix: Rebecca Boots.

Thomas Kennard   110.254   KE   £22.5.3   Oct 16 1772
    List of debts.
    Administratrix: Sarah Kennard.

Handy Beauchamp   110.255   SO   £100.0.9   Apr 3 1772   Aug 19 1772
    Appraisers: William Addams, David Lankford.
    Creditors: Planner Williams, Smith Horsey.
    Next of kin: Levin Beauchamp, Beauchamp Davis.
    Administratrix: Mary Beauchamp.

Stephen Bordley   110.257   KE   £830.1.6   1772
    Appraisers: James McClean, James Piner (dec'd by Mar 14 1772).
    Creditors: John Cadwalader, Richard Lloyd for Mr. James Anderson.
    Next of kin: Henry Bordley (uncle), Arthur Miller (uncle).
    Appraisers (on Mar 14 1772): James McClean, Emory Sudler.
    Administrators: William Bordley, Anthony Bordley.

Caleb Jackson   110.262   KE   £18.6.8   Jun 12 1766   Nov 5 1772
    Appraisers: Jarvis James, Joseph McHand.
    Creditors: Thomas Smyth.
    Next of kin: James Hull, Gideon Greenwood.
    Administrator/Executor: Thomas Smyth, gentleman.

George Greenwood   110.262   KE   £55.0.0   Jun 12 1765   Nov 5 1772
    Appraisers: Jarvis James, Joseph McHand.
    Creditors: Thomas Smyth.
    Next of kin: James Hull, Gideon Greenwood.
    Administrator: Thomas Smyth.

Thomas Bowers   110.263   KE   £235.5.8   Oct 26 1772   Nov 6 1772
    Appraisers: Charles Groome, St. Leger Everett.
    Creditors: John Weir, William Bordley.
    Next of kin: Pearce Bowers, William Bowers.
    Executor: Thomas Bowers.

William Cleaver   110.264   KE   £18.10.3   Dec 2 1772
    List of debts.
    Administratrix: Ann Cleaver, wife of John Frazier.

William Cleaver   110.265   KE   £22.14.3   Nov 14 1772   Dec 2 1772
    Appraisers: Charles Copper, Hezekiah Dunn.
    Creditors: Charles Copper, Elisabeth Cain.
    Next of kin: Benjamin Cleaver, Mary Cleaver.
    Administratrix: Ann Cleaver, wife of John Frazier.

John Garland   110.265   KE   £377.3.6   Aug 28 1772   Dec 9 1772
    Appraisers: William Hazel, Samuel West.
    Creditors: Mr. Griffin Miller, Nathan Menering.
    Next of kin: Elias Deal, James Garland.
    Administratrix: Rebecca Garland.

Elisabeth Hall   110.268   KE   £78.5.0   May 8 1772   Jun 29 1772
    Appraisers: Oliver Smith, A. Comegys.
    Next of kin: John Hall, Martha Hall.
    Administrator: Christopher Hall.

Ebenezar Blackiston   110.269   KE   £184.13.8   Jun 30 1772
    Appraisers: Michael Strong, Daniel Farrel.
    Creditors: Thomas Smyth, John Page.
    Next of kin: Stephen Blackiston, Michael Blackiston.
    Executrix: Henrietta Blackiston.

Robert Meeks   110.271   KE   £630.4.4   Mar 20 1772   Aug 19 1772
    Appraisers: Robert Buchanan, Charles Groome.
    Creditors: William Ringgold, Smyth & Sudler.
    Next of kin: Susannah Meeks, Ann Meeks.
    Executrix: Mary Meeks.

Michael Chandler   110.275   KE   £202.14.1   May 21 1772   Aug 9 1772
    Appraisers: Joseph Rasin, John Duyer.
    Creditors: Donaldson Yates, Abraham Cannell.
    Next of kin: Thomas Chandler, Nathaniel Chandler.
    Administrator: Tahponah Chandler.

Michael Reed   110.277   KE   £12.1.11   Apr 30 1772   Nov 11 1772
    Appraisers: Charles Hynson, Jr., Richard Hosier.
    Creditors: Nathaniel Aiken.
    Next of kin: Joseph Reed, Mary Reed.
    Administrator: William Reed.

Dr. John Smyth   110.278   --   £320.8.1   Sep 24 1772   Nov 21 1772
    List of debts.
    Executors: William Smyth, James Robert Blunt.

Dr. John Smyth   110.280   --   ----   Nov 16 1772
    List of debts.
    Executors: William Smyth, James Robert Blunt.

Adam Hall   110.283   TA   ----   Sep 6 1772
    List of debts.
    Administrators: Ebenezar Mackie, Robert Campbell.

Thomas Skinner   110.285   TA   £13.0.6   Apr 13 1772   Nov 10 1772
    Appraisers: Daniel Sherwood, William Trippe.
    Executor: Peter Denny.

Peter Harwood   110.285   TA   ----   Nov 3 1772
    List of debts.
    Administratrix: Mary Harwood (Quaker).

William Haley   110.287   QA   £10.14.8   Apr 10 1772   Sep 18 1772
    Appraisers: James O'Bryon, Basil Warfield.
    Creditors: Francis Clinton, William Carman.
    Administrator: William Evans.

Charles Goldsborough, Esq.   110.288   TA   £247.1.0   Dec 3 1772
    List of debts.
    Administrator: James Tilghman.

Mr. Andrew Fenia   110.289   QA   £29.4.0   1772   Sep 3 1772
    Appraisers: Samuel Walters, Gideon Emory.
    Creditors: John Keir, John Crawford for Speirs & French & Co.
    Next of kin: Margret Hambleton, Ann Turbut.
    Administrator: John Wilson.

William Webb   110.291   QA   £102.4.5   May 8 1772   Dec 12 1772
    Appraisers: Giles Hicks, John Casson.
    Creditors: James Kemp, Tilghman & Nicols.
    Next of kin: Mary Webb, James Webb.
    Executor: John Dwiggins.

William Kirkham   110.293   QA   £213.10.1   May 13 1772   Sep 12 1772
    Appraisers: Giles Hicks, William Dickinson.
    Creditors: Ann Downes, Francis Orrel.
    Next of kin: Rachel Meads, Rebecca Cooper.
    Executors: James Townsend, Charles Manship, Jr.

James Chapman   110.297   TA   ----   Oct 13 1772
    List of debts.
    Executor: James Chapman.

Mr. Barnaby Doherty   110.299   TA   £317.9.6   Jul 9 1772   Oct 20 1772
(merchant)
    Appraisers: Robert Pickering, Joseph Bewley.
    Creditors: James Wrightstone, Jr., Benjamin Sands.
    Administrator: John Doherty.

Patrick Conerly   110.302   DO   £40.7.1   Jul 4 1772   Aug 12 1772
    Appraisers: George Waters, Joseph Wright.
    Creditors: James Murray, Charles Dickinson.
    Next of kin: Jeremiah Connelly, Terry Connelly.
    Administratrix: Elisabeth Conerly.

Elisabeth Ealey   110.304   TA   ----   Nov 11 1772
    List of debts.
    Executor: Thomas Tibbol.

Matthew Kirwan   110.305   DO   £18.15.7   Aug 25 1772   Sep 7 1772
    List of debts.
    Appraisers: Benjamin Todd, Henry Lake.
    Executrix: Judah Kirwan.

William Wright, Sr.   110.306   DO   £61.15.6   Jul 1 1772   Sep 4 1772
    Appraisers: John True, Thomas Smith.
    Creditors: Henry Steele, Sarah Addams.
    Next of kin: Edmund Wright, Levin Wright.
    Administrator: Jacob Wright.

Addam Hill   110.308   TA   £1798.8.2   Sep 6 1772
    List of debts.
    Administrators: Ebenezar Mackie, Robert Campbell.

James Farguson   110.309   DO   £46.7.0   Oct 2 1772
(also Talbot County)
    List of debts.
    Administratrix: Rosannah Farguson.

Zebulon Keene   110.310   DO   £39.15.15   Oct 14 1772
    List of debts.
    Executor: Richard Keene.

Zebulon Keene   110.310   DO   £8.6.5   Nov 14 1772
    List of debts.
    Executor: Richard Keene.

William Ailett   110.311   QA   £11.2.0   Apr 27 1772   Nov 9 1772
    Appraisers: John Fisher, Anthony Harrington.
    Creditors: Tilghman & Nicols, William Bordley.
    Next of kin: Mathew Ailett, James Ailett.
    Administratrix: Frances Ailett.

Daniel Sherwood   110.312   TA   £0.14.9   Aug 28 1772
    List of debts.
    Administrator: Hugh Bin (?).

Robert Polk   110.312   DO   £379.14.2   Aug 10 1772
    List of debts.
    Surviving Executor: Daniel Polk.

John Prichard/Pritchard   110.313   TA   £39.17.9   Apr 14 1772   Nov 10 1772
    Appraisers: Christopher Birkhead, Peter Stevens.
    Mentions: Prichard Delehay, Samuel Chamberlain, Jr., John Pritchard, John
        Higgins.
    Administrator: Richard Pritchard.

Stephen Bryon   110.315   KE   £530.5.6   Nov 5 1772
(also Queen Anne's County)
    Appraisers: Henry Carter, Thomas Elliott.
    Creditors: Emory Sudler, James Hutchings, Jr.
    Next of kin: Richard Goodman, Marmaduke Goodman.
    Administratrix: Hannah Bryon.

James Garner   110.317   QA   £97.10.11   Oct 5 1772   Oct 1 1772
    Appraisers: Giles Hicks, Jeremiah Colston.
    Creditors: Benson Stainson, Henry Casson.
    Next of kin: Parrish Garner, Joseph Garner.
    Administratrix: Alice Garner.

Zebulon Pritchett   110.319   DO   £150.1.0   May 18 1772   Aug 3 1772
    Appraisers: Naboth Hart, Benjamin Todd.
    Creditors: Robert Hanson.
    Next of kin: Henry Pritchett.
    Administratrix: Jane Pritchett.

James Farguson   110.321   DO   £31.1.0   Aug 20 1772
    List of debts.
    Administratrix: Rosannah Farguson.

William Langrell   110.322   DO   £3.12.3   Sep 7 1772   Sep 19 1772
    List of debts.
    Appraisers: Henry Lake, Naboth Hart.
    Administrator: William Langrell, Jr.

Thomas Griffith   110.322   DO   £80.19.3   Nov 26 1772   Feb 15 1773
    Appraisers: Joseph Robson, Henry Keene.
    Creditors: Mathew Travers, John Byrn.
    Next of kin: Mary Pattison, John Pattison.
    Administratrix: Elisabeth Griffith.

Thomas Wheeler   110.324   DO   £10.1.6   Jan 1 1773
    Appraisers: William Jones, Benjamin Woodward.
    Creditors: William Graham.
    Next of kin: Thomas Wheeler, Charles Wheeler.
    Administratrix: Mary Wheeler.

Stephen Quinnerly   110.325   DO   £137.18.7   Oct 25 1772   Jan 19 1773
    Appraisers: John Dehorty, Marcy Fountain.
    Creditors: Thomas White for Col. Edward Lloyd, Thomas Baynard.
    Next of kin: Rebecca Quinnelle, Priscilla Quinelle.
    Administrator: Edgar Rumbly.

Joseph Stewart   110.328   DO   £31.11.0   May 11 1772   Feb 2 1773
    Appraisers: William Jones, Benjamin Woodward.
    Creditors: Michael Burke, Henry Wright.
    Next of kin: James Stewart, Thomas Stewart.
    Administratrix: Elisabeth Stewart.

Henry Keene   110.330   DO   £23.19.3   Dec 17 1772
    List of debts.
    Executors: John Keene, Benjamin Keene.

James Breeding   110.331   DO   £79.18.11   Nov 28 1772   Dec 16 1772
    Appraisers: Nathaniel Potter, Nicholas Fountain.
    Creditors: Nichols & Chamberlain, Thomas Baynard.
    Next of kin: Robert Bishop, John Breeding.
    Administratrix: Margaret Breeding.

Rebecca Barnett   110.335   QA   £41.7.6   Jan 18 1772   Jan 13 1773
    Appraisers: John Wright, John Atkinson.
    Creditors: Jacob McGonegill, James Smith.
    Next of kin: Sarah Thompson, Robert Smith.
    Administrator: Robert Smith.

Jacob Boone   110.337   QA   £7.2.6   Aug 17 1770   Mar 4 1773
    List of debts.
    Executrix: Hannah Boone.

Isaac Turner   110.338   QA   £107.4.8   Feb 21 1773
    List of debts.
    Administratrix: Hannah Turner.

James Caradine   110.339   QA   £14.6.9   Jul 31 1770   Feb 23 1773
    Appraisers: William Blackiston, Nal. Burroughs.
    Creditors: Gilpin & Hann, Chaney Clough.
    Next of kin: Samuel Carradine, Samuel Dyne Belton.
    Administrator: John Fisher.

William Harris   110.340   QA   £308.6.6   Apr 23 1772   Jan 15 1773
    Appraisers: B. Gould, Vachel Downes.
    Creditors: Philemon Downes for James Anderson, Richard Willson for Robert Brown.
    Next of kin: Thomas Harris, C. Garnett.
    Administratrix: Elisabeth Harris.

Nathan Bowen   110.344   BA   £369.15.7   Feb 12 1771   1773
    Appraisers: Henry Stevenson, Nicholas Haill.
    Creditors: Jonathon Plowman, William Lux.
    Next of kin: Nathan Bowen, Jehu Bowen.
    Executrix: Mary Bowen.

John Orrick   110.346   BA   £161.5.9   Jan 27 1773
    List of debts.
    Administratrix: Carroline Orrick.

John Orrick   110.348   BA   £37.11.6   Jan 27 1773
    List of debts.
    Administratrix: Carroline Orrick.

Peter Butler   110.350   BA   £145.14.6   Nov 17 1771   Mar 4 1773
    Appraisers: Jacob Johnson, Samuel Price.
    Creditors: Thomas Talbot, John Bacon.
    Executrix: Jane Butler.

Hannah Hughes   110.352   BA   £75.10.0   May 30 1772   Jan 13 1773
    Appraisers: John Hart, Mark Alexander.
    Creditors: Henry Stevenson.
    Next of kin: Susannah Norwood, Rebecca Carter.
    Executrix: Arania, wife of Patrick Kennedy.

Joseph Lewis   110.354   BA   £41.15.3   Feb 20 1773
    List of debts.
    Administrator: Clement Lewis.

Mr. John Ensor, Jr.   110.354   BA   £967.11.9   Nov 16 1771   Jan 18 1773
    Appraisers: William Aisquith, Mordecai Gist.
    Creditors: Nicholas Merryman, Thomas Jones.
    Next of kin: Abraham Eason, Joseph Ensor.
    Administrator: Nathaniel Griffith.

George Ensor   110.361   BA   £225.19.5   Feb 5 1773
    Appraisers: Nicholas Merryman, Mordecai Price.
    Creditors: John Merryman, Jr., Nathan Griffith (administrator for John Ensor,
        Jr., deceased).
    Next of kin: Humprey Chilicate, Darby Ensor.
    Executors: George Ensor, Elisabeth Ensor.

Thomas Goldsmith   110.362   BA   £16.1.0   Jul 13 1771   Mar 3 1773
    Appraisers: John Howard, Robert Bishop.
    Creditors: John Dale, Jr., William Bond (son of Jos.).
    Next of kin: William Copeland Goldsmith, Sarah Toomey.
    Administratrix: Lilly Goldsmith.

Abraham Musgrove (taylor)   110.363   BA   £22.4.6   Dec 9 1772   Mar 11 1773
    Appraisers: Conrad Small, John Stoler.
    Creditors: Job Greene, Richard Parker.
    Next of kin: John Musgrove.
    Administrator: William Spencer.

Thomas Rutter   110.365   BA   £110.6.6   Apr 1 1773
    Appraisers: Richard Clark, John Woodward.
    Creditors: John Cattely, John Ashburner.
    Next of kin: Thomas Rutter, Joseph Rutter.
    Administrator/Executor: Hannah Rutter.

James Chilicate   110.367   BA   £224.16.10   Dec 18 1770   Mar 13 1773
    Appraisers: John Bond, Sr., William Tipton.
    Creditors: John Merryman, Jr., John Griffith & Bros.
    Next of kin: John Chilcoate, Humphrey Chilcoate.
    Administrators: John Chilicate, Sarah Chilicate.

Joseph Lewis   110.368   BA   £2.8.5   Feb 20 1773
    List of debts.
    Administrator: Clement Lewis.

William Hagan   110.369   CH   £735.6.0   Oct 10 1772   Dec 16 1772
    Appraisers: Thomas Bowling, Joshua Sanders.
    Creditors: Edward Johnson, Robert Young for John Glassford & Co.
    Next of kin: John Hagan, Joseph Hagan.
    Executor: Joshua Mills.

Mrs. Ann Brooke   110.372   CH   £314.15.0   Jun 9 1772   Jan 8 1773
    Appraisers: Francis Ware, S. Hanson, Jr.
    Creditors: Robert Mundale for John Glassford & Co.
    Next of kin: C. Brooke. (no other kin of age)
    Administrator: Leonard Brooke.

Baker Brooke   110.373   CH   £864.13.0   Jun 20 1771   Jan 8 1773
    Appraisers: Henry Hagan, Samuel Hanson, Jr.
    Creditors: John Craigh for John and James Jemmison.
    Next of kin: C. Brooke. (no other kin of age)
    Executor: Leonard Brooke.

Joseph Chick   110.377   CE   £194.17.6   Sep 12 1772
    Appraisers: Thomas Bouldin, Jesse Bouldin.
    Mentions: Mrs. Mary Chick, Rebecca Chick, Andrew Wallace.
    Administratrix: Mary Chick.

Elisabeth Armstrong   110.379   CE   £3.9.2   Nov 3 1772
    List of debts.
    Administrator: James Glasgow.

John Riddle   110.380   CE   £46.14.5   Aug 31 1772   Oct 17 1772
    Appraisers: Jonathon Hartshorn, Samuel Miller.
    Mentions: Samuel Riddle, George Riddle.
    Administratrix: Jennett Riddle.

Robert Makey/Marky   110.381   CE   £169.4.9   Sep 29 1772   Oct 31 1772
    Appraisers: Moses Andrews, Joseph Wallace.
    Creditors: James Coun (?).
    Next of kin: David Marky, William Marky.
    Executor: James Markey.

Jane Michel/Mitchell   110.383   CE   £12.9.7   Jul 11 1772
    Appraisers: Thomas Cord, John Cather.
    Executor: William Kirkpatrick.

Joseph Chick   110.384   CE   £64.18.1   Sep 12 1772
    List of debts.
    Administratrix: Mary Chick.

Henry Hendrickson   110.385   CE   £218.9.4   Apr 14 1772   Oct 14 1772
    Appraisers: William Wamsley, John Money.
    Creditors: Augustine Hendrickson.
    Next of kin: Andrew Boyce, Buthew Etherington.
    Executors: Augustine Hendrickson, John Hendrickson.

Elisabeth Armstrong   110.387   CE   £17.12.4   Oct 21 1760   Nov 3 1772
     Appraisers: Jonathon Hartshorn, Thomas Underhill.
     Mentions: William McClure, Esther Brown.
     Administrators: James Glasgow.

Mr. Roger Brooke, Sr.   110.389   CA   £1511.4.7   Apr 15 1772   Sep 29 1772
     Appraisers: John Brome, Isaac Clare.
     Creditors: Samuel Gray for Mr. William Mollison, Francis Kirshaw.
     Next of kin: Elisabeth Brooke, Ann Brooke.
     Legacies: Michael Taney, Elisabeth Brooke, Sarah Brooke, Boyer Brooke, Ann
        Brooke, Dorothy Brooke.
     Mentions: widow and 8 children.
     Executors: Elisabeth Brooke, Roger Brooke, Basil Brooke, John Brooke.

Alexander Kelly   110.397   KE   £245.14.7   Dec 21 1772
     List of debts.
     Administrator: Nathaniel Comegys.

Mr. John Wallis (of John)   110.398   KE   £175.10.8   Oct 16 1772
     Appraisers: John Eccleston, John Maxwell.
     Creditors: James Black, Thomas Ringgold.
     Next of kin: Francis Wallis, Hannah Wallis.
     Administrators: Henrietta Wallis, Henry Wallis (Quaker).

John Wallace   110.399   KE   £144.5.11   Nov 4 1772
     Appraisers: James McClain, James Claypoole.
     Creditors: A. Calder, John Green.
     Executors: James Anderson, Thomas Bedingfield Hands, John Bolten.

Augustine Boyer   110.400   KE   £1285.9.7   Nov 6 1772
     Appraisers: Daniel Massey, Alexander Baud.
     Next of kin: Nathaniel Boyer, Thomas Boyer.
     Executors: Thomas Boyer, Augustine Boyer, Jr.

Bridget Wise   110.405   KE   £8.12.6   Dec 2 1772
     List of debts.
     Administrator: John McGowin.

Alexander McClain   110.406   KE   £13.17.6   Jan 6 1773
     List of debts.
     Sureties: Samuel Lowman, Richard Willis.
     Next of kin: Alexander McClain (son).
     Mentions: John Page.

Ebenezar Blackiston   110.406   KE   £15.2.0   Dec 22 1772
     Executrix: Henrietta Blackiston.

Thomas Bowers   110.407   KE   £50.6.11   Dec 29 1772
     Cash received.
     Executor: Thomas Bowers.

Ann Blackiston   110.407   KE   £8.0.0   Feb 16 1773
     List of debts.
     Executor: Joseph Blackiston.

Dorcas Hollis   110.408   KE   £78.17.4   May 6 1772   Jan 6 1773
     Appraisers: William Hodges, John Beck.
     Creditors: William Elborn, Thomas Smyth (adminstrator of Richard Graham).
     Next of kin: Hannah Kelly, Thomas Jerrum.
     Executor: John Page.

Thomas Spencer   110.411   KE   £33.0.11   Jan 27 1773
     Appraisers: James Dunn, Charles Hynson, Sr.
     Creditors: Peregrine Frisby.
     Next of kin: Mary Duffee, Thomas Spencer.
     Administrator: Isaac Perkins.

Rudulph More   110.412   KE   £436.4.9   Nov 9 1772   Jan 3 1773
     Appraisers: John Eccleston, John Comegys.
     Creditors: Thomas Gilpin & Co.
     Executor: Ealie More.

Bridget Wise   110.414   KE   £2.2.6   Dec 2 1772
     List of debts.
     Administrator: John McGowan.

Ebenezar Blackiston   110.415   KE   ----   Dec 22 1772
     List of debts.
     Administratrix/Executrix: Henrietta Blackiston.

John Ritter   110.415   FR   £57.3.6   Mar 9 1772   Feb 3 1773
    Appraisers: Johannes Hirschurn, Georg Hirschurn.
    Creditors: Samuel Beall.
    Next of kin: Abraham Ritter, Marget Ritter.
    Executor: Conrad Ritter.

Josiah Chapline   110.416   FR   £212.6.6   Jan 14 1773
    Appraisers: George Walls, Posthumous Clagett.
    Creditors: Ephraim Gaither, John Duncan.
    Next of kin: Joseph Chapline, William Good.
    Administrator: Moses Chapline.

Jacob Powles   110.418   FR   £183.18.5   Dec 27 1772
    Appraisers: Jacob Downes, John Eberle.
    Creditors: Levin Hardie, Keiser Kremer.
    Next of kin: Nicholas Paulus.
    Executors: Susannah Powles, George Striker.

Henry Broome   110.420   CA   £438.19.11   Apr 8 1771   Feb 3 1773
    Appraisers: Samuel Hun, Joseph Wilson.
    Creditors: Edward Hall & Co., Thomas Freeman.
    Next of kin: John Brome, Thomas Brome.
    Administratrix: Ann Broome.

William Blackburn   110.422   CA   £153.13.9   Dec 14 1770 Jan 19 1773
    Appraisers: Samuel Dare, Isaac Clare.
    Creditors: Edward Hall & Co., Elisabeth Darrumple.
    Next of kin: David Blackburn, John Blackburn.
    Administratrix: Elenor Blackburn.

Capt. Robert Brice   110.425   AA   £81.2.0   Feb 15 1772 Jan 11 1773
    Appraisers: John Campbell, Allen Quynn.
    Creditors: Charles Brown & Co., John Davidson.
    Administratrix: Frances Brice.

Robert Davis   110.428   AA   £918.16.0   Jan 12 1773
    Appraisers: Thomas Gassaway, Sr., Richard Burgess.
    Creditors: Brown Pirkens & Buchanan, James Dirk & Stewart.
    Next of kin: Robert Pain Davis, Sarah Davis.
    Administratrix: Sarah Davis.

John Worthington   110.432   AA   £61.17.3   Mar 3 1773
    List of debts.
    Executor: John Worthington.

Robert Gilchrist   110.433   BA   £1.16.1   Dec 18 1772
    Appraisers: Christopher Randall, Robert Weir.
    Mentions: William Gilchrist, Robert Gilchrist.
    Administrator: John Welch.

Thomas Watkins   110.434   AA   £20.3.7   Jan 14 1773
    Appraisers: William Woodward, John Hall (son of Edward).
    Creditors: Thomas Harwood, Jr., John Brice, Robert Couden.
    Next of kin: Liddia Johnson, Rachel Watkins.
    Executor: Vachel Sewell.

William Chalmers   110.434   QA   £90.17.5   Aug 10 1771 Dec 10 1772
    Appraisers: Thomas Barnes, Jr., Arthur Emory, Jr.
    Creditors: Emory Sudler, Emory Sudler for Smyth & Sudler, Johnson Eareckson.
    Next of kin: John Bell, James Chalmers.
    Administrator: William Stevens.

Thomas Taylor   111.1   DO   £760.8.0   Aug 21 1772
    Appraisers: Arthur Whitely, John Anderson.
    Creditors: Landon Ball, Daniel Sulivane, Jr.
    Next of kin: John Taylor, Sarah Taylor.
    Executors: Sarah Taylor, William Taylor.

John Long   111.7   WO   £119.7.10   Jul 21 1770 Dec 11 1771
    Appraisers: John Teague, William Smook.
    Creditors: Ebenezar Campbell, William Fassitt.
    Next of kin: Daniel Long, Jesse Long.
    Administratrix/Executrix: Elisabeth ------ (no surname given).

Mary Hurly   111.9   DO   £84.1.9   May 27 1772 Nov 12 1772
    Appraisers: Arthur Addison, Curtis Darby.
    Next of kin: Darby Hurly, John Hurly.
    Administrator: Daniel Walter.

William Robertson   111.11   SO   £2.19.0   Mar 4 1772   Sep 23 1772
    Appraisers: George Gilliss, Joseph Venables.
    Administrator: William Badly.

Henry Grimes   111.12   SO   £102.13.5   Aug 8 1772   Nov 4 1772
     Appraisers: George Gilliss, Joseph Venables.
     Creditors: Hugh McBryde & Co., John Paremore.
     Next of kin: Ezekiel Graham, Mary Graham.
     Executrix: Ann Grimes.

George Cunningham   111.16   CE   £60.10.0   Feb 6 1771
     List of debts.
     Administratrix: Sarah Cunningham.

William Bavington   111.16   CE   £200.3.9   ----
     List of debts.

David Clark   111.17   CE   £462.7.0   Oct 18 1770   Jan 23 1771
     Appraisers: James Boyles, James Bolden.
     Creditors: Moses Scott, Hugh Matthews.
     Next of kin: Thomas Clark, Jeme Janvier.
     Administrator: William Clark.

William Hicks Travers   111.19   DO   £246.4.10   Sep 25 1772   Nov 12 1772
(also William Hicks Traverse)
     Appraisers: Thomas Creaton, John Budd.
     Creditors: William Traverse, Robert Dowson.
     Next of kin: John Hicks Traverse, Ann Traverse.
     Administrators: Priscilla Traverse, William Traverse, Jr.

Samuel Nicholson   111.21   WO   £33.12.3   May 25 1771   Dec 10 1771
     Appraisers: Daniel Coe, Charles Banister.
     Creditors: Samuel Handy, Peleg Walter.
     Next of kin: Charles Nicholson, Jacob Rogers.
     Administratrix: Tabitha Nicholson.

John Benston   111.23   SO   £273.2.10   Jun 29 1771
     Appraisers: William Fleming, Javis Ballard.
     Creditors: William Miles, William Furniss.
     Next of kin: William Benston, Saul Ward.
     Executors: Rebeckah Benston, Matthais Miles.

Charles Smith   111.27   SO   £231.14.0   Feb 15 1772   Sep 7 1772
     Appraisers: William Stewart, Hugh Porter.
     Creditors: Sarah McClaster, Henry Jackson & Co.
     Administratrix: Mary Smith.

Thomas Darrack   111.31   KE   £1327.2.6   Sep 1772   Nov 24 1772
(of Georgetown)
     Appraisers: James Pearce, John Noohes.
     Creditors: Thomas Browning, James Darrack.
     Next of kin: David Kennedy, James Darrack.
     Administrators: Charlotte Darrack, John Darrack.

Andrew Usher   111.45   KE   £64.15.9   Aug 31 1772   Nov 5 1772
     Appraisers: Jesse Corden, Abraham Woodland.
     Creditors: Joseph Ireland, James Black.
     Next of kin: Charles Harbert, John Findley.
     Administratrix: Hannah Usher.

John Milton   111.46   KE   £15.2.0   Jul 22 1771   Dec 2 1772
     Appraisers: John Steward, Charles Silden.
     Creditors: Mary Lorain.
     Next of kin: Mary Milton, Abraham Milton.
     Administrator: Joseph Milton, Jr.

Bridget Wise   111.47   KE   £10.12.7   Oct 14 1771   Aug 18 1772
     Appraisers: John Blackiston, Luke Shores.
     Creditors: Thomas Gilpin & Co.
     Next of kin: Catharine McGavin, Judith Weyilet.
     Administrator: John McGavin.

John Donaldson   111.48   KE   £19.16.5   Mar 25 1772   Aug 18 1772
     Appraisers: John Eccleston, Samuel Wallis.
     Creditors: William Rogers.
     Next of kin: Mary Little.
     Executor: John Maxwell.

Paul Whichcote   111.50   KE   £495.10.11   May 12 1772   Jul 30 1772
     Appraisers: Richard Frisby, James Smith.
     Creditors: Richard Lloyd for Mr. James Anderson, Thomas Ringgold.
     Next of kin: Martha Whichcote, Jr., Richard Williss, Jr.
     Administratrix: Martha Whichcote.

John Reed (gentleman)   111.52   KE   £431.6.3   Mar 19 1772   Aug 17 1772
    Appraisers: James Smith, William Sipley.
    Creditors: Morgan & Slubey, Thomas Ringgold.
    Next of kin: John Reed, Sr., Sarah Terray.
    Executors: Hannah Reed, Samuel Reed.

Isaac Boots   111.54   KE   £203.2.2   Jun 2 1772   Aug 23 1772
    Appraisers: Samuel West, William Chiffin.
    Next of kin: William Boots, Joseph Boots.
    Administratrix: Rebecca Boots.

Samuel Hodges   111.56   KE   £217.11.11   May 10 1772   Jul 1 1772
    Appraisers: John Williamson, Thomas Pernam.
    Creditors: William Ringgold, Sr., John Blackiston.
    Next of kin: James Hodges, Stephen Hodges.
    Administrator: William Hodges.

William Crew   111.60   KE   £10.14.3   Apr 18 1772   Aug 5 1772
    Appraisers: Robert Coney, Samuel Thomas.
    Creditors: Smyth & Sudler.
    Next of kin: Thomas Smith Carpenter, Ann Smith.
    Administrator/Executor: Abraham Milton (Quaker).

John Sherwood   111.61   QA   £6.10.5   Aug 20 1772
    List of debts.
    Administratrix: Catharine Sherwood.

Richard Sootton   111.61   QA   £44.15.11   May 6 1772   Jun 25 1772
    Appraisers: H. Elbert, John Lambden.
    Creditors: Thomas Sudler, Joseph Sudler.
    Next of kin: Esther Davis, James Sootton.
    Administratrix: Lydia Sootton.

John Cooper   111.63   QA   £173.0.6   May 19 1772   Nov 19 1772
    Appraisers: Thomas Pennington, Giles Hicks.
    Creditors: Charles Goldsborough.
    Next of kin: Sharpless Cooper, Benjamin Cooper.
    Executor: Thomas Cooper.

William Ridgaway   111.66   QA   £236.7.8   Mar 12 1772   Nov 25 1772
    Appraisers: Richard Mason, John Atkinson (dec'd by Nov 25 1772).
    Creditors: Thomas Gilpin & Co., Richard Tilghman.
    Next of kin: Tobias Burke, William Ridgaway.
    Administrator: Samuel Ridgaway.

Edward Slay   111.69   QA   £22.16.11   Aug 20 1772   Sep 12 1772
    Appraisers: Richard Mason, William Winchester Mason.
    Creditors: Joseph Quillin, James Countiss.
    Next of kin: Mary Ford, Robert Copes.
    Administratrix: Sophia Slay.

John Atkinson   111.70   QA   £788.16.4   May 28 1772   Sep 12 1772
    Appraisers: B. Gould, Richard Mason.
    Creditors: Thomas Ringgold, William Robertson.
    Next of kin: Julyanna Taubman, Julyanna Laived (?).
    Executor: Carpenter/William

Peter Harwood   111.74   TA   £0.18.9   Nov 3 1772
    List of debts.
    Administratrix: Mary Harwood (Quaker).

Henry Keen   111.75   DO   £789.2.4   May 21 1772   May 27 1772
    Appraisers: Thomas Creaton, Henry Lake.
    Creditors: Betty League, Philemon Howell.
    Next of kin: Benjamin Keen, John Keen.
    Executors: Benjamin Keen, John Keen, Jr.

Robert Polk, Jr.   111.78   DO   £523.4.11   Aug 10 1772
    List of debts.
    Administratrix: Betty Polk, wife of Manuel Manlove.

William Noble   111.84   DO   £185.11.8   Jan 6 1772   Mar 9 1772
    Appraisers: Risdon Moore, Robert Clarkson.
    Creditors: Thomas Watkins, John Long.
    Next of kin: Hanary Camplin, Mathew Corey.
    Executrix: Mary Ann Noble.

John Brice   111.87   QA   £20.7.10   Dec 10 1771   Oct 8 1772
    Appraisers: Benjamin Gould, William Pryor.
    Mentions: Thomas Gilpin & Co., Hannah Miles.
    Administrator: William Clark.

Abraham Clark   111.89   DO   £10.1.1   Nov 9 1772
    List of debts.
    Executor: Benoni Banning.

James Safford   111.89   DO   £25.4.2   Nov 11 1772
    List of debts.
    Executrix: Mary Safford.

Beauchamp Turpin   111.90   DO   £4.5.0   Aug 13 1772
    List of debts.
    Executrix: Mary Turpin.

Robert Polk   111.91   DO   £489.10.2   Aug 10 1772
    List of debts.
    Executor: Daniel Polk.

Hollady Smith   111.92   DO   £193.5.3   Oct 4 1771   Nov 13 1772
    Appraisers: Edward White, Thomas Smith.
    Creditors: Ann Eareckson, Stevens Martin & Goldsborough.
    Next of kin: Solomon Smith, Rachel Cake.
    Executrix: Sarah Smith.

Joseph Alford   111.94   DO   £285.2.2   Nov 18 1771   Feb 2 1772
    Appraisers: Peter Edmondson, John Chezum.
    Creditors: William Richardson, Jr. for Edward Lloyd, Esq. (executor for Edward
        Lloyd), James Murray.
    Next of kin: Edward Alford, Joseph Alford.
    Executor: Maccabeus Alford.

Edward Needles/Nedels   111.97   TA   £955.15.9   May 21 1772   Nov 10 1772
    Appraisers: L. Comerford, D. Wilson.
    Creditors: Moses Allen, Matthais Gale.
    Next of kin: Nancy Needles, George Dudley.
    Executrix: Ann Nedels.

Mary Cannon   111.103   DO   £91.17.9   Dec 16 1771   Mar 30 1772
    Appraisers: Risdon Moore, Edward Wright.
    Creditors: William Cannon, Julius Aug. Jackson.
    Next of kin: Sarah Hitch, Francis Lank.
    Administrator: Jonathon Nicols.

Daniel Sherwood (planter)   111.104   TA   £12.8.0   Aug 28 1772
    List of debts.
    Administrator: Hugh Nice.

Thomas Simmons   111.105   DO   £0.6.10   Oct 28 1772
    List of debts.
    Administratrix: Bridget Simmonds.

Francis Hayward   111.105   DO   £6.1.11   Aug 31 1772
    List of debts.
    Administratrix: Mary Hayward.

Edward Soward   111.106   DO   £31.6.3   Jan 4 1773   Feb 1 1773
    Appraisers: Thomas Linthicum, John Spedden.
    Creditors: John Trippe, Gilbert North.
    Next of kin: Mary Soward, Charles Soward.
    Administrator: John Soward, Jr.

Thomas Hayward   111.108   DO   £118.7.2   Sep 16 1772   Jan 8 1773
    Appraisers: Levin Travers, Willis Newton.
    Creditors: Robert Gilmor, Garner Bruffett.
    Next of kin: Betty Hayward, Thomas Hayward.
    Executrix: Sarah Hayward.

Richard Richardson   111.112   DO   £4.16.11   Sep 11 1772   Feb 10 1773
    Appraisers: Thomas Vickars, Jr., William Thomas.
    Creditors: John Crawford, Richard Sanders.
    Next of kin: Rachel Cox, Priscilla Cox.
    Administrator: Benjamin Woodward.

John Lecompt   111.114   do   £115.18.1   1772   Dec 17 1772
    List of debts.
    Executrix: Mary, wife of James Shaw.

John Vinson   111.116   DO   £57.3.10   Dec 1 1772   Dec 10 1772
    Appraisers: Thomas Linthicum, William Bennett.
    Creditors: Joseph Payne, John Spedden.
    Next of kin: James Vinson, Mary Cantwell.
    Administratrix: Betty Vinson.

Roger Hurly   111.119   DO   £1.5.7   Nov 30 1772
    List of debts.
    Administrator: Matthew Hurly.

Mary Griffith   111.120   DO   £407.0.9   Nov 19 1772   Dec 18 1772
    Appraisers: Henry Lake, Benjamin Todd.
    Creditors: George Paul, Peter Kirwan.
    Next of kin: George Goote, John Frames.
    Executor: Aaron Atkinson (Quaker, of Talbot County).

Sarah Baker   111.122   QA   £40.4.0   Mar 19 1772   Dec 3 1772
    Appraisers: Basil Warfield, William Price.
    Creditors: Christopher Cross Routh, James Chetham.
    Next of kin: Esther Johnson, Sarah Walker.
    Administrator: John Walker.

James Ruth   111.124   QA   £17.12.10   Feb 22 1773
    List of debts.
    Administratrix: Mary, wife of Thomas Smith.

Michael Green   111.125   QA   £32.8.0   May 22 1772   Mar 2 1773
    Appraisers: James Obryon, Basil Warfield.
    Creditors: Hannah Clayton, James Costin.
    Next of kin: John Green, Henne Green.
    Executrix: Sarah Green.

John Ensor, Jr.   111.126   BA   £2467.15.8   Jan 18 1773
    List of debts.
    Administrator: Nathan Griffith.

Mr. Christopher Carnan   111.133   BA   £1793.11.10   Jan 12 1770   Jan 18 1773
    Appraisers: William Aisquith, Samuel Owings, Jr.
    Creditors: John Stevenson, H. D. Gough.
    Next of kin: Prudence Gough, George Carnan.
    Executrix: Elisabeth Carnan.

Barnet Holtzinger   111.146   BA   £716.13.4   Aug 7 1772
    Appraisers: Mordecai Hammond, Phillip Grayble.
    Next of kin: George Holtzinger (son), daughter who married Thomas Hartley.
    Executors: Martin Eichelberger, Frederick Eichelberger, Leslaff Holtzinger.

Frances Divers   111.157   BA   £139.17.9   Mar 13 1773
    Appraisers: Thomas Davis, William Allender.
    Creditors: J. Beale Howard, Edward Day.
    Next of kin: Christopher Divers, Ananias Divers.
    Administratrix: Mary Divers.

William Towson   111.159   BA   £526.5.2   Aug 11 1772   Apr 1 1773
    Appraisers: Nathan Nicholson, William Britten.
    Creditors: John Smith, Benjamin Griffith & Co.
    Next of kin: Dinah Towson, Ezekiel Towson.
    Administrator/Executor: Thomas Baily.

Mr. John Boswell   111.163   CH   £437.13.0   Dec 21 1772   Dec 23 1772
    Appraisers: Richard Tubman, John Hanson.
    Next of kin: William Boswell, Joseph Boswell.
    Administrators: Sarah Boswell, Charles Mankin.

Richard Brook   111.165   CH   £981.17.7   May 6 1771   Jan 8 1773
    Appraisers: Edward Edelin, Joshua Sanders.
    Creditors: Hugh Gardner for George and Andrew Buchanan & Co., John Craig for John
      and James Jameson.
    Next of kin: Marsham Queen, Catharine Brook.
    Executor: Leonard Brook.

Elisabeth Armstrong   111.168   CE   £15.16.0   Nov 3 1772
    List of debts.
    Administrator: James Glasgow.

Frederick Ellsbury   111.169   CE   £11.7.9
    Cash received.
    Executrix: Rebecca Ellsbury.

John Eliason   111.169   CE   £1.10.2   Oct 2 1772
    List of debts.
    Administratrix: Lydia, wife of John Montgomery.

William Bavington   111.170   CE   £20.12.5   Nov 28 1772
    List of debts.
    Administrators: John Bavington, Augustine Beedle.

Frederick Ellsbury   111.170   CE   £2.7.1   Nov 28 1772
    Executrix: Rebecca Ellsbury, wife of Robert Whitesides.

William Bavington   111.171   CE   £8.0.3   Jul 22 1772   Sep 30 1772
    List of debts.
    Administrators: John Bavington, Augustine Beedle.

Joseph Cluck   111.171   CE   £14.18.5   Sep 12 1772
    List of debts.
    Administratrix: Mary Cluck.

Elisabeth Mitchell   111.172   CE   £9.15.8   Jul 7 1772
    List of debts.
    Executor: Edward Mitchell.

John Eliason   111.173   CE   £278.16.6   Oct 2 1772
    List of debts.
    Administrator: Lydia, wife of John Montgomery.

George Lewis   111.174   CE   £303.17.11   Aug 12 1772   Nov 14 1772
    Appraisers: James Boyle, Peregrine Vandegrift.
    Creditors: Ephraim Thompson, Jr.
    Next of kin: Bat. Hetherington, Jr., Mary Mason.
    Administratrix: Sarah Lewis.

Edward Furroner   111.176   CE   £334.11.0   Sep 4 1772
(of Warwick Town)
    Appraisers: Augustine Beedle, Robert Lusby.
    Creditors: William Rumsey.
    Next of kin: Sarah Ward, Alleydenor Jones.
    Administrators: Edward Furroner, Elisabeth Furroner.

John Latham   111.180   CE   £170.15.1   Nov 9 1771   Nov 14 1772
    Appraisers: Andrew Laurenson, Peregrine Vandegrift.
    Creditors: Samuel Veazey, Samuel Bayard, Jr.
    Next of kin: Sarah Robart, John Latham.
    Administrators: Elisabeth Latham, Joseph Ensot.

Daniel Finney   111.184   CE   £63.10.4   Sep 12 1772
    Appraisers: Samuel Gilpin, Robert Bond.
    Mentions: Agnes Cummings, James Eokin.
    Next of kin: John Finney, Catron Finney.
    Administratrix: Elisabeth Finney.

James Kirkpatrick   111.185   CE   £27.11.0   Oct 17 1772   Dec 12 1772
    Appraisers: William Foster, William Brumfield.
    Executor: Richard Cazier.

Elisabeth Mitchell   111.186   CE   £33.5.0   Jul 7 1772
    List of debts.
    Executor: Edward Mitchell.

Sarah Handly   111.187   CE   £15.8.0   Jun 23 1772   Nov 25 1772
    Appraisers: James Cosden, John Reyland.
    Administrator: Thomas Savin, Sr.

John Culpepper   111.188   CA   £15.5.9   May 29 1771
    Appraisers: Samuel Dare, Isaac Clare.
    Creditors: Edward Hall, James Somervell.
    Next of kin: John Culpepper, John Conwill.
    Administrator: Michael Culpepper.

Richard Deal   111.189   CA   £540.18.11   Jul 16 1771   Oct 2 1772
    Appraisers: Edward Gantt, Joseph Kent.
    Creditors: Charles Graham, David Arnold.
    Next of kin: Jacob Deale, John Deall.
    Executrix: Sarah Deal.

Samuel McHard   111.192   KE   £35.17.6   Jan 16 1773   Jan 27 1773
    List of debts.
    Administratrix: Mary McHard, wife of James Byrn/Bryan.

Augustine Boyer   111.193   KE   £266.11.10   Jan 9 1773
    List of debts.
    Executors: Thomas Boyer, Augustine Boyer, Jr.

Thomas Newcomb   111.195   KE   £28.9.6   Dec 7 1771   Feb 5 1773
    Appraisers: Isaac Spencer, Jesse Cosden.
    Creditors: Thomas Gilpin & Co., James Blade.
    Next of kin: George Vansant Newcomb, William Salisbury Newcomb.
    Administratrix: Mary Newcomb, wife of Thomas Barnes.

Henry Russell   111.196   KE   £5.13.4   Apr 7 1772   Jan 6 1773
     Appraisers: Morgan Hewitt, Nathan Hutcheson.
     Creditors: Judith Brice.
     Administrator/Executor: John Page.

Alexander McClean   111.197   KE   £2.0.0   Jun 1 1772   Jan 6 1773
     Appraisers: William Frisby, Marmaduke Tilden.
     Creditors: Thomas Worten, Matthew Aiken.
     Next of kin: Isabella Watt.
     Administrator: John Page.

George Little   111.198   KE   £639.15.10   Sep 8 1772   Jan 2 1773
     Appraisers: J. Maawell, Samuel Wallis.
     Creditors: Henry Wallis, William Slubey, Jr.
     Next of kin: George Little, Adam Little.
     Executrix: Mary Little.

Mr. Jacob Bourne   111.201   CA   £413.0.0   Sep 19 1771 Jan 7 1773
     Appraisers: Samuel Gray, Young Parran (dec'd by Jan 7 1773).
     Creditors: Edward Hall & Co., James Somervell.
     Next of kin: Jesse Jacob, Betsy Bourne.
     Executrix: Esther Bourne.

Edward Norwood   111.204   BA   £943.16.2   Apr 17 1772 Feb 17 1772
     Appraisers: John Dorsey, Joshua Griffith.
     Creditors: John Stewart & Campbell, Russel & Reoly.
     Next of kin: Samuel Norwood, Ruth Norwood.
     Executor: Edward Norwood.

Elisabeth Galwith   111.207   AA   £103.19.9   Dec 15 1772 Mar 12 1773
     Appraisers: John James, John Watkins, Jr.
     Creditors: Thomas Lane, John Plummer.
     Next of kin: John Galwith, Sarah Galwith.
     Executor: Jonas Galwith.

Thomas Willett   111.209   PG   £28.15.9   May 18 1772 Nov 26 1772
     Appraisers: Charles Burgess, Peter Young.
     Creditors: Nathaniel Magruder, Magruder & Hepburne.
     Next of kin: Ninian Willett, Ninian Willett, Jr.
     Administrator: John Read Magruder.

Thomas Key   111.210   SM   £3.5.7   Mar 21 1773
     List of debts.
     Administrator: Philip Key.

Ann Aisquith   111.211   BA   £64.1.3   Sep 7 1771   Feb 25 1773
     Appraisers: William Goodwin, B. Griffith.
     Creditors: Henry Stevenson.
     Next of kin: Joseph Hopewell, Mary Rogers.
     Administrator: William Aisquith.

Charles Pennington   111.213   AA   £47.14.2   1772   Mar 19 1773
     Appraisers: Hezekiah Foreman, William Rickords.
     Creditors: Daniel Seward, Na. Hammond.
     Next of kin: Charles Pennington, John Smith.
     Administrator: William Pennington.

Joseph Stevens   111.215   AA   £18.9.6   Dec 23 1772
     Appraisers: John Marriott, Augustine Garnbull, Jr.
     Creditors: Samuel Haw. Howard, Thomas Harwood, Jr.
     Next of kin: Charles Stevens, John Stevens.
     Administrator: Vachel Stevens.

William Worthington   111.216   AA   £366.2.2   Jul 11 1772
     List of debts.
     Executor: John Davis.

Robert Gilchrist   111.217   BA   £871.14.10   Dec 31 1772
     List of debts.
     Administrator: John Whelsh.

Robert Gilchrist   111.218   BA   £114.12.9   Dec 18 1772
     List of debts.
     Administrator: John Welsh.

Thomas Key   111.219   SM   £67.8.5   Mar 22 1773
     Appraisers: John Shanks, Jr., John Mason.
     Creditors: Wilfred Veale, U. Woott.
     Next of kin: Jane Briscoe, Susannah Gardiner Key.
     Administrator: Philip Key.

Mr. Richard Snowden   111.220   AA   £1866.1.11   Sep 5 1772   Feb 19 1772
    Appraisers: William Coale, Richard Stringer.
    Creditors: Edward Gaither, Jr. for Mr. Stephen West, Na. Hammond for Philip
        Hammond.
    Next of kin: Henry Snowden, Thomas Snowden.
    Administratrix: Elisabeth Snowden.

Corker Hammond   111.222   KE   £140.9.6   Dec 17 1772   Mar 6 1773
    Appraisers: A. Calder, Joseph Ringgold.
    Creditors: Morgan & Slubey, Jr., Richard Lloyd.
    Next of kin: Ann Hamon, Hannah Forman.
    Administratrix: Hannah Hammond.

Abraham Cannell   111.226   KE   £620.18.8   Dec 5 1772   Mar 16 1773
    Appraisers: Charles Groome, Thomas Wilkins.
    Creditors: Thomas Bowan, John Thompson.
    Next of kin: Martha Shawn, Monica Cannell.
    Administrators: Jerom Cannell, Isaac Cannell.

Simon Worrel/Worrell   111.228   KE   £902.4.3   Mar 13 1773
    Appraisers: William Apsley, Thomas Wilkins.
    Creditors: Samuel Sinnett, Robert Anderson.
    Next of kin: Rebecca Sutton, William Worrell.
    Administrator/Executor: Priscilla Worrell.

Frederick Hanson   111.232   KE   £1142.5.10   Mar 10 1773
    Appraisers: Ebenezar Blackiston, N. Ricketts.
    Creditors: Richard Graham (executor of John Graham), James Mackiston.
    Next of kin: Mary Crew, Gustavius Hanson.
    Executors: Mary Hanson, John Page, Richard Miller.

Ann Milbourn   111.237   WO   £13.18.7   Mar 4 1772   Nov 4 1772
(widow of Thomas Milbourn)
    Appraisers: Powell Patty, Annanias Hudson.
    Next of kin: Presgrave Kennett, Turvile Kennett.
    Administrator: Kendal Kennett.

Thomas Flint   111.238   WO   £137.15.4   Nov 12 1771   Oct 8 1772
    Appraisers: Stephen Roach, Joshua Sirman.
    Creditors: John Nelms, Parker Selby.
    Next of kin: Betty Flint, Nancy Flint.
    Administratrix: Sarah Flint.

Robinson Lingo   111.241   WO   £277.2.1   May 15 1772   Oct 8 1772
    Appraisers: Edward Northen Nelms, George Parsons, Jr.
    Creditors: George Parsons, Sr., Andrew Smith.
    Next of kin: John Lingo, Priscilla Lingo.
    Executor: Joseph Dashiell, Smith Lingo.

John Collier   111.244   WO   £97.13.9   Apr 11 1772   Dec 4 1772
    Appraisers: John Campbell, Powell Patty.
    Creditors: Ebenezar Campbell, William Fassitt.
    Next of kin: Kendall Collier, Joseph Ironshire.
    Executrix: Tabitha Collier.

Purnel Fletcher Smith   111.247   WO   £104.1.11   Mar 15 1772
    Appraisers: James Rownd, Charles Rackliff.
    Creditors: John Postly, Edward Dymock.
    Next of kin: James Smith, John Smith.
    Executrix: Sarah Smith.

Stephen Whiett/White   111.249   WO   £23.13.4   Nov 7 1772
    Appraisers: John Dale, Powell Patty.
    Administratrix: Comfort, wife of Solomon Long.

Amy Morgan   111.250   WO   £1.11.0   Nov 19 1772
    Appraisers: William Holland, Thomas Harney.
    Administrator/Executor: Avery Morgan.

Joseph Massey   111.250   WO   £12.5.0   Nov 19 1772
    Appraisers: William Holland, David Wharton.
    Executrix: Hannah, wife of Avery Morgan.

James Davis   111.251   WO   £247.12.10   May 14 1772   Nov 5 1772
    Appraisers: Stephen Roach, George Parsons.
    Next of kin: Samuel Davis, James Davis, Jr.
    Executrix: Sabra, wife of John Perdue.

Jonathon Mudd   111.254   CH   £173.1.5   Apr 5 1773   Apr 9 1773
    Appraisers: Leonard Boarman, Raphael Boarman, Jr.
    Creditors: John Winter, William Burtles.
    Next of kin: Benjamin Higdon, William Higdon, Jr.
    Administratrix: Ann Mudd.

Elisabeth Clements   111.257   --   £2.8.3   Dec 1 1772   Mar 18 1773
    Appraisers: Thomas McPherson, Daniel McPherson, Jr.

Thomas Hungerford   111.257   CH   £97.0.0   Dec 11 1772   Mar 9 1773
    Appraisers: George Clk. Smoot, Theophilus Yates.
    Creditors: Thomas Contee, Phil. Findal.
    Administrator: John Marshall.

Jarman Gillett   111.258   WO   £115.6.1   Nov 20 1772
    Appraisers: William Mills, Elisha Jones.
    Creditors: Joseph Stevenson, James Smith.
    Next of kin: Margaret Warington, Sarah Stevenson.
    Executrix: Agnes Gillett.

George Parker   111.262   WO   £338.1.6   Mar 30 1772
    Appraisers: Joseph Scrogin, Jonathon Cathell.
    Creditors: John Parker, William McBryde.
    Next of kin: John Parker, Elisha Parker.
    Executor: Jacob Parker.

Cornelius Leslie   111.264   CE   £38.3.1   Mar 17 1773   Mar 21 1773
    Appraisers: John Stump, James Spear.
    Administrator: John Touchstone.

Maj. Andrew Pearce   111.265   CE   £884.13.5   Sep 29 1772
    Appraisers: Barnet Vanhorn, Augustine Beedle.
    Creditors: J. G. Bouchell, Hugh Matthews.
    Next of kin: Rachel Pearce, Daniel Pearce.
    Administrators: Cassandra Pearce, William Rumsey.

Thomas Biddle   111.270   CE   £19.2.6   Apr 17 1773
    List of debts.
    Executor: Elisabeth Biddle, Thomas Biddle.

John Armstrong   111.271   CE   £213.5.2   Feb 10 1773   Mar 11 1773
    Appraisers: Benjamin Bravard, Jeremiah Taylor.
    Creditors: Tobias Rudolph, William Miller.
    Next of kin: Edward Armstrong, Mary Armstrong.
    Administrators: Rebecca Armstrong, Noble Biddle.

Maj. Andrew Pearce   111.274A   CE   £7.15.0   Sep 29 1772   Mar 15 1773
    Appraisers: Barnet Vanhorn, Augustine Beedle.
    Creditors: J. G. Bouchell, Hugh Matthews.
    Next of kin: Rachel Pearce, Daniel Pearce.
    Administrators: Cassandra Pearce, William Rumsey.

Mr. Thomas Siverson   111.274B   CE   £191.6.9   Feb 23 1773   Mar 11 ----
    Appraisers: John Ward Veazey, James Wroth.
    Creditors: John Ward Veazey, John Gray.
    Next of kin: Mary Siverson, Rebecca Siverson.
    Executor: Ezekiel Siverson.

Thomas Biddle   111.276   CE   £524.3.8   Mar 15 1773   Apr 17 1773
    Appraisers: Alexander Stuart, Alexander Clark.
    Creditors: James Bouldin, Jr., Benjamin Chrisfield.
    Next of kin: Thomas Biddle, Dom. Biddle.
    Executors: Elisabeth Biddle, Thomas Biddle.

John Carslake (planter)   111.279   TA   £102.16.8   Dec 20 1769   Apr 2 1773
    Appraisers: Robert Pickering, Joseph Bewley.
    Creditors: Francis Baker, William & Joseph Bordley.
    Next of kin: Elisabeth Naylor, Mary Downes.
    Administratrix: Henrietta Carslake.

Denny Besswick/Beswick   111.281   TA   £172.2.6   Nov 25 1772   Mar 9 1773
    Appraisers: George Dudley, Benedict Hutchins.
    Creditors: James Wilson, William Whitby.
    Next of kin: William Besswick, Richard Besswick.
    Executrix: Rachel Beswick.

Thomas Bruff   111.281   TA   £110.12.0   Feb 24 1772   Jan 12 1773
(also Queen Anne's County)
    Appraisers: Edward Trippe, John Young.
    Creditors: Nicols & Chamberlaine, John Gordon.
    Next of kin: Susannah Bruff, Mary Bruff.
    Executor: Joseph Bruff.

Rev. Andrew Lendrum   111.288   BA   £1203.14.5   Apr 23 1772   Apr 28 1773
    Appraisers: Greenbury Dorsey, Samuel Griffith.
    Creditors: Amos Garrett, A. Tasker.
    Next of kin: Mary Lendrum, Lucundra Lendrum.
    Administrators: Robert Burgess Lendrum, John Lee Webster.

William Stevenson   111.295   FR   £145.14.0   Dec 16 1773   Mar 16 ----
    Appraisers: Abraham Hayter, James Galt.
    Creditors: John McAllister, John Buchanan.
    Next of kin: Margaret Stevenson, Katharine Stevenson.
    Executor: James Watson.

Elisabeth Clements   111.298   CH   £431.16.10   Nov 21 1771   Jan 13 1772
    Appraisers: Thomas McPherson, Daniel McPherson.
    Creditors: A. Hamilton for Mssrs. Simpson & Bierd & Co., Ignatius Middleton.
    Next of kin: John Clements (son of Francis), Thomas Clements.
    Executor: George Clements.

John Norris   111.302   BA   £191.14.2   Jun 30 1772   May 6 1773
(son of Benjamin)
    Appraisers: William Jones, Daniel Scott.
    Creditors: Richard Dallam (administrator of Richard Adair), Aquila Hall.
    Next of kin: Joseph Norris (son of Benjamin), Abram Norris.
    Administrators: Benjamin Norris, Susanna Norris.

Nicholas Hasselback   111.304   BA   £1675.18.0   Jan 10 1772   Apr 4 1773
    Appraisers: Thomas Worthington, ------ Strieper.
    Next of kin: Catharine Hasselback, Ma---- --alenastein.
    Administratrix: Catharine Hasselback.

Andrew Welter/Wealthy   111.311   BA   £144.5.5   Dec 10 1772   Mar 30 1773
    Appraisers: John Showell, Stephel Calyea.
    Creditors: Jacob Shearman, John Weavers.
    Next of kin: Morrilis Daher, Catharine Stone.
    Executors: Frederick Decker, Jacob Rupe.

Aquila McComas   111.314   BA   £3.4.0   Apr 7 1773
    List of debts.
    Executrix: Sarah McComas.

Barnet Johnson   111.315   BA   £1.0.7   May 1 1773
    List of debts.
    Executrix: Heather Johnson.

William Johnson   111.316   BA   ----   May 1 1773
    List of debts.
    Executors: Thomas Johnson, Edmund Bull.

Thomas Jackson   111.316   BA   £20.10.1   Nov 19 1763   Apr 24 ----
    Appraisers: Luke Raven, Christopher Dale.
    Creditors: Mark Alexander, William Lux for Christopher Grahame (executor of J.
       Dick).
    Next of kin: Henry Jackson, William Clark.
    Administrator: Samuel Clark.

Richard Jones   111.317   BA   £9.19.3   Apr 12 1773
    List of debts.
    Executor: John Hendrickson.

Henry Pearson   111.318   BA   £30.4.3   Mar 30 1773
    List of debts.
    Executor: John Boyd.

Nicholas Riley   111.319   KE   £594.15.2   Mar 5 1773   May 24 1773
    Appraisers: James Pearce, Robert Moody.
    Creditors: William Rogers, John Voorhees.
    Next of kin: Benjamin Riley, Sarah Huff.
    Executor: William Riley.

Jonathon Leatherbury   111.323   KE   £342.1.9   Sep 23 1772   May 8 1773
    Appraisers: James McClean, James Claypool.
    Creditors: Smith & Ringgold, Thomas Smyth.
    Next of kin: Sarah Piner, Mary Leatherbury.
    Executor: Peregrine Leatherbury.

Richard Briscoe   111.326   --   £38.7.8
    List of debts.
    Mentions: George Marchant (who has run away).
    Administratrix/Executrix: Judah Briscoe.

Joseph Cooper   111.327   KE   £25.9.11   Mar 4 1773   May 25 1773
    Appraisers: Charles Hynson, Jr., Richard Hosier.
    Creditors: John Aspenall, Jane Connaway.
    Administrator: Matthew Aiken.

John Hill   111.328   KE   £23.7.1   Apr 9 1773
    Appraisers: Bartin Wilkens, Charles Tilden.
    Creditors: Thomas Smyth, James McClean.
    Executrix: Elisabeth Walker.

William Saunders/Sanders   111.329   KE   £10.18.3   Aug 26 1771   Apr 24 1773
    Appraisers: William Smith, Nathaniel Knock.
    Creditors: Thomas Gilpin & Co., William Clark.
    Next of kin: Charles Sanders, Joseph Sanders.
    Administrator: George Sanders.

Jervis/Jarvis James   111.331   KE   £561.15.10   Jun 1 1772   May 17 1773
    Appraisers: William Frisby, Marmaduke Tilden.
    Creditors: George Leyburn, Morgan & Slubey, Jr.
    Executrix: Sarah James.

Charles Brown   111.335   DO   £1103.5.10   Mar 5 1773   Apr 6 1773
    Appraisers: Robert Clarkson, David Nutter.
    Creditors: R. Mitchell for John Mitchell, Jonathon Brady.
    Next of kin: Charles Brown, Curtis Brown.
    Executor: Tilghman Brown.

Mary Ennalls   111.339   DO   £232.3.6   Feb 19 1772   Mar 2 1773
    Appraisers: Roger A. Hooper, Levin Travers.
    Creditors: James Sullivane, Robert Harrison.
    Next of kin: Henry Ennalls, Henrietta Ennalls.
    Administrator: Thomas Ennalls.

Alexander Morton   111.346   DO   £203.5.3   Mar 10 1773
    List of debts.
    Administrator: John Fisher.

James Hignutt   111.349   DO   £3.15.0   Mar 13 1771   Mar 12 1773
    Appraisers: Nathaniel Potter, Edward Smith.
    Creditors: Moses Cranner, Benjamin Harrison.
    Next of kin: Marsey Wheatley, Sarah Kirkman.
    Executors: John Hignutt, Daniel Hignutt.

Thomas Taylor   111.350   DO   £16.11.8   Mar 30 1773
    List of debts.
    Executors: Sarah Taylor, William Taylor.

William Allford   111.351   DO   £621.3.7   Feb 12 1773   Mar 15 1773
    Appraisers: William Haskins, James Wing.
    Creditors: Charles Blair, Nathan Ferriss.
    Next of kin: Isaac Nicols, Jr., Stephen Fleharty.
    Executrix: Mary Allford.

John Saulsbury   111.356   DO   £35.6.0   Mar 11 1773
    Appraisers: John Cooper, Jacob Rumbly.
    Creditors: Nicols & Chamberlaine, John Saulsbury.
    Next of kin: James Saulsbury, John Saulsbury.
    Administratrix: Olive Saulsbury.

Thomas Taylor   111.357   DO   £50.8.4   Mar 30 1773
    List of debts.
    Executors: Sarah Taylor, William Taylor.

Thomas Murphy   111.358   DO   £82.10.4   Nov 26 1772   Apr 9 1773
    Appraisers: John Budd, Edmund Barnes.
    Creditors: Joseph Robsson, Robert Harrison.
    Next of kin: James Murphy, Joseph Murphy.
    Administratrix: Dorothy Murphy.

Andrew Gibb   111.360   --   £326.9.9
    List of debts.
    Administratrix: Isabel Gibb.

Solomon Timmons   111.365   WO   £99.18.6   Apr 16 1773
    Appraisers: John Dale, Joseph Ironshire.
    Creditors: J. Atkinson, John Postly.
    Next of kin: Joseph Timmons, Samuel Inneurs.
    Administratrix: Rebecke Timmons.

Solomon Russell   111.367   WO   £242.1.4   Sep 15 1772   Mar 25 1773
    Appraisers: Edward Northen Nelms, George Parsons, Jr.
    Creditors: George Handy, James Houston.
    Next of kin: Alexander Russell, Price Russell.
    Administrator: Josiah Russell.

Andrew Ferguson   111.376   WO   £222.1.1   Jan 1773   Apr 16 1773
    Appraisers: Samuel Handy, Peter Chaille.
    Creditors: Adam Spence, Neil McMullin.
    Next of kin: Joseph Ferguson.
    Executrix: Elisabeth Ferguson.

James Cathell   111.379   WO   £345.3.0   May 12 1772   Apr 23 1773
    Appraisers: Stephen Roach, Samuel Davis.
    Creditors: William Winder, John Wilkins.
    Next of kin: John Cathell, David Cathell.
    Executor: James Cathell.

Alexander Massey   111.384   WO   £838.14.2   Aug 29 1772   Jun 9 1773
    Appraisers: Wolton Purnell, Isaac Murray.
    Creditors: Henry Franklin, James Wilson.
    Next of kin: Eleanor Franklin, David Fassett.
    Executor: John Masse.

William Crockett   111.389   WO   £75.7.1   Jul 9 1772   May 31 1773
    Appraisers: Jonathon Boyce, John Ellegood.
    Creditors: Joseph Vaughan, Richard Crockett.
    Next of kin: John Crockett, Wurder Crockett.
    Executors: Richard Crockett, Elisabeth Crockett.

Nathaniel Hopkins Murray   111.391   WO   £281.1.4   Apr 13 1771   Apr 8 1773
    Appraisers: Matthew Outten, Levi Hopkins.
    Creditors: James Rownds, Benton Harris.
    Next of kin: Levin Hopkins, Samuel Hopkins.
    Administrator: George Martin.

Warran/Warren Hadder, Sr.   111.397   WO   £62.12.8   Mar 1 1773   Jun 8 1773
    Appraisers: Joseph Ironshire, Isaac Evans.
    Creditors: John Postly.
    Next of kin: John Hadder, William Lowes, Jr.
    Executrix: Elisabeth Hadder.

Thomas Meeds/Meedes   111.400   QA   £521.2.2   Dec 22 1772   Jun 6 1773
    Appraisers: Giles Hicks, Jeremiah Colston.
    Creditors: Tilghman & Nicols, John Clark.
    Next of kin: John Meeds, John Meeds, Jr., Thomas Meeds.
    Executrix: Rachel Meeds.

William McNee   111.403   QA   £10,17.11   Sep 17 1772   May 6 1773
    Appraisers: Matthew Chilton, John Casson (dec'd by May 6 1773).
    Creditors: Henry Casson, Joshua Clark.
    Next of kin: Mary Thawley.
    Administrator/Executor: Bartholomew Feddeman.

Moses Swift   111.404   QA   £60.6.3   Mar 8 1773   May 27 1773
    Appraisers: William Winchester Mason, William Clark.
    Creditors: Henry Casson, Thomas Matthes.
    Next of kin: James Swift, Anane Marchant.
    Executor: Isaac Bays.

John Pickerson   111.407   QA   £21.14.3   Oct 15 1772   May 6 1773
    Appraisers: Philemon Green, James Miller.
    Creditors: Phil. Downes for Mr. James Anderson, Robert Pickering for Edward
        Lloyd, Esq.
    Next of kin: Thomas Kenton, Solomon Kenton.
    Administrator: Henry Downes.

Benjamin Baxter   111.409   BA   £74.19.2   May 28 1772   Mar 31 1773
    Appraisers: William Wilkinson, Josias Brown.
    Creditors: Thomas Gash, Andrew Buchanan.
    Next of kin: Edmund Baxter, Thomas Gash.
    Administratrix: Rachel Baxter.

Hugh McKenny/Kenned   111.412   BA   £45.7.11   Jun 17 1773   Jun 25 1773
    Appraisers: Thomas Long, Richard Clark.
    Creditors: Edward Harris, Duncan Carmichael.
    Next of kin: Agness Lavery, Ellenor Loluwry (?).
    Administratrix: Margaret Lowry.

Hugh McKenny   111.414   BA   £18.19.5   Jun 25 1773
    List of debts.
    Administratrix: Margaret Lowry.

Hugh McKenny   111.415   BA   £8.19.1   Jun 25 1773
    List of debts.
    Administratrix: Margaret Lowry.

Rev. Mr. Caspar Kirchner   111.415   BA   £19.8.2   Jun 1 1773
    Appraisers: Christoph Wiesenthal, George Lindenberger.
    Creditors: Wilhelm Loeble/Loble, Morie Wewler.
    Executor: Christian Kirchner.

Ephraim Gover   111.417   BA   £36.15.2   Jun 21 1773
    List of debts.
    Executrix: Elisabeth Gover.

Benjamin Denny   111.419   BA   £74.15.6   Jun 20 1773
    List of debts.
    Executor: John Craddock, Thomas Craddock.

Jonathon Massey   111.419   BA   £10.0.2   Jun 9 1773
    List of debts.
    Administratrix: Cassandra, wife of Jonathon Woodland.

Jonathon Massey   111.420   BA   £85.2.6   Jun 9 1773
    List of debts.
    Administratrix: Cassandra, wife of Jonathon Woodland.

Mr. John Carvill, Jr.   111.421   KE   £859.10.8   Mar 27 1773   Jun 3 1773
    Appraisers: John Wickes, James Dunn.
    Creditors: Thomas Ringgold, James Anderson.
    Next of kin: J. C. Hynson, Richard Hynson.
    Administratrix: Ann Carvill.

Nathaniel Miles   111.427   KE   £220.12.11   Jun 5 1773
    List of debts.
    Administratrix/Executrix: Hannah Miles.

Isaac Heather   112.1   WO   £37.9.0   Apr 7 1771   Sep 25 1772
    Appraisers: John Teague, William Smock.
    Creditors/Next of kin: Mary Collins, Rachel Heather.
    Administratrix: Mary, wife of John Burbage.

John Schoolfield   112.2   WO   £334.17.2   Apr 6 1772   Sep 11 1772
    Appraisers: John Teague, Joshua Bratton.
    Creditors: Samuel Smyly, Henry Bishop.
    Next of kin: Robert Schoolfield, Betty Schoolfield.
    Executor: Thomas Schoolfield.

Mary Truitt   112.5   WO   £31.19.9   Nov 30 1771   Sep 25 1772
    Appraisers: John Teague, John Houston.
    Creditors: Henry Bishop, William Brittingham, Jr.
    Next of kin: Comfort Mumford, Tabitha Patrick.
    Legacies: William Truitt, daughter Sarah Turner, daughter Ann Evans, daughter
        Tabitha Patrick, daughter Elisabeth Beathards, daughter Comfort Mumford,
        daughter Mary Turner, daughter Rhoda Turner. ,pi /Beathards/Elisabeth
    Executor: William Truitt.

John Kelly   112.8   WO   £28.13.2   Aug 17 1772   Nov 11 1772
    Appraisers: John Ellegood, George Benston.
    Creditors: Samuel Smith, Cornelius Rogers.
    Next of kin: John Smith, Daniel Kelly.
    Administrator: Obediah Smith.

George Thompson   112.9   WO   £161.9.6   Jul 25 1772   Aug 3 1772
    Appraisers: Joseph Cannon, Peter Dolbee.
    Creditors: Simon Kollock, George Gibbins.
    Next of kin: James Thompson, Jantzan Pahlar.
    Executor: Jesse Thompson.

William Bevans/Beavens   112.11   WO   £71.12.10   Jan 6 1772   Dec 4 1772
    Appraisers: Daniel Cottingham, Solomon Townsend.
    Creditors: William Holland, John Atkinson.
    Next of kin: Rowland Beavens, William Beavens.
    Executrix: Sarah Beavens.

Susannah Gwinn   112.13   CH   £15.1.0   Mar 9 1773
    Appraisers: Joseph Joy, Notly Dutton.
    Creditors: John Scrogin, Benjamin Lesly Corry for John Corry.
    Next of kin: Mary Stone, Jane Hungerford.
    Administrator: Edward Warren.

Edward Derrick   112.14   CH   £7.12.0   Apr 13 1772   Feb 20 1773
(stranger to Charles County)
    Appraisers: George Jenkins, Robert Sinnet.
    Administrator: John Derrick.

John Clinkscales   112.15   CH   £19.19.1   Feb 23 1772   Mar 23 1773
    Appraisers: Theophilus Hanson, Edward Milstead, Jr.
    Creditors: Robert Mundell for John Glassford & Co., Knox & Baille.
    Next of kin: Adam Clinkscales, Mary Clinkscales.
    Administratrix: Frances Clinkscales.

William Payn/Payne   112.16   CH   £30.4.8   Jan 22 1772   Mar 23 1773
    Appraisers: Moses Hobart, James Cottrell.
    Creditors: Benjamin Douglass for Mr. Thomas Contee, Hugh Gardner for George and
        Andrew Buchanan.
    Administrator: Basil Payne.

Benjamin McCoy   112.17   CH   £136.10.11   Mar 28 1772   Mar 2 1773
    Appraisers: Francis Ware, Samuel Tubman.
    Creditors: Barnes & Redgate, W. Thompson.
    Next of kin: John McCoy, Peter Harrout Thisby.
    Administratrix: Mary Reeves (formerly Mary McCoy).

Charles Wharton   112.19   WO   £188.7.9   Jun 18 1772   Nov 20 1772
    Appraisers: James Burnitt, Elishe Jones.
    Creditors: Daniel Young, Elisabeth Melton.
    Next of kin: John Tull, Sr., Stephen Tull.
    Executrix: Sarah Boston (late Sarah Wharton).

Michael Milbourn   112.21   WO   £268.2.4   Jun 25 1772   Oct 23 177x
    Appraisers: Thomas Merrill, James Paterson.
    Creditors: Samuel Henderson, Howell Gladden.
    Next of kin: Caleb Milbourn, Sr., Jonathon Milbourn.
    Administrator: Caleb Milbourn.

James Harris   112.25   QA   £117.19.2   Nov 25 1772   Apr 1 1773
    Appraisers: Basil Warfield, John Chairs.
    Creditors: Thomas Ringgold, William Mumford.
    Next of kin: Rachel Mumford, Thomas Harris.
    Executrix: Rebecca Harris.

George Merchant   112.27   QA   £39.18.9   Mar 1 1773   Apr 17 1773
    Appraisers: William Winchester Mason, Isaac Bays.
    Creditors: Henry Casson, Solomon Dill.
    Next of kin: Sarah Marchant, Wealthyam Bannard.
    Administrator: Samuel Martindale.

Robert Brody   112.28   QA   £442.3.4   Aug 31 1772   Apr 17 1773
    Appraisers: Richard Mason, Thomas Baggs.
    Mentions: James Brody, John Wallace.
    Mentions: Richard Siste, William Brody.
    Executrix: Margaret Brody.

Charles Brown   112.31   QA   £228.17.2   Feb 18 1768   Apr 29 1773
    Appraisers: Thomas Claland, Jacob Seth.
    Executrix: Priscilla Brown.

Phineas Hodgson   112.32   CE   £100.19.6   Mar 29 1773
    List of debts.
    Administrator: John Hodson.

Thomas Biddle/Biddel   112.33   CE   £20.4.0   Apr 17 1773
    List of debts.
    Executors: Elisabeth Biddel, Thomas Biddel.

Enoch Janney   112.33   CE   £6.13.0   Jan 7 1773   Feb 10 1773
    Appraisers: Andrew Lawrenson, William Taylor.
    Mentions: Isaac Janney, Thomas Janney.
    Administrator: William Domagan.

Mr. Robert Mercer   112.34   CE   £16.0.0   Jan 15 1773   Jan 26 1773
    Appraisers: John Roberts, John Money.
    Mentions: Rebecca Severson.
    Next of kin: Ann Caulk, Frances Mercer.
    Executrix: Ann Mercer.

Jesse Boldin   112.35   CE   £664.15.7   Aug 24 1772   Jan 23 1773
    Appraisers: Robert Thompson, Jr., Benjamin Bravard.
    Creditors: Elijah Boldin.
    Next of kin: James Boldin, Nathan Boldin, Elijah Boldin.
    Administratrix: Mary Boldin.

John Garey   112.39   TA   £119.5.7   Nov 16 1771   Apr 15 1773
    Appraisers: Richard Grason, Richard Skinner.
    Creditors: Francis Kinnemont, William Pagan.
    Next of kin: Ann Benson, William Garey.
    Administratrix: Mary Ann Garey.

Clemane/Clement Sails   112.41   TA   £14.3.4   Aug 1 1772   Mar 2 1773
    Appraisers: Thomas Martin, John Barnett.
    Creditors: Charles Crookshanks, John Cox.
    Next of kin: Gabriel Sailes.
    Executor: Nathaniel Cox.

Thomas Loveday   112.42   TA   £247.10.8   Nov 3 1772   Mar 3 1772
    Appraisers: Daniel Sherwood, George Dudley.
    Creditors: Edward Lloyd, Nicols & Chamberlain.
    Next of kin: Mary Rice, Sally Loveday.
    Executrix: Ann Loveday.

William Dawson (bricklayer)   112.43   TA   £11.9.1   Aug 13 1772   Mar 2 1773
    Appraisers: John Denny, John Auld.
    Creditors: Philemon Auld, Mathew Tilghman.
    Next of kin: Ailce Dawson, William Dawson.
    Administrator: Thomas Harrison.

John Loveday   112.45   TA   £386.14.1   May 25 1772   Mar 3 1773
    Appraisers: George Dudley, Edward Clark.
    Creditors: Matthais Gale, Peter Parrott.
    Next of kin: Mary Rice, Hugh Rice, Sally Loveday.
    Administratrix: Sarah Loveday.

Mrs. Rebecca Perry   112.48   FR   £649.13.6   Jun 15 1772   May 18 1773
    Appraisers: Archibald Orme, James Orme.
    Creditors: David Lynn, T. Spricht (?) Wootton.
    Next of kin: Alexander Offutt, John Willson.
    Executor: James Perry.

James Perry   112.50   FR   £38.6.0   May 18 1773
    Appraisers: Archibald Orme, Brooke Beall.
    Next of kin: John Hilleary, Martha Perry.
    Executor: James Perry.

Thomas Drane   112.50   PG   £173.7.8   Feb 2 1772   May 7 1773
    Appraisers: Samuel White, Abiezer Plummer.
    Creditors: John Sprigg, Jeremiah Crabb.
    Next of kin: Peter Meglauglin, Cansande Drane.
    Administratrix: Susannah Drane.

Capt. John Cromwell   112.52   AA   £108.6.6   Jan 1 1773   May 3 1773
    Appraisers: William Randall, Bale Owings.
    Executor: George Risteace (of Baltimore County).

Henry Child   112.53   AA   £840.9.0   Dec 8 1772   Apr 27 1773
    Appraisers: John Brown, Isaac Hall.
    Creditors: Bennett Darnall, Thomas Tillard & Co.
    Next of kin: William Child, Zachariah Child.
    Administrators: William Child, Samuel Child.

Rezin Todd   112.56   AA   £119.7.4   Jan 26 1773   Apr 7 1773
    Appraisers: John David, Hezekiah Foreman.
    Creditors: N. Hammond.
    Next of kin: Mary Todd.
    Administratrix: Sarah Todd.

Dr. James Spavold   112.58   BA   £172.8.11   Aug 19 1772   Apr 26 1773
    Appraisers: Joseph E. Butler, Joseph Corole Hall.
    Creditors: John Rogers, John Lee Webster.
    Executor: Amos Garret.

John Crider   112.61   FR   £107.8.7   Apr 16 1773
    Appraisers: David Shriver, Michael Hebner.
    Administratrix: Barbara Crider (a Dunker).

Edward Shaw   112.63   FR   £364.3.3   Feb 9 1773   Mar 17 1773
    Appraisers: Anthony Livers, Richard Lilly.
    Creditors: Thomas Ogle, James Ogle.
    Next of kin: James Ogle, William Ogle.
    Executrix: Sarah Shaw.

Mathew Clark   112.65   FR   £290.7.2   Nov 23 1772   Mar 20 1773
    Appraisers: Joseph Smith, Christian Orndorstz.
    Creditors: John Stall.
    Executors: John Ingram, Elisabeth Clark.

Christopher Willson   112.67   FR   £36.12.0   Dec 23 1772   Apr 12 1773
    Appraisers: Simon Meredith, Michael Waggoner.
    Creditors: David Plara, Thomas Willson.
    Next of kin: Susanna Willson, Thomas Willson.
    Administrator: James Kinsler.

Michael Milbourn   112.68   WO   £48.0.0   Jun 23 1772
    vide folio 21.

Mr. Young Parran   112.68   CA   £3413.16.2   May 4 1772   Mar 16 1773
    Appraisers: James Somervell, Samuel Gray.
    Creditors: Edward Hall, James McLaran.
    Next of kin: John Parran, Moses Parran.
    Executor: Richard Parran.

George Ross   112.75   FR   £544.3.6   Dec 1 1772   Mar 20 1773
    Appraisers: Joseph Smith, John Reynolds.
    Creditors: James Snowden, Archibald Sheerer.
    Next of kin: Oth. Hold. Williams, Elie Williams.
    Administrator: Dr. David Ross.

Mrs. Barbara Brooke   112.77   CA   £639.11.4   May 7 1772   Mar 15 1773
    Appraisers: Isaac Clare, John Clare.
    Creditors: Robert Young for James Gordon & Co., William Allen for William
        Molleson.
    Next of kin: Ann Crompton, Thomas Bond.
    Executrix: Ann Bond.

Stockett Sunderland   112.82   CA   £202.9.4   May 2 1772   Mar 15 1773
    Appraisers: William Dare, Michael Catterton.
    Creditors: Charles Grahame, John Hamilton Smith.
    Next of kin: Benjamin Sunderland, Thomas Sunderland.
    Administratrix: Lydia Sunderland.

Christopher Hance   112.85   CA   £87.0.4   Mar 23 1773
    Appraisers: Philip Dossey, John Ireland.
    Creditors: Alexander Ogg, Joseph Ireland.
    Next of kin: Benjamin Hance, Jr., James Hance.
    Administrator: Aaron Williams, Jr.

Charles Clagett   112.86   CA   £65.5.6   Dec 2 1772   Mar 17 1773
    Appraisers: Alexander Somervell, Samuel Gray.
    Creditors: James Somervell, Edward Hall.
    Next of kin: Samuel Dare, William Dare.
    Executrix: Mary Cladgett.

Mr. Phillip Dowell   112.87   CA   £388.16.1   Feb 12 1771   Mar 23 1773
    Appraisers: Joseph Kent, Richard Ward.
    Creditors: Thomas Reynolds, Charles Grahame.
    Next of kin: Elisabeth Cox, Susannah Dowell.
    Executors: John Dowell, Mary Dowell.

Samuel Ward   112.89   CA   £233.6.9   Nov 1 1770   Feb 4 1773
    Appraisers: Samuel Dare, Isaac Clare.
    Creditors: James Somervell, Nathaniel Dare.
    Next of kin: James Ward, John Ward.
    Administrators: Mary Ward, Edward ------.

Richard Crosby   112.90   CA   £36.10.17   Jul 1 1772   Mar 26 1773
    Appraisers: William Lyles, Benjamin Skinner.
    Creditors: Philip Hodgkin, Jr. for John Campbell, John Hamilton Smith.
    Next of kin: Mary Crosby, Joseph Crosby.
    Administrator: Mordecai Smith.

Mr. Francis King   112.92   PG   £382.2.5   Dec 11 1771   Apr 9 1773
    Appraisers: Ignatius Wheeler, Thomas Dent.
    Creditors: John Baynes, Allen Bowie.
    Next of kin: Benjamin King, Margaret King.
    Administratrix: Frances King.

James Barnes   112.96   PG   £583.8.3   Feb 1773   Mar 23 1773
    Appraisers: Abraham Boyd, Walter Evans.
    Creditors: William Deakins, Jr. for William Mollison, Robert Ferguson for John
        Glassford & Co.
    Next of kin: David Barnes, John Barnes.
    Administrator: Thomas Barnes.

Mr. George Hardy   112.100   PG   £160.3.9   Mar 24 1773
    List of debts.
    Executor: Thomas Dent.

Mr. Henry Hardy   112.102   PG   £24.10.0   Mar 24 1773
    List of debts.
    Executor: Thomas Dent.

Mr. George Hardy   112.104   PG   £313.13.11   Mar 24 1773
    List of debts.
    Executor: Thomas Dent.

Francis King   112.105   PG   ----   Apr 9 1773
    List of debts.
    Administrator: Francis King.

Thomas Reccords   112.115   SO   £110.1.7   Jul 8 1771   Oct 9 1771
    Appraisers: Esme Bayley, Joshua Hitch.
    Creditors: Jonathon Cathell, Joshua Humphries.
    Next of kin: Alexander Records, Lamee Records.
    Administratrix: Sarah Records.

Francis King   112.119   PG   £59.19.11   Apr 9 1773
    List of debts.
    Administrator: Francis King.

William Willett   112.122   PG   ----   Mar 9 1773
    List of debts.
    Executrix: Mary Willett.

Jonathon Oden   112.123   PG   £533.12.3   Sep 8 1772   Mar 24 1773
    Appraisers: Jel. Belt, John Wilson.
    Creditors: William Murdock, William Sydebotham.
    Next of kin: Vincent Oden, Susanna Oden.
    Administratrix: Elisabeth Oden.

Henry Whitaker   112.126   PG   £323.4.8   Oct 21 1772   Feb 2 1773
    Appraisers: Abraham Jones, James Drane.
    Creditors: John Read Magruder, Archibald Allen.
    Next of kin: Alexander Whitaker, Susanna Whitaker.
    Administrator: Robert Whitaker.

Mrs. Elisabeth Osborn   112.128   PG   £37.13.11   Dec 10 1772   Mar 1 1773
    Appraisers: Nathaniel Magruder, Basil Magruder.
    Creditors: J. Sprigg, Thomas Hamilton.
    Next of kin: Miss Tomsoline Alen (niece).
    Mentions: William Moodie.
    Administrator: William Osborn.

Benjamin Ramsey Hodges   112.131   PG   £904.9.0   Dec 1 1772   Feb 22 1773
    Appraisers: Edward Sprigg, David Crawford.
    Creditors: Thomas Philpot (by his attorney Frank Leek), J. Sprigg.
    Next of kin: Charles Hodges, Thomas Ramsey Hodges.
    Executrix: Deborah Hodges.

Mr. George Hardey   112.134   PG   £807.14.7   Jul 3 1772   Mar 20 1772
    Appraisers: John Wynn, Luke Marbury.
    Creditors: Richard Brooke, Thomas Clagett for Oswald Denniston & Co. (surviving
        partners of David Dalyell, George Oswald & Co.)
    Next of kin: Henry Hardey, Anthony Hardey.
    Executor: Thomas Dent.

Mr. William Willet/Willett   112.140   PG   £327.9.1   Jan 30 1773   Mar 29 1773
    Appraisers: Nathaniel Magruder, Peter Young.
    Creditors: Edward Willett, William Nickols.
    Next of kin: Ninian Willett, Sr., William Willett.
    Executrix: Mary Willett.

Benjamin Ramsey Hodges   112.143   PG   ----   Mar 28 1770
    List of debts.
    Executrix: Deborah Hodges.

James Knight   112.144   SO   £101.6.2   Feb 12 1773   Apr 26 1773
    Appraisers: George Gilliss, Joseph Venables.
    Creditors: Joseph Venables, Hugh McBryde & Co.
    Next of kin: Jonathon Knight, Nehemiah Knight.
    Executrix: Elisabeth Knight.

John Hopkins   112.146   SO   £162.4.0   Oct 8 1772   Apr 7 1773
    Appraisers: George Dashiell, William Stewart.
    Creditors: John Evans, Sr., John Evans (son of John).
    Next of kin: Elisabeth Hopkins, Grace Hopkins.
    Executor: Stephen Hopkins.

Richard Venables   112.148   SO   £12.16.6   Jun 12 1771   Apr 12 1773
    Appraisers: George Gilliss, John Phillips.
    Creditors: Alexander Laing, John Daugharty.
    Next of kin: Joseph Venables, Wil. Venables.
    Administrator: Benjamin Venables.

Levin Gilliss   112.150   SO   £666.10.6   Aug 26 1772   May 8 1773
    Appraisers: William Polk, William Jones.
    Creditors: G. Dashiell, John Sheriff.
    Next of kin: Mary Gilliss, Sarah Gilliss.
    Executrix: Sarah Gilliss.

Josiah Elliss/Ellis   112.155   SO   £52.2.3   Oct 19 1772   Apr 12 1773
    Appraisers: Jacob Bell, Joshua Hitch.
    Creditors: George Handy, Hezekiah Blades.
    Next of kin: Joseph Ellis, Levin Ellis.
    Executor: Stephen Ellis.

Cornelius Ward   112.156   SO   £49.16.3   Dec 31 1773   May 5 1773
    Appraisers: William Fleming, Stephen Mitchell.
    Creditors: John Shirreff, Joseph Ward.
    Next of kin: Matthew Ward, Jesse Ward.
    Administratrix: Sarah Ward.

William Montgomery   112.158   DO   £453.1.9   Jun 10 1773
    List of debts.
    Executrix: Nelly Montgomery.

Henry Trippe   112.167   DO   £138.4.6   Jun 7 1773
    List of debts.
    Executor: John Dickinson.

William Montgomery   112.168   DO   £249.14.2   Feb 27 1773   Jun 10 1773
    Appraisers: Nathaniel Potters, Robert Clarkson.
    Creditors: John Maslin, Jr., Ezekiel Pritchett.
    Next of kin: Richard Liden, Sarah Liden.
    Executrix: Nelly Montgomery.

Levin Woolford   112.174   DO   £248.11.11   Sep 17 1772   Jun 7 1773
    Appraisers: Thomas Ennalls, Jonathon Patridge.
    Creditors: Thomas Muse, Levin & Robert Woolford (executors of John Woolford).
    Next of kin: Thomas Woolford, William Woolford.
    Administrator: James Woolford 3rd.

James Wallace   112.178   DO   £0.19.5   Jul 3 1773
    List of debts.
    Executor: Arthur Whitely.

Christopher Nutter   112.179   DO   £29.12.9   Jun 2 1773
    List of debts.
    Executrix: Eleanor, wife of William Polk.

Thomas Cannon   112.180   DO   £282.4.9   Mar 31 1773   Jun 9 1773
    Appraisers: George Waters, James Cavender.
    Creditors: Peter Hubbert, Isaac Bradley.
    Next of kin: Joseph Cannon, Absolom Cannon.
    Executrix: Sarah Cannon.

Jacob Pattison   112.184   DO   £2212.9.6   Nov 18 1772   Jul 22 1773
    Appraisers: James Tootell, Thomas Creaton.
    Creditors: Daniel Sulivane, Jr., William Wheland.
    Next of kin: Richard Pattison, Jeremiah Pattison.
    Executrix: Sarah Pattison.

Jacob Pattison   112.191   DO   £862.13.1   Jul 22 1773
    List of debts.
    Executrix: Sarah Pattison.

Priscilla Pollock   112.194   DO   £605.14.1   Apr 20 1773   Jul 3 1773
    Appraisers: George Walles, Henry Hooper.
    Creditors: John Mithell, Samuel Griffith.
    Next of kin: Edward Roberts, William Roberts.
    Administrator: Francis Roberts.

Henry Keene   112.200   DO   £6.16.9   May 17 1773
    List of debts.
    Executors: John Keene, Benjamin Keene, Jr.

Solomon Matkin   112.201   DO   £2.17.2   May 17 1773
    List of debts.
    Administrator: Ezekiel Johnson.

Richard Webster   112.202   DO   £49.7.9   Mar 23 1773   Jun 2 1773
    Appraisers: Nathaniel Potter, Abraham Collins.
    Creditors: William Douglass, Richard Ozment.
    Next of kin: John Webster.
    Executor: Solomon Webster.

Richard Webster   112.205   DO   £0.6.9   Jun 2 1773
    List of debts.
    Executor: Solomon Webster.

Thomas Dawson   112.206   DO   £78.6.5   May 10 1773   Jun 10 1773
    Appraisers: Nathaniel Potter, Joseph Godwin.
    Creditors: Tharp & Ralston, Jonathon Bready.
    Next of kin: Richard Dawson, Rebekah Smith.
    Executrix: Sarah Dawson.

Kendall Jacobs   112.209   DO   £370.9.6   May 26 1773   Jun 31 1773
    Appraisers: Robert Clarkson, William Cannon.
    Creditors: Jonathon Stewart, Barthol Twiford.
    Next of kin: John Jacobs, Curtis Jacobs.
    Executors: Sarah Jacobs, William Jacobs.

Christopher Nutter   112.213   DO   £704.8.9   Mar 26 1773   Jun 2 1773
    Appraisers: Robert Clarkson, William Willson.
    Creditors: Levin Crapper, Betty Manlove.
    Next of kin: David Nutter, Mary Cannon.
    Executrix: Eleanor, wife of William Polk.

John Edgell   112.218   DO   £47.7.0   Mar 29 1773   Jun 2 1773
    Appraisers: Maccabeus Alford, Peter Edmondson.
    Next of kin: James Edgell, Abraham Edgell.
    Administratrix: Elisabeth Edgell.

Charles Walker   112.220   DO   £59.15.9   Jun 17 1773
    Appraisers: John Stevens, Arthur Whitely.
    Creditors: Daniel Sulivane, Jr., William Ennalls.
    Next of kin: Elisabeth Hogans, Priscillah Walker.
    Administrator: Philemon Lecompte.

John Polk   112.223   DO   £496.5.5   May 26 1773   Jun 2 1773
    Appraisers: Robert Clarkson, Elijah Adams.
    Next of kin: Anne Laws, Daniel Polk, Betty Manlove.
    Administrator: William Polk.

Edward Trippe   112.225   DO   £2019.1.9   Jul 19 1773
    Appraisers: William Haskins, Thomas Noel.
    Creditors: James Murray, Thomas Muir.
    Next of kin: Mary Hindman, Elisabeth (sister to Edward Trippe) wife of B.
        Ennalls.
    Executrix: Margaret Trippe.

David Pollock   112.233   DO   £1086.8.8   Mar 26 1773   Jun 1 1773
    Appraisers: Henry Hooper, George Waters.
    Creditors: John Pollock, John Collings.
    Next of kin: John Pollock, Joseph Pollock.
    Executors: John Collings, Alexander Laws.

John Chandler   112.243   CH   £226.13.7   May 11 1773   Jun 21 1773
    Appraisers: Henry Smith Hawkins, George Keech.
    Creditors: Barnes & Redgate, Robert Mundell for John Glassford & Co.
    Next of kin: Stephen Chandler, Samuel Cox.
    Administrator: Stephen Chandler.

Thomas Posey, Jr.   112.245   CH   £28.18.4   May 3 1773   Jun 22 1773
    Appraisers: Robert Hendley Court, William Barker.
    Creditors: Knox & Baillie (creditor of Thomas Posey {son of Richard} dec'd),
        Ignatius Ratcliff.
    Next of kin: Elisabeth Posey, Ignatius Byrn.
    Administratrix: Ann Posey.

Mr. Christopher Haw   112.246   CH   £826.15.0   Jul 9 1773
    Appraisers: Edward Edelin, Thomas Richard Cooksey.
    Creditors: Meverell Look, Samuel Love.
    Next of kin: Samuel Briscoe, Philip Briscoe.
    Executrix: Sarah Price Haw.

Francis Spong   112.250   CH   £6.14.0   Jun 22 1773
    Appraisers: Thomas Simmes, James Vineyard.
    Creditors: Robert Mundell for John Glassford & Co.
    Administratrix: Elisabeth Spong.

Walter Dodson   112.251   CH   £435.15.8   Jun 30 1773
     Appraisers: Edward Edelin, Samuel Turner.
     Creditors: James Craik, Henry Boarman.
     Next of kin: Jacob Dodson, John Dodson.
     Executrix: Henrietta Dodson.

Samuel Wickham   112.254   FR   £428.17.6   Mar 24 1773   Aug 17 1773
     Appraisers: Benjamin Ogle, Jr., C. Beatty.
     Creditors: James Sterett & Son.
     Next of kin: James Calhoun, Henry Wickham.
     Executor: Joseph Wood, Jr.

Samuel Wickham   112.262   FR   £122.6.2   Jun 1 1773   Aug 17 1773
     List of debts.
     Executor: Joseph Wood, Jr.

Emmanuel Brandiller   112.267   FR   £100.18.6   Mar 29 1773   Sep 14 1773
(also Emmanuel Braishway)
     Appraisers: Christopher Burkard, James Rohrer.
     Creditors: John Gance, Phillip Shridt.
     Next of kin: Jacob Young.
     Administrator: Christian Hyple.

Robert Stockton   112.270   FR   ----   Aug 19 1773
     List of debts.
     Administrator/Executor: William McClary.

William Durbin   112.271   FR   £166.18.4   Aug 19 1773
     Appraisers: David Shriver, George Brown.
     Creditors: R. Crexall, Elisabeth Rogers.
     Next of kin: Samuel Durbin, Thomas Durbin.
     Executrix: Mary Durbin.

Peter Little   112.274   FR   £670.4.3   May 27 1773   Sep 10 1773
     Appraisers: Abraham Hayter, Jacob Good.
     Creditors: Mathis Nus, Weud Cadobel (?).
     Next of kin: Johann Heinrich Klein, Frietrich Klein.
     Executor: Michael Little.

William Howard   112.277   FR   £54.10.10   May 5 1773   Aug 12 1773
     Appraisers: Richard Davis, Basil Williams.
     Creditors: Rignal Pratter, Caspar Mantz.
     Next of kin: Clement Howard.
     Executor: James Howard.

James Reynolds   112.279   FR   £74.15.3   Apr 30 1773   Aug 17 1773
     Appraisers: William Witherow, Adam Kerr.
     Mentions: Joseph Ramsey, William Reynolds.
     Administrators: Mary Reynolds, William Reynolds.

John Hughs   112.280   FR   £25.3.0   Sep 10 1773
     Appraisers: Richard Richardson, Thomas Johnson.
     Creditors: Philip Thomas, John Hanson, Jr.
     Next of kin: Levi Hughs, Rachel Mokes.
     Administrator: John Hughs.

William Norris   112.281   FR   £47.19.6   Aug 19 1773
     Cash received.
     Administrator: Catharine, wife of Simon Mustitle.

John Hughs, Sr.   112.283   FR   £33.7.1   Sep 10 1773
     List of debts.
     Administrator: John Hughs, Jr.

Matthew Leany/Laney   112.284   FR   £71.11.2   Mar 30 1773   Aug 18 1773
     Appraisers: Henry Counce, Jonathon Hays.
     Creditors: Christopher Edelin for Christian Lownds, Normand Bruce for Ann Ormd.
        Key (executrix of Francis Key).
     Next of kin: Margaret Laney, Magdalene Laney.
     Executor: John Laney.

Samuel Blackmore   112.286   FR   £73.0.11   Apr 12 1773   Aug 18 1773
     Appraisers: Charles Harding, Elias Harding.
     Creditors: Robert Henderson for John Glassford & Co., Thomas Crumpkin & Co.
     Next of kin: Samuel Blackmore, Ann Blackmore.
     Executor: James Blackmore.

Henry Baward/Boward   112.288   FR   £66.6.5   Apr 24 1771   Jul 20 1773
     Appraisers: Henry Shryock, William Keyser.
     Creditors: Martin Kerr, Jonathon Heyes.
     Administratrix: Ann Boward.

John Boyer   112.290   FR   £38.4.2   May 12 1773
    Cash received.
    Administrator: Paul Boyer.

William Durbin   112.290   FR   £76.6.5   Aug 19 1773
    List of debts.
    Executrix: Mary Durbin.

Elisabeth Offutt   112.291   FR   £521.13.4   Jun 23 1773   Aug 21 1773
    Appraisers: Andrew Heugh, John Fleming.
    Creditors: T. Sprigg Wootton, John Ferguson.
    Next of kin: Hannah Offutt, Hezekiah Offutt.
    Executors: Mordecai Offutt, Nathaniel Magruder.

William Aydelord/Aydelott   112.295   WO   £74.10.2   Jun 11 1773   Aug 14 1773
    Appraisers: William Holland, John Adelott.
    Creditors: Joseph Aydelott.
    Next of kin: Samuel Aydelott, John Aydelott.
    Executrix: Mary Aydelott.

William Whittington   112.298   WO   £2143.2.0   Dec 19 1769   Aug 31 1773
    Appraisers: John Selby, Peter Chaille.
    Creditors: Neil McMullen, J. Bishop.
    Next of kin: Benton Harris, Betty Harris.
    Executrix: Mary King Whittington.

John Morris   112.302   WO   £218.17.4   Jul 25 1773   Aug 27 1773
    Appraisers: Stephen Roach, Joshua Sturgis.
    Next of kin: Samuel Morris, Jonathon Morris.
    Executrix: Mary Morris.

Nathaniel Ramsey   112.305   WO   £558.13.5   Jan 19 1773   Aug 5 1773
    Appraisers: Adam Bravard, Isaac Evans.
    Creditors: Littleton Downes, Zadock Purnell.
    Next of kin: Nanny Martin.
    Administratrix: Sarah Ramsey (surviving administrator).

Obedia Messex   112.310   WO   £147.16.5   Jun 5 1773   Aug 4 1773
(also Obediah Messick)
    Appraisers: Samuel Shelton Sloss, Elijah Cannon.
    Creditors: John Collings, Richard Crockett.
    Next of kin: Job Ingram, George Messick.
    Executrix: Comfort Messick.

Tabitha Townsend   112.313   WO   £70.17.2   Dec 28 1772   Aug 27 1773
    Appraisers: William Selby, Jr., George Martin.
    Creditors: John Coudry, Major Townsend.
    Next of kin: Sophia Atkinson, Rachel Cutler.
    Administrator: John Townsend.

William Kellam   112.315   WO   £105.5.6   Jul 1773   Aug 5 1773
    Appraisers: John Waples, Paul Thoroughgood.
    Creditors: George Messick, Bartholomew Johnson.
    Next of kin: John Kellam, Tabitha Kellam.
    Executor: Thomas Kellam.

Levin Townsend   112.319   WO   £30.16.9   Mar 2 1771   Aug 20 1773
    Appraisers: Philip Quinton, James Townsend.
    Creditors: Samuel Handy, George Haywood.
    Next of kin: Mathew Outten, George Martin.
    Administrators: Levin Hopkins, Levin Hill.

Joshua Atkinson   112.321   WO   £571.15.0   May 12 1773   Jul 9 1773
    Appraisers: Nehemiah Tilghman, John Fleming.
    Creditors: John Atkinson, Joseph Scott.
    Next of kin: John Atkinson, J. B. Schoolfield.
    Executrix: Sarah Atkinson.

Rhoda Houston   112.325   WO   £197.17.11   Mar 19 1773   Jul 16 1773
    Appraisers: Levin Vaughan, James Windser.
    Next of kin: Robert Houston, Jr., John Houston.
    Executors: John Collins.

Ezekiel Dubberly   112.330   WO   £73.13.2   Mar 23 1773   Jun 8 1773
    Appraisers: Elisha Jones, William Aydelott.
    Creditors: John Neille, John Jones.
    Next of kin: John Jones, John Duberly.
    Executrix: Jemima Dubberly.

Reubin Lynch   112.333   WO   £43.1.1   Jun 14 1773   Aug 4 1773
    Appraisers: John Cod, John Tull.
    Creditors: Joshua Hill, Turvile Kennett.
    Next of kin: Levi Linch, Sarah More.
    Administratrix: Hannah Linch.

Solomon Timmons   112.336   WO   £99.18.6   Feb 2 1773   Apr 16 1773
    Appraisers: John Dale, Joseph Ironshire.
    Creditors: M. J. Atkinson, John Postly.
    Next of kin: Samuel Timmons, Joseph Timmons.
    Administratrix: Rebeckah Timmons.

Obediah Gault   112.338   WO   £82.15.3   Feb 10 1773   Aug 4 1773
    Appraisers: Josiah Mitchell, John Dale.
    Creditors: John Postly, John Campbell.
    Next of kin: William Gault, Ann Gault.
    Executor: Moses Freeman.

John Harper   112.341   WO   £87.10.9   Jun 25 1773
    Appraisers: Joshua Duer, Joseph Merrill.
    Creditors: John Harper, Samuel Adams.
    Next of kin: Edward Harper, Mary Pilchard.
    Administratrix: Catharine Harper.

Salley Corbin   112.342   WO   £29.6.8   Mar 6 1773   Aug 1 1773
    Appraisers: J. B. Schoolfield, James Williams.
    Creditors: child (died in her minority).
    Next of kin: (of Somerset County) did not sign.
    Administrator/Executor: James Brodwatters.

Jonathon Jacobs   112.343   WO   £45.2.3   Jun 2 1773   Aug 5 1773
    Appraisers: William Holland, Levin Dirickson.
    Creditors: John Waples, Caleb Wyatt.
    Next of kin: John Hemmons, Elisabeth Hemmons.
    Administrator: Abraham Jacobs.

William Aydelott   112.346   WO   £74.11.2   Jun 11 1773   Aug 4 1773
    Appraisers: William Holland, John Aydelott.
    Creditors: James Aydelott.
    Next of kin: Samuel Aydelott, John Aydelott, Sr.
    Executrix: Mary Aydelott.

Gideon Jones   112.348   WO   £19.7.4   Aug 27 1773
    Appraisers: Bowdoin Robins, William Holland.
    Creditors: Parker Selby, John Purnell Robins.
    Next of kin: Rebecca Vearet.
    Administrator: Fisher Walton.

William Warran   112.349   WO   £17.14.9   Mar 28 1772   Aug 7 1773
    Appraisers: Joseph Ironshire, Isaac Evans.
    Creditors: Ebenezar Campbell.
    Next of kin: Thomas Warran, Richard Warran.
    Administrator: John Postly.

Joseph Bigsby   112.351   WO   £5.1.9   Sep 1 1772   Aug 7 1773
    Appraisers: Adam Bravard, Josiah Dale.
    Creditors: Levi Pepper.
    Administrator: John Postly.

Mary Kirby   112.352   WO   £373.18.6   Jun 4 1772   Aug 5 1773
    Appraisers: Josiah Mitchell, John Stewart.
    Creditors: Turvile Kennett, John Lindell.
    Next of kin: Isabela Miller, Sarah Miller.
    Executrix: Sarah Kirby.

John Wilson   112.355   BA   £227.6.0   Jun 7 1773   Jun 28 1773
    Appraisers: John Walters, John Presbury.
    Creditors: J. Beale Howard, Stephen Walters.
    Next of kin: Thomas Wilson, James Wilson.
    Administratrix: Cordelia Wilson.

Micajah Greenfield   112.357   BA   £578.4.3   May 7 1773   Jul 31 1773
    Appraisers: Greenbury Dorsey, John Wood.
    Creditors: William West (creditor to estate of James Tayler).
    Next of kin: Plina Adams, James Greenfield.
    Executors: James Osborn, Mary Greenfield.

Blackledge Woodland   112.361   BA   £120.10.7   Jun 24 1773   Aug 5 1773
    Appraisers: John Day (son of Edward), Samuel Ricketts.
    Creditors: Henry Wetherall, J. Beale Howard.
    Next of kin: Jonathon Woodland, Martha Daney.
    Executrix: Elisabeth Woodland.

Katharine North   112.364   BA   £85.4.0   Feb 2 1773   Feb 10 1773
    Appraisers: John Mariny, Moses Galloway.
    Creditors: Henry Stevenson, Mordecai Gist.
    Administratrix: Mary Stansbury.

William Debrular   112.365   BA   £51.5.3   Jun 21 1773
    Appraisers: Henry Wetherall, Jonathon Woodland.
    Mentions: Cordelia Presbury, Micajah Debrular.
    Mentions: John Beale Howard, Buchanan & Cowan.
    Administrator: William Debrular.

William Towson   112.366   BA   £56.9.8   Aug 22 1773
    Appraisers: Nathaniel Nicholson, Abraham Britten.
    Creditors: Benjamin Griffith & Bro., John Smith.
    Next of kin: Ezekiel Towson, Dinah Towson.
    Executor: Thomas Baily.

John Talbott (son of John)   112.367   BA   £431.1.9   Dec 23 1771   Jul 29 1773
    Appraisers: Thomas Talbott, Jacob Johnson.
    Creditors: Jonathon Plowman, Benjamin Griffith & Bro.
    Next of kin: Thomas Talbott, Benjamin Talbott.
    Administrators: Sophia Talbott, John Talbott.

Archibald Mossman   112.370   BA   £14.4.5   Jul 29 1773   Jul 30 1773
    Appraisers: Thomas Conestable, David McClellan.
    Creditors: John McClelan, George Pristman.
    Next of kin: Christian Mossman.
    Administrator: Thomas Beard.

Robert Kay   112.371   BA   £36.2.1   Aug 20 1766   Aug 6 1773
    Appraisers: John Paca, Aquila Hall.
    Creditors: Amos Garrett.
    Administrator: John Lee Webster.

William Jones   112.373   BA   £241.6.5   Aug 6 1773
    Appraisers: John Wilson, Hugh Whiteford.
    Mentions: Jacob Jones.
    Mentions: Thomas Steel, John Wilson & Co.
    Executor: William Jones.

Joseph Beaumont   112.376   BA   £716.14.10   Sep 11 1773
    Appraisers: H. Courtenay, William Richardson.
    Mentions: Richard Button, Joseph Magoffin.
    Executrix: Elisabeth Beaumont.

John Backer/Baker   112.382   BA   £16.6.6   Aug 9 1773
    Appraisers: Samuel Messer Smith, Jacob Welsch.
    Creditors: Jacob Welsch, Johannes Stanwer.
    Next of kin: Peter Backer, Elisabeth Backer.
    Administrator: Evet. Baker.

William Towson   112.383   BA   £40.18.6   Aug 13 1773
    List of debts.
    Executor: Thomas Baily.

Thomas Kelly   112.384   BA   £24.16.6   Aug 30 1773
    Appraisers: William Wilson, William Ramsey.
    Creditors: Peter Langlin, John Stevenson.
    Next of kin: Mary Martin.
    Executrix: Martha Martin.

William Wright   112.385   BA   £62.3.7   Nov 11 1772   Jun 16 1773
    Appraisers: Abraham Andrew, Moses Galloway.
    Creditors: Abraham Inloes, John Skinner for James Russell & Co.
    Next of kin: William Wright, Joseph Wright.
    Administratrix: Sophia Hughs (late Sophia Wright).

John Legate   112.387   BA   £81.18.8   Dec 1 1772   Aug 1 1773
    Appraisers: Jacob Johnson, William Parrish.
    Mentions: Archibald Buchanan.
    Next of kin: Joseph Leggitt, Sutten Leggitt.
    Administratrix: Ann Legate.

John Anderson   112.389   BA   £143.19.11   Mar 2 1773   Jun 26 1773
    Appraisers: Daniel Curtis, Richard Jones.
    Creditors: Buchanan & Cowan, Belinda Talbot (executrix of Thomas Talbot, dec'd).
    Next of kin: William Anderson, Benjamin Anderson.
    Administratrix: Isabella Anderson.

John Anderson   112.391   BA   £16.13.1   Jun 26 1773
    List of debts.
    Administratrix: Isabella Anderson.

John Legate   112.391   BA   £6.8.2   Aug 1 1773
    List of debts.
    Administratrix: Ann Legate.

Thomas Hatton   112.392   BA   £35.9.6   Aug 20 1773
    List of debts.
    Administratrix: Catharine Hatton.

Thomas Kelly   112.393   BA   £3.19.3   Sep 10 1773
    List of debts.
    Executrix: Martha Martin.

William Debrular   112.394   BA   £8.6.6   Jun 1 1773
    List of debts.
    Executor: William Debrular.

William Towson   112.395   BA   £42.10.5   Aug 13 1773
    List of debts.
    Executor: Thomas Bayly.

John Read Jenifer   112.396   SM   £615.18.0   Jun 10 1773
    Appraisers: George Leigh, Massey Leigh.
    Creditors: Archibald Campbell for James Gordon & Co., Jenifer Taylor.
    Next of kin: Samuel Jenifer, Ann Read.
    Administratrix: Elisabeth Jenifer.

Phillip Abel/Abell   112.398   SM   £57.4.0   Nov 2 1772   Jul 1 1773
    Appraisers: Philip Clark, Bennet Medley.
    Next of kin: Samuel Abell, Jr., Samuel Abell youngest.
    Administratrix: Ann Dradon Abell.

Mrs. Mary Hart   112.400   SM   £50.10.2   May 7 1773
    Appraisers: Gerard Bond, William Mills.
    Creditors: James Bate, Raphael Lancaster.
    Next of kin: Thomas Allston, Jr., Elisabeth Woodward.
    Administrator: Thomas Allston.

John Simmons   112.402   SM   £159.10.11   Sep 21 1773
    Appraisers: Ignatius Taylor, James King.
    Creditors: Hugh Hopewell.
    Next of kin: James Milbourne, A. Milbourne.

    Thomas Tenneson   112.405   SM   £3.11.3   Feb 16 1773
    Appraisers: Michael Jenifer, Matthais Jones.
    Administrator: Jesse Tenneson.

William Doxey   112.406   SM   £116.12.7   Aug 14 1772   Jun 22 1773
    Appraisers: George Biscoe, Matthais Jones.
    Next of kin: Ann Davis, Aaron Davis.
    Administrator/Executor: James Doxey.

Thomas Redman   112.409   SM   £120.4.9   Jan 14 1773   Jul 10 1773
    Appraisers: John Thompson, Jr., William Martin.
    Creditors: William Burnett, Archibald Campbell for John Glassford & Co.
    Next of kin: William Gaulsbery.
    Administratrix: Sarah Redman.

Richard Weaklin/Wheatly   112.412   SM   £67.17.2   Sep 17 1772   May 1 1773
    Appraisers: Joshua Graves, Sinha Wilson.
    Next of kin: Thomas Wavolen.
    Administrator: Thomas Green Alvey.

John McPherson   112.414   SM   £29.9.7   Jul 20 1773
    List of debts.
    Administratrix: Rachel McPherson.

John French   112.415   SM   £47.12.7   Aug 9 1773
    Appraisers: Enoch Fenwick, Francis Boarman,
    Next of kin: James French, Martin French.
    Administrator/Executor: Ignatius French.
Executrix: Elisabeth Simmons.

Bennett Fenwick   112.416   SM   £10.9.7   Jan 1 1773
    List of debts.
    Executor: Richard Fenwick.

William Joseph, Jr.   112.417   SM   £54.14.6   Jan 20 1773   Sep 17 1773
    Appraisers: John Hooper Brome, John Cartwright.
    Creditors: Richard Boarman.
    Next of kin: William Joseph, Clement Joseph.
    Administrator: Thomas Reeder.

Benjamin Williams   112.418   SM   £0.7.2   Jul 1 1773
    List of debts.
    Executor: Benjamin Williams.

Bennett Fenwick   112.419   SM   £5.2.9   Jan 1 1773
    List of debts.
    Executor: Richard Fenwick.

Jesse Boldin   112.419   CE   £55.8.6   Jul 20 1773   Jul 24 1773
    List of debts.
    Administratrix: Mary, wife of John Smith.

Richard White   112.422   CE   £159.8.5   Jun 24 1773
    List of debts.
    Administrator: John Gray.

George Ankrim   112.423   CE   £8.19.5   Jun 26 1773
    List of debts.
    Executor: Archibald Ankrim.

Robert Mackey   112.424   CE   £6.0.0   Jun 28 1773
    List of debts.
    Executor: James Mackey.

Sarah Bordley   112.424   CE   £75.5.11   Jun 19 1773
    List of debts.
    Administratrix: Cassandra Pearce.

George Ankrim   112.425   CE   £2.7.0   Jun 26 1773
    List of debts.
    Executor: Archibald Ankrim.

Robert Mackey   112.425   CE   £77.18.8   Jun 28 1773
    List of debts.
    Executor: James Mackey.

Sarah Bordley   112.426   CE   £0.18.10   Jun 19 1773
    List of debts.
    Administratrix: Cassandra Pearce.

Silvester Ryland   112.426   CE   £27.1.0   Jun 24 1773
    List of debts.
    Administrator: James Cosden.

Henry Pennington   112.427   CE   £16.10.0   Jun 23 1773
    List of debts.
    Executrix: Mary Pennington.

Richard Biddle   112.427   CE   £58.7.2   Jul 17 1773
    List of debts.
    Executors: Augustine Biddle, Dominick Biddle.

Richard White   112.428   CE   £6.17.6   Jul 8 1772   Jun 24 1773
    Appraisers: James Coppin, Alexander Wilkinson.
    Creditors: William Rogers, Archibald Wright.
    Administrator: John Gray.

Hartley Sappington   112.430   CE   £434.17.2 Jun 22 1773   Aug 7 1773
    Appraisers: John Ward Veazey, James Porter.
    Creditors: Richard Sappington, Charles Phillipshill.
    Next of kin: Richard Sappington, Richard Pearce.
    Executor: Benjamin Sappington.

Edward Trippe   112.433   DO   ----   Jul 19 1773
    vide folio 225.
    Executrix: Margaret Trippe.

Mr. James Walmsley   113.1   CE   £88.10.10 Apr 16 1773   Jun 23 1773
    Appraisers: John Ward Veazey, John Beedle.
    Creditors: Benjamin Pryce, Ephraim Pryce.
    Next of kin: William Walmsley, Nicholas Walmsley.
    Administrator: William Walmsley, Jr.

James Burgin   113.3   KE   £142.4.3   Jun 13 1773   Aug 17 1773
    Appraisers: Christopher Hall, Joseph Redgrave.
    Creditors: Isaac Spencer, James Davis.
    Next of kin: Philip Burgin, Joshua Burgin.
    Executor: Oliver Smith.

Samuel White   113.5   KE £3.2.6   Aug 18 1773   Sep 1 1773
    Appraisers: Gilbert Falconar, John Spearman.
    Creditors: Gilpin & Jurey.
    Next of kin: John White.
    Administrator: John Dean.

Benjamin Daws   113.6   KE £23.16.2   Aug 10 1773
    Appraisers: Samuel Dickinson, Solomon Semans.
    Creditors: William Wood, James Davis.
    Administratrix: Margaret Daws.

James Fields   113.7   KE £9.19.0   Jul 20 1773   Aug 25 1773
    Appraisers: Thomas Croome, William Cowarden.
    Creditors: Christopher Fields, Coter Griffith.
    Next of kin: Christopher Fields, James Fields.
    Administrator: Joseph Fields.

Mary Meeks   113.8   KE £55.19.9   Mar 16 1773   Aug 21 1773
(widow of Francis Meeks)
    Appraisers: William Sipley, William Copper.
    Creditors: Priscillah Worrell, Kinwin Wroth.
    Next of kin: Thomas Lahill, Hannah Lahill.
    Administrator: Kinwin Wroth.

John McGinnis   113.9   KE £6.12.6   Nov 13 1772   Aug 14 1773
    Appraisers: William Smith, William St. Clair.
    Creditors: John Dean, Isaac Spencer.
    Administrator: Francis Senan.

Michael Chambers   113.9   KE £91.18.0   Jun 8 1773   Aug 28 1773
    Appraisers: Thomas Boyer, Nathel Boyer.
    Creditors: John Crawford, Jacob Paterson.
    Next of kin: Marget Reed, Hewerm (?) Chaird.
    Executor: William Hynson French.

John Kennard   113.11   KE £17.3.9   Nov 1772   Aug 17 1773
    Appraisers: James Smith, Samuel Sterrett.
    Creditors: Robert Anderson, Richard Lloyd for Mr. James Anderson.
    Next of kin: Daniel Kennard, Stephen Kennard.
    Administratrix: Ann Kennard.

John Spencer   113.11   KE £7.3.2   Aug 18 1773
    List of debts.
    Administrator: Isaac Spencer.

John Spencer   113.11   KE £201.1.6   Jul 19 1773   Aug 18 1773
    Appraisers: Ebenezar Reyner, Robert Maccwill.
    Administrator: Isaac Spencer.

Isaac Handy   113.12   SO £629.15.2   Nov 24 1772   Sep 13 1773
    Appraisers: John Span Conway, Littleton Airs.
    Creditors: George Handy, Sr., William Waland.
    Next of kin: Joseph Handy, Ann Handy.
    Executor: George Handy.

Joseph Surman   113.16   SO £70.6.11   Jan 7 1773   Sep 10 1773
    Appraisers: Thomas Irving, John Piper.
    Creditors: James Anderson, Richard Trilley.
    Next of kin: Marget Anderson, Sarah Anderson.
    Administrator: John Leatherbury.

Joshua Surman   113.18   SO £38.13.1   May 26 1773   Sep 7 1773
    Appraisers: Stephen Roach, Francis Adams.
    Creditors: Isaac Surman, Mary Morres.
    Next of kin: Isaac Surman, Edward Surman.
    Executor: David Ragling.

Thomas Disharoon   113.19   SO £71.1.4   Feb 24 1773   Aug 19 1773
    Appraisers: Stephen Roach, John Chambers.
    Creditors: Robert Dashiell, George Handy.
    Next of kin: George Disharoon, Obediah Disharoon.
    Executor: Francis Disharoon.

Levi Wood   113.20   SO £74.3.9   Mar 12 1773   Aug 17 1773
    Appraisers: William Adams, William Moore.
    Creditors: George Dashiell, Planner Williams.
    Next of kin: William Wood, Martha Wood.
    Executor: Leah Wood.

Ann Wood   113.21   SO   £285.17.0   Mar 12 1773   Aug 17 1773
    Appraisers: William Adams, William Moore.
    Creditors: Planner Williams, ------ Moore.
    Next of kin: William Wood, Martha Wood.
    Administratrix/Executrix: Leah Wood (executrix of Levi Wood).

John Anderson   113.23   SO   £87.5.10   Jan 21 1773   Sep 9 1773
    Appraisers: John Piper, George Dashiell.
    Creditors: Joshua Morris, James Bounds.
    Next of kin: James Anderson, Isaac Anderson.
    Administrator: John Anderson.

Francis Humphreys   113.25   TA   £423.11.5   Jun 15 1771   Jun 1 1773
    Appraisers: Joseph Bewley, William Beswick (dec'd by Jun 1 1773).
    Creditors: Thomas Jones.
    Next of kin: Thomas Baker.
    Administratrix: Martha Humphreys.

Dr. Daniel Killum   113.28   TA   £16.3.1   Jun 8 1773   Jul 6 1773
    Appraisers: John Stevens, Edward Trippe.
    Executrix: Mary, wife of Thomas Dawson.

Abraham Brumwell   113.28   TA   £20.4.3   Aug 26 1773   Aug 23 1773
    Appraisers: John Denny, David Fairbank.
    Creditors: Joseph Hopkins, Thomas Dodson.
    Next of kin: Present but refused to sign.
    Administrator: William Grace.

Barnaby Dougerty/Dougherty   113.30   TA   £671.1.11   Aug 3 1773
    List of debts.
    Administrator: John Dougherty.

Andrew Skinner   113.38   TA   £137.6.6   Aug 20 1773
    List of debts.
    Administratrix: Ann, wife of Hugh Price.

Andrew Skinner   113.40   TA   £54.11.2   Aug 20 1773
    List of debts.
    Administratrix: Ann, wife of Hugh Price.

David Killum   113.41   TA   £264.14.0   Jul 6 1773
    List of debts.
    Executrix: Mary, wife of Thomas Dawson.

David Killum   113.46   TA   ----   May 18 1773   Jul 6 1773
    List of debts.
    Executrix: Mary, wife of Thomas Dawson.

Samuel Bowman   113.56   TA   £6.9.0   Aug 24 1773
    List of debts.
    Executrix: Ann Bowman.

John Blades   113.57   TA   £12.8.2   Oct 30 1773
    List of debts.
    Administrators: Elisabeth Blades, John Blades.

Grace Morgan   113.57   TA   £41.12.11   Feb 15 1773   Nov 1 1773
    Appraisers: Samuel Thomas, George Dudley (dec'd by Nov 1 1773).
    Creditors: Tilghman & Nicols.
    Next of kin: William Benny, Sarah Spuron (?).
    Administrator: James Tennant.

Elisabeth Lawrence   113.59   TA   £55.8.4   Jun 10 1773   Oct 3 1773
    Appraisers: Solomon Neale, Robert Neale.
    Creditors: Sharp & Dawson, Stevens Martin & Goldsborough.
    Next of kin: George Hunt, Mary Lizard.
    Administrator: Thomas Dawson.

Joseph Parratt (joyner)   113.61   TA   £67.0.10   Apr 24 1770   Sep 21 1773
    Appraisers: Robert Comerford, William Troth.
    Creditors: John Johnston, Robert Goldsborough.
    Next of kin: Richard Parratt, James Parratt.
    Administrator: Perry Parratt.

William Elston   113.62   TA   £150.9.0   Sep 21 1773
    Appraisers: James Barnwill, Richard Turbutt.
    Creditors: James Lloyd Chamberlaine, William Nicols.
    Next of kin: John Shannahan, Elisabeth Shannahan.
    Administratrix: Mary, wife of Perry Parratt.

John Waters   113.63   TA   £304.6.5   Sep 17 1773   Nov 6 1773
    Appraisers: Joseph Bewley, John Baker.
    Creditors: Robert Goldsborough, Nicols & Goldsborough.
    Administratrix: Sarah Waters.

William Holmes   113.65   TA   £61.15.5   Aug 21 1766   Aug 20 1773
    Appraisers: William Trippe, Thomas Skinner.
    Creditors: Matthew Jenkins, Ralph Holmes.
    Next of kin: Solomon Holmes, Ralph Holmes.
    Administratrix: Leah, wife of James Jones.

William Holmes   113.68   TA   £16.12.4   Jul 20 1769   Aug 20 1773
    Appraisers: William Trippe, Henry Bowdle.
    Creditors: Matthew Jenkins, Ralph Holmes.
    Next of kin: Solomon Holmes, Ralph Holmes.
    Administratrix: Leah, wife of James Jones.

John Cullen   113.69   TA   £111.16.9   Aug 19 1773   Aug 24 1773
    Appraisers: Abner Turner, James Kemp.
    Creditors: Tilghman & Nicols, Richard Johns (executor of P. Comerford).
    Next of kin: John Cullin, David Cullin.
    Administratrix: Elisabeth Cullen.

Andrew Skinner   113.71   TA   £868.12.8   Feb 18 1769   Aug 20 1773
    Appraisers: James Benson, Thomas Ray.
    Creditors: James Lloyd Chamberlaine, Daniel Skinner.
    Next of kin: Richard Skinner, Daniel Skinner.
    Administratrix: Ann, wife of Hugh Rice.

Benedict Hutchings   113.74   TA   £588.15.8   May 6 1773   Nov 4 1773
    Appraisers: Richard Johns, Solomon Neall.
    Creditors: George Parrott, Nicols & Chamberlaine.
    Next of kin: Isiah Parratt Hix, Pheby Hicks.
    Executor: Samuel Thomas.

Edward Nedles/Nedels   113.78   TA   £17.7.2   Jun 22 1773   Jun 22 1773
    Appraisers: D. Wilson (Quaker), P. Comerford (dec'd).
    Creditors: Matthais Gale, Moses Allen.
    Next of kin: Nancy Hambleton, John Nedles.
    Executrix: Ann Nedels.

Hannah Turner   113.79   TA   £25.4.9   Feb 1 1773   Aug 8 1773
    Appraisers: Aaron Parrott, Richard Johns.
    Creditors: Orson Warren, Ann Bowman.
    Next of kin: William Warren, Orson Warren.
    Administrator: Joseph Turner.

James Barnett   113.80   TA   £156.18.11   Aug 2 1773   Nov 6 1773
    Appraisers: John Stevens, Charles Bullen.
    Creditors: H. Lloyd.
    Next of kin: Richard Barnett, Susannah Parratt.
    Administratrix: Jean Barnett.

James Robinson   113.82   TA   £27.4.2   Jun 23 1773   Oct 6 1773
    Appraisers: Solomon Neall, Henry Troth.
    Mentions: Rachel Harrison, John Burkham.
    Next of kin: Lambert Robinson, Rebekah Burkham.
    Administrator: Levin Milles.

Henry Clark   113.83   TA   £329.19.5   Jun 18 1773   Aug 3 1773
    Appraisers: Richard Johns, George Burgess.
    Creditors: James Lloyd Chamberlaine, Aaron Atkinson.
    Next of kin: Caleb Clark, Joshua Clark.
    Administratrix: Jean Clark.

David Merrick   113.86   TA   £174.7.8   May 15 1773   Nov 16 1773
    Appraisers: Thomas Jenkins, Mr. Lewis Barnet.
    Creditors: Thomas Welsh, William Stevens.
    Next of kin: John Merrick, Andrew Merrick.
    Administratrix: Elisabeth Merrick.

Layronce Porter   113.89   TA   £112.13.11   Jul 23 1766   Oct 16 1773
    Appraisers: Fiddeman Rolle, Edward Trippe.
    Creditors: Matthew Tilghman.
    Next of kin: Ann Porter, Elisabeth Porter.
    Executrix: Sophia, wife of John Blyth.

George Garnet   113.92   QA   £216.17.4   Apr 8 1773
    List of debts.
    Administrator: Turbutt Wright.

Ann Blackiston   113.92   KE   £60.7.9   Feb 5 1773   Feb 10 1773
    Appraisers: Nathaniel Miller, Richard Miller.
    Creditors: John Hage, Thomas Ringgold.
    Next of kin: George Blakiston, John Blackiston.
    Executor: James Blackiston.

Thomas Talbot   113.93   CA   £24.17.8   Apr 15 1771 Jul 9 1773
    Appraisers: William Harris, Jr., Thomas Cleverly Dare.
    Creditors: James Weems, William Harris.
    Next of kin: Joseph Talbot, William Alnutt.
    Executors: John Talbot, Philip Talbot.

Josias Sunderland   113.94   CA   £477.15.1   May 30 1772
    Appraisers: William Dare, Michael Catterton.
    Creditors: John Hamilton Smith, Charles Grahame.
    Next of kin: Thomas Sunderland, Lewis Stockett.
    Executor: Benjamin Sunderland.

John Gatrall   113.97   FR   £20.2.6   Feb 22 1773 Feb 26 1773
    Appraisers: Robert Owen.
    Executrix: Rachel, wife of Benjamin Griffith.

Mr. Samuel Offutt   113.97   FR   £23.5.6   May 19 1762 Jun 8 1773
    Appraisers: William Pritchett, Andrew Heugh.
    Administrator: Nathaniel Magruder (son of Alexander).

Samuel Offutt   113.97   FR   £0.18.4   Jun 8 1773
    List of debts.
    Administrator: Nathaniel Magruder (son of Alexander).

John Orme   113.98   FR   £249.6.8   Apr 18 1773 May 14 1773
    List of debts.
    Administrator/Executor: James Orme, Lucy Orme.

William Reed   113.103   AA   £277.0.8   Nov 4 1772   Sep 8 1773
    Appraisers: Thomas N. Stockett, Thomas Watkins.
    Creditors: Thomas Duckett for Thomas Philpot, John Nelson Gray.
    Next of kin: James Reed, William Reed, Jr.
    Executrix: Eleanor Reed.

Hezekiah Foreman   113.106   AA   £209.0.1   Apr 8 1773
    Appraisers: Clark Rockhold, John Davis.
    Creditors: John Shaw, Robert Couden.
    Next of kin: Joseph Foreman, Rachel Foreman.
    Executrix: Mary Foreman.

Walter Pumphrey   113.107   AA   £324.7.3   Mar 12 1773
    Appraisers: Elijah Robeson, Daniel Smith.
    Creditors: Nicholas Maccubbin, Thomas Harwood, John Brice.
    Next of kin: David Meroshaw, Greenbury Pumphrey.
    Administratrix: Rezin Pumphrey.

George Connoway   113.109   AA   £330.8.2   May 1 1773   Jul 27 1773
    Appraisers: W. Gambrill, ------ Watts.
    Creditors: Robert Couden, John Brice.
    Next of kin: Vachel Conaway, Elijah Robosson.
    Executrix: Rachel Connaway.

John Schneider   113.111   AA   £55.17.3   Oct 24 1771 Jul 27 1773
    Appraisers: Jesse M. Hard, Thomas Hewitt.
    Creditors: Elias Boyer & Co., Harwood & Brice.
    Administrator: Thomas Harwood, Jr.

John Jevens   113.112   AA   £33.16.3   Aug 31 1770 Jul 27 1773
    Appraisers: Thomas Hyde, William Wilkins.
    Creditors: John Marriott, Philip Hammond, Jr.
    Administrator: Thomas Harwood, Jr.

Basil Wheeler   113.114   AA   £37.7.1   Sep 1 1773
    List of debts.
    Administratrix: Rebeccah Wheeler.

Nicholas Norman   113.114   AA   £85.5.7   Aug 9 1773
    List of debts.
    Executor: Nicholas Norman.

James Holladay/Holliday   113.115   AA   £23.9.3   Mar 31 1773
    List of debts.
    Administratrix: Sarah Holliday.

James Holliday/Hollyday   113.115   AA   £20.15.0   Mar 30 1772
        Appraisers: Samuel Lane, Thomas Deale.
        Executrix: Sarah Hollyday.

John Beard   113.116   AA   £9.14.0   Mar 11 1773   Jul 14 1773
        Appraisers: William Ijams (son of George), William Ijams.
        Next of kin: Richard Beard, Rachel Beard.
        Administrator: Joseph Bird.

John Pennington   113.116   AA   £15.7.0   Jan 29 1773   Mar 6 1773
        Appraisers: William Ricketts, Hezekius Foreman.
        Creditors: Daniel Soward, Milka Floyad.
        Next of kin: William Haycraft, William Pennington.
        Administratrix: Eleanor Pennington.

John Cromwell   113.117   AA   £181.17.1   Apr 6 1773
(son of Joshua)
        Appraisers: William Gambrill, Benjamin Gambrill.
        Creditors: Philip Hammond, Jr., Lancelot Jacques.
        Next of kin: Oneal Cromwell, Joshua Cromwell.
        Executrix: Comfort Cromwell.

John McDonald   113.118   AA   £551.4.9   Jan 26 1773   Sep 15 1773
        Appraisers: Alexander Warfield, Nicholas Worthington.
        Creditors: Lancelot Jacques, Denton Jacques.
        Next of kin: two brothers (unnamed) who came to Maryland by Sep 15 1773.
        Executor: Robert Couden.

Joseph Brown   113.121   AA   £34.15.6   Jul 29 1771   Jun 18 1773
        Appraisers: Thomas Hyde, Thomas Harwood, Jr.
        Creditors: Colin Campbile, James Dicke & Stewart.
        Administrator: James Dundass.

Mrs. Priscilla Woodward   113.122   AA   £170.17.5   Mar 16 1773   May 1 1773
        Appraisers: Alexander Warfield, Nicholas Worthington.
        Creditors: William Noke.
        Next of kin: Mary Ridgley, Thomas Woodward.
        Executor: William Woodward.

Mr. James John Mackall   113.125   CA   £7554.2.10   Mar 4 1772   Jul 12 1773
        Appraisers: Alexander Somervell, Samuel Gray.
        Creditors: Edward Hall & Co., William Allein for William Mollison.
        Next of kin: James Mackall, Thomas Mackall.
        Executor: John Mackall.

David Furnie/Fourney   113.131   FR   £162.11.0   Oct 1772   Sep 15 1773
        List of debts.
        Executor: John Stull.

David Furnie/Fourney   113.133   FR   ----   Oct 1772   Sep 15 1773
        List of debts.
        Executor: John Stull.

Charles Leatherbury   113.137   QA   £125.3.11   May 11 1772   Sep 14 1773
        Appraisers: William Pryor, Benjamin Gould.
        Creditors: Gilpin & Jurey, Joseph Sudler.
        Next of kin: Thomas Leatherbury, Pen. Leatherbury.
        Administratrix: Elisabeth, wife of William Simmonds.

John Smith   113.139   CE   £1028.6.0   Feb 11 1773   Sep 1 1773
        Appraisers: Jonathon Hartshorn, William McClure.
        Creditors: William Currer, Samuel Reynolds.
        Next of kin: Margaret Smith, Moses Haslett.
        Executor: David Smith.

John Smith   113.140   CE   £104.7.3   Sep 2 1772   Sep 1 1773
        (date of death cited as Sep 2 1772)
        List of debts.
        Executor: David Smith.

Timothy Tool   113.141   QA   £243.9.6   Mar 17 1772
        Appraisers: John Fisher, John Costin.
        Creditors: Henry Casson, Hannah Clayton.
        Next of kin: James Tool, Sarah Tool.
        Executor: William Phillips.

Mr. James John Mackall   113.144   CA   £18.0.0   Sep 2 1773   Sep 18 1773
        Appraisers: Alexander Somervell, Samuel Gray.
        Executor: John Mackall.

Mrs. Theodosia Key   113.144   SM   £317.10.5   Apr 24 1773   Apr 29 1773
    Appraisers: Girard Bond, John Shanks.
    Creditors: Thomas Bond, James Jordan for John Glassford & Co.
    Next of kin: Phillip Key, Susanna Gardiner Key.
    Administrator: Normand Brull.

John Orme   113.147   FR   £426.19.7   Jul 20 1772   May 14 1773
    Appraisers: Thomas Johns, William Deakins, Jr.
    Creditors: John Ferguson, Stephen Wist.
    Next of kin: Archibald Orme, Ebenezar Edn. Orme.
    Executors: James Orme, Lucy Orme.

Lewis Derochburne   113.151   QA   £247.13.11   Apr 8 1771
    Appraisers: Samuel Blunt (dec'd), Thomas Barnes, Jr.
    Creditors: Philip Downes for Mr. James Anderson, Joseph Derochburne.
    Next of kin: Margaret Derochburne, Joseph Derochburne.
    Administrator: William Coursey.

Lewis Derochburne   113.154   QA   £298.0.3   Oct 16 1772   Oct 14 1773
    Appraisers: Thomas Barnes, Jr., Arthur Emory, Jr.
    Creditors: Philip Downes for Mr. James Anderson, Joseph Derochburne.
    Next of kin: Margaret Derochburne, Joseph Derochburne.
    Administrator: William Coursey.

James Peters   113.155   QA   £21.3.6   Aug 9 1773   Nov 26 1773
    Appraisers: Benjamin Gould, Abner Dudley.
    Next of kin: Jonathon Peters, William Peters.
    Administrator: John Peters.

John Bryan   113.156   QA   £35.16.5   Oct 9 1769   Nov 3 1773
    Mentions: Hezekiah Betts, James Roberts.
    Creditors: Smyth & Sudler, Henry Bolton.
    Mentions: Robert Thompson, Ephraim Thompson.
    Executrix: Tabitha Bryan.

Abraham Oldson   113.158   QA   £281.19.8   Jun 30 1772   Sep 6 1773
    Appraisers: James O'Bryan, Basil Warfield.
    Creditors: William Minor, John Walten.
    Next of kin: John Holdson, James Holdson.
    Executor: Thomas Oldson.

John Tillotson   113.160   QA   £820.2.9   Apr 27 1772   Sep 13 1773
    Appraisers: Basil Warfield, James O'Bryan.
    Creditors: James Hollyday, James Chetham.
    Next of kin: John Tillotson, Sarah Tillotson.
    Executrix: Sarah Tillotson.

William Bush   113.163   QA   £122.2.9   Sep 29 1773   Nov 20 1773
    Appraisers: John Costin, James Chetham.
    Creditors: Christopher Cross Routh, Charles Goldsborough.
    Next of kin: George Bush, Jamme Hargadine.
    Executrix: Elisabeth Bush.

Thomas Jump   113.165   QA   £197.19.8   1773   Nov 4 1773
    Appraisers: Giles Hicks, Jeremiah Colston.
    Creditors: Tilghman & Nicols, Henry Casson.
    Next of kin: Leavin Jump, Abraham Jump.
    Executrix: Isabella Jump.

Richard Cooper   113.166   QA   £1217.17.0   1773   Oct 21 1773
    Appraisers: Giles Hicks, Jeremiah Colston.
    Creditors: Phillip Feddeman, Tilghman & Nicols.
    Next of kin: George Cooper, John Hall.
    Executrix: Ann Cooper.

Charles Clayton (Gent.)   113.171   QA   £563.17.6   Aug 10 1773   Nov 8 1773
    Appraisers: John Bordley, John Seeders.
    Creditors: Clement Sewell, William M. Lead.
    Next of kin: Sarah Chaires, Mary Clayton.
    Administratrix: Elisabeth Clayton.

James Reed   113.175   QA   £287.10.10   1773   Oct 28 1773
    Appraisers: Giles Hicks, Jeremiah Colston.
    Creditors: Tilghman & Nicols, Robert Browne for Priscilla Browne.
    Next of kin: Abraham Reed, Isaac Reed.
    Administratrix: Rachel Reed.

James Hart   113.177   QA   £67.6.0   Jun 2 1773   Nov 24 1773
    Appraisers: John Colston, James Chetham.
    Creditors: Christopher Cross Routh, Thomas Reed.
    Next of kin: Augustin Hart, Patrick Hart.
    Administratrix: Henrietta Hart.

Agnes Peaters/Peters   113.178   QA   £130.4.8   Jun 9 1773   Nov 26 1773
      Appraisers: Benjamin Gould, Abner Dudley.
      Creditors: Gilpin & Jurey, Thomas Ford.
      Next of kin: Jonathon Peters, John Peters.
      Executor: William Peters.

Mary Eagles   113.181   QA   £143.18.4   Mar 26 1771   Sep 24 1773
      Appraisers: Valentine Burroughes, Richard Heather.
      Creditors: C. Tilghman, ------ Needham.
      Next of kin: Elisabeth Eagles, Mary Dyre Eagles.
      Executor: John Fisher.

Thomas Hughs   113.184   QA   £5.7.6   Sep 7 1773   Dec 6 1773
      Appraisers: William Winchester Mason, William Carman.
      Creditors: Vining & Varnum.
      Next of kin: Joseph Morris.
      Administrator: Thomas Bartlett.

Thomas Meeds   113.185   QA   £10.2.4   Aug 3 1773   Oct 28 1773
      Appraisers: Giles Hicks, Jeremiah Colston.
      Mentions: John Meeds, Lida Meeds.
      Executrix: Rachel Meeds.

Mrs. Ann Walters   113.185   QA   £207.16.8   Feb 13 1773   Oct 16 1773
      Appraisers: Charles Downes, Jr., Charles Clayton (dec'd Oct 16 1773).
      Administrator: Robert Walters.

Charles Eareckson   113.182   QA   £468.11.6   Mar 5 1773   Oct 14 1773
      Appraisers: Jacob Carter, John Elliott.
      Creditors: Benjamin Tolson, John Jones.
      Next of kin: William Eareckson, Charles Eareckson.
      Executrix: Elisabeth Eareckson.

Matthew Griffith   113.190   QA   £571.2.2   Apr 21 1773   Dec 8 1773
      Appraisers: John Fisher, Anthony Harrington.
      Creditors: John Griffith, Christopher Cross Routh.
      Next of kin: William Griffith, William Elliot Griffith.
      Executrix: Ruth Griffith.

Peter Countis/Countiss   113.193   QA   £74.5.3   Sep 4 1773   Dec 9 1773
      Appraisers: Richard Mason, William Carman.
      Creditors: Christopher Cross Routh, James Countiss.
      Next of kin: James Roe, Sarah Williams.
      Administratrix: Sarah Countiss.

John Saterfield/Satterfield   113.195   QA   £7.8.4   Aug 10 1773   Aug 26 1773
      Appraisers: Matthew Chilton, William Parratt.
      Creditors: Henry Casson, Benson Stainton.
      Next of kin: Hinson Satterfield, Solomon Satterfield.
      Administrator: Joseph Everett.

Richard Smyth   113.196   QA   £26.6.6   Aug 21 1773   Aug 26 1773
      Appraisers: Caleb Clements, John Seeders.
      Creditors: Philip Downes for Mr. James Anderson, Richard Wilson for Robert
        Browne.
      Next of kin: John Green Smith, William Smith, Jr.
      Administrator: William Smith.

William Baynard   113.197   QA   £19.0.4   1770   Jun 17 1773
      List of debts.
      Administratrix: Sophia Baynard.

Jonathon Baker   113.198   QA   £17.9.6   Aug 17 1773
      Appraisers: Thomas Baggs, Samuel Hunter.
      Creditors: Henry Casson, James Chetham.
      Next of kin: William Collings, Ann Baker.
      Administrator: Thomas Archer Price.

James Sudler   113.199   QA   £1288.19.9   Apr 8 1773   Jul 22 1773
      Appraisers: Tobias Wells, Thomas Bannister.
      Creditors: John Barnes & Co., Philip Downes for Mr. James Anderson.
      Next of kin: James R. Blunt, Susannah Walters.
      Executrix: Elisabeth Sudler.

Nicholas Price   113.206   QA   £65.17.2   Jan 8 1773   Jul 28 1773
      Appraisers: Giles Hicks, Jeremiah Colston.
      Creditors: Joshua Clark, Stevens Martin & Goldsborough.
      Next of kin: Elisabeth Manor, Nicholas Price.
      Administratrix: Margaret Price.

John Leith   113.207   QA   £70.2.8   May 12 1773   Aug 7 1773
     Appraisers: William Winchester Mason, Isaac Baggs.
     Creditors: Gideon Emory, Solomon King.
     Next of kin: Alexander Leith, John Leith.
     Administratrix: Sarah Leith.

William Willson   113.209   QA   £219.5.10   Mar 31 1773   Jun 17 1773
     Appraisers: Tobias Wells, Arthur Emory, Jr.
     Creditors: Thomas Elliott Hutchings, Sarah Legg.
     Next of kin: John Legg, James Legg, Mary Ann Goodhand, John Wilson.
     Administratrix: Rebeccah Willson.

James Sylvester   113.211   QA   £136.18.4   Aug 6 1773
     Appraisers: William Bell, Ezekiel Hunter.
     Creditors: Tilghman & Nicols, Henry Casson.
     Next of kin: Thomas Sylvester, Neriah Satterfield.
     Executrix: Deborah Sylvester.

William Harrington   113.213   QA   £134.7.2   Apr 19 1773   Aug 7 1773
     Appraisers: Richard Mason, Samuel Jackson.
     Creditors: William M. Molliston, Henry Casson.
     Next of kin: Nathan Harrington, John Price.
     Administrator: Henry Harrington.

Benjamin Harris   113.216   QA   £67.0.7   Apr 7 1773   Aug 9 1773
     Appraisers: Abner Dudley, James Roberts.
     Creditors: Isaac Spencer, Joseph Sudler.
     Next of kin: Charles Harris, William Harris.
     Administrator: Thomas Taylor.

Thomas Meredith   113.217   QA   £46.14.11   Aug 9 1773   Aug 11 1773
     Appraisers: James Kent, Basil Warfield.
     Executors: John Meredith, Margaret Meredith, Thomas Meredith.

John Matterford   113.218   QA   £15.13.1   Jul 24 1773   Aug 18 1773
     Appraisers: John Culbreth, John West.
     Creditors: Henry Casson, Robert Hall & John Jones.
     Next of kin: Nathan Hirrentin, Prudence Mountiell.
     Administrator: Richard Smith.

Richard Taylor   113.220   QA   £196.0.4   Jul 1 1772   Aug 9 1773
     Appraisers: James Hackett, William Hackett.
     Creditors: Samuel Wallis, John Rochester.
     Next of kin: Elisabeth Taylor, Martha Taylor.
     Administratrix: Elisabeth Taylor.

John Baggs, Jr.   113.222   QA   £43.3.9   Mar 6 1773   Aug 11 1773
     Appraisers: Richard Mason, William Winchester Mason.
     Creditors: Stevens Martin & Goldsborough, John Jenkinson.
     Next of kin: John Baggs, Tibbels Baggs.
     Administratrix: Rebecca Baggs.

Robert Scrivener   113.223   QA   £471.13.11   Mar 9 1773   Aug 19 1773
     Appraisers: Basil Warfield, James Chetham.
     Creditors: Thomas Ringgold, Bishop & Walters.
     Next of kin: Mary Meredith, Charles Scrivener.
     Executrix: Juliana Scrivener.

Edward Dyer   113.225   QA   £621.9.1   Mar 18 1773   Aug 25 1773
     Appraisers: Richard Mason, Vachel Downes.
     Creditors: Thomas Ringgold, Warner Mifflin.
     Next of kin: Sarah Dyer, Nathaniel Dyer.
     Administrator: Edward Dyer.

Humphrey Spry   113.228   QA   £27.2.2   Apr 24 1773   Jul 13 1773
     Appraisers: Joseph Boon, Samuel Wallis.
     Creditors: Joseph Sudler, Samuel Thompson.
     Next of kin: Jehu Spry, Abraham Spry.
     Administratrix: Mary Spry.

Charles Bradley   113.229   QA   £50.11.1   Jan 20 1772   Aug 27 1773
     Appraisers: John Fisher, Anthony Harrington.
     Creditors: Henry Casson, Richard Mason.
     Next of kin: Thompson Bradley, Charles Bradley.
     Executor: Nathaniel Bradley.

Henry Wright Pratt   113.230   QA   £276.2.11   Sep 7 1772   Aug 26 1773
     Appraisers: John Costin, James Chetham.
     Creditors: C. Tilghman, J. Nicholson, Jr.
     Next of kin: Nathan Pratt, Solomon Pratt.
     Administratrix: Hester, wife of Elbert Downes.

Samuel Blunt   113.232   QA £673.11.1   Sep 2 1772   Jul 15 1773
    Appraisers: Thomas Barnes, Jr., Arthur Emory, Jr.
    Creditors: Philip Downes for James Anderson, Richard Willson for Robert Browne.
    Next of kin: Denjamin Blunt, James R. Blunt.
    Administratrix: Sarah Blunt.

Boon Chance   113.235   QA £1.15.9   May 3 1773   Aug 6 1773
    Appraisers: Richard Mason, William Winchester Mason.
    Creditors: Edward White, Absolom Chance.
    Next of kin: Batchelder Chance, Peter Chance.
    Administrator: William Boon.

Edward Brown   113.236   QA £13.0.10   Nov 11 1773
    Appraisers: Isaac Winchester, Henry Carter.
    Creditors: Thomas Elliott Hutchings.
    Next of kin: Morgan Brown, James Brown.
    Administrator: William Ringgold.

Edward Brown, Jr.   113.236   QA £1582.1.9   Nov 12 1773
    List of debts.
    Administrator: William Ringgold.

Edward Brown, Jr.   113.241   QA £591.11.11   Nov 12 1773
    List of debts.
    Administrator: William Ringgold.

Elijah Miers   113.243   SO £7.14.4   Aug 1 1773   Oct 19 1773
    Appraisers: Joseph Venables, Joshua Huffinton.
    Creditors: John Graham, John White.
    Next of kin: Sarah Cimmey, Joseph Melson.
    Administrator: John Miers.

Teague Riggin   113.244   SO £263.19.3   May 20 1773 Oct 19 1773
    Appraisers: William Fleming, Isaac Coston.
    Creditors: John Shiriff, Elisha Parkinson.
    Next of kin: John Riggin, Benton Riggen.
    Administrators: Hannah Riggin, Teague Riggen.

Michael Tharp   113.247   SO £24.9.6   Sep 15 1773 Nov 17 1773
    Appraisers: Joseph Venables, Joshua Huffington.
    Creditors: Samuel Cooper.
    Next of kin: Thomas Cooper.
    Administratrix: Eunice Tharp.

Nathaniel Waller   113.250   SO £35.5.6   Oct 22 1773 Nov 17 1773
    Appraisers: James English, George Parsons.
    Creditors: Jonathon Beech, William Winder.
    Next of kin: Nathaniel Waller, Joseph Waller.
    Administrator: John Waller.

Samuel Revel   113.252   SO £9.11.11   Sep 1 1773   Nov 18 1773
    Appraisers: James Bounds, George Kibble.
    Creditors: Benjamin Cottman, Joseph McVeigh.
    Next of kin: John Newman, William Revell.
    Administratrix: Esther Revel.

Zadock Martin   113.255   QA £16.5.6   1770   Sep 16 1773
    Appraisers: John Wilson, William Carradine.
    Administrator: John Kerr.

Dr. George Garnet   113.256   QA £759.2.9   1772   Apr 7 1773
    Appraisers: John Wilson, William Carradine.
    Creditors: Philip Downes for Mr. James Anderson, James Brice for Sarah Brice.
    Next of kin: Mary M. Hard, Martha Crane.
    Administrator: Turbutt Wright.

James Hayman   113.260   WO £88.12.1   Oct 16 1771 Sep 7 1773
    Appraisers: Stephen Roach, Jonathon Cathell.
    Creditors: Peter Waters, John Harris Hayman.
    Next of kin: David Hayman, John Hayman.
    Executrix: Margaret Hayman.

Sophiah Stockley/Schoolfield   113.263   WO £48.12.9   May 30 1772 Nov 2 1773
    Appraisers: James Patterson, Elisha Jones.
    Creditors: James Houston, Esther Dickenson.
    Next of kin: Sarah Benson, John Brittingham.
    Administrator: James Houston.

Benjamin Vinson   113.264   WO   £263.3.9   Sep 9 1773
    Appraisers: Peter Dobbe, John Collins.
    Creditors: Isaac Cooper, Thomas Wells.
    Next of kin: Ann Vinson, Prisse Vinson.
    Executor: George Vinson.

Charles Watson   113.267   WO   £262.2.2   Sep 24 1773
    Appraisers: Bowdoin Robins, David Dixon.
    Creditors: John Atkinson, James Stevenson.
    Next of kin: Nathan Watson, Robert Watson.
    Administratrix: Elisabeth Watson.

John Smith   113.269   WO   £22.15.5   Feb 11 1773   Nov 2 1773
    Appraisers: William Boyce, John Connoway.
    Creditors: Jonathon Dolbie, Joseph Smith.
    Next of kin: Joseph Smith, Sothy Johnson.
    Executrix: Mary Smith.

Samuel Ward   113.270   WO   £10.14.6   Aug 23 1773   Nov 3 1773
    Appraisers: John Tull, John Hayward.
    Creditors: Levin Dirrikson, Joseph Godfrey.
    Administratrix: Bridget Ward.

Elisha Gray   113.272   WO   £224.15.3   Jul 19 1773   Nov 4 1773
    Appraisers: John Gibbons, John Cox.
    Creditors: Bridget Gray, James Gray.
    Next of kin: Bridget Gray, James Gray.
    Administrator: William Jordain Hale.

Joseph Smith   113.275   WO   £278.7.10   Sep 10 1773
    Appraisers: Matthew Hopkins, Samuel Taylor.
    Creditors: John Postly, Edward Dymock, Belitha Collings.
    Next of kin: Elisha Collins.
    Executrix: Sarah Smith.

Jacob Pain   113.277   WO   £210.4.6   Nov 3 1773
    Appraisers: William Aydelott, David Dixon.
    Creditors: Esther Dubsby.
    Next of kin: Moses Pain, John Pain.
    Executrix: Tabitha Pain.

John Handcock   113.280   WO   £6.12.7   Nov 22 1772   Sep 11 1773
    Appraisers: John Miller, Polig Walter.
    Creditors: Polig Walter, Rackclif Conner.
    Next of kin: refused to sign.
    Administrator: William Holland.

David Hudson   113.281   WO   £45.17.3   Aug 21 1773   Nov 3 1773
    Appraisers: John Cox, Caleb Wyatt.
    Creditors: John Waples.
    Next of kin: Lot Hudson, Anne Wyatt.
    Executrix: Esther Hudson.

George Truitt   113.284   WO   £277.17.10 May 23 1772   Feb 12 1773
    Appraisers: Adam Brevard, William Richards.
    Mentions: Levin Bradford, Edward Dymock.
    Next of kin: Cakziah Powell, Nehemiah Truitt.
    Administratrix: Mary Truitt.

John Hammond   113.287   WO   £142.4.3   May 26 1772   Feb 12 1773
    Appraisers: John Tigue, John Purnall.
    Creditors: Martha Bowin, Elijah Morris.
    Next of kin: Edward Hammond, William Hammond.
    Administratrix: Leah Smock (late Leah Hammond).

John Swain   113.289   WO   £123.10.6   Jun 23 1772   Mar 24 1773
    Appraisers: John Ellegood, James Winser.
    Creditors: Peter Hubbert, Clemence Bayley.
    Next of kin: William Swain, Ann Swain.
    Executrix: Anne Swain.

Lewis Dickerson   113.293   WO   £110.2.5   Apr 11 1772   Mar 5 1773
(also Levi Dickeson)
    Appraisers: Elisha Jones, Jacob Payne.
    Creditors: Jonathon Watson, Henry Schoolfield.
    Next of kin: Isaac Dickeson, James Dickeson.
    Administrator: Joshua Dickeson.

Mary Townsend   113.296   WO   £210.9.6   Jan 10 1772   Mar 5 1773
    Appraisers: John Gibbins, William Tingle.
    Creditors: William Holland, Joshua Hall.
    Next of kin: John Townsend, Mary Townsend.
    Executor: Luke Townsend.

Solomon Brittingham   113.298   WO   £350.11.0   Jun 3 1772   Apr 2 1773
    Appraisers: John Purnell Robins, John Teague.
    Creditors: Samuel Handy, John Atkinson.
    Next of kin: William Brittingham, Belitha Brittingham.
    Executrix: Mary Brittingham.

William Fassitt   113.300   WO   £1361.19.1   Jun 23 1772   Feb 12 1773
    Appraisers: Adam Bravard, Adam Spence.
    Creditors: Edward Dymock, Samuel Mills.
    Next of kin: John Fassitt, John Fassitt, Jr.
    Executrix: Mary Fassitt.

William Smock   113.304   WO   £378.8.7   Mar 30 1772   Sep 12 1773
    Appraisers: James Rownd, John Marshall.
    Creditors: William Laughinghouse, Samuel Smyly.
    Next of kin: John Smock, Hinve Smock.
    Executrix: Mary Smock.

John Thompson   113.308   WO   £20.7.2   Jan 15 1773   Mar 2 1773
    Appraisers: Joseph Melson, Benjamin Phillips.
    Creditors: Phillip Short, John Wingate.
    Next of kin: James Thompson, William Thompson.
    Administratrix: Ann Thompson.

Mary Walton   113.310   WO   £297.14.1   Feb 26 1773   Mar 3 1773
    Appraisers: Bowdoin Robins, Outten Sturgis.
    Creditors: Fisher Walton, Robert Forman.
    Next of kin: Mathew Selby, Parker Selby.
    Administrator: Thomas Marshall.

John Tull   113.313   WO   £131.7.11   Aug 19 1772   Mar 27 1773
    Appraisers: John Coe, Reubin Linch.
    Creditors: Joshua Hill, Parker Selby (sheriff).
    Next of kin: Mary Collings, Mary Aydlott.
    Executor: John Tull.

Edward Cary   113.317   WO   £201.3.10   Jan 10 1773   Mar 3 1773
    Appraisers: Simon Kollock, Thomas West.
    Creditors: Joseph Melson, James Anderson.
    Next of kin: James Thompson, Ann Thompson.
    Administrator: George Messick.

Jonathon Cathell   113.320   WO   £288.1.3   May 19 1772   Mar 26 1773
    Appraisers: Stephen Roach, Joseph Venables.
    Creditors: William Winder, James Houston.
    Next of kin: James Thompson, James Cathell.
    Administrator: Daniel Cathell.

Ann Dashiell   113.329   WO   £461.18.9   May 10 1773   Apr 30 1773
    Appraisers: William Polk, Benjamin Cottman.
    Creditors: Ephraim Stevens, Samuel Collins Adams.
    Next of kin: Ephraim Stevens, Matthais Dashiell.
    Executor: James Robertson.

Rachel Hitch   113.333   SO   £43.12.5   Feb 27 1773   Nov 30 1773
    Appraisers: Atkadozi (sic) Johnson, Thomas Stanford.
    Creditors: Charles Hayman, Ann Hayman.
    Next of kin: Leah Hitch, Richard Nicholson.
    Administrator: Benjamin Hitch.

William Braughton   113.335   SO   £129.2.3   Jun 4 1773   Dec 7 1773
    Appraisers: John Pollit, George Waters.
    Creditors: Thomas Hayward, Richard Dashiell.
    Next of kin: John Broughton, Jr., Hannah Riggen.
    Administrator: John Braughton.

William Brown, Sr.   113.337   SO   £1.10.8   Jun 20 1773   Jul 20 1773
    Appraisers: William Winder, John Phillips.
    Administrator: Robert Brown.

Levin Gilliss   113.338   SO   £1.5.0   Jul 13 1773   Jul 21 1773
    Appraisers: William Polk, William Jones.
    Executrix: Sarah Gilliss.

William Pollit   113.339   SO   £724.2.5   Apr 23 1772   Jul 10 1773
    Appraisers: William Jones, William Polk.
    Creditors: Alexander McLaughlin, John Sherreff.
    Next of kin: Philip Graham, Nancy Pollot.
    Administrator: Thomas Pullitt.

Thomas Toadvine/Todvine   113.344   SO   £52.9.4   Aug 7 1772   Feb 26 1773
    Appraisers: Stephen Roach, Obediah Disharoon.
    Creditors: John Houston, Dixen Todvine.
    Next of kin: Henry Todvine, Dixon Todvine.
    Executors: Stephen Todvine, Arnold Todvine.

Windom Scot/Scott   113.346   SO   £30.6.2   Nov 27 1772   Feb 24 1773
    Appraisers: Joseph Venables, William Brown.
    Creditors: John White.
    Next of kin: Keziah Schoot, Sary Scott.
    Executor: Mitchell Scott.

Benjamin Byrd   113.349   SO   £63.2.1   Apr 6 1773   Jun 23 1773
    Appraisers: Thomas Stanford, Joseph Humphries.
    Creditors: Joshua Byrd, Matthais Miles.
    Next of kin: Joshua Byrd, Benjamin Byrd.
    Administrator: Thomas Byrd.

Thomas Handy   113.352   SO   £430.8.6   Sep 3 1772   Jun 16 1773
    Appraisers: Esme Bayly, Thomas Stanford.
    Creditors: William Handy.
    Next of kin: George Handy, William Handy.
    Administratrix: Betty Handy.

Phillip Addams   113.359   SO   £388.2.4   Jul 7 1772   Jun 29 1773
    Appraisers: Teague Riggon, Purnell Outten.
    Creditors: Fountain Beauchamp, Jr., Levi Addams, Jr.
    Next of kin: Elisabeth Matthews, Tabitha Addams.
    Executor: William Addams.

David Greer   113.362   SO   £90.10.0   Nov 12 1772   Nov 18 1772
    Appraisers: William Horsey, James Englis.
    Creditors: Charles Right, ------ Dashiell (sheriff).
    Next of kin: Jonathon Buck, William Greer.
    Administratrix: Jane Greer.

Solomon Long   113.365   SO   £945.10.6   Feb 19 1772   Jan 26 1773
    Appraisers: Isaiah Tilghman, William Furness.
    Creditors: Lambert Hyland, William Mitchell.
    Next of kin: Rebecca Mitchell, Christan Howard.
    Administrators: David Long, Solomon Long.

Edward Cullen   113.372   SO   £113.19.0   Jan 27 1773   Mar 31 1773
    Appraisers: George Dashiell, John Span Conway.
    Creditors: Henry Jackson & Co., William Allen, Jr.
    Administratrix: Mary Cullen.

John Twilly/Twilley   113.376   SO   £188.3.5   Oct 24 1772   Apr 6 1773
    Appraisers: George Wailes, John Wailes.
    Creditors: George Handy, William Giels.
    Next of kin: Nowy Winwright, Betty Wilson.
    Administratrix: Eloner Twilley.

William Gray   113.380   SO   £249.8.0   Apr 7 1773
    Appraisers: Robert Elzey, William Hath.
    Creditors: John Shirreff, William Miles.
    Next of kin: James Smith, Edward Smith.
    Administratrix: Sarah, wife of Charles Vaughan.

Louther Dashiell   113.383   SO   £157.15.1   Dec 23 1772   Feb 9 1773
    Appraisers: William Polk, Benjamin Cotman.
    Creditors: Alexander McLaughlin, John Sherriff.
    Next of kin: Anna Dashiell, Arthur Dashiell, Jr.
    Administrator: James Robertson.

Elisabeth Elzey   113.386   SO   £114.5.2   Jan 3 1770   Nov 18 1772
    Appraisers: George Day Scott, Jesse Dashiell.
    Creditors: John Elzey, ------.
    Next of kin: Nelly Jones.
    Administrators: William Stewart, Benjamin Venables.

Elias Taylor   113.389   SO   £126.6.8   Mar 25 1772   Dec 15 1772
    Appraisers: Purnell Outten, Isaac Marshall.
    Creditors: George Dashiell (sheriff), Isaac Mitchell.
    Next of kin: Dennis Taylor, Loillen (??) Taylor.
    Administrator/Executor: Sarah Taylor.

Joshua Hitch, Jr.   113.391   SO   £223.12.1   Sep 19 1771   Feb 9 1773
    Appraisers: Esme Bayly, Joseph Dashiell.
    Creditors: James Houston, William McBryde.
    Next of kin: John Caldwell, Joshua Hitch.
    Administrators: Sarah Hitch, Robert Hitch.

Samuel Cox   113.394   SO   £257.10.0   Aug 31 1772   Mar 17 1773
    Appraisers: Killiam Lankford, John Whittington.
    Creditors: Aaron Sterling, John Johnson.
    Next of kin: Sarah Fleming, Elisabeth Henderson.
    Executrix: Martha Cox.

Samuel Haynie   113.397   SO   £249.12.2   Jun 1 1772   Feb 27 1773
    Appraisers: Joseph Towgood, John Towney.
    Creditors: Joshua Hitch, Gillis Polk.
    Next of kin: James Haynie.
    Executrix: Judith Haynie.

William Lingo   113.399   SO   £83.18.9   Sep 18 1772   Dec 30 1772
    Appraisers: Joseph Scrogin, Richard Waller.
    Creditors: ------ Dashiell, William McBryde.
    Next of kin: Smith Lingo, John Lingo.
    Administratrix: Leah Lingo.

Thomas Dunn   113.401   SO   £35.15.2   Jan 13 1773   Feb 10 1773
    Appraisers: Hugh Porter, John Dougherty.
    Creditors: James Hunt, Henry Gale.
    Next of kin: George Bennett, Benjamin Mezick.
    Administrator: Richard Dunn.

Jacob Franklin   113.403   AA   £15.7.0   Apr 7 1773   Sep 29 1773
    Appraisers: Thomas Harwood, Isaac Hall.
    Creditors: Steward & Johns, Henry Darnall, P. Manner.
    Next of kin: William Norris, John Franklin.
    Executor: Jacob Franklin.

Elisabeth Jinner/Ginners   113.408   AA   £47.13.6   Nov 19 1773
    Appraisers: James Deall, Thomas Norris.
    Creditors: Steward & Johns.
    Next of kin: Benjamin Atwell, Joseph Atwell.
    Administrator: Jacob Cutler.

Andrew Craig (blacksmith)   113.409   AA   £122.0.8   Sep 28 1773
    Appraisers: Stephen Steward, Jacob Franklin (dec'd by Sep 28 1773).
    Creditors: Henry Darnall, P. Manner, Thomas Norris.
    Next of kin: Ann Cigel, Elisabeth Cudge.
    Administrator: Richard Johns.

John Ashley   113.411   AA   £65.18.3   Mar 24 1773   Nov 4 1773
    Appraisers: John Gray (son of John), John Gray (son of Joshua).
    Creditors: N. Hammond, Thomas Hammond, John Brice.
    Next of kin: William Ashley, Sarah Cromwell.
    Administrator: Zachariah Ashley.

John Brown   113.413   AA   £1029.8.10   Nov 23 1773   Dec 17 1773
    Appraisers: ------ Watts, John Marriott.
    Creditors: Nicholas Maccubbin, N. Hammond.
    Next of kin: Marget Brown, Sarah Brown.
    Executrix: Elisabeth Brown.

Charles Griffith   113.416   AA   £2107.16.2   Oct 25 1771   Dec 14 1773
    Legacies to: John Griffith, Charles Griffith, Mary White, Catharine Worthington,
        granddaughter Catharine Worthington, granddaughter Elisabeth Worthington.
    Appraisers: Gerrard Hopkins, Johns Hopkins.
    Creditors: William Noke, John Clapham.
    Next of kin: Charles Griffith, William Griffith.
    Executors: John Griffith, Nicholas Worthington.

Samuel Meek/Meeke   113.422   AA   £42.0.0   Nov 11 1773
    Appraisers: John Marriott, A. Gambrill.
    Creditors: William Yieldhale, Samuel Harsly Howard.
    Next of kin: Jane Meek, Christopher Meek.
    Administrator: Vachel Stevens.

Abraham Simmons   113.423   AA   £830.2.6   Apr 20 1773   Nov 6 1773
    Appraisers: Richard Green, Richard Richardson.
    Creditors: Henry Darnall, P. Manner, William Brogdin for John Buchanan.
    Next of kin: Richard Simmons, William Simmons.
    Administratrix: Abigail Simmons.

Ralph Cobey   113.426   CH   £40.4.0   Aug 5 1773   Oct 23 1773
        Appraisers: Richard Barnes, Theodore Hanson.
        Creditors: Barnes & Redgate, Richard Barnes.
        Next of kin: John Cobey, Mary Cobey.
        Executor: John Russell.

Thomas King   113.427   CH   £64.12.0   Sep 16 1773   Nov 17 1773
        Appraisers: Peter Dent, Thomas Marshall.
        Creditors: Richard Clagett, Peter Campbell for John Glassford & Co.
        Next of kin: John King, Susanna Murphy.
        Administratrix: Eleanor King (widow).

Joseph Chunn   113.429   CH   £214.11.3   Oct 28 1773
        Appraisers: Stephen Compton, John Wilder.
        Creditors: James Jordan for John Glassford & Co.
        Creditors/Next of kin: Lancelot Chunn, Henry Chun.
        Administrator: Benjamin King.

Walter Trueman Stoddert   113.431   CH   £750.11.6   Nov 10 1772   Jun 7 1773
        Appraisers: Robert Handy, Richard Speake.
        Creditors: Barnes & Redgate, Robert Mundell for John Glassford & Co.
        Next of kin: Benjamin Tindall, Kenhelm Stoddert.
        Administratrix: Marget Stoddert.

Justinian Cooksey, Jr.   113.433   CH   £38.1.2   Aug 10 1773   Aug 29 1773
        Appraisers: Hatch Dent, John Dintson.
        Creditors: Richard Lee, Zephaniah Turner for Barnes & Redgate.
        Next of kin: Justinian Cooksey, Thomas Richard Cooksey.
        Administrator: Samuel Cooksey.

Gerrard Neal/Neale   114.1   CH   £1327.4.0   Aug 20 1773   Oct 25 1773
        Appraisers: Stephen Compton, T. Harris.
        Creditors: Joseph Addison, Robert Mundell for John Glassford & Co.
        Next of kin: John Neale, Raphaele Neale.
        Administratrix: Ann Neale.

Mr. Jacob Bourne   114.4   CA   £246.9.3   Aug 17 1772   Nov 11 1773
        Appraisers: Samuel Gray, Richard Parran.
        Creditors: Edward Hall & Co.
        Next of kin: Betty Hance, Susannah Bourne.
        Executrix: Ester Bourne.

Edward Wood   114.6   CA   £163.4.3   Jan 8 1772   Dec 22 1773
        Appraisers: William Ireland, Frisby Freeland.
        Creditors: Rebecca Arnold, E. Johnson.
        Next of kin: Benjamin Wood, Elisabeth Wood.
        Administrator: Benjamin Wood.

Leonard King   114.9   CA   £17.3.0   Jan 14 1772   Dec 23 1773
        Appraisers: Henry Harrison, Michael Callerton.
        Creditors: Samuel Harrison for Brown & Co., Frances Woolf.
        Next of kin: Thomas Dawel, Margrett King.
        Administrator: Charles King.

John Pardoe   114.10   CA   £11.4.4   Mar 25 1773   Dec 1773
        Appraisers: Isaac Clare, Joseph Wilson.
        Creditors: E. W. Hall & Co., Samuel Gray.
        Next of kin: Sarah Williams for John Pardo.
        Administrator: Basil Brooke.

Thomas Green Martin   114.11   SM   £295.10.1   Nov 22 1773
        Appraisers: Kenelm McWilliams, Joseph W. Walker.
        Creditors: James Jordan for John Glassford & Co., John Gibson.
        Next of kin: Thomas Lee, Jr., Thomas Lee, Sr.
        Administrator/Executor: Samuel Lee.

Thomas Manley   114.13   SM   £71.15.0   Nov 9 1772   Mar 9 1772
        Appraisers: George Leigh, Massey Leigh.
        Creditors: John McLean, Mordecai Jones.
        Next of kin: Priscilla Hernson, Mary Allison.
        Administratrix: Ann Manley.

Bennett Wheeler   114.15   SM   £451.8.4   May 4 1773   Oct 10 1773
        Appraisers: John Shanks, Gerard Bond.
        Creditors: James Jordan for John Glassford & Co., Ignatius Wheeler.
        Next of kin: Ignatius Wheeler, Susannah Shardith (?).
        Administratrix: Jane Wheeler.

Thomas Allen   114.18   CA   £13.11.9   Dec 11 1772   Nov 30 1773
    Appraisers: Mordecai Smith, John Targyhill.
    Creditors: Henry Darnall, Portland Manner, James Jenness.
    Next of kin: Hannah Hanest, Jane Gover.
    Administrator: Martin Morris, Rachel Allen.

------   114.20   £173.11.3
Reference Liber WF#1 Folio 98.
    List of debts.

Frances Humphrey   114.24   TA   £423.11.5   Jun 15 1771   Jun 5 1773
    Appraisers: Joseph Bewley, William Beswick (dec'd by 5 June 1773).
    Creditors: Thomas Jones.
    Next of kin: John Baker.
    Administratrix: Martha Humphrey.

John Myers   114.28   FR   £52.1.9   Nov 18 1773
    Appraisers: Conrod Grosh, Michael Romer.
    Creditors: Henry Lazarus.
    Administratrix: Catharine Myers.

John Medcaff   114.29   SM   £40.14.5   Aug 7 1773   Oct 10 1773
    Appraisers: Enoch Fenwick, John Ford.
    Creditors: Archibald Campbell for John Glassford & Co., Nathaniel Ford.
    Next of kin: George Howard, John Wimsatt.
    Administratrix: Elisabeth Medcaff.

Caleb Able (Cabbel Abell)   114.31   SM   £127.16.8   Nov 10 1773
    Appraisers: Thomas Tarlton, William Wise.
    Creditors: Edward Abell.
    Next of kin: Caleb Abell, John Abell Younger.
    Administratrix: Mary Abell.

John Mattingly   114.34   SM   £23.14.5   Jul 9 1773   Nov 5 1773
    Appraisers: Henry Sewell, Samuel Molson.
    Creditors: Nathaniel Ford.
    Next of kin: James Mattingly, Robert Mattingly.
    Administratrix/Executrix: Ann Matting.

Thomas Newton   114.36   SM   £181.10.6   Sep 15 1772   Jan 11 1773
    Appraisers: Samuel Abell, Sr., Robert Wimsatt, Jr.
    Creditors: Henrietta Howden.
    Next of kin: Elender Howard, Joseph New.
    Executors: Susannah Newton, William Newton.

Stephen Chilton   114.38   SM   £279.10.10   Nov 3 1773
    Appraisers: William Hobb, John Taylor.
    Creditors: Grace Guyther, Vernon Hobb.
    Next of kin: Stephen Chilton, George Chilton.
    Executrix: Ann Chilton.

Baston Dotts   114.41   PG   £160.10.9   Feb 17 1773   May 24 1773
    Appraisers: John Lowe, Jr., Josiah Wade.
    Creditors: Daniel McPherson, Thomas Dent.
    Administrator: Edward Magruder.

Mr. Edward Carteel   114.44   PG   £26.11.8   Apr 10 1773   Jun 14 1773
    Appraisers: James Moore, Sr., John ----aurn.
    Creditors: Peter Campbell for John Glassford & Co., Stephen West.
    Next of kin: Machash Carteel, Charity Carteel.
    Executrix: Cassandre Carteel.

Catharine Scarse   114.47   PG   £21.2.0   Aug 18 1773
    Appraisers: John Lowe, Jr., Daniel Hurley.
    Creditors: Zachariah Scott, David Scearse.
    Next of kin: Nathaniel Scearse.
    Administrator: Shadrack Scarse.

Danes Dawson   114.49   PG   £11.6.8   Sep 18 1773   Sep 19 1773
    Appraisers: Richard Evelin, John Lowe.
    Creditors: Edward Magruder, Bedder Phillips.
    Next of kin: Ann Dawson, Thomas Dawson.
    Administrator: John Dawson.

Samuel Riddle   114.50   PG   £148.18.3   Oct 15 1773
    Appraisers: Abraham Boyd, Josias Share.
    Creditors: William Dealins, Jr., Robert Dirk.
    Next of kin: James Riddle, Benjamin Ray.
    Executrix: Lucy Riddle.

Mr. James Magruder   114.52   PG   £1064.5.8   Mar 18 1773   Jul 13 1773
    Appraisers: Benjamin Brookes, Charles Burgess.
    Creditors: Allen Bowie, Judsan Coolidge for John Buchanan.
    Next of kin: Samuel Magruder 3rd, Nathaniel Magruder.
    Administratrix: Mary Magruder.

John Corry   114.58   CH   £1165.7.11   Feb 1 1773
    Appraisers: Edward Edelen, Leonard Hall.
    Creditors: John Craig for Alexander Cunningham & Co., James Brown for Barnes &
        Redgate.
    Next of kin: Mary Corry, Margaretta Corry.
    Executrix: Elisabeth Corry.

James McIntosh   114.67   FR   £13.6.0   Oct 11 1773   Dec 21 1773
    Mentions: Benedict Green, Hezekiah Magruder.
    Mentions: Daniel Pharoutish (?).
    Administrator: Daniel McIntosh.

Rev. Archibald Avan   114.67   FR   £72.3.2   Mar 29 1773   Nov 9 1773
    Appraisers: Conrad Grosh, Thomas Price.
    Creditors: Charles Betty, Philip Thomas.
    Next of kin: Ann Dobie.
    Administratrix: Magdalin Avan.

Peter Bergh   114.70   FR   £248.4.0   Aug 6 1773   Nov 12 1773
    Appraisers: John Stoner, Valentine Creager.
    Creditors: Paulish Wolf, Conrad Grosh.
    Next of kin: Johannes Berg, Wilhelm Berg.
    Administrators: Catharine Barrish, Peter Barrish.

Joshua Hickman   114.72   FR   £145.9.3   Dec 8 1773
    Appraisers: Benjamin Gatton, James Fyfe.
    Creditors: James Gillen, Contee Hanson.
    Next of kin: Solomon Hickman, Atte Hickman.
    Administratrix: Eleanor Hickman.

Richard Blue   114.74   PG   £13.3.7   Aug 27 1772
    List of debts.
    Administrator: Joseph Witchol.

Sarah Pye   114.75   CH   £913.1.7   Sep 21 1773   Nov 10 1773
    Appraisers: William Jenkins, Benjamin McPherson.
    Creditors: Robert Mundel for John Glassford & Co., Jesse Matthews.
    Next of kin: Edward Edelen, Jr., Henrietta Harmersley.
    Executor: Joseph Edelen.

Christian Deal   114.82   BA   £55.13.0   Nov 10 1773
    List of debts.
    Executrix: Elisabeth, wife of Joseph Miller.

Isaac Cord   114.84   BA   £41.4.2   Nov 3 1773   Nov 6 1773
    Appraisers: George Chauncy, Anthony D------.
    Mentions: Speirs French & Co., Henry Garland.
    Administrator: James Osbourn, Jr.

John Rutledge   114.86   BA   £109.3.9   Oct 11 1773   Nov 3 1773
    Appraisers: Moses Galloway, Abraham Andrew.
    Creditors: William Andrew, John Skinner for Mssrs. James Russel & Co.
    Next of kin: Kesiah Parks, John Bullidge.
    Executor: Abraham Rutledge.

Nathan Harrington   114.89   BA   £209.11.10   Aug 25 1773   Apr 21 1773
    Appraisers: John Daughaday, H. Stevenson.
    Creditors: Andrew Buchanan.
    Next of kin: Abel Harrington, William Harrington.
    Administratrix: Temperance Harrington.

John Stone   114.91   BA   £22.9.6   Nov 25 1773
(Name cited in the attestation section of inventory is John Jones.)
    Appraisers: Benjamin Amoss, John Stewart.
    Creditors: James Talbott, Underwood Guyton.
    Administrator: Samuel Jones.

John Anderson   114.93   BA   £434.10.6   Oct 9 1773
    Appraisers: Robert Bryarly, Mordecai Amos.
    Next of kin: William Anderson.
    Administratrix: Catharine Anderson.

Aquila Price   114.97   BA   £313.0.6   Mar 15 1773   Jun 31 1773
    Appraisers: Jeremiah Johnson, Oliver Mathew.
    Creditors: Johnathon Plowman, John Merryman, Jr.
    Next of kin: John Price, Benjamin Price.
    Administrator: Mordecai Price.

William Wheeler   114.101   BA   £166.13.3   Jan 2 1772   Mar 18 1773
(son of William)
    Appraisers: John Daughaday, Nathan Wekmer.
    Creditors: H. Stevenson, Benjamin Rogers.
    Mentions: Richard Wheeler.
    Administratrix: Ruth Wheeler.

Andrew Bergenboyle/Bergupile 114.104   BA   £137.11.4   Aug 10 1773   Oct 20 1773
    Appraisers: John ------, Alexis Semmon, Sr.
    Mentions: Catorn Beargupil, Johann ------.
    Mentions: Georg Marthezn (?), Crist---orbor Jenbil.
    Executors: William Bergenboyle, Henry Warebrum.

Barnett Johnson   114.109   BA   £609.10.6   Nov 12 1771   May 1 1773
    Appraisers: Henry Wilson, Edmund Bull.
    Creditors: Samuel Webb, Buchanan & Cowan.
    Next of kin: Thomas Johnson, John Johnson.
    Executrix: Hester Johnson.

James Billingsley   114.112   BA   £930.18.3   May 3 1773
    Appraisers: Thomas Baker Rigon, Edmund Bull.
    Next of kin: Francis Billingslea, Walter Billingslea.
    Administratrix: Ruth Billingsley.

James Helly   114.117   BA   £788.3.7   Apr 18   Nov 5 1773
    Appraisers: Jacob Johnson, John Stewart.
    Creditors: Jonathon Plowman, Felix O'Meill.
    Next of kin: John Sheel, Mary Sheel.
    Administrator: John Shield.

Samuel Shaw   114.121   BA   £93.7.2   Aug 14 1773   Nov 4 1773
    Appraisers: William Webb, Edward Morgan.
    Creditors: Joseph Buttler, Buchanan Smith.
    Administrators: Francis Miel, Arminta Shaw.

Edward Garrettson   114.124   BA   £737.8.3   May 11 1773   Nov 29 1773
    Appraisers: Greenbury Dorsey, Samuel Griffith.
    Creditors: Edward Cruisanks.
    Next of kin: Robert Brown, Sarah Garrettson.
    Administrator: Elijah Blackstone.

John Henry   114.129   BA   £1575.4.5   Mar 5 1771   Oct 4 1773
    Appraisers: Greenbury Dorsey, Samuel Griffith.
    Creditors: George Stewart, William Young, Jr.
    Next of kin: Archibald Beaty, Jane Beaty.
    Administratrix: Mary Henry.

Robert Gardner   114.135   CA   £301.0.7   Jan 7 1772   Nov 18 1773
    Appraisers: Alexander Somervell, Isaac Clare.
    Creditors: Samuel Gray, Edward Hale & Co.
    Next of kin: Dennis Freeman, Mary Grimes.
    Executor: John Gardner, Kinsly Gardner.

John Morton Jordan   114.139   AA   £1820.15.8   Oct 11 1771   Dec 1 1773
of Annapolis
    Appraisers: Thomas Hyde, Thomas Harwood, Jr.
    Creditors: James Dick & Stewart, Robert Ruth.
    Next of kin/Administrator: Reuben Merriwether.

John Morton Jordan   114.152   AA   £612.7.6   Jun 1773   Dec 2 1773
of Annapolis
    Appraisers: Thomas Hyde, Thomas Harwood, Jr.
    Mentions: Mrs. Dorothea Jordan (widow).
    Administrator: Reuben Merriwether.

John Morton Jordan, Esq.   114.160   AA   £657.17.8   Dec 2 1773
    Mentions: Robert Smith, Dorothea Jordan (widow).

John Morton Jordan   114.167   AA   £657.17.8   Dec 3 1773
    List of debts.
    Administrator: Reuben Merriwether.

Manuel Manlove   114.169   DO   £1141.10.3   Jul 13 1773   Aug 12 1773
     Appraisers: Robert Clarkson, William Carmon.
     Creditors: Levin Crapper, John Parker.
     Next of kin: Jonathon Manlove, Boaz Manlove.
     Executrix: Betty Manlove.

John Wheeler   114.175   DO   £46.17.11   Sep 27 1773
     List of debts.
     Executor: George Wheeler.

John Wheeler   114.179   DO   £148.1.8   Sep 27 1773
     List of debts.
     Executor: George Wheeler.

Mary Cluck   114.182   CE   £79.15.0   Dec 4 1772   May 3 1773
     Appraisers: James Bolden, Benjamin Bravard.
     Creditors: Thomas Huggins, Thomas Bravard.
     Next of kin: Thomas Bravard.
     Administrators: Thomas Frisby Henderson, Jeremiah Taylor.

Elisabeth Glassford   114.183   KE   £243.7.6   Apr 30 1773   Jun 26 1773
     Appraisers: Peter Massey, William Merritt.
     Creditors: James Black.
     Next of kin: James Black, Elisabeth Fleming.
     Administrator: John Wallis.

Mrs. Sarah Boardley   114.187   CE   £657.3.3   Nov 8 1769   Jun 19 1773
     Appraisers: John Mercer, Sylvester Nowland.
     Creditors: Augustine Beedle, Hugh Matthews.
     Next of kin: Rachel Pearce, Henry W. Pearce.
     Administratrix: Cassandra Pearce.

John Smith   114.194   KE   £42.10.1   Jun 28 1773
     Appraisers: Ebenezar Black, Jr., Thomas Crow.
     Creditors: Richard Lloyed for Mr. James Anderson, John Bolton.
     Next of kin: Philip Smith, T. Smyth.
     Administrator: Michael Strong.

Michael Chandler   114.196   KE   £44.5.6   Mar 27 1773   Jun 17 1773
     Appraisers: John Dyer, Joseph Rasin.
     Creditors: Donaldson Yeates, Isaac Camull (?).
     Next of kin: Thomas Chandler, Nathaniel Chandler.
     Administratrix: Tahpenah (?) Chandler.

James Piner   114.197   KE   £347.5.6   Jun 19 1773
     Appraisers: Simon Wilmore, N. Ricketts.
     Creditors: William Ringgold, Thomas Ringgold, Jr.
     Next of kin: Thomas Wilkins, Bartens Wilkins.
     Administratrix: Ann Piner.

Mary Wilson   114.200   KE   £13.2.5   Jun 17 1773
     List of debts.
     Executor: George Wilson.

Susannah Brown   114.200   KE   £7.11.5   Mar 31 1773   Jun 25 1773
     Appraisers: Charles Groome, William Cowarden.
     Creditors: James Wroth.
     Next of kin: David Brown, Nicholas Brown.
     Administrator: Robert Brown (Quaker).

Mr. Samuel Mansfield   114.201   KE   £206.8.3   Mar 9 1773   Aug 9 1773
     Appraisers: H. Maawell (sic), Hezekiah Cooper.
     Creditors: John Lambert Wilmer, Donaldson Yeates.
     Next of kin: Mary Mansfield, Ann Mansfield.
     Administrator: Samuel Mansfield.

Mary Wilson   114.207   KE   £160.11.5   Oct 30 1771   Jun 17 1773
     Appraisers: Abraham Freeman (dec'd by 11 May 1773), James Pearce.
     Creditors: William Rogers, Archibald Wright.
     Next of kin: Melicent Rodgers, Rachel Downes.
     Executor: George Wilson.

Mr. George Little   114.209   KE   £236.2.6   Jun 9 1773   Aug 9 1773
     Appraisers: H. Maxwell, Samuel Wallis.
     Creditors: Henry Wallis, William Slubey, Jr.
     Next of kin: Adam Littel, George Littel.
     Executrix: Mary Littel.

Mr. Augustine Boyer   114.210   KE   £335.12.2   Nov 4 1773   Dec 9 1773
     Appraisers: Daniel Massey, Alexander Baird.
     Next of kin: Thomas Boyer.
     Executors: Thomas Boyer, Augustine Boyer, Jr.

John Dougherty   114.211   KE   £241.13.3   Feb 1772   Jun 22 1773
    Appraisers: Rassin Gale, Macall Medford.
    Next of kin: Donaldson Yeates, Mary Daughterte, Issebella Denning, John Denning.
    Administrators: John Earle, Mary Earle.

Dennis Shehawn   114.213   KE   £20.0.0   Jun 10 1773
    List of debts.
    Administrator/Executor: Michael Jobson.

Daniel Smith   114.214   KE   £23.17.2   Jul 21 1773
    List of debts.
    Administrator: Isaac Cannel.

Mr. John Wallace   114.215   KE   £73.6.8   Aug 20 1770   Jun 16 1773
of Chestertown
    List of debts.
    Executors: James Anderson, Thomas Bendly Hands, John Bolton.

Daniel Smith   114.216   KE   £187.12.7   Jul 27 1773
    List of debts.
    Administrator: Isaac Cannel.

Jane Cann   114.218   KE   £116.0.1   Aug 26 1773   Oct 15 1773
    Appraisers: Charles Groome, George Lamb.
    Creditors: Frances Cann, Jeremiah Cannel.
    Next of kin: John Ricketts, Roger Hates.
    Executors: Abraham Haynes & wife.

Charles Steward   114.219   KE   £60.10.0   Aug 13 1773   Oct 11 1773
    Appraisers: William Hozel.
    Mentions: James Ankragh, William Reed.
    Mentions: Samuel West, John Steward.
    Administratrix: Sarah Steward.

Nathaniel Chandler   114.221   KE   £81.1.10   Aug 10 1773   Nov 18 1773
    Appraisers: Joseph Rasin, John Duyer.
    Creditors: Donaldson Yeates, Isaac Cannell.
    Next of kin: Thomas Chandler, Phebe Gale.
    Executor: Marmaduke Medford.

Abraham Freeman   114.224   KE   £1167.3.4   Mar 1 1773   May 11 1773
    Appraisers: Robert Maxwell, Barten Piner.
    Creditors: John Voorhees, Mary Freeman.
    Next of kin: Isaac Freeman, Mary Freeman.
    Administrators: Avarilla Freeman, John Sutton.

Paul Whichcote   114.234   KE   £82.18.9   May 13 1773   May 27 1773
    Appraisers: Richard Frisby, James Smith.
    Creditors: Richard Lloyd, Thomas Ringgold.
    Next of kin: Richard Williss, Jr., Martha Whichcote.
    Administratrix: Martha Whichcote.

Michael Reed   114.234   KE   £4.18.3   May 26 1773
    List of debts.
    Administrator/Executor: William Reed.

Thomas Perkins   114.235   KE   £138.13.9   Aug 27 1773   Sep 1 1773
    List of debts.
    Executors: Jonathon Turner, Ebenezar Reyner.

Mr. Philip Rasin   114.236   KE   £125.8.0   Feb 27 1773   Jun 10 1773
    Appraisers: Henry Maxwell, John Duyer.
    Creditors: Abraham Rasin.
    Next of kin: Abraham Rasin, Joseph Rasin.
    Executors: John Rasin, Thomas Rasin.

Mary Kinnard   114.236   KE   £49.19.4   Jun 8 1773   Jun 10 1773
    Appraisers: Robert Buchanan, Luke Griffith.
    Next of kin: Stephen Shinwood, Jean Williamson.
    Executor: Daniel Kinnard.

Capt. John Carvil   114.237   KE   £1042.11.1   Apr 1 1773   Jun 3 1773
    Appraisers: John Wickes, James Dunn.
    Creditors: Thomas Ringgold, Morgan & Slubey.
    Next of kin: Thomas Hynson, Richard Hynson.
    Administratrix: Ann Carvil.

Shaderick Wotters   114.248   QA   £162.3.0   Aug 1773   Mar 9 1774
(also Shadrack Wootters)
        Appraisers: Giles Hicks, Jeremiah Colston.
        Creditors: Henry Casson, Tilghman & Nicols.
        Next of kin: Mary Cinnamon, Jonathon Wotters.
        Executrix: Hannah Wooters.

John Brown   114.251   QA   £268.13.1   1772   Mar 9 1774
        Appraisers: John Wilson, John Hammond.
        Creditors: Robert J. Earle, Elisha Brown.
        Next of kin: Mary Wright, Charles Brown.
        Administrator: Nathan Brown.

Phillemon St. Tee   114.256   QA   £4.14.10   Dec 27 1773   Mar 24 1774
        Appraisers: John R. Emory, Edward Chetham.
        Creditors: Hannah Clayton, Sarah Coale.
        Next of kin: Sophia Wright, James St. Tee.
        Administrator: John Watson.

Vallentine Burroughs   114.258   QA   £185.10.11   Oct 29 1773   Mar 24 1774
        Appraisers: Andrew Graham, Richard Heathers.
        Creditors: John Dean, Thomas Gilpin & Co.
        Next of kin: Elijah Burroughs, Frances Burroughs.
        Administratrix: Rebecca Burrus.

Mrs. Sarah Blake   114.260   QA   £916.14.10   Jun 1771   Jan 8 1774
        Appraisers: John Wilson, William Carradine.
        Creditors: William Leed for Speirs & Markie & Co., Charles Goldsborough.
        Next of kin: Elisabeth Blake, Henrietta Maria Blake.
        Administrator: Charles Blake.

John Tolson   114.267   QA   £392.0.6   Sep 20 1773   Mar 24 1774
        Appraisers: Richard Mason, William Bell.
        Creditors: Thomas Sylvester, Tilghman & Nicols.
        Next of kin: Benjamin Tolson, John Elliott.
        Executrix: Mary Tolson.

James Satterfield   114.272   QA   £485.3.9   Aug 11 1773   Apr 7 1774
        Appraisers: John Fisher, Anthony Harrison.
        Creditors: Tilghman & Nicols, Christopher Cross Routh.
        Next of kin: Rachel Tarbutton, Als Sylvester.
        Administratrix: Margaret Satterfield.

Margaret Dolvin   114.279   QA   £73.9.7   Nov 30 1773   Mar 17 1774
        Appraisers: Charles Price, James Cox.
        Creditors: James Davidford, John Walker.
        Next of kin: James Dolvin, Richard Dolvin.
        Administrator: Phillemon Green.

John Downey   114.279   QA   £48.13.0   Dec 17 1773   Mar 17 1774
        Appraisers: B. Gould, Abner Dudley.
        Creditors: Eleazer McComb, George Wimson.
        Next of kin: Thomas Downey, Jr., Thomas Downey.
        Administratrix: Tabitha Downey.

Charles Higgins   114.283   QA   £117.5.1   Aug 17 1773   Mar 16 1774
        Appraisers: James O'Bryan, Basil Warfield.
        Creditors: Arthur Emory, Jr., Robert J. Earle & Co.
        Next of kin: Elisabeth Runney, Sarah Ford.
        Administratrix: Margaret Higgins.

Edward Dyer   114.285   QA   £3.15.0   Feb 10 1774   Mar 24 1774
        Appraisers: Richard Mason, Vachel Downs.
        Administrator: Edward Dyer.

Folio 286 does not exist.

Michael Devanns   114.287   PG   £24.0.8   Sep 5 1773   Mar 23 1774
        Appraisers: Thomas Boteler, John Sayer.
        Creditors: Alexander Howard Magruder, Alexander Howard Magruder (sic).
        Next of kin: James Devanns, Mice Devanns.
        Administrator: Aaron Williams.

Philip Evans   114.289   PG   £229.16.3   Mar 23 1774
        Appraisers: Thomas Wilcoxon, Jr., Henry Berkley.
        Creditors: William Lydebotham, Robert Dick.
        Next of kin: Ann Evans, Marah Sayer.
        Executor: John Evans.

Barton Dots   114.294   PG   £2.5.0   Feb 12 1774   Mar 24 1774
        Appraisers: John Lowe, Jr., Josiah Wade.
        Administrator: Edward Magruder.

Niniam Willett   114.294   PG   £60.16.6   Dec 1 1773   Feb 24 1774
    Appraisers: Peter Young, Thomas Clagett.
    Creditors: John Read Magruder for John Buchanan & Son, Thomas Belt 3rd.
    Next of kin: Ninian Willett, Charles Willett.
    Executor: Isaac Willett.

Thomas Upton   114.297   PG   £15.5.0   Mar 24 1774
    Appraisers: Thomas Wilcoxon, Jr., Azariah Gatton.
    Creditors: Richard Pousonby for Mssrs. Cunningham Findley & Co.
    Next of kin: Jhn Upton.
    Executrix: Martha Upton.

James Knott   114.300   PG   £387.8.6   Aug 12 1773   Feb 28 1774
    Appraisers: Alexander Jackson, John Pearre.
    Creditors: Leonard Mattingly, Joseph Smith.
    Next of kin: Frances Knott, Ann Buchanan.
    Administratrix: Sarah Knott.

Mr. Thomas Lowe   114.304   PG   £285.0.9   Jan 3 1774   Mar 23 1774
    Appraisers: Ignatius Wheeler, Patrick Beall.
    Creditors: Mssrs. Oswald Pennistern & Co., Thomas Clagget, John Payne for self
        and John Lowe.
    Next of kin: James Lowe, Henry Love, Jr.
    Executrix: Verlinda Lowe.

James Knott   114.308   PG   £236.1.5   Feb 28 1774
    List of debts.
    Administratrix: Sarah Knott.

Susanna Rigg   114.310   CH   £17.3.6   Feb 8 1774   Mar 8 1774
    Appraisers: John Marshall, Joshua Jay.
    Mentions: Andrew Buchanan for self & George Buchanan, Thomas Smyth.
    Mentions: David Philpott, John Philpot.
    Executor: Thomas Rigg.

Richard Neele/Neale   114.311   CH   £428.3.7   Dec 10 1772   Mar 22 1774
    Appraisers: Edward Smock. T. Harris.
    Creditors: James Jordan, John Lancaster.
    Next of kin: Bennett Neale, Joseph Neale.
    Administratrix: Ann Neale (administratrix of Gerard Neale).

Richard Neale   114.314   CH   £353.2.5   Mar 22 1774
    Appraisers: Edward Smock, T. Harris.
    Creditors: John Craig for Cunningham Findley & Co., Andrew Buchanan for George
        and Andrew Buchanan.
    Next of kin: Bennett Neale, Joseph Lancaster.
    Administratrix: Ann Neale.

Thomas Ricketts   114.317   CE   £34.8.6   Jan 21 1774   Feb 14 1774
    Appraisers: Joseph Gilpin, Ebenezar Hollingsworth.
    Mentions: John Ricketts.
    Executor: Benjamin Ricketts.

Michael Wallace   114.319   CE   £571.19.5   Dec 22 1773
    List of debts.
    Executors: David Wallace, Sarah Wallace.

Michael Wallace   114.325   CE   £79.8.6   Dec 22 1773
    List of debts.
    Executors: David Wallace, Sarah Wallace.

Michael Wallace   114.326   CE   £519.16.11   Dec 22 1773
    Appraisers: Tobias Rudulph, John Strawbridge.
    Mentions: John Wallace, Sarah Wallace.
    Mentions: Richard Bond, Samuel Gilpin.
    Administrators/Executors: Sarah Wallace, David Wallace.

Francis Fulton   114.332   CE   £48.1.11   Sep 18 1773   Jan 29 1774
    List of debts.
    Executrix: Ann Fulton.

Francis Fulton   114.336   CE   £23.2.11   Dec 22 1773
    List of debts.
    Executrix: Ann Fulton.

Samuel Dougherty   114.337   CE   £60.13.0   Feb 26 1774
    List of debts.
    Administrator: William King.

Samuel Dougherty   114.339   CE   £20.7.0   Jan 21 1774   Feb 26 1774
    Appraisers: Richard Bond, Amos Alexander.
    Creditors: John Strawbridge, Joseph Wallace.
    Administrator: William King.

Thomas Norton   114.340   CE   £37.6.7   Dec 27 1773
    List of debts.
    Executor: Nathan Norton.

Samuel Dougherty   114.342   CE   £23.5.5   Feb 26 1774
    List of debts.
    Administrator: William King.

Mr. James Hart   114.343   CE   £696.11.3   Jan 13 1774   Mar 3 1774
    Appraisers: Nicholas George, Benjamin Mauldin.
    Next of kin: John Hankey.
    Executors: Ann Hart, Robert Hart.

Mary Campbell   114.347   CE   £48.5.7   Jun 5 1773   Mar 5 1774
    Appraisers: Tobias Rudulph, Ebenezar Campbell.
    Creditors: Thomas Frisby Henderson, Robert Buchanan.
    Next of kin: Ebenezar Campbell.
    Administrator: John Campbell Chambers.

Thomas Baird/Beard   114.349   CE   £557.11.2   Dec 21 1773   Mar 8 1774
    Appraisers: Charles Heath, James Coppen.
    Executor: Lewis Beard.

Jesse Bouldin/Boldin   114.353   CE   £85.11.1   Jan 29 1774
    List of debts.
    Administratrix: Mary, wife of John Smith.

Jesse Boldin/Bouldin   114.356   CE   £48.18.10   Jan 29 1774
    List of debts.
    Administratrix: Mary, wife of John Smith.

Francis Fulton   114.357   CE   ----   Jan 28 1774
    Appraisers: Patrick Ewing, Samuel Gillispie.
    Creditors: James Porter, Thomas Brown.
    Next of kin: Samuel Fulton, Alexander Fulton.
    Administratrix: Ann Fulton (widow).

Thomas Norton   114.359   CE   £239.9.3   Dec 27 1773
    List of debts.
    Executor: Nathan Norton.

Ephraim Vaughan   114.360   SO   £4.10.7   Apr 26 1774
    Appraisers: George Wailes, Barkley Townsend.
    Executrix: Betty Vaughan.

Ann Dashiel   114.361   SO   £13.14.8   Mar 22 1774   Jun 8 1774
    Appraisers: William Polk, Benjamin Cottman.
    Executor: James Robertson.

Daniel Dixe   114.363   SO   £43.2.1   May 9 1774   Jun 14 1774
    Appraisers: Purnell Outten, William Flemming.
    Administrator: Ezekiel Lankford.

Thomas Banks   114.365   SO   £22.4.2   Mar 29 1773
See also Folio 437.
    Appraisers: Thomas Lankford, Affradozi Johnson.
    Creditors: William McBryde, William Horsey.
    Next of kin: Josiah Banks, Robert Banks.

Mr. Isaak Handy   114.367   SO   £826.15.0   Jun 17 1774
    Appraisers: James Robertson, Robert Elzey.
    Creditors: George Handy, John Shireff for Speirs & French & Co.
    Next of kin: George Handy, William Handy.
    Administratrix: Esther Handy.

Isaac Handy   114.374   SO   £74.19.8   Jun 17 1774
    List of debts.
    Administratrix: Esther Handy.

Benjamin Warrington   114.375   SO   £69.11.4   Mar 7 1774   May 23 1774
See also Folio 436.
    Appraisers: John Piper, William Turpin.
    Creditors: William Winder, Robert Brown.
    Next of kin: Sarah Warrington, Esther Warrington.
    Administratrix: Charity Warrington.

Isaac Dickerson   114.384   SO   £171.3.3   Dec 3 1773   May 31 1774
    Appraisers: Purnell Outten, Jacob Addams.
    Creditors: Caleb Jones, Elijah Mathews.
    Next of kin: Joshua Dickerson, Sarah Dickerson.
    Executor: James Dickerson.

Mr. Charles Woolford   114.385   SO   £821.1.6   Jul 27 1772   May 31 1774
    Appraisers: Levin Dashiel, James Robertson.
    Creditors: Levin Dashiel, Levin Ballard.
    Next of kin: Levin Woolford, Levin Ballard.
    Administratrix: Mary Ann Woolford.

Thomas Walker   114.394   SO   £64.14.3   Oct 13 1773   May 18 1774
    Appraisers: George Wailes, Richard Waller.
    Creditors: George ------, John ----well.
    Next of kin: James Walker, Mark Walker.
    Administratrix: Sophia Walker.

Thomas Pryor   114.397   SO   £274.14.1   Jan 4 1774   May 17 1774
    Appraisers: Ezekiel Gilliss, Revel Horsey.
    Creditors: Francis King, Levin Gun.
    Mentions: Randal Prior, Rorly (?) Wallston.
    Administratrix: Esther Pryor.

Jacob Fury/Furry   114.402   CH   £117.1.11   Mar 2 1774
    List of debts.
    Administrator/Executor: Rachel Furry.

Samuel Love   114.408   CH   £230.17.9   Dec 3 1772   Apr 26 1774
    Appraisers: Bennett Dyson, Thomas Reeves.
    Executor: Samuel Love.

Timothy Flannagin/Flanagan   114.411   CH   £455.6.3   Apr 6 1772   Mar 10 1774
    Appraisers: William Winter, Jr., Warren Dent.
    Creditors: Robert Mundell for John Glassford & Co., Ignatius Ryon.
    Next of kin: Bartholomew Flanagan, James Fitzgerald.
    Executor: Gerard Fowke.

Joseph Garner   114.415   CH   £798.9.10   Apr 11 1774   May 27 1774
    Appraisers: Thomas McPherson, Daniel McPherson.
    Creditors: Philip Webster, G. R. Brown.
    Next of kin: Joseph Garner, John Garner.
    Executor: Charles Garner.

John Andrews   114.420   CH   £135.6.9   Jun 14 1774
    Appraisers: John Craw, T. Harris.
    Creditors: Thomas Hungerford, Thomas James.
    Administratrix: Eleanor Andrews.

Henry Clements   114.422   CH   £309.11.11   Apr 5 1774   May 11 1774
    Appraisers: Alexander McPherson, Daniel McPherson.
    Creditors: Alexander Hamilton for James Brown & Co., Leonard Green.
    Next of kin: Thomas Clements, John Clements of Fra.
    Administrators: Christiana Clements, George Clements.

Thomas Nash   114.426   CH   £42.8.7   May 7 1774
    Appraisers: Zack Chunn, Lam Turner.
    Creditors: Bennett Watkins, Barnes & Redgate.
    Next of kin: Pha Delmno Sims (sic), Mark Sims.
    Administratrix: Ann Nash.

Mr. James Neale   114.428   CH   £990.0.2   Apr 14 1774   Jun 30 1774
    Appraisers: Joshua Sanders, Edward Boarman, Jr.
    Creditors: James Jordan for John Glassford & Co., Hugh McBryde.
    Next of kin: Henry Gardiner, William Gardiner.
    Administrators: Raphael Lancaster and his wife Tocesia.

Thomas Reeves   114.433   CH   £74.17.8   Jun 1 1774   Jun 18 1774
    Appraisers: Thomas Richard Cooksey, William Compton.
    Creditors: Bennett Dyson, Daniel Murphey.
    Next of kin: Samuel Reeves, Gerard Dyson.
    Administratrix: Mary Reeves.

Elisabeth Ford   114.435   CH   £0.12.2   Jan 15 1773   Jun 14 1774
    Appraisers: T. Harris, George ------ Smoot.
    Administrator: Charles Allison Ford.

Benjamin Warrington   114.436   SO
Continuation of Folio 375.
    Administratrix: Charity Warrington.

Thomas Banks   114.437   SO   Jul 5 1774
Continuation of Folio 365.
     Administrator: Henry Banks.

Charles Carroll, Jr.   115.1   PG   £1061.5.8   May 17 1773   Aug 24 1773
     Appraisers: Richard Henderson, William Beakins.
     Creditors: William Deakins, Jr. for William Molleson, John Turnbull.
     Next of kin: Notley Young, Ignatius Digges.
     Administratrix: Mary Carroll.

Joseph Wright   115.8   FR   £166.7.6   Nov 6 1773   Nov 20 1773
     Appraisers: Upton Sheredine, Daniel Richards.
     Creditors: Christopher Edelin, David Moore (son of John).
     Next of kin: Philip Wright, Amos Wright.
     Executrix: Rebecca Wright.

Birckhead Sharp   115.12   TA   £427.13.3   May 6 1771   Aug 10 1773
     Appraisers: Daniel Sherwood, John Stevens.
     Creditors: Henry Hollyday, Nicholas Goldsborough.
     Next of kin: Samuel Sharp, Nancy Sharp.
     Daughters: Margaret, Mary, Catharine, Elisabeth, Lydia.
     Executrix: Margaret Sharp.

Frances Gibson   115.18   TA   £467.10.5   Dec 19 1768   Aug 4 1773
     Appraisers: John Bracco, Thomas Ross.
     Creditors: John Gordon, James Hays Chamberlaing.
     Next of kin: Sarah Kinlnmont, Jonathon Gibson.
     Administratrix: Frances Gibson.

John Dyus   115.23   TA   £21.12.10   Jul 6 1773
     Appraisers: James Barnwell, Sr., Samuel Register.
     Creditors: Matthais Gale, John Merchant.
     Next of kin: Joseph Newman.
     Executor: John Merchant, Jr.

William Austin   115.24   TA   £237.2.8   May 11 1773   Jul 6 1773
     Appraisers: Solomon Neal, Henry Troth.
     Creditors: Sharp & Dawson.
     Next of kin: Henry Austin, Richard Austin.
     Administrators: Ann Austin, Thomas Austin.

John Hudson   115.27   TA   £20.13.6   May 29 1773   Jul 30 1773
     Appraisers: John Stevens, Thomas Jenkins.
     Creditors: William Stevens, William Maynadier.
     Next of kin: Ann Burgess.
     Administratrix: Sarah Hudson.

Thomas Tenant/Tennant   115.28   TA   £90.1.1   Jan 28 1773   Apr 27 1773
(carpenter)
     Appraisers: Jonathon Nicols, Henry Banning.
     Creditors: Samuel Chamberlaine, Thomas Harrison.
     Next of kin: James Tennant.
     Administratrix: Mable Tennant.

James Brown (joyner)   115.31   TA   £109.18.9   Apr 1 1773   Aug 3 1773
     Appraisers: Charles Bullen, Mr. Lewis Barnett.
     Creditors: John Stevens, William Stevens.
     Next of kin: Sarah Brown, William Brown.
     Administratrix: Cassandra Brown.

John Blades   115.34   TA   £142.17.6   May 7 1773   May 25 1773
     Appraisers: T. Sherwood, Henry Banning.
     Creditors: Thomas Harrison, Philip Weathrak.
     Next of kin: Edmund Blades, Dorothy Blades.
     Administrators: Elisabeth Blades, John Blades.

George Millington   115.37   TA   £287.4.3   Jun 5 1773   Aug 17 1773
     Appraisers: Joseph Bewley, James Gibson.
     Creditors: Tilghman & Nicols.
     Next of kin: Isaac Millington, Rachel Lane.
     Executrix: Hannah Millington.

John Higgins   115.40   TA   £247.11.3   May 29 1773   Aug 3 1773
     Appraisers: John Stevens, Thomas Jenkins.
     Creditors: William Stevens, William Maynadier.
     Next of kin: James Saywell Higgins, Sarah Hughson.
     Executrix: Bridget Higgins.

Edward Clark   115.45   TA   £316.7.2   May 30 1773   Jul 27 1773
    Appraisers: Richard Johns, George Burgess.
    Creditors: Edward Parkinson, Peter Parrott.
    Mentions: "for executors of Matthais Gale & Gale & Fearn".
    Next of kin: Mary Dudley, Rebekah Clark.
    Executors: Caleb Clark, Joshua Clark.

Peter Deny/Denny   115.49   TA   £1062.3.8   Mar 15 1773   Jul 27 1773
    Appraisers: Henry Troth, Solomon Neall.
    Creditors: Moses Allen, Milt Cagan for Speirs & French & Co.
    Next of kin: Lyded Denness, Thomas Elliott.
    Executor: Perry Parrot.

Richard Turbut   115.56   TA   £586.15.11   May 15 1772   Jun 8 1773
    Appraisers: Aaron Parratt, George Dudley.
    Creditors: William Hayward, Robert Goldsborough.
    Next of kin: Vincent Price, Elisabeth Turbull.
    Administratrix: Sarah Turbut.

John Tylor   115.60   TA   £87.17.4   Dec 5 1772   Jun 8 1773
    Appraisers: George Dudley, Benedick Huckens.
    Creditors: Matthais Gale, Ann Needles.
    Next of kin: Thomas Tylor, Elijah Tylor.
    Administratrix: Elisabeth Emerson (widow of John Tylor).

Dr. Lodman Elbert   115.62   TA   £841.9.2   Aug 7 1772   May 25 1773
    Appraisers: Richard Pickering, Joseph Bewley.
    Creditors: James Loyd Chamberlain, William Hayward.
    Next of kin: Rebeca Downes, Mary Ann Garey.
    Administrator: Henry Elbert.

John Baily/Bailey   115.69   TA   £4.7.11   Jun 4 1773   Jun 10 1773
    Appraisers: Thomas Rag, John Young.
    Administrator: John Mather.

John Baily   115.70   TA   ----   Jun 10 1773
    List of debts.
    Creditors: Thomas Mansfield, Mary Ann Garey.

Peter Sharp   115.70   TA   £481.6.7   Nov 8 1769   Jun 8 1773
    Appraisers: Thomas Jenkins, Tristram Bowdle.
    Creditors: John Traup, Stevens & Martin.
    Next of kin: Christopher Birckhead, Rachel Edmondson.
    Administrator: Pollard Edmondson.

Richard Fairbrother   115.74   TA   £47.5.4   May 22 1772   Jul 13 1773
    Appraisers: William Sharp, Matthew Lewis Barnett.
    Creditors: John Stevens for Elisabeth Loyd, Thomas Jenkins.
    Next of kin: Mary Fairbrother.
    Administrators: Elisabeth Fairbrother, Philip Mackey.

William Stevens   115.77   TA   £300.11.9   Nov 1 1772   Jul 6 1773
    Appraisers: Howell Powell, Daniel Sherwood.
    Creditors: Charles Crookshanks for Speirs & French & Co., Nicholas Pamphilon.
    Next of kin: Peter Stevens, Ann Jenkins.
    Administratrix: Sarah Stevens.

Barnaby Dougherty   115.80   TA   £179.18.2   Jul 27 1772   Apr 30 1773
    List of debts.
    Administrator: John Dougherty.

William Coburn/Cobourn   115.83   TA   £0.8.0   Oct 6 1773
    List of debts.
    Administrator: James Lloyd Chamberlaine.

William Coburn   115.84   TA   £16.17.7   Aug 29 1770   Oct 6 1773
    Appraisers: Thomas Barrow, James Barrow.
    Creditors: John Hall, John Bracco.
    Next of kin: Solomon Coburn, Anne Coburn.
    Administrators: William Nicols, James Lloyd Chamberlaine.

Col. Thomas Chamberlaine   115.86   TA   £13.1.11   Sep 17 1773
    List of debts.
    Executor: James Lloyd Chamberlaine.

Francis Chaplin   115.86   TA   £26.6.5   May 12 1773   Aug 17 1773
    Appraisers: Nicholas Goldsborough, Samuel Dickinson.
    Creditors: Mary Chaplin, Charles Crookshanks.
    Next of kin: Joseph Chaplin, Mary Hancock, Elisabeth Chaplin.
    Administrator: Thomas Jenkins.

Richard Clark   115.88   TA   £32.2.4   Feb 19 1773   Jul 6 1773
    Appraisers: Christopher Birckhead, Samuel Abbatt.
    Creditors: William Stevens, William Arrington.
    Administrator: William Clark.

Vincent Helsby   115.89   TA   £167.18.8   Jun 21 1773   Jul 6 1773
    Appraisers: John Stevens, John Mullikin.
    Creditors: Charles Crookshanks for Speirs & French & Co., Samuel Sharp.
    Next of kin: Elisabeth Hills, John Helsby.
    Administratrix: Mary Helsby.

John Catrop   115.94   TA   £247.11.10   May 22 1773   Aug 24 1773
    Appraisers: Solomon Neall, Henry Troth.
    Creditors: Sarah Turbutt, Thomas Dawson.
    Next of kin: Elisabeth Neall, John Catrop.
    Administratrix: Ruth Catrop.

Mary Broadaway   115.98   TA   £123.18.6   May 28 1773
    Appraisers: George Wilson, Caleb Clark.
    Creditors: George Wilson.
    Next of kin: Ann Cooper, Ann Frampton.
    Administrator: Abner Broadaway.

James Wallace   115.100   DO   £159.11.1   Jul 13 1773
    List of debts.
    Executor: Arthur Whitely.

William Wright   115.104   DO   £3.9.6   May 27 1773
    List of debts.
    Administrator: Jacob Wright.

William Wright, Jr.   115.104   DO   £8.17.2   Jun 3 1773
    List of debts.
    Administratrix: Sarah Wright.

Solomon Camper   115.106   DO   £62.15.9   Apr 3 1773   Jun 14 1773
    Appraisers: Peter Edmondson, John Valliant.
    Creditors: Matthais Gale, William Ennalls.
    Next of kin: John Camper, Mary Caulk.
    Administratrix: Philadelphia Camper.

Henry Keen/Keene   115.108   DO   £21.11.8   May 17 1773
    List of debts.
    Executors: John Keene, Benjamin Keene, Jr.

Capt. Henry Keene   115.109   DO   £84.2.11   Nov 16 1772   May 17 1773
    Appraisers: Henry Lake, Thomas Creaton.
    Creditors: Mary Keene, Betty Longue.
    Next of kin: Benjamin Keene, Matthew Keene.
    Executor: Benjamin Keene.

Moses Lecompt   115.110   DO   £6.1.10   May 21 1773
    List of debts.
    Executor: William Lecompte.

John Wheeler   115.111   DO   £16.0.11   Apr 26 1773
    List of debts.
    Administratrix: Mary Wheeler.

William Byus, Jr.   115.112   DO   £1.6.0   Jun 5 1773
    List of debts.
    Executor: William Byus.

William Phillips   115.113   DO   £25.15.5   Jun 28 1773
    List of debts.
    Executor: Ezekiel Keene.

Henry Navey   115.114   DO   £4.6.0   Jun 2 1773
    List of debts.
    Administratrix: Mary Navey.

Robert Polk   115.114   DO   £587.3.3   Jun 3 1773
    List of debts.
    Executor: Daniel Polk.

John Wheeler   115.115   DO   £66.5.7   Jul 2 1772   Apr 9 1773
    Appraisers: Benjamin Woodard, Thomas Vickars.
    Creditors: Daniel Sulivane, Jr., Nansey Wheeler, Charles Wheeler.
    Next of kin: Elisabeth Ross.
    Administratrix: Mary Wheeler.

Richard Soward   115.120   DO   £58.8.9   Aug 1 1773   Aug 12 1773
    Appraisers: Thomas Linthicum, John Spedden.
    Creditors: Harrison & Sprigg, Richard Coney.
    Next of kin: Charles Soward, John Soward.
    Administratrix: Sarah Soward.

John Rider Nevitt   115.122   DO   £673.16.3   Nov 1772   Sep 17 1773
    Appraisers: John Stevens, John Tootell.
    Creditors: John Henry, Henry Hooper 2nd.
    Next of kin: Sarah Muir, Emelia Green.
    Administratrix: Sarah Ennalls Nevitt.

John Pike   115.127   DO   £29.13.1   Jul 28 1773   Aug 16 1773
    Appraisers: Gideon Gambell, James Brown.
    Creditors: Richard Able Battson, William Tickle.
    Next of kin: Sarah Pike, Grace Pike.
    Administrator: William Smith.

John Lane   115.128   DO   £158.3.6   Jun 14 1773   Sep 13 1773
    Appraisers: Roger Ashcom Hooper, Willis Newton.
    Creditors: James Sulivane, Harrison & Sprigg.
    Next of kin: William Lane, Bretanna Lane.
    Administratrix: Lucy Lane.

Joseph Shenton   115.132   DO   £173.8.4   Jul 12 1773   Sep 26 1773
    Appraisers: Henry Lake, Thomas Creaton.
    Creditors: Patrick Leyburn, John Tubman.
    Next of kin: Charles Shenton, Charles Keene.
    Executor: Abraham Meekins.

Thomas Mace   115.134   DO   £41.10.1   Aug 9 1773   Oct 27 1773
    Appraisers: Roger Jones, Stevens Woolford.
    Creditors: Landon Ball, Nicholas Mace.
    Next of kin: Thomas Mace.
    Executors: Edmund Mace, John Mace.

Thomas Addams/Adams   115.137   DO   £55.10.7   Aug 6 1773   Sep 13 1773
    Appraisers: Nathaniel Potter, John Hooper.
    Creditors: William Richardson, Charles Dickinson.
    Next of kin: Elijah Adams, Bartholomew Adams.
    Administratrix: Rhody Adams.

John Briley   115.140   DO   £61.8.1   Jun 1773   Aug 16 1773
    Appraisers: John True, Jacob Wright.
    Creditors: James Murray, Robert Gilmor.
    Next of kin: Joseph Kerbuy, Samuel Briley.
    Administratrix: Isabel Briley.

George Hutton   115.142   DO   £120.0.0   Aug 19 1772   Aug 11 1773
    Appraisers: Nathaniel Potter, William Fountain.
    Next of kin: William Hutton, George Hutton.
    Executrix: Mary Hutton.

Richard Minner   115.146   DO   £123.7.3   Jun 17 1773   Aug 11 1773
    Appraisers: Peter Edmondson, Maccabeus Alford.
    Creditors: Edward Parkinson, Charles Blair.
    Next of kin: William Minner, Edward Minner.
    Administrator: Richard Clark.

William Fountain   115.148   DO   £558.3.0   May 5 1773   Aug 11 1773
    Creditors: Michael Nelson, David Peterkin Woolford.
    Next of kin: Nathaniel Potter, Zabdiel Potter.
    Executor/Executrix: Major Fountain.

John Ghow   115.152   DO   £33.16.3   Jun 25 1773   Aug 11 1773
    Appraisers: Peter Edmondson, Maccabeus Alford.
    Creditors: Thomas Noel, Charles Blair.
    Next of kin: William Gow.
    Administratrix: Mary Gowe.

James Eccleston   115.154   DO   £134.17.10   Sep 2 1772   Jul 26 1773
    Appraisers: Winlock Russum, Jacob Wright.
    Creditors: Thomas Mace, Daniel Sulivane, Jr.
    Next of kin: Charles Eccleston, Joseph Eccleston.
    Administrator: William Eccleston.

Thomas Andrew   115.156   DO   £120.4.0   Jun 12 1773   Aug 12 1773
    Appraisers: Henry Dickinson, Peter Richardson.
    Creditors: Richard Stanford, James Murray.
    Next of kin: Betty Brown, Rebecah Brannock Andrew.
    Administratrix: Elisabeth Andrew.

Richard Wallace   115.157   DO   £74.10.11   Jul 12 1773   Aug 11 1773
    Appraisers: Benjamin Keene, John Keene.
    Creditors: Joseph Wallace, John Wells.
    Next of kin: Joseph Wallace, Charles Wallace.
    Executor: Ann Wallace.

Benjamin Murray   115.160   DO   £19.18.4   Apr 3 1773   Aug 11 1773
    Appraisers: John True, James Wright.
    Creditors: Patrick Braughan, Robert Gilmor.
    Next of kin: Sarah Wallis, Sarah Hutten.
    Administratrix: Margaret Murray.

Thomas Stack   115.162   DO   £91.16.9   Aug 17 1773   Sep 13 1773
    Appraisers: Anderton Eaton, Philip French.
    Creditors: Charles Blair, R. Moore.
    Next of kin: Catrun Ross, Patrick Stack.
    Administratrix: Ann Stack.

Andrew McGhee   115.165   DO   £2433.2.11   Mar 26 1773   Jul 16 1773
    Appraisers: Thomas Firmin Eccleston, Robert Gilmor.
    Creditors: Charles Dickinson, Thomas Noel.
    Executor: Peter Richardson.

Henry Penington   115.188   CE   £368.2.7   Jun 21 1773   Jun 23 1773
    Appraisers: Peregrine Ward, John Stoops.
    Creditors: Thomas Cooper, John Stockton.
    Next of kin: Mary Pennington, Joseph Hutchison.
    Executor: Mary Penington.

William Freeman   115.191   KE   £693.11.7   Mar 5 1773   Jul 28 1773
    Appraisers: Robert Maxwell, William Merritt.
    Creditors: William Henry, James Jones.
    Next of kin: Ann Freeman, Mary Freeman.
    Executor: Isaac Freeman.

Mr. John Caulk   115.195   KE   £561.5.5   Jul 19 1773   Oct 9 1773
    Appraisers: James Dunn, Nathan Hutcheson.
    Creditors: John Page, James Anderson, John Caulk.
    Next of kin: Temperance Bowers, Jesse Cazier, Richard Caulk.
    Executor: Asenah Caulk.

James Piner   115.200   KE   £26.14.10   Aug 21 1773
    List of debts.
    Administratrix: Ann Piner.

Frederick Perkins   115.200   KE   £848.9.5   Apr 2 1773   Jun 12 1773
    Appraisers: John Eccleston, Charles Groome.
    Creditors: Thomas Ringgold, Peregrine Frisby, Macal Medford.
    Next of kin: Susannah Piner, Jonathon Turner.
    Administrator: Isaac Perkins.

John Williams   115.206   KE   £465.16.8   Aug 23 1773   Dec 10 1773
    Appraisers: Charles Groome, St. Leger Everett.
    Creditors: John Voorhey, James Wilmer, Donaldson Yeates.
    Next of kin: Ann Howell, Sarah Briscoe.
    Executor: MaCall Medford.

Francis Day   115.209   DO   £64.18.4   May 1 1773   Nov 29 1773
    Appraisers: William Harper, Levin Kirkman.
    Creditors: James Sulivane, Samuel Davidson.
    Administrator: James Austen/Austin (see also folio 436.)

Nathan Manship   115.212   DO   £106.11.6   Oct 2 1773   Nov 8 1773
    Appraisers: James Wing, William Richardson.
    Creditors: Matthais Gale, Nathan Manship.
    Next of kin: Charles Manship, Nathan Manship.
    Administratrix: Eleanor, wife of Thomas Peirry.

William Burn   115.214   DO   £74.1.0   Sep 2 1773   Dec 9 1773
    Appraisers: Jonathon Patridge, Jonathon Bestpitch.
    Creditors: Harrison & Sprigg, Murray & Sulivane.
    Next of kin: Elisabeth Burn, Thomas Burn.
    Administrator: Henry Steuart.

Thomas Hayward (son of John)   115.216   DO   £75.1.9   Aug 17 1773   Dec 6 1773
    Appraisers: John Lecompte, Willis Newton.
    Creditors: Thomas Ennalls 3rd, John Greenwood.
    Next of kin: John Hayward, ------.
    Administratrix: Adday Hayward.

Richard Wallace   115.219   DO   £10.0.0   Sep 16 1773   Oct 25 1773
    Appraisers: Benjamin Keene, John Keene.
    Creditors: Joseph Wallace, John Wells.
    Next of kin: Joseph Wallace, Charles Wallace.
    Executrix: Ann Wallace.

Robert Johnson   115.220   DO   £48.8.5   Aug 23 1773   Nov 3 1773
    Appraisers: Patrick Brohawn, John King, Jr.
    Creditors: John Byrn, James Granlee.
    Next of kin: Ezekiel Johnson, William Johnson.
    Administratrix: Elisabeth Johnson, Jr.

Thomas John Marshall   115.222   DO   £739.19.2   Jul 27 1773   Nov 29 1773
    Appraisers: John Dickenson, John Anderton.
    Creditors: Henry Hooper 2nd, Henry Steele.
    Next of kin: John Darby.
    Executor: John Marshall.

Joshua Ricards   115.228   DO   £47.11.3   Feb 16 1773   Nov 29 1773
    Appraisers: George Wallace, Ezekiel Brown.
    Creditors: Betty Manlove, Robert Mitchell.
    Next of kin: Archibald Ricards, Charles Ricards.
    Administrator: Joseph Ricords.

Francis Brown   115.230   DO   £86.18.5   Mar 6 1773   Nov 12 1773
    Appraisers: Henry Hooper, George Wallace.
    Creditors: Hamilton & Blair, Clement Bayley.
    Next of kin: Ezekiel Brown, Charles Brown.
    Administrator: Anderton Brown.

Obediah Dawson   115.232   DO   £17.5.4   Apr 2 1773   Dec 20 1773
    Appraisers: Roger A. Hooper, Thomas Pitt.
    Creditors: John Hooper.
    Next of kin: John Hooper, Anthony Dawson.
    Administrator: John Dawson.

Hugh Spedding   115.234   DO   £13.9.5   Dec 16 1773
    List of debts.
    Executrix: Lauranna, wife of William Bennett.

Thomas McCraikin   115.234   DO   £25.0.9   Dec 7 1773
    List of debts.
    Administratrix: Nancy McCraikin.

Thomas Andrew, Jr.   115.235   DO   £4.5.7   Oct 26 1773
    List of debts.
    Administratrix: Elisabeth Andrew.

Thomas Andrew, Jr.   115.235   DO   £12.19.2   Aug 1773   Aug 12 1773
    List of debts.
    Administratrix: Elisabeth Andrew.

Thomas McCrakin   115.237   DO   £42.12.7   Dec 7 1773
    List of debts.
    Administratrix: Nancy McCrakin.

Joseph Alford   115.238   DO   £1.7.0   Aug 30 1773
    List of debts.
    Executor: Maccabeus Alford.

Thomas Hayward   115.238   DO   £1.1.2   Sep 17 1773
    List of debts.
    Executrix: Sarah Hayward.

William Fountain   115.239   DO   £144.17.5   Oct 11 1773
    List of debts.
    Administratrix: Major Fountain.

James Eccleston   115.241   DO   £123.13.1   Sep 8 1773
    List of debts.
    Administrator: William Eccleston.

Francis Brown   115.241   DO   £6.13.6   Nov 12 1773
    List of debts.
    Administrator: Anderton Brown.

William Alford   115.242   DO   £0.11.10   Aug 12 1773
    List of debts.
    Executrix: Mary Alford.

Mary Griffith   115.243   DO   £2.9.6   Feb 19 1774
(also cited as Elisabeth Griffith)
     List of debts.
     Executor: Aaron Atkinson.

William Heath   115.243   QA   £9.9.6   Jun 17 1774
     List of debts.
     Administratrix: Esther, wife of William Featherston.

John Lockerman   115.244   QA   £89.13.5   Apr 20 1774
     List of debts.
     Administrator: John Goldsborough.

John Casson   115.245   QA   £7.19.8   Jun 17 1774
     List of debts.
     Administratrix: Sarah Casson.

Col. William Hopper   115.246   QA   £2251.0.6   May 18 1772   May 24 1774
     Appraisers: Basil Warfield, James O'Bryon.
     Creditors: William M. Leeds for Speirs & French & Co., James Hollyday.
     Next of kin: Joseph Nicholson.
     Mentions: Ruth Spry.
     Executors: William Hopper, James Bordley.

James Emory   115.251   QA   £71.10.9   Mar 1773   May 30 1774
     Appraisers: John Hammond, David Lindsey.
     Creditors: Patrick O'Bryon, William Minor.
     Next of kin: Ann Emory, Rebecah Clements.
     Executor: Charles Emory.

Charles Leatherbury   115.252   QA   £39.2.0   Mar 5 1774   Jun 8 1774
     Appraisers: Benjamin Gould, William Pryor.
     Son: Thomas Leatherbury.
     Administratrix: Elisabeth Simmonds.

Joseph Young   115.253   QA   £172.0.7   Mar 23 1774   Jun 9 1774
     Appraisers: James Hackett, Benjamin Gould.
     Mentions: Elisabeth Comb, Absalam Meraday, Catharine Marsh, Mary Ann Jackson.
     Executor: James Ruth.

Thomas Roe   115.256   QA   £178.3.9   Oct 7 1773   Apr 18 1774
     Appraisers: Solomon Mason, William Cannon.
     Creditors: William Molleston, Christopher Cross Routh.
     Next of kin: James Baggs, Davis Loe/Roe.
     Administratrix: Hannah Roe.

Jacob Seth, Gentleman   115.258   QA   £1189.12.8   Jul 19 1773   May 13 1774
     Appraisers: J. Bordley, John Seeden.
     Creditors: John Kerr, Hemsley & Tilghman.
     Next of kin: John Seth, Susannah Clayland.
     Administratrix: Mary Seth.

James Gwin   115.265   QA   £53.18.10   May 10 1773   May 2 1774
     Appraisers: John Fisher, Anthony Harrington.
     Creditors: William McLeod, James Davidson.
     Next of kin: Elisabeth Holding, Caleb Holding.
     Administratrix: Hannah Gwinn.

William Newman   115.267   QA   £109.19.2   Apr 8 1774   Jun 15 1774
     Appraisers: Benjamin Gould, William Pryor.
     Creditors: Joseph Sudler, John Dean.
     Next of kin: Daniel Newman, Nathaniel Newman, Jr.
     Executrix: Elisabeth Newman.

William Chears/Chaires   115.270   QA   £52.1.4   Sep 3 1773   Jun 15 1774
     Appraisers: Richard Mason, William Cannon.
     Creditors: William Robertson, John Wallace.
     Next of kin: Thomas Chears, Mary Hurlock, Mary Ann Matthews.
     Administratrix: Henrietta Chaires.

John Casson   115.272   QA   £291.6.2   1773   Jun 17 1774
     Appraisers: William Bell, Benjamin Sylvester.
     Creditors: Henry Casson, Tilghman & Nicols.
     Next of kin: Henry Casson, Robert Casson, Robert Cleland.
     Administratrix: Sarah Casson.

William Nutrel   115.275   QA   £20.8.1   Mar 30 1772
     Appraisers: Henry Downes, Jr., Richard Small.
     Creditors: Henry Casson, William Molleston.
     Next of kin: Nathan Nutrel, Ann Nutrel.
William Nutrel   £14.15.8   Dec 17 1772   May 4 1774
     Appraisers: Henry Downes, Jr., Giles Hicks.
     Administrator: Robert Casson.

Leonard Piles   115.277   PG   £575.19.6   May 19 1774   Jul 11 1774
     Appraisers: W. Dorsett, Thomas Clagett.
     Creditors: John Read Magruder, Richard Brooke.
     Next of kin: Francis Piles, Linny Piles.
     Executrix: Elisabeth Piles.

John Mackey   115.281   PG   £27.15.0   Feb 21 1774   Jun 16 1774
     Appraisers: Allen Bowie, William Dorsett.
     Next of kin: Henrietta Mackie, James Mackay.
     Administrator: Judson Cooledge.

Ann Batson   115.281   AA   £393.8.5   Feb 25 1774   May 11 1774
     Appraisers: Thomas Gassaway, Edward Gaither, Jr.
     Creditors: William Simmons, Jr., Jeremiah Chapman Simmons.
     Next of kin: Edward Tillard, William Tillard.
     Administrators: Ann Tillard, William Fisher.

Thomas Dashiell   115.283   SO   £481.16.10   Jul 10 1773   May 23 1774
     Appraisers: Isaac Hopkins, William Stewart.
     Creditors: Henry Jackson & Co., Levin Dashiell.
     Next of kin: Mary Mynck, Arthur Dashiell.
     Administratrix: Jane Dashiell.

Ephraim Vaughan   115.289   SO   £276.16.5   Nov 20 1773   Mar 16 1774
     Appraisers: George Wailes, Barkley Townsend.
     Creditors: Isaac Cooper, Caleb Balding.
     Next of kin: Jethro Vaughan, Levin Vaughan.
     Executrix: Betty Vaughan.

Robert Chambers   115.293   SO   £40.1.8   Apr 19 1773   Apr 26 1774
     Appraisers: Stephen Roach, Francis Disharoon.
     Creditors: Alexander McLauglin.
     Next of kin: Sarah Chambers, Alice Chambers.
     Administrator: John Chambers.

John Conant   115.294   SO   £6.6.1   May 29 1773   Apr 28 1774
     Appraisers: Henry Gale, John Phillips.
     Creditors: Henry Jackson & Co.
     Next of kin: William Giles.
     Administrator: Jones Bounds.

Elgate Hitch   115.297   SO   £326.13.9   Feb 19 1773   Apr 12 1774
     Appraisers: Esme Bayly, Thomas Stanford.
     Creditors: James Bounds, George Handy.
     Next of kin: Joshua Byrd, Thomas Byrd.
     Executor: Robert Hitch.

Southey Whittington   115.301   SO   £391.2.0   Dec 10 1773   Mar 16 1774
     Appraisers: Elijah Coulbourn, Lazarus Lankford.
     Creditors: Michael Holland, Jr., John Gunby.
     Next of kin: Benjamin Polk, Isaac Whittington.
     Executor: Southing Whittington.

William Giles   115.304   SO   £220.1.3   Apr 5 1773   Mar 16 1774
     Appraisers: William Nutter, John Phillips.
     Creditors: Thomas Loyd, John Phillips.
     Next of kin: William Giles, Mary Hawes.
     Executor: John Harris.

Joseph Seraghim/Serogin   115.311   SO   £314.4.6   Mar 16 1774
     Appraisers: William Winder, Thomas Stanford.
     Creditors: William McBryde, John Shireff.
     Next of kin: Samuel Seragin, Robert Seragin.
     Executor: John Serogin.

Mr. Rensher Roberts Grandee   115.317   SO   £106.11.0   Jul 30 1773   Mar 16 1774
     Appraisers: George Jones, William Waller.
     Creditors: Henry Jackson & Co., William White.
     Next of kin: Bettey Martin, Sarah Robards.
     Executrix: Mary Roberts Grandee.

Benjamin Wilpper   115.322   BA   £26.4.3   Mar 19 1773   Jan 27 ----
    Appraisers: Danid Shields, Aaron Nattison.
    Creditors: John Read, B. Hiesenthal.
    Next of kin: Mary Wilpper.
    Administrator: William Edwards.

Susannah Kirk   115.325   BA   £55.9.3   Apr 25 1772   Jan 17 1774
(alias Susannah Bryan/Brian)
    Appraisers: John McNabb, Thomas Ewing.
    Mentions: David Stewart, Cornelius Clopper, Jr.
    Administrator: George Woolsey.

Francis Phillips   115.328   BA   £22.19.3   Jun 22 1773   Feb 2 1774
    Appraisers: Samuel Owings, Charles Wells.
    Creditors: Philip Rogers, Thomas Jones.
    Administrator: Joseph Baxter.

Benjamin Wilpper   115.330   BA   £52.15.5   Jan 27 ----
    List of debts.
    Administrator: William Edwards.

Samuel Bayles/Bailiss   115.332   BA   £203.14.7   Dec 28 1773
    Appraisers: William Wilson, Charles Gilbert.
    Creditors: John Wilson for self & Co., William Ramsay.
    Next of kin: Nathaniel Bayles, Jonas Bayles.
    Executors: Benjamin Bailiss, Samuel Bailiss.

Nicholas Merryman   115.333   BA   £52.17.9
    List of debts.
    Administrator: Samuel Merryman.

Benjamin Wilpper   115.334   BA   £8.6.7   Jan 27 ----
    List of debts.
    Administrator: James Edwards (or William Edwards).

Samuel Ground   115.334   KE   £1337.5.7   Oct 22 1773   Feb 1 1774
    Appraisers: Richard Frisby, Luke Griffith.
    Creditors: Thomas Ringgold, Robert Anderson.
    Next of kin: Ann Hosier, Margaret Waltham.
    Administrator: Charles Groome.

Charles Ringgold, Jr.   115.341   KE   £37.19.10   Mar 17 1774
    Appraisers: James Dunn, John Caulk.
    Creditors: Thomas Ringgold for self & Sedgely Hillhouse.
    Next of kin: Randolph (no surname given).
    Administrator: Thomas Slipper.

Charles Ringgold   115.342   KE   £488.11.2   Jan 10 1774   Mar 10 1774
    Appraisers: John Hatchem, James Glenn.
    Creditors: Philip Smith.
    Next of kin: Mary Hynson.
    Executrix: Sarah Ringgold.

Thomas Brown   115.346   KE   £39.9.10   Nov 16 1773   Mar 10 1774
    Appraisers: James Smith, Nathaniel Beding.
    Creditors: Thomas Smith, Smyth & Ringgold.
    Next of kin: William Brown, Joseph Brown.
    Administratrix: Martha, wife of William Crabbin.

Stephen Boyer   115.347   KE   £24.10.0   Feb 18 1774   May 5 1774
    Appraisers: Peter Massey, Robert Maxwell.
    Creditors: William Henry, Isaac Spencer.
    Next of kin: Thomas Boyer, Richard Boyer.
    Administratrix: Mary Boyer.

Zerobabel Massay   115.348   KE   £106.0.6   Apr 10 1774   Apr 26 1774
    Appraisers: George Little, John Whittington.
    Creditors: Rebecah Marly, Elijah Massy.
    Next of kin: Elisabeth Massy, Robert Marly.
    Administratrix: Mary Rochester.

Mr. Michael Chambers   115.350   KE   £12.0.6   Mar 20 1774   Apr 15 1774
    Appraisers: Thomas Boyer, Nathaniel Boyer.
    Creditors: John Crawford, James Meullan.
    Next of kin: Cathern Mare, Marget Reed.
    Executor: William Hynson French.

Edward Comegys   115.350   KE   59.8.9   Jan 19 1774   Mar 9 1774
    Appraisers: Jesse Cosden, William Smith.
    Creditors: Thomas Pratt, Thomas Smyth.
    Next of kin: Charrity Pratt, John Burnside.
    Executors: Sarah Comegys, Isaac Spencer.

Mrs. Frances Dunn   115.351   KE   £473.12.2   Apr 5 1773   Feb 19 1774
    Appraisers: John Caulk, J. C. Hanson.
    Creditors: Thomas Ringgold, Richard Spencer.
    Next of kin: John Wickes, John Wickes, Jr.
    Administrators: James Dunn, Samuel Wicks.

John Wilson   115.355   KE   £681.1.3   Nov 23 1773   Feb 12 1774
    Appraisers: Peter Massy, Christopher Hall.
    Creditors: William Rogers, William Henry.
    Next of kin: James Wilson, Rachel Wilson.
    Executrix: Sarah Wilson.

Thomas Rasin (Quaker)   115.360   KE   £473.8.4   Jun 11 1772   Dec 24 1773
    Appraisers: Peter Massy, John Wilson.
    Creditors: John Voorhees, Gavin Murray for Jamison Johnstone & Co.
    Next of kin: Abraham Rasin, Sarah Rasin.
    Administrator: William Rasin.

Thomas Rasin (Quaker)   115.364   KE   £15.8.0   Dec 24 1773
    List of debts.
    Administrator: William Rasin.

Thomas Rasin (Quaker)   115.365   KE   £203.16.9   Aug 26 1773   Dec 24 1773
    Appraisers: Peter Massy.
    Creditors: John Voorhees, Gavin Murray for Jamison Johnstone & Co.
    Next of kin: Abraham Rasin, Sarah Rasin.
    Administrator: William Rasin.

Edward Brown   115.365   KE   £90.6.2   Aug 20 1773   Apr 26 1774
    Appraisers: Philip Davis, James Claypoole.
    Creditors: William Bowdle, Morgan & Slubey.
    Next of kin: John Hawkins, Maremy Gould.
    Administratrix: Elisabeth Brown.

John McGinis   115.368   KE   £5.7.10   Jan 19 1774
    List of debts.
    Administrator/Executor: Francis Lennan/Lenan.

John McGinnis   115.369   KE   £13.1.4   Jan 19 1774
    List of debts.
    Administrator/Executor: Francis Lennan/Lenan.

James Field   115.369   KE   £5.0.3   Mar 21 1774
    List of debts.
    Administrator: Joseph Field.

Rudulph Moore   115.370   KE   £21.10.6   Jan 1 1774
    List of debts.
    Mentions: Rebecca Harding, Alice Harding.
    Executrix: Alice, wife of Reuben Harding.

Rudulph Moore   115.370   KE   £313.12.5   Jan 1 1774
    List of debts.
    Executrix: Alice, wife of Reuben Harden.

John Kennard   115.371   KE   £9.2.2   May 2 1774
    List of debts.
    Executrix: Ann Kennard.

James Graham   115.371   KE   £418.1.4   Jan 12 1774   Apr 7 1774
    Appraisers: Jacob Jones, Jonathon Turner.
    Creditors: Christopher Hall, Joseph Mann.
    Next of kin: John Beazy, Andrew Graham.
    Executrix: Rebecca Graham.

Nathaniel Ward   115.375   CE   £620.4.4   Mar 28 1774   Jun 14 1774
    Appraisers: Edward Veazey, Benjamin Pryce.
    Creditors: Hugh Matthews, Thomas B. Veazey.
    Next of kin: John Ward, William Ward.
    Administrator: Thomas Beedle.

Augustine Biddle   115.378   CE   £537.5.5   May 10 1774
    Appraisers: Andrew Miller, Benjamin Bravard.
    Creditors: Samuel Morrison.
    Next of kin: Thomas Biddle, John Barrington.
    Administrators: John Biddle, Jesse Biddle.

Augustine Biddle   115.382   CE   £8.4.7   May 18 1774
    List of debts.
    Administrators: John Biddle, Jesse Biddle.

Augustine Biddle   115.382   CE   £148.2.0   May 18 1774
     List of debts.
     Administrators: John Biddle, Jesse Biddle.

William Sheerswood   115.383   CE   £144.12.8   Mar 25 1774   May 30 1774
(also William Shearswood)
     Appraisers: Edward Dougherty, Andrew Welsh.
     Creditors: William Currer, Samuel Wilson.
     Next of kin: Lydia Sharf.
     Executor: William Shearswood.

Alphonso Cozden/Cosden   115.385   CE   £718.4.1   May 17 1774   Jun 20 1774
     Appraisers: John Ward Veazey, John Ward.
     Creditors: Sturgis & Shields, Thomas Cosden.
     Next of kin: Thomas Cosden, James Cosden.
     Mentions: Mr. William Ward, Daniel Charles Heath.
     Executors: Elisabeth Cosden, Nicholas Walmsley.

Hannah Bauck   115.389   KE   £95.19.8   Apr 15 1761   May 28 1774
     Appraisers: Thomas Browning, James Pierce.
     Creditors: John Wilson, Richard Wilson.
     Next of kin: Isaac Freeman, Jr.
     Executor: Isaac Freeman.

Moses Alford   115.390   KE   £11.17.11   Mar 24 1774   Jun 2 1774
     Appraisers: Charles Groome, Luke Griffith.
     Creditors: Morgan & Slubey, Robert Anderson.
     Next of kin: Aquilla Attox, Barney Corse.
     Executor: Isaac Perkins.

Jane Cole   115.391   KE   £301.11.1   May 6 1774   Jun 13 1774
     Appraisers: Macall Medford, Jonathon Turner.
     Creditors: George Vincent Newcomb, Elisabeth Cop.
     Next of kin: John Mitchell, Jr., Elisabeth Cop.
     Executor: John Mitchell.

John Caulk   115.393   KE   £91.8.6   Apr 27 1774   May 25 1774
     Appraisers: James Dunn, Nathan Hutcheson.
     Creditors: James Anderson, John Page.
     Next of kin: Richard Caulk, Temperance Bower.
     Executrix: Arsennah Griffith.

Francis Stevens   115.394   KE   £14.12.5   May 9 1774
     Appraisers: Abraham Wilson, Samuel Thomas.
     Creditors: Daniel Farrell, Thomas Smith.
     Next of kin: William Stephens, John Ball.
     Administratrix: Hester Stevens.

Charles Steward   115.395   KE   £22.9.0   Apr 18 1774   May 30 1774
     Appraisers: William Hazel, Samuel West.
     Mentions: Frances Steuart, John Stewart, William Reed.
     Administratrix: Sarah Steward.

Thomas Lorain   115.396   KE   £259.9.4   May 28 1774
     List of debts.
     Administrator/Executor: James McLane.

Philip Burgin   115.399   KE   £54.3.4   Apr 7 1774   May 9 1774
     Appraisers: Joseph Redgrave, Christopher Hall.
     Creditors: John Woodshier, Pearce & Clark.
     Next of kin: George Vansant, Jesse Burgin.
     Administrator: Joshua Burgin.

Christian Chiffins   115.401   KE   £41.16.18   Dec 31 1773   May 23 1774
     Appraisers: William Blackiston, Benjamin Blackiston.
     Creditors: David Kennedy, John Darrach.
     Next of kin: Elisabeth Woodeson, Jacob Lycan.
     Executor: James Chiffins.

Martha Cole   115.402   KE   £830.19.4   Oct 11 1773   May 6 1774
     Appraisers: Robert Maxwell, Jonathon Turner.
     Creditors: Donaldson Yeates, Bouldin & Hoard.
     Next of kin: John Mitchell, Jr., Fs. Sinah Cole.
     Executor: John Mitchell.

William Sanders   115.407   KE   £6.17.6   Jun 20 1774
     List of debts.
     Administrator/Executor: William Sanders.

Thomas Lorain   115.408   KE   £603.12.0   May 28 1774
     Mentions: Mary Lorain.
     Executrix: Mary, wife of James McLane/McClean.

James Thomas   115.412   KE   £7.4.9   Jun 16 1774
    List of debts.
    Executrix: Mary, wife of Acquilla Page.

Moses Alford   115.412   KE   £73.6.2   Jun 2 1774
    List of debts.
    Executor: Isaac Perkins.

Moses Alford   115.413   KE   £18.2.2   Jun 2 1774
    List of debts.
    Mentions: Daniel Kennard.
    Executor: Isaac Perkins.

Frances Dunn   115.414   KE   £7.10.0   May 28 1772
    List of debts.
    Administrator/Executor: James Dunn.

Hannah Burk   115.414   KE   £1.14.3   May 28 1774
    List of debts.
    Executor: Isaac Freeman.

John Carvill   115.414   KE   £8.16.1   May 11 1774
    List of debts.
    Administratrix: Ann Carvill.

Capt. John Carvill   115.415   KE   £9.19.2   May 11 1774
    List of debts.
    Administratrix: Ann Carvill.

Capt. John Carvill   115.415   KE   £136.3.0   Mar 3 1774   May 11 1774
    Appraisers: John Wickes, James Dunn.
    Creditors: Morgan & Slubey, Thomas Ringgold.
    Next of kin: J. C. Hanson, Richard Hynson.
    Administratrix: Ann Carvill.

Nicholas Riley/Ryley   115.416   KE   £125.18.9   May 17 1774
    Appraisers: James Pearse, Robert Hoody.
    Creditors: William Rogers, John Voorhees.
    Next of kin: Sarah Huff, Benjamin Riley.
    Executor: William Ryley.

Nicholas Ryley   115.416   KE   £206.9.5   May 17 1774
    List of debts.
    Executor: William Ryley.

John Carvill, Jr.   115.417   KE   £45.10.0   Mar 3 1774   May 11 1774
    Appraisers: John Wickes, James Dunn.
    Creditors: James Anderson, Thomas Ringgold.
    Next of kin: J. C. Hanson, R. Cruckshank.
    Administratrix: Ann Carvill.

John Carvill, Jr.   115.417   KE   £2.2.10   May 11 1774
    List of debts.
    Administratrix: Ann Carvill.

Daniel McDearmott/McDermot   115.418   KE   £75.3.9   Jun 27 1774
    Appraisers: J. Wilson, John Wilson.
    Creditors: James Brady, Archibald Wright.
    Administratrix: Helen McDermot.

Moses Tenant/Tennant   115.421   KE   £61.11.0   May 18 1774   Jun 14 1774
    Appraisers: John Eccleston, William Maxwell.
    Creditors: Jonathon Worth, Henry Wallis.
    Next of kin: John Tennant, Elisabeth Tennant.
    Administrator: William Tennant.

Thomas Price   115.422   KE   £9.5.1   Jun 17 1774
    Appraisers: Joshua Lamb, Abraham Rasin.
    Mentions: Isaac Cammill.
    Executor: Nathaniel Horrell.

Thomas Perkins, Jr.   115.423   KE   £306.7.4   Mar 13 1774   Jun 25 1774
    Appraisers: Joshua Lamb, Hezekiah Cooper.
    Next of kin: Susannah Piner, Sarah Wickes.
    Administrators: Ebenezar Ryner, Jonathon Turner.

Mr. George Slye/Sly   115.425   Sm   £5139.19.5   Jul 28 1773   Apr 20 1774
    Appraisers: William Jordan, John Shanks, Jr.
    Mentions: George Plowden, Jane Craycroft.
    Executrix: Clare Sly.

Andrew Mills   116.1   SM   £478.4.5   1772   Apr 29 1773
     Appraisers: John Miller, Joshua Merrill.
     Creditors: James Jordan for James Jordan & Co., John Briscoe for James Buchanan &
          Co.
     Next of kin: Zachariah Bond, Thomas Bond.
     Executors: James Mills, Charles Mills.

John Somerville   116.2   --   £24.11.7   Dec 7 1773
     List of debts.
     Executor: Alexander Somerville.

John Somerville   116.3   CA   £1463.12.8   Dec 6 1773
     List of debts.
     Executor: Alexander Somerville.

James Kelly   116.11   BA   £132.14.3   Nov 5 1773
     List of debts.
     Executor: John Shields.

James Kelly   116.11   BA   £119.13.1   Nov 5 1773
     List of debts.
     Executor: John Shields.

John Mayner   116.12   BA   £61.5.7   Oct 5 1773
     List of debts.
     Executor: John Lawson.

James Sloane   116.13   BA   £8.8.1   Oct 7 1773
     List of debts.
     Administratrix: Jane Sloane.

James Sloane   116.14   BA   £69.1.10   Oct 7 1773
     List of debts.
     Administratrix: Jane Sloane.

Henry Pearson   116.15   BA   £113.8.0   Mar 30 1773
     List of debts.
     Executor: John Boyd.

Thomas Jackson   116.16   BA   £14.13.2   Apr 24 1773
     list of debts.
     Administrator: Samuel Clark.

Thomas Jackson   116.17   BA   £10.14.1   Apr 24 1773
     list of debts.
     Administrator: Samuel Clark.

James Coale/Cole   116.18   BA   £79.5.2   Sep 15 1772   May 5 1773
     Appraisers: Charles Gilbert, Kent Mitchell.
     Creditors: Amos Garrett (executor of James Spavold).
     Next of kin: Thomas Gilbert, William Arnold.
     Executors: Jane Cole, James Cole.

Jacob Mohler   116.21   BA   £473.11.0   Sep 18 1773   Sep 28 1773
(clock and watchmaker)
     Appraisers: John Belsner.
     Creditors: George Lindenberger, Andene Hog.
     Executors: Elisabeth Mohler, Peter Shits.

Richard Crawley   116.24   BA   £9.3.0   Aug 4 1770   Apr 22 1773
     Appraisers: William Smith, William Robertson Presbury.
     Creditors: William Presbury.
     Administratrix: Thomas Presbury.

Edward Harriss/Harris   116.25   BA   £156.9.9   Nov 16 1773
(Quaker)
     Appraisers: Isaac Griest, John Smith.
     Creditors: George Fletcher, Henry Stevenson.
     Next of kin: Thomas Harris.
     Administrator: William Davis.

James Sloane   116.28   BA   £47.3.2   Oct 30 1773   Oct 7 1773
     Appraisers: William McComas, Joshua Amos.
     Creditors: William Fisher, Jr.
     Next of kin: very young children.
     Administratrix: Jane Sloane.

Mark Guishard   116.29   BA   £455.14.6   Sep 14 1772   Mar 26 1773
     Appraisers: Benkid Wilson, Abraham Britton.
     Creditors: Buchanan & Cowan.
     Mentions: Archibald Buchanan.
     Administratrix: Sarah Guishard.

Dr. Thomas Bond   116.31   CA   £748.8.7   Feb 19 1773   Dec 2 1773
    Appraisers: Edward Gantt, Charles Grahame.
    Creditors: William Allen for Patrick Sim Smith, William Molleson.
    Next of kin: Benjamin Mackall, John Bond.
    Executrix: Elisabeth Bond.

Jesse Bolden   116.35   CE   £100.0.0   Mar 6 1773   Jul 12 1773
    Appraisers: Jesse Hollingsworth, Isaac Griest.
    Creditors: Elijah Boldin.
    Next of kin: James Bouldin.
    Administratrix: Mary, wife of John Smith.

George Cunningham   116.36   CE   £354.17.0   May 29 1773   Jun 23 1773
    Appraisers: John Stoops, Alexander Williamson.
    Administratrix: Sarah Cunningham.

Benjamin Vinsand/Vansandt   116.37   CE   £77.8.7   Nov 19 1772
    Appraisers: Silvt. Nowland, Benjamin Nowland.
    Next of kin: William Grear, Benjamin Sappington.
    Administratrix: Rachel Vansandt.

William Callender   116.39   CE   £46.19.9   Nov 15 1773
    List of debts.
    Executrix: Elisabeth, wife of Andrew Welsh.

Thomas Stewart   116.39   CE   £8.16.10   Dec 9 1773
    List of debts.
    Administrator: Benjamin Stuart.

Samuel Adere   116.40   CE   £34.12.5   Nov 20 1773
    List of debts.
    Executrix: Hannah Adere.

John Eliason   116.40   CE   £82.7.2   Nov 6 1773
    List of debts.
    Administratrix: Mary Eliason.

William Jones   116.41   CE   £91.19.6   Jul 29 1773   Dec 8 1773
    Appraisers: Benjamin Nowland, Stephen Ryland.
    Creditors: Charles Phillipshill, Richard Thompson.
    Next of kin: Mary Page, Thomas Robwith.
    Administratrix: Rebecca Jones.

Thomas Steuart   116.43   CE   £196.16.9   Aug 18 1773   Dec 9 1773
    Appraisers: Adam Vance, Alexander Clarke.
    Creditors: Mary Fares.
    Next of kin: William Stuart, Alexander Stuart, Jr.
    Administrator: Benjamin Steuart.

John Eliason   116.45   CE   £49.15.5   Nov 6 1773
    List of debts.
    Administratrix: Mary Eliason.

Richard Wallace   116.45   CE   £74.3.9   Jul 23 1773   Sep 17 1773
    Appraisers: Barnet Vanhorn, John Hood.
    Creditors: John McLean.
    Next of kin: William Price, Mary Rothwill, Thomas Brison.
    Administratrix: Ann Wallace.

Alldridge/Aldridge Ryland   116.47   CE   £82.17.9   Jun 28 1773   Oct 9 1773
    Appraisers: John Stockton, Benjamin Price/Pryce.
    Creditors: John Price, Sturgis & Shields.
    Next of kin: Fredies Ryland, Jehu Ryland.
    Administrator: Jeremiah Sutton.

John Hays/Hayes   116.49   CE   £61.6.5   Aug 16 1773   Nov 10 1773
    Appraisers: John Ward, John Beadle.
    Mentions: Ruth Tharp, James Hayes.
    Administratrix: Sarah Hayes.

William Cather/Cauther   116.51   CE   £244.16.9   Aug 5 1773   Nov 27 1773
    Appraisers: Jonathon Hardshorn, James Glasgow.
    Creditors: William Allen.
    Next of kin: Elebeth Cather.
    Executor: Robert Cauther.

John Eliason   116.53   CE   £121.18.10   Mar 15 1773   Sep 7 1773
    Appraisers: Barnet Vanhorn, James Boyles.
    Creditors: Elias Eliason, William Rumsey.
    Next of kin: Cornelius Eliason, Andrew Eliason.
    Administratrix: Mary Eliason.

Samuel Adere   116.55   CE   £240.5.0   Nov 20 1773
    List of debts.
    Executor: Hannah Adere.

William Callender   116.56   CE   £15.16.2   Nov 15 1773
    List of debts.
    Executrix: Elisabeth, wife of Andrew Welsh.

William Makin   116.57   --   £688.14.11
    List of debts.

Mr. Francis Key   116.59   CE   £1424.7.1   Oct 4 1773
    List of debts.
    Administratrix: Ann Arnold Key.

Mr. Francis Key   116.60   CE   £281.16.9   Oct 4 1773
    List of debts.
    Administratrix: Ann Arnold Key.

Robert Wamsley   116.61   CE   £449.5.10   Apr 15 1772   Oct 14 1772
    Appraisers: James Wroth, John Money.
    Creditors: John Veazey, Sr., ------ Earle.
    Next of kin: William Wamsley, William Wamsley (sic).
    Executors: Alethia Wamsley, Nicholas Wamsley.

Samuel Adear/Adere   116.87   CE   £353.6.2   Mar 25 1773   Jun 26 1773
    Appraisers: James Bouldin, Jr., Edward Armstrong.
    Creditors: William Fulton, Andrew Crew, Jr.
    Next of kin: William Adair, John Adare.
    Executrix: Hannah Adere.

Richard Biddle   116.90   CE   £563.13.0   Apr 21 1773   Jul 17 1773
    Appraisers: Benjamin Bravard, Andrew Miller.
    Creditors: Samuel Morrison.
    Next of kin: Noble Biddle, Thomas Biddle.
    Executors: Augustine Biddle, Dominick Biddle.

George Little   116.94   KE   £31.10.3   Nov 11 1773
    List of debts.
    Executrix: Mary Little.

Simon Worrell   116.94   KE   £10.15.10   Dec 9 1773
    List of debts.
    Administratrix: Priscilla Worrell.

Rudolph Moore   116.95   KE   £153.9.8   Oct 26 1773   Dec 9 1773
    Appraisers: John Eccleston, William Comegys.
    Creditors: Gilpin & Jurey.
    Executrix: Ealce, wife of Rhubin Hardin.

Nathan Manning   116.96   KE   £100.8.7   Sep 4 1773   Dec 8 1773
    Appraisers: James Chiffins, George Blackiston.
    Creditors: William Thomas Gould, Sarah Boughman, Frances Medith.
    Administratrix: Elisabeth Manning.

William Greenlee   116.98   KE   £57.2.9   Oct 30 ----
    Appraisers: George Blackiston, James Chiffins.
    Mentions: Robert Greenlee, Joseph Mydith.
    Mentions: William Hazel, Martha Ashford.
    Executor: Samuel Greenlee.

Thomas Darrack   116.99   KE   £1439.7.4   Nov 11 1773
    List of debts.
    Administrators: Charlotte Darrack, John Darrack.

Moses Alford   116.107   KE   £584.17.4   Feb 3 1773   Oct 20 1773
    Appraisers: Luke Griffith, Charles Groome.
    Creditors: Mary Kennard, Morgan & Stubey, Robert Anderson.
    Next of kin: Barney Carse, Aquilla Attix.
    Executor: Isaac Perkins.

William Ashley   116.111   KE   £66.8.5   Aug 30 1773   Nov 25 1773
    Appraisers: Richard Willis, Kinvin Wroth.
    Creditors: ------ Bolton, Stephen Pacol.
    Next of kin: Edward Ashley, Mary Greenfield.
    Administratrix: Sophia Ashley.

John McDonald   116.113   AA   £104.16.10   May 17 1774
    List of debts.
    Executor: Robert Couden.

Ann Middleton   116.115   AA   £574.10.9   Jan 26 1774   Apr 14 1774
    Appraisers: Thomas Hyde, Na. Hammond.
    Creditors: Thomas Harwood, Jr., John Brice.
    Next of kin: Ellin Alkin, Joseph Middleton.
    Executor: Gilbert Middleton.

Joseph Jacobs   116.121   AA   £1400,6.8   Apr 12 1774
    Appraisers: Elijah Robosson, Jacob Walters (dec'd by April 12 1774).
    Creditors: John Stevenson, John Davis.
    Next of kin: Richard Jacobson, Richard Jacobs (son of Richard).
    Executors: Joseph Jacobs, Richard Jacobs.

Thomas Gassaway, Sr.   116.126   AA   £869.8.8   Apr 13 1774   Jun 30 1774
    Appraisers: Gerrard Hopkins, Jonathon Selman.
    Creditors: James Dick, Richard Tootell.
    Next of kin: Ann Rawlings, Henry Gassaway.
    Executrix: Mary Gassaway.

Henry Fuller   116.131   AA   £79.7.5   Jun 15 1774
    Mentions: Clark Rockhold, John Gray (son of Joshua).
    Creditors: Lancelot Jacques, Thomas Hyde.
    Mentions: Aaron Johnson, Greenberry Johnson.
    Administratrix: Sarah Fuller.

Charles Todd   116.133   AA   £17.14.2   Apr 23 1774   May 11 1774
    Appraisers: John Campbell, John Rawlins.
    Creditors: Na. Hammond, Richard Tootell.
    Next of kin: Burle Boone, Rachell Todd.
    Administrator: John Brice.

Martha Tillard   116.134   AA   £229.10.2   Jan 12 1774   May 11 1774
    Appraisers: Richard Richardson, Richard Green.
    Creditors: Thomas Morton, Jr., Richard Green.
    Next of kin: William Simmons, Jr., Abraham Fisher.
    Executors: Thomas Tillard, William Tillard.

Mr. Benjamin Williams   116.136   AA   £569.9.11   Nov 28 1772   May 17 1774
    Appraisers: Benjamin Selby, Elijah Green.
    Creditors: Nicholas Maccubbin, Thomas Harwood, Jr.
    Next of kin: Joshua Williams (son of Henry), Benjamin Williams (son of John).
    Administratrix: Comfort, wife of John Griffith.

Ann Batson   116.140   AA   £371.13.9   Apr 9 1774   May 11 1774
    Appraisers: Richard Richardson, Richard Green.
    Creditors: William Simmons, Jr., Jeremiah Chapman.
    Next of kin: Edward Tillard, William Tillard.
    Administrators: Thomas Tillard, William Fisher.

William Carter   116.141   AA   £18.6.5   Oct 14 1773   Apr 16 1774
    Appraisers: Richard Beard, Jr., Edward Lee.
    Creditors: John Shaw, Rebecca Walsh.
    Next of kin: William Carter, Rebecca Carter.
    Administrator: Gassaway Watkins.

Francis Crickmore   116.143   AA   £15.5.3   Jun 11 1773   Jun 15 1774
    Appraisers: William Nok, John Campbell.
    Creditors: Jordan Steiger, Samuel ---- Howard.
    Administratrix: Elisabeth Crickmore.

Dr. James Thompson   116.144   AA   ----   Feb 24 1774
    List of debts.
    Executor: William Smith.

Dr. James Thompson   116.146   AA   £113.18.9   Feb 24 1774
    List of debts.
    Executor: William Smith.

John Davidge   116.148   AA   £138.10.1   Mar 19 1774
    List of debts.
    Executrix: Honour, wife of Joseph Wilkins.

John Davidge   116.149   AA   £44.4.9   Mar 22 1774
    List of debts.
    Executrix: Honour, wife of Joseph Wilkins.

Edmund Maw   116.150   AA   £319.1.3   Mar 1 1774
    List of debts.
    Administratrix: Elisabeth Maw.

Daniel Kent   116.150   AA   £40.2.11   Mar 4 1774
    List of debts.
    Administrator: Joseph Joyce.

Priscilla Woodward   116.151   AA   £107.1.2   Mar 11 1774
    List of debts.
    Executor: William Woodward.

Mrs. Ann Dorsey   116.151   AA   £23.14.9   Mar 9 1774
    Appraisers: John Dorsey, William Coale.
    Mentions: Sarah Dorsey, Nicholas Dorsey, Thomas Dorsey.
    Executor: Joshua Dorsey.

Elisabeth White   116.152   AA   £27.0.6   Nov 27 1773 Feb 26 1774
    Appraisers: William Woodward, John Marriott.
    Creditors: Richard Tootell, Richard Couden.
    Next of kin: Gaither Simpson, Ann Simpson.
    Administrators: Joshua Ridgly, Cornelius Barry.

Edmund Maw   116.153   AA   £318.6.9   Apr 14 1772 Mar 1 1774
    Appraisers: John Campbell, Robert Reith.
    Creditors: Thomas Hyde, Nathaniel Hammond.
    Next of kin: John Maw (nephew), Elinor Maw (neice), James Maw (nephew).
    Administratrix: Elisabeth Maw.

Daniel Kent   116.155   AA   £2.5.0   Jul 16 1773 Mar 3 1774
    Appraisers: Thomas Mayo, Joseph Hansbury.
    Mentions: H. Stevenson, William Irwin, Thomas Worthington.
    Executor: Joseph Joyce.

Samuel Burgess   116.156   AA   £691.13.4   Jan 30 1773 Feb 22 1774
    Appraisers: Isaac Hall, Thomas Deale.
    Creditors: Thomas Tillard, Henry Darnell, P. Mannon.
    Next of kin: Marmaduke Wyvill, Benjamin Burgess.
    Administratrix: Jane Burgess.

Charles Pettebone   116.160   AA   £523.13.2   Jun 29 1773 Feb 22 1774
    Appraisers: ------ Watts, John Merriken.
    Creditors: Na. Hammond, Sarah Brice.
    Next of kin: Thomas Stinchcombe, Nathaniel Stinchcombe.
    Administratrix: Ann Pettebone.

John White   116.163   AA   £166.19.4   Nov 27 1773 Jan 29 1774
    Appraisers: William Woodward, John Marriott.
    Creditors: Brice B. Worthington, Richard Mackubin.
    Next of kin: Gaither Simpson, Ann Simpson.
    Mentions: Alexander Mlten (?).
    Executors: Joshua Ridgly, Cornelius Barry.

William Hewitt   116.167   AA   £138.13.0   Dec 18 1773 Jan 10 1774
    Appraisers: John Campbell, Francis Fairbrother.
    Creditors: Charles Bryan, John Sands.
    Administrator: John Hewitt.

James Riddle   116.168   BA   £134.16.9   Feb 20 1774 Mar 16 1774
    Appraisers: Mark Alexander, George Lindenberger.
    Creditors: Robert Walsh, Nathaniel Smith.
    Next of kin: Ann Riddle.
    Administrator: William Richardson.

Aquila Price   116.170   BA   £114.0.6   Jan 12 1774 Mar 13 1774
    Appraisers: Oliver Mathew, Jeremiah Johnson.
    Creditors: John Merryman, Jr., Jonathon Plowman.
    Next of kin: John Price, Benjamin Price.
    Administrator: Mordecai Price.

Hugh Frazier   116.171   BA   £129.17.6   Nov 14 1772 Mar 3 1774
    Appraisers: James Calhoun, David Mitchell.
    Creditors: Philip Rogers, David Mitchell.
    Next of kin: James Frazier.
    Administratrix: Ruth Frazier.

Benjamin Norriss/Norris   116.174   BA   £524.19.9   May 21 1772 Mar 5 1774
    Appraisers: John Love, John Taylor.
    Creditors: Thomas Smithson, John Archer.
    Next of kin: Joseph Norris, Abram Norris.
    Executor: Joseph Norris.

Gilbert Crockett   116.175   BA   £348.3.0   Mar 4 1774
    List of debts.
    Executor: William Webb.

Gilbert Crockett   116.180   BA   £123.17.7   Apr 13 1772   Mar 4 1774
    Appraisers: Greenberry Dorsey, Samuel Griffith.
    Creditors: Samuel Webb, Samuel Lee.
    Next of kin: Mary Harrison, Samuel Crockett.
    Executor: William Webb.

Dennis Garret Cole   116.183   BA   £328.13.4   Jun 19 1773   Mar 4 1774
    Appraisers: William Tipton, John Bond.
    Creditors: Mordecai Cole, John Price.
    Next of kin: Thomas Cole, Henry Cole.
    Executors: John Price (Quaker), Stephen Gill.

Michael Wellman   116.186   SM   £66.0.1   Oct 23 1773   Dec 14 1773
    Appraisers: Peter Urquhar, McKlore Hammett.
    Creditors: Archibald Campbell for John Glassford & Co.
    Next of kin: Susanna Peacock.
    Executor: Elisabeth Wellman.

Thomas Redman   116.188   SM   £19.17.3   Feb 18 1774
    List of debts.
    Administratrix/Executrix: Sarah Redman.

John Wheatly   116.189   SM   £3.3.7   Jan 1 1774
    List of debts.
    Administratrix/Executrix: Elisabeth Wheatly.

Thomas Redman   116.190   SM   £19.3.0   Feb 3 1774
    List of debts.
    Administratrix/Executrix: Sarah Redman.

John Mills, Sr.   116.191   SM   £177.13.4   Dec 16 1774   Apr 28 1774
    Appraisers: William Jordan, Samuel Maddox.
    Creditors: William Fraser, John Masson for Cunningham & Co.
    Next of kin: James Mills, Susanna Mills.
    Administrator/Executor: John Mills the youngest.

James Walker   116.193   SM   £36.10.7   Sep 12 1773   Mar 21 1774
    Appraisers: William Hamersley, Samuel Maddox.
    Creditors: Sarah Knott, James Jordan for John Glassford & Co.
    Next of kin: Henry Walker, Mary Walker.
    Administratrix/Executrix: Susanna Walker.

Dr. Henry Jerningham   116.195   SM   £545.5.3   Apr 20 1774
    Appraisers: William Hamersley, Gerard Bond.
    Creditors: James Jordan for John Glassford & Co., John Briscoe for James Buchanan
        & Co.
    Executrices: Katharine Jerningham, Frances Henrietta Jerningham.

John Pavat   116.198   SM   £44.9.0   Nov 22 1773   Mar 1 1774
    Appraisers: Samuel Theobalds, Robert Armstrong.
    Administrator/Executor: Robert Bennett.

Michael Conely   116.199   SM   £1.17.0   Dec 4 1773   Mar 3 1774
    Appraisers: Robert Armstrong, John Smith.
    Administrator: William Langley.

John Goldsmith   116.200   SM   £170.6.2   Dec 31 1773   Mar 7 1774
    Appraisers: Samuel Maddox, John Hornell.
    Creditors: James Jordan for John Glassford & Co., William Bond.
    Next of kin: Ann Goldsmith, John Goldsmith.
    Administrator/Executor: John Tippett (son of William).

Dennis Tippett/Tippet   116.202   SM   £178.5.3   Oct 21 1773   Dec 14 1773
    Appraisers: Zachariah Bond, John Hornell.
    Creditors: John Mills the youngest for James Buchanan & Co., Margaret Tippet.
    Next of kin: Butler Tippet, James Tippet.
    Administrators/Executors: Notley Tippet, Joseph Tippet.

William Ennis   116.204   SM   £86.2.7   Jan 20 1774   Mar 2 1774
    Appraisers: William Hammitt, Thomas Tarlton.
    Creditors: Thomas Tarlton, John Block.
    Next of kin: Henny Ennis, William Ennis.
    Executors: Mary Ennis, William Martin.

John Briscoe Davis   116.206   SM   £80.17.8   Feb 21 1774   Apr 20 1774
    Appraisers: William Kilgour, Truman Greenfield.
    Creditors: Maxwell & Tubman.
    Mentions: Mary Davis, Rachel Wood Davis.
    Administrator: Lawson Davis.

William Moore   116.209   SM   £35.4.3   Mar 8 1774   Apr 10 1774
    Appraisers: Thomas Nicholls, John Mills.
    Creditors: Matthew Blair for Cunningham Findley & Co.
    Mentions: John More, Elisabeth Moore.
    Administrator/Executor: William Moore.

William Oard   116.210   SM   £216.0.8   Nov 4 1773   Apr 5 1774
    Appraisers: Matthew Tennison, Stephen Tarlton.
    Creditors: Basel Smith, James Jordan for John Glassford & Co.
    Next of kin: Thomas Oard, Jesse Oard.
    Administratrix/Executrix: Eleanor Oard.

Mr. Richard Collis/Colliss   116.212   SM   £161.1.6   Jun 23 1773   Feb 10 1774
    Appraisers: William Hamersley, James Eden.
    Creditors: John Mills for James Buchanan & Co., James Jordan for John Glassford &
        Co.
    Next of kin: Yonell Attwell.
    Administratrix: Elisabeth Colliss.

Elinor Graves   116.214   SM   £274.14.6   Apr 26 1773   Apr 23 1774
    Appraisers: Jeremiah Jordan, James Sotheron Briscoe.
    Creditors: Archibald Campbell for John Glassford & Co.
    Next of kin: John Graves, Jr., Sarah Tippett.
    Administrator: Seneca Nelson.

Thomas Mattingly, Jr.   116.216   SM   £274.5.10   Jul 20 1773
    Appraisers: Robert Thompson, Cyrus Venles.
    Creditors: James Jordan for John Glassford & Co., Catharine Jernigham.
    Next of kin: Ann Mattingly, Ruth Mattingly.
    Executor: Clement Mattingly.

Rebecca Swan   116.218   SM   £1.5.0   Nov 30 1771   Apr 5 1774
    Appraisers: Justinan Joseph, William Hambleton.
    Administrator/Executor: Leonard Soale.

William Dunlop   116.219   DO   £96.5.9   Jun 22 1773   Jan 12 1774
    Appraisers: John Anderton, Thomas Smith.
    Creditors: William Eccleston, James Sulivane.
    Administrator: Charles Eccleston.

Mark Hurley   116.225   DO   £188.3.6   Jun 2 1772   Mar 9 1774
    Appraisers: Arthur Addison, Custis Darby.
    Creditors: John White, Thomas Ennalls.
    Next of kin: Elijah Hurly, Constantine Hurly.
    Administrator: John Hurley.

Thomas Gray   116.229   DO   £68.14.1   Mar 16 1773   Jan 10 1774
    Appraisers: Winlock Russam, Joshua Willis.
    Creditors: John Andrew, James Murray.
    Next of kin: William Gray (eldest brother), Rachel Dean (eldest sister).
    Executor: Thomas Gray.

Samuel Cheezum   116.232   DO   £25.16.9   Sep 18 1773   Jan 4 1774
    Appraisers: John Valliant, Richard Collison.
    Creditors: William Perry, Peter Richardson for MGhee & Richardson.
    Next of kin: Daniel Chezum, Rebakah Chezum.
    Administrator: John Cheezum.

Thomas Clarkson   116.233   DO   £2.10.6   Nov 14 1769   Feb 7 1774
    Appraisers: Isaac Nicolls, Ambros Goslen.
    Creditors: Obed Outen.
    Next of kin: Barzillai Clarkson, Binniah Clarkson.
    Administrator: Curtis Cannon.

Joseph Harper   116.234   DO   £84.8.8   Dec 11 1773   Jan 24 1774
    Appraisers: Henry Lake, Benjamin Keen.
    Creditors: Adam Trotwill, William Donnock.
    Next of kin: Joseph Harper, Priscila Harper.
    Administratrix: Rachel Harper.

Nicholas Fountain   116.236   DO   £88.3.1   Oct 12 1773   Mar 7 1774
    Appraisers: James Johnson, Abraham Collins.
    Creditors: Matthais Gale, Daniel Sulivane.
    Next of kin: Nathaniel Potter, Zabdiel Potter.
    Administratrix: Mary Ann Fountain.

Sarah Thomas   116.240   DO   £4.3.5   Jul 12 1773   Jan 31 1774
    Appraisers: George Waters, James Wright.
    Creditors: Isaac Sim.
    Next of kin: Patience Sulivane, Elisabeth Brinsfield.
    Administrator: Jonathon Hurlock.

Sarah Thomas   116.241   DO   £60.0.0   Jan 31 1774
    List of debts.
    Administrator: Jonathon Hurlock.

John Grainger   116.242   DO   £17.0.9   Aug 1 1773   Feb 15 1774
    Appraisers: Thomas Linthicum, John Spedden.
    Creditors: Levin Ball, D. Sulivane, Jr.
    Next of kin: Elisabeth Adams, Ann Ross.
    Administratrix: Elisabeth Harrington.

Sarah Cannon   116.244   DO   £55.5.0   Sep 11 773   Jan 17 1774
    Appraisers: James Cavendar, David Polk.
    Creditors: Isaac Spencer.
    Next of kin: Jesse Merrill, Henry Hooper.
    Administrator: Benjamin Cannon.

Levin Robinson   116.245   DO   £139.19.2   Jun 27 1773   Mar 10 1774
    Appraisers: Joseph Robinson, Patrick Brohawn.
    Creditors: Sarah Madkins, Harrison & Sprigg.
    Next of kin: John McNamara, Leeth Robinson.
    Executrix: Nancy Robinson.

Stephen Quinley   116.247   DO   £7.10.3   Nov 9 1773   Feb 17 1774
    Appraisers: John Dehorty, Mary Fountain.
    Creditors: Thomas White for Col. Edward Lloyd, Thomas Baynard.
    Mentions: Rebecca Quineley, Priscilla Quineley.
    Administrator: Edgar Rumbly.

James Cary/Carey   116.250   DO   £2.16.9   Sep 3 1773   Mar 10 1774
    Appraisers: Samuel Griffith, Charles Brown, Jr.
    Next of kin: William Laws, Alexander Laws.
    Administrator: John Woodgate.

Henry Feddey   116.252   DO   £5.1.0   Sep 20 1773   Feb 23 1774
    Appraisers: Joseph Godwin, Constantine Cannon.
    Creditors: Jonathon Bready, Jonathon Morgan.
    Next of kin: Rachel Elderig, Debro Fedey.
    Administrator: John Martin.

Charles Caffey   116.253   DO   £53.3.2   Jul 29 1773   Feb 25 1774
    Appraisers: Benjamin Hines, Ezekiel Johnson.
    Creditors: John Bennett, Peter Grimes.
    Next of kin: John Mills, Peter Grimes.
    Administratrix: Mary, wife of Joseph Clarkson.

William Caffey   116.255   DO   £48.9.11   Jul 23 1773   Feb 28 1774
    Appraisers: Benjamin Heine, Ezekiel Johnson.
    Creditors: John Bennett, Peter Grimes.
    Next of kin: Elisabeth Grimes, John Mills.
    Administratrix: Mary, wife of Joseph Clarkson.

Robert Griffith   116.257   DO   £140.14.11   Jan 23 1773   Feb 5 1774
    List of debts.
    Administrator: John Griffith.

John Williams   116.259   KE   £52.14.8   Aug 15 1774
    List of debts.
    Executor: Macaul Medford.

Frederick Hanson, Jr.   116.260   KE   £33.10.8   Jun 17 1774
    List of debts.
    Executors: John Page, Richard Miller.

John Hembrey   116.262   KE   £12.7.8   Aug 18 1774   Aug 27 1774
    List of debts.
    Administrator: John Page.

William Greenlee   116.262   KE   £4.7.0   Aug 5 1774
    List of debts.
    Executor: Samuel Greenlee.

Robert Meeks   116.263   KE   £17.16.5   Aug 8 1774
    List of debts.
    Executrix: Mary Meeks.

John Williams   116.264   KE   £2.11.11   Aug 15 1774
    List of debts.
    Executor: Macall Medford.

John Clark   116.264   KE   £0.8.8   Aug 9 1774
    List of debts.
    Administrator: William Clark.

Thomas Darrack   116.265   KE   £298.19.8   Jan 9 1774   Jun 29 1774
    List of debts.
    Administrators: Charlotte Darrack, John Darrack.

John Reid (son of Joseph)   116.267   KE   £5.0.0   Jun 27 1774
    List of debts.
    Administratrix: Araminta Reid.

Amos Reed   116.267   KE   £293.5.0   Dec 23 1773   Jul 30 1774
    Appraisers: John Lamb, William Maxwell.
    Creditors: John Eccleston, James Black.
    Next of kin: Joseph Reed, George Reed.
    Administratrix: Hannah Reed.

Israel Hughes   116.269   KE   £23.14.1   Jun 24 1774   Sep 2 1774
    Appraisers: James Piper, James Claypoole.
    Creditors: William Bordley, Morgan & Stubey.
    Administrator: William Hughston.

George Leybourn   116.270   KE   £239.7.3   Mar 11 1774   Aug 15 1774
    Appraisers: James Claypoole, James Piper.
    Creditors: A. Frisby.
    Next of kin: Joshua Lamb, John Corhe.
    Executor: Robert Amery.

Mrs. Rachel Hutcheson   116.274   KE   £261.12.2   Apr 20 1774   Jul 9 1774
    Appraisers: Morgan Huett, Nathaniel Miller.
    Next of kin: Nathaniel Hutcheson, Rachel Glanvil.
    Executor: John Hutcheson.

Elisabeth Boyer   116.278   KE   £272.17.0   Jun 28 1774   Aug 11 1774
    Appraisers: Samuel Davis, Daniel Massey.
    Next of kin: Nathaniel Boyer, Thomas Boyer.
    Executor: Augustine Boyer.

John Hembrey   116.279   KE   £10.15.0   Mar 9 1774   Aug 27 1774
    Appraisers: Morgan Huett, Nathaniel Hutcheson.
    Creditors: Richard Brice.
    Administrator: John Page.

Edward Coley   116.279   KE   £160.9.8   Jun 14 1774   Aug 8 1774
    Appraisers: Samuel Griffith, Thomas Crew.
    Creditors: James Maslin, Thomas Smyth.
    Next of kin: John Coley, Wolman Spencer.
    Administrator: John Wales

Mr. Benjamin Jackson   116.281   KE   £763.3.4   May 30 1774   Aug 6 1774
    Appraisers: John Eccleston, William Maxwell.
    Creditors: Thomas Smyth, Morgan & Stubey.
    Next of kin: Elisabeth Seegar, Samuel Seegar.
    Administratrix: Mary Jackson.

David Scott   116.284   KE   £327.12.5   Apr 13 1774   Jul 4 1774
    Appraisers: Peter Massey, Christopher Hall.
    Creditors: John Voorhees, Solomon Austin.
    Next of kin: Charles Haley, son John Scott.
    Administrator: John Moffett.

William Hamlin   116.288   KE   £19.5.6   May 18 1774   Jul 23 1774
    Appraisers: William Pearce, James Wroth.
    Creditors: Isaac Cannell, William Stuart.
    Next of kin: Martha Sulivane, Edward Beck.
    Administratrix: Mary, wife of Edward Beck.

Dennis Garret Cole   116.289   BA   £330.13.4   Jun 19 1773   Mar 5 1774
    Appraisers: William Tiplin, John Bond.
    Creditors: Mordecai Coles, John Price, Jr.
    Next of kin: Thomas Cole, Sr., Hennery Cole.
    Executors: John Price, Stephen Lull.

Thomas Talbott   116.292   BA   £1946.2.2   Sep 7 1773   May 6 1774
    Appraisers: Thomas Franklin, J. Beale Howard.
    Creditors: Jonathon Plowman, Dix Stansbury.
    Next of kin: Edmund Talbott, Joseph Slade.
    Executrix: Belinda Talbott.

Cordelia William Wilson   116.299   BA   £226.8.6   Mar 6 1774
    Appraisers: Henry Wetherall, William Debrunler.
    Creditors: J. Beale Howard, Mary Scott.
    Next of kin: Josias Smith.
    Administrator: Samuel Smith.

Hugh Watts (sailmaker)   116.302   BA   £207.17.3   Mar 24 1774   Apr 9 1774
    Appraisers: Cornelius Howard, Thomas Worthington.
    Next of kin: John Clegg.
    Administratrix: Margaret Watts.

John Leonard Moore   116.304   BA   £11.9.8   Apr 15 1774
    Appraisers: Morrice Wersler, Benjamin Griffith.
    Creditors: George Michael Rittlemeyer, Peter Machinkinnon.
    Administrator: John Henry Gilbert.

Henry Fitch   116.306   BA   £1.13.2   Apr 7 1774
    List of debts.
    Administratrix: Ruth, wife of Joseph Hill.

Balser Meyers/Myers   116.307   BA   £525.16.10   Jan 28 1772   May 9 1774
    Appraisers: Mark Alexander, Christopher Rais.
    Next of kin/Creditors: C. Jasterett, John Smith, Margaret Myers.
    Executors: Frederick Myers, John Stoler.

Benjamin Norris, Jr.   116.310   --   £190.8.4   Apr 13 1772   Oct 12 1772
(son of Benjamin)
    Appraisers: Thomas Bond, John Stevens.
    Creditors: J. Beale Howard for executors of Mr. David McCulloch, Benjamin
        Griffith & Co.
    Next of kin: Joseph Norris (son of Benjamin), Abram Norris.
    Administratrix: Mary Norris.

Mr. Samuel Bailey   116.313   BA   £409.12.0   Nov 20 1773
    Appraisers: Thomas Sellers, Thomas Worthington.
    Mentions: John Bailey, Kerenhappuk Hamilton, A. Stenhouse, Benjamin Nicholson,
        Ridgely & Nicholson.
    Executors: Charles Ridgely, Alexander Wells.

John Gough   116.315   BA   £12.2.6   Apr 21 1771   Apr 1 1774
    Appraisers: James Cox, Mark Alexander.
    Mentions: James Edwards, Murdock Kennedy.
    Administrator: Alexander Stanhouse.

Mr. Josephus Murray   116.316   BA   £493.6.5   Dec 6 1773
    Appraisers: Samuel Worthington, Nathan Cromwell.
    Creditors: Shadrack Murray, William Lyon & Walker.
    Next of kin: Shadrack Murray, George Ashmer.
    Executors: Christopher Murray, Ruth Murray.

Robert Stevenson/Stephenson   116.317   BA   £173.6.2   Jun 22 1773   Nov 30 1773
    Appraisers: Samuel Smith, John McAdow.
    Creditors: Joseph E. Butler for Speirs & French & Co., William Young, Jr.
    Next of kin: John Stephenson, Robert Stevenson.
    Administratrix: Ann Stephenson.

Nicholas Hyland   116.318   CE   £2084.6.0   May 2 1774   Jul 26 1774
    Appraisers: Thomas Savon, Thomas Price.
    Creditors: Tobias Rudulph, Abraham Mitchell.
    Next of kin: Nicholas Hyland, Meliscent Williamson.
    Executor: Isaac Hyland.

John Ford   116.324   CE   £199.9.2   Jun 19 1774   Aug 12 1774
    Appraisers: Benjamin Bravard, Richard Thompson, Jr.
    Creditors: Tobias Rudulph, Abraham Mitchell.
    Next of kin: Richard Ford, George Ford.
    Executors: Mary Ford, John Ford.

Peter Slyter/Sluyter   116.326   CE   £601.13.1   Mar 22 1774   Aug 13 1774
    Appraisers: Thomas Bouldin, Thomas Wallace.
    Creditors: Solomon Hearsey, William Rumsey.
    Next of kin: Peter Baynard, Samuel Baynard, Jr.
    Administrator: Henry Sluyter.

Martha Harper   116.329   CE   £418.10.11   Dec 11 1773   Aug 9 1774
    Appraisers: Barnet Vanhorn, John Hood.
    Creditors: Cornelius Eliason.
    Next of kin: Elisabeth Harper.
    Administrators: Abraham Eliason, Elias Eliason.

Eleanor McCoy   116.331   CE   £524.9.7   Aug 5 1774   Aug 6 1774
(wife of James McCoy)
    Appraisers: Alexander Clark, Barnet Vanhorn.
    Creditors: Benjamin All, Richard Boulden Ford.
    Next of kin: Sarah McCoy, Gracy Vanes.
    Executors: Adam Vance, Benjamin Armstrong.

Thomas Moor/Moore   116.334   CE   £240.12.3   Feb 26 1774   1774
    Appraisers: Robert Thompson, James Moor.
    Mentions: Isaac Bowen, Alexander Clark, Samuel Morrison, Thomas Bettel.
    Administrators: Julian Moore, Peregrine Moore.

Daniel Finney   116.335   CE   £3.11.1   Aug 27 1774
    List of debts.
    Administratrix: Eleanor Finney.

Mary Chick   116.336   CE   £98.8.4   Sep 3 1774
    List of debts.
    Mentions: Thomas Frisby Henderson, Jeremiah Taylor.

Hartly Sappington   116.336   CE   £17.14.4   Aug 9 1774
    List of debts.
    Executor: Benjamin Sappington.

Mr. James Hart   116.337   CE   £272.1.10   Jun 4 1774   Aug 4 1774
    Appraisers: Nicholas George, Benjamin Mauldin.
    Executors: Anna Hart,Robert Hart.

John Ford   116.338   CE   £16.15.2   Aug 12 1774
    List of debts.
    Executors: Mary Ford, John Ford.

James Hart   116.338   CE   £14.4.7   Aug 4 1774
    List of debts.
    Executors: Ann Hart, Robert Hart.

William Mallard   116.339   SO   £64.10.11   Sep 9 1774
    Appraisers: L. Woolford, John Irving.
    Creditors: Samuel Wilkins, Samuel Hyland.
    Administrator: John Sheriff.

Bell Maddux   116.341   SO   £119.14.11   Apr 14 1774 Aug 17 1774
    Appraisers: Purnell Outten, William Cottingham.
    Creditors: Planner Williams, Caleb Jones.
    Next of kin: Paul Maddux, Lazarus Maddux.
    Executor: Bable Maddux.

Isaac Moore   116.344   SO   £99.4.1   Apr 18 1774 Aug 23 1774
    Appraisers: Solomon Bird, Stephen Ward.
    Creditors: Littleton Sterling, John Parker.
    Next of kin: John Moore, Jemima Moore.
    Executor: Isaac Moor.

William Miles   116.347   SO   £54.3.5   Mar 7 1774   Aug 17 1774
    Appraisers: Elijah Coulbourn, Prewell Kersey.
    Creditors: Henry Miles, Stacy Miles.
    Next of kin: Henry Miles, Jr., Henry Miles.
    Administratrix: Bettey Miles.

Jacob Giles   116.349   SO   £106.5.8   Dec 21 1773 Aug 17 1774
    Appraisers: George Wailes, John Wailes.
    Creditors: William McBryde, John Phillips.
    Next of kin: Isaac Giles, William Giles.
    Administratrix: Eunice Giles.

Joseph Ward   116.351   SO   £376.1.11   Jan 20 1774 Jul 26 1774
    Appraisers: Purnell Outten, Elijah Coulbourn.
    Creditors: Planner Williams, John Ward.
    Next of kin: Mary Ward, John Ward.
    Administratrix: Ann Ward.

Jacob Gibson   116.354   SO   £89.7.8   Feb 24 1774 Sep 21 1774
    Appraisers: George Jones, Gowen Wright.
    Creditors: Henry Jackson for Gale Jackson & Stewart, John Jones.
    Next of kin: Jacob Gibson, Elisabeth Gibson.
    Administratrix: Ann Gibson.

George Martin   116.357   SO   £56.11.9   Apr 13 1774 Sep 10 1774
    Appraisers: James English, Ebenezar Waller.
    Creditors: John Roberts, Levin Fletcher.
    Next of kin: Lisabeth Martin, Bridget Carter.
    Administrator: William Martin.

Edward Stevenson   116.360   SO   £55.16.0   Aug 11 1774 Sep 18 1774
    Appraisers: William Jones, John Elzey, Jr.
    Creditors: John Winder, Henry Jackson & Co.
    Administratrix: Mary Waggaman.

John Shiles   116.364   SO   £15.4.10   Aug 26 1774   Sep 22 1774
    Appraisers: George Day Scott, Robert Collier.
    Creditors: Henry Jackson & Co., Thomas Irving.
    Next of kin: Thomas Shiles, Sarah Shiles.
    Administrator: John Shiles.

Capt. John Ladelar   116.369   CH   £1432.16.6   Apr 6 1774
    Appraisers: John Marshall, George Clk. Smoot.
    Creditors: John Anderson, Theophilus Gates.
    Next of kin: Joseph Irving.
    Administratrix: Elisabeth Ladelar.

Ann McDonald   116.371   CH   £371.7.8   Apr 13 1774   Jul 18 1774
    Appraisers: George Tubman, Peter Dent.
    Creditors: Robert Mundell for John Glassford & Co., G. R. Brown.
    Next of kin: Virlinder McDonald, Deborah McDonald.
    Administrator: Alexander McDonald.

John Miles   116.374   CH   £32.8.10   Jun 13 1774   Jul 28 1774
    Appraisers: T. Powling, Thomas Lockett.
    Creditors: Edward Semmes, Peter Campbell for John Glass ford & Co.
    Next of kin: Eleanor Mills, William Miles.
    Administratrix: Sarah Miles.

Benjamin Branson   116.376   CH   £27.14.11   Aug 12 1774
    Appraisers: John Marshall, Joshua Doy.
    Creditors: Samuel Jonas, F. Smyth.
    Next of kin: Michael Branson, John Branson.
    Administratrix: Hewyean Branson.

Elisabeth Posey/Possey   116.377   CH   £88.5.11   Jul 21 1774
    Appraisers: Benjamin Philpott, George Keech.
    Creditors: Robert Reston for George and Andrew Buchanan, Moses Hobert.
    Next of kin: Daniel Cam. Hobert, Ann Povey.
    Administrator: Edward Hobert.

Henry Miles   116.379   CH   £109.0.1   Jun 6 1774   Jul 25 1774
    Appraisers: Thomas Darnall, Thomas Harvin.
    Next of kin: (son) William Miles, (son) Henry Miles.
    Administratrix: Eleanor Miles.

Marmaduke Semmes   116.383   CH   £187.14.3   Aug 17 1774
    List of debts.
    Executrix: Henrietta Semmes.

Jonathon Mudd   116.384   CH   £0.13.0   Aug 26 1774
    Appraisers: Leonard Boarman, Raphael Boarman.
    Administratrix: Ann Mudd.

Thomas Willin/Willing   116.384   SO   £64.13.1   Apr 22 1773   Feb 22 1774
    Appraisers: William Steuart, W. Dashiell.
    Creditors: Henry Jackson & Co., Isaac Atkinson.
    Next of kin: Thomas Willin, Mary Willin.
    Executor: George Willin.

Mary Surman   116.389   SO   £3.19.6   Sep 1 1773   Mar 1 1774
    Appraisers: John Piper, George Dashiell.
    Creditors: John Anderson, John Nelson.
    Next of kin: Leah Surman, Sarah Anderson.
    Administrator: George Bennett.

Margaret Smith   116.391   SO   £19.17.9   Jul 8 1773
    Appraisers: William Fleming, Joseph Ward.
    Creditors: William Furniss, Teague Riggin.
    Next of kin: John Smith, William Smith.
    Executor: Edward Smith.

William Dean   116.393   DO   £30.12.3   Aug 26 ----   Oct 12 1774
    List of debts.
    Executor: Edward Dean.

John Madkin   116.396   DO   £59.3.5   Sep 3 1774   Oct 3 1774
    Appraisers: Edmund Mace, Roger Woolford.
    Creditors: Landon Ball, Benjamin Baruck.
    Next of kin: Sarah Matkins, Theador Matkins.
    Administrator: William Madkins.

Thomas Moore   116.401   DO   £209.10.4   Oct 17 1774
    Appraisers: Charles Eccleston, Thomas Smith.
    Mentions: Mary McCallister, Leving Hubbard.
    Creditors: Thomas Steuart (minor), William Veach.
    Next of kin: Nehemiah Hubbard, James McCallister of Andrew.
    Executor: Thomas Moore, Jr.

John Frames   116.404   DO   £241.5.9   Jun 24 1774   Sep 19 1774
    Appraisers: John Darby, William Trippe.
    Creditors: Samuel Davidson for Speirs & French & Co., Thomas Smith.
    Next of kin: William White, George Inote (?).
    Executrix: Mary Frames.

William Moore   116.407   DO   £19.3.19   Oct 17 1774
    Appraisers: Charles Eccleston, Thomas Smith.
    Creditors: James Sulivane, William Veach.
    Next of kin: Elisabeth Thomas, James Moore.
    Administrator: Thomas Moore, Jr.

Stephen Quinnerly   116.409   DO   £0.7.6   Oct 15 1774   Oct 17 1774
    List of debts.
    Appraisers: John Dehorty, Marcy Fountain.
    Administrator: Edgar Rumbly.

Margaret Ennalls   116.409   DO   £1385.19.10   May 23 1774
    Appraisers: Hugh Eccleston, Thomas Pitt.
    Creditors: Archibald Patison for Speirs & French & Co., Thomas Muse.
    Next of kin: James Murray, Henry Murray.
    Administratrix: Mary Maynadier.

Dr. William Wheland   116.415   DO   £748.15.1   Feb 2 1774   Aug 29 1774
    Appraisers: Charles Muir, Ralph Green.
    Creditors: John Henry, Henry White.
    Next of kin: Michael Willcox, Elisabeth Wheland Smith.
    Administrator: James Wheland.

William Clarkson   116.421   DO   £271.11.5   Feb 10 1774
    Appraisers: Risdon Moore, George Waters.
    Creditors: Ambros Goslin, Robert Gilmer.
    Next of kin: Richard Clarkson, Abraham Clarkson.
    Administrator: Richard Clarkson, Jr.

John Clarrage   116.425   DO   £50.2.9   Aug 3 1774   Sep 15 1774
    Appraisers: James Shaw, John Hedon.
    Creditors: Anthony Manning, John Hodson.
    Next of kin: Henry Claridge, Jr., Henry Clarrage.
    Administratrix: Elisabeth Clarrage.

Richard Willis   116.427   DO   £76.9.8   Dec 7 1773   May 16 1774
    Appraisers: Benjamin Woodard, Edmund Mace.
    Creditors: Patrick Leybury, Edward Staplefort.
    Next of kin: John Willis, Benjamin Mekins.
    Administratrix: Rachel Willis.

Josias Mace   116.430   DO   £89.19.11   Jun 17 1774   Aug 29 1774
    Appraisers: Thomas Creaton, Ezekiel Johnson.
    Creditors: Ezekiel Keene, John King, Jr.
    Next of kin: Mark Meekins, Mary Meekins.
    Executrix: Ann Mace.

Mr. John Enson   116.432   BA   £380.8.11   Apr 27 1773   Sep 15 1773
    Appraisers: William Aisquith, Mark Alexander.
    Creditors: Nathan Griffith (Administrator to John Enson, Jr.), Jonathon Plowman.
    Next of kin: Elisabeth Enson (wife of John Enson, deceased), Orpah Markland.
    Executor: Abraham Enson.

William Ottey, Esq.   117.1   BA   £702.19.3   Feb 11 1773   Jul 1774
    Appraisers: Zachariah McCubbin, Thomas Lloyd.
    Creditors: Edward Cooke.
    Next of kin: William Hammond.
    Administratrix: Ann Ottey.

Mr. Abraham Raven   117.15   BA   £860.18.3   May 1 1773   Dec 9 1773
    Appraisers: William Aisquith, Ezekiel Towson.
    Creditors: Abraham Resteau for Archibald Buchanan, Benjamin Griffith & Brothers.
    Next of kin: Elisabeth Cromwell, William Resteau.
    Administratrix: Sarah Resteau.

Abraham Green   117.23   BA   £46.9.6   Apr 18 1774   Jun 4 1774
    Appraisers: A. Eaglestone, Edward Brown.
    Creditors: Charles Gurts, Thomas Jones.
    Next of kin: Solomon Green, Moses Green.
    Administrator: Daniel Davis.

John Doyl/Doyle   117.26   BA   £49.1.10   May 21 1774
    Appraisers: Robert McAllister, Peter Chenoweth.
    Creditors: Robert Jordan, John Stevenson.
    Next of kin: Richard Doyl, Jonathon Doyl.
    Administratrix: Elisabeth Doyle.

Isaac Maglamary/Maglamore   117.29   WO   £31.11.3   Sep 14 1772
    Appraisers: Stephen Roach, George Parson, Jr.
    Creditors: Samuel Davis, William McClemming.
    Next of kin: David Magee, Methe Altend (?).
    Administratrix: Ann Maglamore.

William Otty   117.32x   BA   £6.8.2   Jul 1 1774
    List of debts.
    Administratrix: Ann Ottey.

Thomas Rutter   117.33   BA   £60.7.9   Dec 8 1773
    List of debts.
    Administratrix: Hannah Rutter.

Thomas Rutter   117.33   BA   £2.13.0   Dec 8 1773
    List of debts.
    Administratrix: Hannah Rutter.

James Riggin   117.34   WO   £144.10.0   Oct 9 1773   Feb 4 1774
    Appraisers: John Fleming, James Ottwell.
    Creditors: William Miles, Philip Dayson.
    Next of kin: Teague Riggin, Nehemiah Townsend.
    Executrix: Elisabeth Riggin.

William Pitts   117.38   WO   £85.1.9   Aug 30 1773   Feb 1 1774
    Appraisers: Dixon Quinton, Elisha Jones.
    Creditors: Ephraim Henderson, Samuel Brittingham.
    Next of kin: John Blades, Samuel Blades.
    Executrix: Mary Pitts.

Elisabeth Morris   117.40   WO   £15.6.3   Feb 2 1773   Mar 2 1774
    Appraisers: Jethro Bowin, Edward Hammond.
    Creditors: Luke Bowin, James Wilson.
    Next of kin: Elisha Morris, Hammond Runnell.
    Administrator: Edward Morris.

Nathaniel Ennis   117.42   WO   £75.11.8   1773   Jan 7 1774
    Appraisers: John Purnell Robins, Samuel Handy.
    Creditors: James Wilson, Joshua Townsend.
    Next of kin: Luke Ennis, Leah Ennis.
    Executor: Jesse Ennis.

Daniel Dikes   117.46   WO   £41.11.8   Dec 13 1773   Mar 2 1774
    Appraisers: Stephen Roach, George Parsons.
    Creditors: Nathaniel Willis, Jacob Parker.
    Next of kin: Daniel Dikes, Stephen Dikes.
    Administrator: Arthur Dikes.

John Nighenburgh   117.48   WO   £35.3.2   Jun 14 1773
(also John Neighenbrough)
    Appraisers: James Rownd, John Marshall.
    Creditors: Edward Dymoke, Zadock Purnell.
    Next of kin: Thomas Neighbrough, Mathew Crapper.
    Administratrix: Luranna Neighbrough.

James Benson   117.51   WO   £93.9.0   Aug 17 1773   Mar 2 1774
    Appraisers: John Collings, Jonathon Bell.
    Creditors: Shadrack Fallin.
    Next of kin: William Newton, Benjamin Wootten.
    Executrix: Betty Benson.

Nathaniel Townsend   117.55   WO   £11.0.8   Aug 31 1773   Feb 18 1774
    Appraisers: Thomas Sturgis, Samuel Hudson.
    Creditors: Joshua Tayler, Parker Dukes.
    Next of kin: Ann Simpson, Comfort Townsend.
    Administrator: John Ball.

John Ruke/Ruark   117.56 WO £81.1.11   Dec 14 1773
  Appraisers: Eleazer Johnson, Samuel Dreaden.
  Creditors: William Horsey, William McBryde.
  Next of kin: Ezekiel Rourk, Sehive (?) Ruke.
  Executrix: Mary Ruark.

William Davis   117.61 WO £176.9.8 Jun 16 1773 Jan 7 1774
  Appraisers: Schoolfield Parker, Elijh Laws.
  Creditors: Samuel Handy, John Davis.
  Next of kin: John Davis, Thomas Davis.
  Executors: Ann Davis, Robert Davis.

Mary Purnell   117.63 WO £113.0.0 Jan 14 1774 Mar 11 1774
(relict of Jeptha Purnell)
  Appraisers: William Lane, William Morris.
  Next of kin: John Selby, Zadock Selby.
  Administrator: Benjamin Purnell.

Ezekiel Porter   117.67 WO £58.3.11   Mar 7 1774
  Appraisers: Nathaniel Ennis, John Marshall.
  Creditors: Charles Rackliff, Samuel Smyly.
  Next of kin: John Porter, Edward Davis.
  Executor: Samuel Ennis.

William Taylor   117.69 WO £5.4.9   Dec 17 1773
  Appraisers: George Martin, Philip Quinton.
  Creditors: Parker Selby (sheriff), William Selby, Jr.
  Next of kin: Solomon Taylor, Sarah Taylor
  Administrator: Thomas Taylor.

Jacob Reed   117.71 WO £143.14.9 May 20 1773 Jan 21 1774
  Appraisers: John Dale, William Farlow.
  Next of kin/Creditors: John David, Adam Brevard.
  Next of kin/Creditors: Joshua Sturgis, James Dale.
  Executrix: Martha Reed.

Joseph Bishop   117.74 WO £96.6.11   Feb 11 1774
(son of Joseph Bishop)
  Appraisers: Samuel Scarborough, Mathew Selby.
  Creditors: James Wilson.
  Next of kin: Joseph Ennis, Charles Bishop.
  Executrix: Elisabeth Bishop.

Pierce Riggin   117.77 WO £95.1.5 Sep 18 1773 Feb 11 1774
  Appraisers: J. B. Schoolfield, William McCuddy.
  Next of kin: Darby Riggin, Clear Riggin, William Miles, Racel (?) Hayman.
  Executrix: Ann Riggin.

Andrew Sanders   117.81 WO £130.4.1   Nov 12 1773
  Appraisers: John Collins, Jonathon Bell.
  Creditors: Elisabeth Filbeg, Shadrack Faly.
  Next of kin: Nathaniel Sanders, Sarah Sanders.
  Executrix: Charity Sanders.

George Robinson   117.85 WO ----   Feb 21 1774
  Appraisers: William Holland, Elisha Cullingham.
  Administratrix: Mary, wife of Samuel Logwood.

Jesse Scott   117.85 WO £51.4.5 Jan 2 1774
  Appraisers: Mathew Outten, Jesse Ennis.
  Creditors: John Selby, William Selby, Jr.
  Next of kin: Elisabeth Scott.
  Administrator: Major Townsend.

William Hambleton   117.87 CH £555.18.6   Feb 1 1774
  Appraisers: Thomas Simms, Raphaele Neale.
  Creditors: Kole Hurrd for John Glassford & Co.
  Next of kin: James Hamilton, Mary Stewart.
  Executor: Patrick Hambleton.

David Stone   117.91 CH £1563.10.10   Feb 26 1774
  Appraisers: William McConchie, Richard Barnes.
  Creditors: Robert Hooe for Hooe Stone & Co., Robert Mundell for John Glassford &
  Co.
  Next of kin: Catharine Scott, Betty Ann Stone.
  Administrators; Elisabeth Stone, Thomas Stone, John Haskins Stone.

Hezekiah Garner   117.97   CH   £84.18.0   Nov 15 1773   Feb 9 1774
    Appraisers: Joshua Posy, Edward Warrin.
    Creditors: Mathew Blair for Cunningham Findley & Co., Philip Gardner for C. T.
    Hey.
    Next of kin: John Gardner, Edward Gardner.
    Administratrix: Jean Garner.

Mr. Marmaduke Semmes   117.99   CH   £1928.17.8   Mar 2 1773   Feb 9 1774
    Appraisers: John Hanson, John Hawkins.
    Creditors: James Craik, John Craig for Alexander Cunningham & Co.
    Next of kin: John Ward, Thomas Semmes, Marmaduke Semmes.
    Executor: Hennerutter Semmes.

Joseph Murrein/Moreign   117.104   DO   £23.19.1   Apr 1 1774   May 23 1774
    Appraisers: Thomas Smith, William White.
    Creditors: Hugh Eccleston, Thomas Ennalls.
    Next of kin: James Murrein, Moses Murrein.
    Administrator: Thomas Moreign.

Mary Turner   117.106   CH   £245.3.7   Sep 18 1773   Jan 21 1774
    Appraisers: Thomas McPherson, Daniel McPherson.
    Creditors: Barnes & Redgate, Robert Mundell for John Glassford & Co.
    Next of kin: Eleanor Beale, Elisabeth Beale.
    Administrator: Zephaniah Turner.

Mary Trivitt   117.112   CH   £30.1.6   Dec 29 1772   Jan 14 1774
    Appraisers: Raphael Boarman, Francis Posey.
    Creditors: Edward Edelon, Samuel Love.
    Administrator: Joseph Gwynn, Jr.

Samuel Hamilton   117.114   CH   £418.13.4   Aug 3 1773   Jan 24 1774
    Appraisers: Alexander McPherson, Philip Webster.
    Creditors: James Craik, Robert Mundell for John Glassford & Co.
    Next of kin: James Hamilton, Patrick Hamilton.
    Administratrix: Elisabeth, wife of Benjamin Nuttly Mitchell.

William Govane   117.119   BA   £844.12.3   Sep 15 1774
    List of debts.
    Administrator: William Smith.

Mary Welsh   117.122   SM   £233.18.11   Feb 16 1774   Sep 26 1774
    Appraisers: George Burroughs, Leonard Wood.
    Creditors: James Forbes, Richard Beavens.
    Next of kin: Vincent Oden, Pagiby Low.
    Administrator: William Waters.

Rizden Smith   117.127   QA   £29.14.3   Jan 17 1772   Oct 8 1774
    Appraisers: Samuel Walters, Robert Tate.
    Administrator: John Kerr.

Philip Weathrall   117.129   TA   £424.8.0   Oct 31 1774
    Balances.
    Administrator: Thomas Place.

Philip Weathrall   117.135   TA   £6.1.7   Sep 10 1774   Oct 31 1774
    Appraisers: Henry Banning, Thomas Harrison.
    Creditors: George Gleave, William N. Gachen.

Winiford Lanham   117.135   PG   £11.10.0   Feb 26 1772   Sep 11 1774
    Appraisers: Henry Humphrey, Samuel Lisby.
    Next of kin: Zadock Jenkins.
    Executor: Edward Lanham.

John Kirkpatrick   117.136   CE   £139.11.6   Aug 4 1770   Oct 12 1774
    Appraisers: Nathaniel Baker, Robert Alison.
    Creditors: Pattrick Hamilton, James McCreary.
    Sons: John Kirkpatrick, James Kirkpatrick.
    Administrator: William Porter.

William Leavens   117.139   AA   £68.11.7   Sep 13 1774
    Appraisers: William Coale, Richard Stringer.
    Creditors: Edward Norwood for Stephen West, M. Pue.
    Administrator: Samuel Dorsey.

Rev. Robert Penney   117.141   AA   £197.16.0   Aug 6 1774   Nov 4 1774
    Appraisers: John Merriken, Richard Weedon.
    Creditors: Richard Tootell, Shaw & Chisholm.
    Administrators: Robert Cowden, Robert McGowan.

Walter Gott   117.144   AA   £660.6.10   Sep 11 1774   Sep 15 1774
    Appraisers: Richard Richardson, Isaac Hall.
    Creditors: Henry Darnal, Peter Mennor, Gilbert Buchanan for John Buchanan & Son.
    Next of kin: John Gott, Ezekiel Gott.
    Administratrix: Ann Gott.

Eliphalet Jacobs   117.148   QA   £63.8.0   1772   Oct 8 1774
    Appraisers: John Wilson, Jacob Seth.
    Creditors: James Davidson.
    Next of kin: Thomas Baker.
    Administrator: John Kerr.

William Burton   117.149   WO   £434.14.10   Apr 27 1774   Aug 3 1774
    Appraisers: Simon Kollock, Elisha Cottingham.
    Creditors: Benjamin Burton, John Gibbins, Jr.
    Next of kin: John Wingate, Jacob Burton.
    Administratrix: Molly Burton.

Richard Murray   117.152   WO   £18.4.8   May 2 1774   Jul 8 1774
    Appraisers: John Tull, John Cox.
    Creditors: William Holland, Levin Dirickson.
    Next of kin: James Murray, David Murray.
    Administratrix: Ann Murray.

Ezekiel Dubberly   117.155   WO   £0.4.2   Jul 15 1774
    Appraisers: William Aydelott, Elisha Jones.
    Administrator/Executor: Jemima Dubberly.

Joshua King   117.155   WO   £65.9.2   Apr 18 1774   Aug 2 1774
    Appraisers: Joseph Dashiell, John Friency.
    Creditors: William Winder, Jr. for William Winder, ------ Hitch for William
    McBryde.
    Next of kin: Mitchell King, Robert King.
    Administrator: Ephraim King.

Charles Henderson   117.159   WO   £10.10.1   Feb 29 1774   Aug 12 1774
    Creditors/Next of kin: Ann Hadder, Leonard Johnson, Parker Selby, Rachel Nuton.
    Executrix: Mary Henderson.

Solomon Townsend   117.161   WO   £466.11.4   Apr 12 1774   Sep 2 1774
    Appraisers: William Allin, J. B. Schoolfield.
    Creditors: John Fleming, Stephen Townsend.
    Next of kin: Samuel Townsend, James Townsend.
    Executors: William Townsend, Solomon Townsend.

Pritchet Delehay   117.167   DO   £154.16.8   Apr 24 1774   May 10 1774
    Appraisers: Roger A. Hooper, Richard Newton.
    Creditors: Archibald Patison for Speirs & French & Co., Thomas Pitt.
    Next of kin: Richard Delehay, James Delehay.
    Administratrix: Lilley, wife of William Saunders.

Lambert Flowers   117.171   DO   £25.19.9   Feb 4 1774   Apr 11 1774
    Appraisers: George Waters, James Richards.
    Creditors: Peter Richardson, Frederick Dell, Charles Flowers.
    Next of kin: John Flowers.
    Administratrix: Rebecca Flowers.

Coventon/Covington Otly   117.174   SO   £68.17.6   Apr 15 1774   Nov 15 1774
    Appraisers: S. Whittington, Killiard Lankford.
    Creditors: Planner Williams, Benjamin Scott.
    Next of kin: James Oteley, John Davis Cox.
    Executrix: Martha Cox.

John Disheroon   117.175   SO   £17.19.9   Oct 15 1772   Nov 14 1774
    Appraisers: William Polk.
    Creditors: William Hath, Arthur Dashiell.
    Next of kin: Frances Disheroon, Joseph Disheroon.
    Executor: Constant Disheroon (surviving executor).

Daniel Richey/Ritchey   117.177   SO   £87.19.1   Jan 21 1774   Nov 5 1774
    Appraisers: William Stewart, John Dougherty.
    Creditors: William Collier, John Cougherty.
    Next of kin: Archibald Ritchie, Margaret Mezick.
    Administratrix: Delilah Ritchey.

Jeremiah Brittingham   117.181   WO   £23.0.3   Feb 20 1773   Sep 2 1774
    Appraisers: Schoolfield Parker, William Purnell.
    Creditors: Samuel Smyly, Joseph Ennis.
    Next of kin: Nathaniel Brittingham, Ann Godfrey.
    Executrix: Patience Brittingham.

Lemuel Smock   117.183   WO   £34.1.3   Apr 18 1773   May 13 1774
    Appraisers: Parker Selby, John Bullay.
    Creditors: Margaret Greig, Samuel Smyly.
    Next of kin: Kendale Smock, William Smock.
    Administrator: Makemmey Smock.

Maclemmy Jones   117.185   WO   £101.18.5   Jun 13 1773   Aug 26 1774
    Appraisers: John Duncan, Thomas Duncan.
    Creditors: Solomon Rogers, Samuel Smyly.
    Next of kin: Elenor Tarr, Mary Sturgis.
    Administrators: Jesse Jones, George Jones.

John Laurence   117.187   WO   £82.4.10   Dec 11 1773   Jun 7 1774
    Appraisers: Caleb Tingle, John Postly.
    Creditors: John Pope Mitchell, Leah Hill.
    Next of kin: Elijha Laurence, Elebath Laurence.
    Executors: Mary Laurence, Henry Laurence.

Ezekiel Porter   117.189   WO   £1.5.12   Jul 4 1774   Jul 8 1774
    Appraisers: John Marshall, Nathaniel Ennis.
    Administrator: Samuel Ennis.

William Roberts   117.190   WO   £95.15.9   Apr 7 1774   Jun 22 1774
    Appraisers: John Dale, Josiah Dale.
    Creditors: John Postly, Nathan Coller.
    Executrix: Elisabeth Roberts.

William Wright   117.193   WO   £59.17.7   Dec 15 1773   Jun 7 1774
    Appraisers: Edmund Northen Nelms, George Parsons.
    Creditors: John Nelms, Joseph Dashiell.
    Next of kin: Thomas Carey, Sophiah Wright.
    Administratrix: Sarrah Wright.

Nicholas Gray, Sr.   117.196   WO   £55.14.3   Apr 15 1774   Jun 24 1774
    Appraisers: John Davis, Josiah Dale.
    Creditors: David Evans, James Willson.
    Next of kin: William Gray, Dannas (?) Gray.
    Executor: John Gray.

Isaac Denson   117.199   WO   £94.16.5   Jan 7 1774
    Appraisers: John Puzey, Marrel Maddux.
    Creditors: George Vinson, Gilliss & Waters.
    Next of kin: Philip Denson, Saul Denson.
    Administratrix: Sarah Denson.

John Turvill Gault   117.202   WO   £188.12.9   1774
    Appraisers: W. Holland, Levin Derickson.
    Creditors: Joseph Dirickson, Henmon Whorton.
    Next of kin: William Gault, David Gault.
    Administratrix: Anjaletta Gault.

Charles Riggen   117.204   WO   £72.11.11   Jun 2 1774   Jun 6 1774
    Appraisers: Jonathon Bell, Robert Hopkins.
    Creditors: Simon Kollock, Joshua Riggen.
    Next of kin: James Riggen, Teague Riggen.
    Executor: William Otwell.

Joseph Robertson/Robinson   117.206   WO   £74.15.3   Mar 14 1774   Jun 6 1774
    Appraisers: Thomas Batson, William Ford Hall.
    Creditors: William Holland, Parker Selby.
    Next of kin: Joshua Robertson, Ester Robertson.
    Executors: Betty Robinson, John Robinson.

William Fooks   117.209   WO   £381.12.4   Aug 3 1774
    Appraisers: Samuel Ingersoll, Joshua Sturgis.
    Creditors: Jesse Fooks, William McBryde.
    Next of kin: Thomas Fooks, John Fooks.
    Executor: Daniel Fooks.

John Campbell   117.213   WO   £1540.9.2   Sep 13 1773   Sep 2 1774
    Appraisers: John Dale, Isaac Murray.
    Creditors: Edward Dymock, David Evans.
    Next of kin: Mary Fassitt, John Brevard.
    Executor: John Campbell.

Arthur Fowler   117.214   WO   £145.12.9   Mar 12 1774   Nov 5 1774
    Appraisers: William Owens, Joshua Polk.
    Creditors: Jonathon Bready, Molton Crapper.
    Next of kin: Arthur Fowler, Jesse Fowler.
    Executors: Mary Fowler, Arthur Fowler.

William Hust   117.220   WO   £84.4.2   May 20 1774   Aug 2 1774
    Appraisers: Charles Polk, Jr., John Griffith.
    Creditors: Levin Crapper, Samuel Cawlk.
    Next of kin: Jesse Fowler, John Hust.
    Administrator: Josiah Hust.

Joseph Morris   117.223   WO   £246.13.11   Feb 16 1774   Jun 28 1774
    Appraisers: Simon Kollock, Richard Jefferson.
    Creditors: Joshua Morris, Simon Kollock.
    Next of kin: Joshua Morris, Dennis Morris.
    Executor: William Morris.

William Sturgis   117.226   WO   £8.1.9   Aug 28 1773   Jul 8 1774
    Appraisers: George Speney, Isaac Kellam.
    Creditors: Hugh Wallis, John Price.
    Next of kin: Stephen Sturgis, Richard Sturgis.
    Administrator: Thomas Sturgis.

Nehemiah Truitt   117.227   WO   £52.18.0   --- 5 1774   Jul 28 1774
    Appraisers: John Postly, Joseph Ironshire.
    Creditors: John Postly, David Evans.
    Next of kin: Sarah Timmons, Ede Truitt.
    Executor: Nehemiah Truitt.

John Pusey/Puzey   117.229   WO   £87.5.8   Mar 10 1774
    Appraisers: John Fleming, Darby Riggen.
    Creditors: John Atkinson, John Caudry.
    Next of kin: John Puzey, Lankford Puzey.
    Executor: Isaac Puzey.

Pages 230 through 299 do not exist.

William Maison/Mason   117.301   WO   £21.8.9   Mar 12 1774   Nov 24 1774
    Appraisers: William Selby, Jr., John Ayres.
    Creditors: George Martin, Mary Whittington.
    Next of kin: James Maison.
    Administrator: Noble Crapper.

John Robins Cord   117.303   WO   £319.19.4   Mar 13 1774   Nov 4 1774
    Appraisers: William Holland, William Tunnell.
    Creditors: George Howard, Adam Brevard.
    Next of kin: Ann Postly, Deligance Richards.
    Executrix: Rhoda Cord.

John Lockwood   117.306   WO   £179.6.1   Apr 18 1774   Sep 9 1774
    Appraisers: Joshua Hall, John Cox/Coe.
    Creditors: Ezekiel Williams, William Hall.
    Next of kin: Benjamin Lockwood, Samuel Lockwood.
    Executrix: Mary Lockwood.

Thomas Purnell   117.309   WO   £3866.16.13   Dec 10 1769   Nov 3 1774
    Appraisers: Peter Chaille, Adam Spence.
    Creditors: John Atkinson.
    Next of kin: Jabez Fisher, Charles Rackliffe.
    Executors: son Thomas Purnell, Thomas Purnell of (sons puaent?).

Henry Blare Johnson   117.313   WO   £129.19.10   Nov 1773   Nov 10 1774
    Appraisers: Peter Dolbie, Jonathon Bell.
    Creditors: George Gibbins, Shadrack Fallin.
    Next of kin: Wittington Johnson, Ann Johnson.
    Executrix: Christian Johnson.

Joseph Nicholson   117.314   WO   £33.16.5   Dec 5 1774
    Appraisers: Peter Chaille, George Martin.
    Mentions: Linsey Joshua Townsend.
    Mentions: John Nicholson, John Snead, Jr., Samuel Linsey.
    Administratrix: Mary, wife of Josiah Robins.

Benjamin Parratt   117.316   TA   £349.13.11   Jun 26 1773   Mar 3 1774
    Appraisers: Richard Johns, Solomon Neally.
    Creditors: Matthais Gale.
    Next of kin: Aaron Parratt, William Parratt.
    Executrix: Mary Parratt.

Elisabeth Halley   117.319   PG   £174.6.8   Sep 14 1773   Nov 24 1774
    Appraisers: J. Hawkings, Zachariah Wade.
    Creditors: John Halley, Peter Campble for John Glassford & Co.
    Next of kin: Samuel Halley, John Halley.
    Executor: Robert Gooden.

James Buckley   117.322   TA   £9.15.8   Jun 7 1773   Apr 5 1774
        Appraisers: Solomon Martin, William Howell Powell.
        Creditors: James Bracco Dylaney, William Stevens.
        Next of kin: Thomas Buckley, James Barnett.
        Administrator: Matthew Jenkins.

William Priestly   117.323   TA   £47.13.11   May 11 1772   Mar 29 1774
        Appraisers: D. Sherwood, John Sherwood.
        Next of kin: David Priestly, Perry Priestly.
        Administrator: Pollard Edmondson.

William Evans   117.325   TA   £284.3.2   Apr 22 1773   Apr 5 1774
        Appraisers: Thomas Ray, Thomas Barrow.
        Creditors: James Lloyd Chamberlaine, William Pasan.
        Next of kin: James Evans, James Gaose.
        Executrix: Mary Evans.

William Evans   117.328   TA   £32.16.4   Apr 5 1774
        List of debts.
        Executrix: Mary Evans.

Jonathon Dobson   117.330   TA   £52.16.4   Jan 1 1774   Apr 19 1774
        Appraisers: Richard Johns, George Burgess.
        Creditors: Mathais Gale, Thomas Work.
        Next of kin: Rebecca Chamber, Hannah Parratt.
        Executor: Aaron Parratt.

Thomas Haddaway   117.331   TA   £213.12.3   May 17 1774
        Appraisers: J. Denny, Sr., Robert Lambdin, Jr.
        Creditors: Matthew Tilghman, Thomas Harrison.
        Next of kin: George Haddaway.
        Executrix: Susannah Haddaway.

John Barker   117.333   TA   £17.16.3   Dec 27 1773   Mar 15 1774
        Appraisers: Henry Troth, Solomon Neall.
        Creditors: Samuel Sharp, Matthais Gale.
        Next of kin: Ruth Catrop, Lemmon John Catrop.
        Administrator: John Catrop.

Edward Neal   117.334   TA   £116.18.5   Feb 11 1772   Mar 1 1774
        Appraisers: George Dudley, P. Denny.
        Creditors: James Lloyd Chamberlaine (surviving partner of Nicols & Chamberlaine).
        Next of kin: Ann Cox, Sophya Edmondson.
        Executor: Robert Neal.

John Bryan   117.338   SM   £52.2.10   Mar 7 1774   May 20 1774
        Appraisers: John Hooper Broom, John Cartwright.
        Creditors: Mathais Blair for Cunningham Findley & Co., James Jordan for John
            Glassford & Co.
        Next of kin: Ignatius Bryan, Elenor Able.
        Administrator: Philip Bryan.

Philip Tenley/Tennely, Jr.   117.340   PG   £36.9.9   Sep 11 1773   Nov 24 1773
        Appraisers: William Boyne, Nathaniel Wallon.
        Creditors: Thomas Clagett for Oswald Deniston & Co., Peter Campbell for John
            Glassford & Co.
        Next of kin: William Tennally, John Tennally.
        Administratrix: Hannah Tennelly.

Thomas Waters   117.341   SM   £257.3.6   Feb 20 1774   May 20 1774
        Appraisers: Robert hammett, John Cox.
        Creditors: Maxwell & Tubman, John Somervell.
        Next of kin: Joseph Waters, Elisabeth Waller.
        Administratrix: Mary Waters.

Vinson/Vincent Patterson   117.344   TA   £126.2.10   May 12 1772   Apr 12 1774
        Appraisers: Charles Pickarring, David Rotemfer.
        Creditors: Daniel Maynadier, Charles Crookshanks.
        Next of kin: Margaret Paddison, Margaret Hall.
        Administratrix: Sarah Patterson.

Abraham Jones   117.347   PG   £786.18.4   Nov 2 1773
        Appraisers: Samuel White, Jeremiah Magruder.
        Creditors: J. Sprigg, Rachel Beckett.
        Next of kin: Edward Jones, Henry Jones.
        Administratrix: Ann Jones.

Benjamin Wakefield   117.351   SM   £149.17.5   Apr 30 1774
        Appraisers: W. Jordan, Garard Bond.
        Creditors: James Jordan for John Glassford & Co., Francis Metcalf.
        Next of kin: Ann Simpson.
        Administrator: George Golott.

John Christian Smith   117.352   FR   £191.17.0   Nov 8 1773   Jan 27 1774
     Appraisers: Adam Sub (?), Stephan Ran--gn.
     Creditors: Conrad Grach, Valentine Lane.
     Next of kin: Philip Smith, Elisabeth Beall.
     Administrators: Margaret Smith, William Smith.

Edward Owen   117.353   FR   £469.19.5   Apr 22 1774   May 27 1774
     Appraisers: William Waters, John Baker.
     Creditors: Barbry Williams.
     Next of kin: Robert Owen, Thomas Owen.
     Executrix: Ruth Owen.

John Spangler   117.355   PG   £57.7.10   Jun 10 1773   May 24 1774
     Appraisers: Johannes Eych, Dewalt Zegen.
     Creditors: Jonathon Hegen, Onchil Cowt.
     Administratrix: Ann Spangler.

Tobias Horine   117.357   FR   £168.10.5   Nov 20 1770   Feb 18 1774
     Appraisers: Thomas Johnson, George Weil.
     Creditors: George Weil.
     Next of kin: Elisabeth Horine, Adam Harnen.
     Executor: Michael Troutner.

Frederick Sheets   117.358   FR   £136.3.4   Jul 30 1773   May 24 1774
     Appraisers: George Hertnegel, Abraham Uch (?).
     Administratrix: Barbara Sheets.

John Wye   117.359   FR   £11.9.6   May 20 1774
     Appraisers: Abraham Hoff, Heinrich Hofmann.
     Creditors: Thomas Beath.
     Executrix: Catharine Wye.

Benjamin Brite   117.360   FR   £56.11.4   Nov 6 1773   Mar 19 1774
     Appraisers: Alexander Clagett, James Harbin.
     Creditors: Samuel Boone.
     Next of kin: Benjamin Ray, John Ray, Jr.
     Administratrix: Fulda Davis.

David Hickman   117.361   FR   £66.19.6   Feb 24 1774
     Appraisers: John Williams, Solomon Stimptson.
     Mentions: George Walter, Moses Jewell.
     Next of kin: Bety Jewell, Dorceteas Hickman.
     Administrator: William Wilson.

Mr. Samuel Norwood   117.362   BA   £1396.12.5   Nov 15 1773   Jun 6 1774
(also Anne Arundel County)
     Appraisers: Charles Croxall, Clement Brook.
     Creditors: Samuel Owings, Edward Norwood for Stephen West.
     Next of kin: Edward Norwood, Samuel Norwood.
     Executor: Charles Ridgeley (son of William).

William Gallion   117.374   BA   £157.7.7   Feb 25 1774   Mar 24 1774
     Appraisers: Greenberry Dorsey, Samuel Griffith.
     Creditors: Robert Megay, Benjamin Hanson, James Gallion.
     Next of kin: Nathan Gallion.
     Administrator: Jacob Gallion.

Nicholas Newell   117.375   FR   £57.17.6   Mar 31 1774   Apr 16 1774
     Appraisers: William Fead, Adam Ridenour.
     Next of kin: John Hedler, Johann Weil.
     Administratrix: Margaret Newell.

John Cook   117.377   FR   £1373.1.3   Sep 24 1772   Jun 7 1774
     Appraisers: Henry Griffith, Richard Brook.
     Creditors: William Baker, William Rickets.
     Next of kin: Mary Cook, Zadock Ford.
     Administrator: Ambrose Cook.

John Pearce   117.378   FR   £545.0.8   Feb 17 1774   May 30 1774
     Appraisers: Walter Beall, William Tannehill.
     Creditors: Henry Roser for John Glassford & Co., Richard Henderson.
     Next of kin: William Pearce, Thomas Pearce.
     Administratrix: Margaret Pearce.

Unckle Unckles   117.382   FR   £46.18.5   Apr 15 1774
     Appraisers: Enoch Davis, Nicholas Umsted.
     Creditors: Thomas Allen Farquhar, Gabriel Esenberg.
     Next of kin: Thomas Farquhar, William Farquhar.
     Executors: John Uncles, William Uncles.

Melchar Leighter   117.384   FR   £106.3.0   May 6 1773   Sep 5 1774
    Appraisers: Henry Fisher, George Srectrer.
    Next of kin: Henry Leider, Andrew Smith.
    Administrator: John Lighter.

Mr. Thomas Emory   117.385   QA   £114.9.0   1766   Jan 29 1774
    Appraisers: John Willson, Charles Clayton.
    Executor: Gideon Emory.

John Hamilton   117.386   CE   £221.12.1   Jun 7 1773   Apr 14 1774
    Appraisers: William Currer, Edward Dougherty.
    Creditors: Benjamin Rumsey, Charles Rumsey.
    Next of kin: John Hamilton, Charles Hamilton.
    Executrix: Jane Hamilton.

Thomas Wells   117.392   QA   £20.9.8   Nov 28 1773 Feb 4 1774
    Appraisers: John Fisher, Anthony Harrington.
    Creditors: Hannah Falkner, Christopher Cross Routh.
    Next of kin: Nathaniel Wells, Easter Needs.
    Administratrix: Hester Wells.

James Fleet   117.393   CA   £14.11.3   Mar 10 1769 Apr 20 1774
    Appraisers: Edward Wood, Leonard Wood.
    Creditors: James Weems, James Weems as administrator of Roger Wheller.
    Next of kin: Rebecca Fleet, Lyttleton Fleet.
    Administrator: John Weems, Jr.

John Emory   117.394   QA   £77.13.8   Oct 11 1773 Jan 8 1774
(son of William Emory)
    Appraisers: B. Gould, Thomas Price.
    Creditors: Peregrine Tilghman, Gideon Emory.
    Next of kin: William Emory (son of William), Sophia Emory.
    Administratrix: Sarah Emory.

Phineas Chew   117.396   CE   £384.16.3   Jun 10 ---- Feb 26 1774
    Appraisers: Edward Dougherty, George Johnson.
    Creditors: Isaac Van Bibber.
    Next of kin: Samuel C. Darsy, Alm. Van Bibber, Isaac Van Bibber.
    Administratrix: Cassandra Chew.

James Baxter   117.398   CE   £479.6.9   May 25 1773 Mar 24 1774
    Appraisers: Nathaniel Baker, Andrew Read.
    Next of kin: Mary Waugh Thomas, Rachel Williams.
    Administrators: William Baxter (dec'd by Mar 24 1774), Joseph Baxter.

Patrick Robertson   117.402   QA   £559.4.4   May 16 1774 Jun 10 1774
(also Caroline County)
    Appraisers: Richard Mason, Vachel Downes.
    Creditors: Robert M. Germant (administrator of Isaac Cox), Charles Goldsborough.
    Next of kin: Alexander Robertson, Margaret Robertson.
    Executor: John Robertson.

Robert Lloyd   117.407   QA   £43.15.9   Apr 13 1773 Feb 7 1774
    Appraisers: William Merodeth Sr., Richard Costin.
    Mentions: Hannah Worman, Susey Hannarloud, Thomas Deford, Robert Reynolds.
    Administrator: Robert Rennols.

William Baxter   117.408   CE   £453.10.8   Jun 19 1773 Mar 24 1774
    Appraisers: John Crookshanks, John Wakefield.
    Creditors: James H. Hamilton, John Veazey, Jr.
    Next of kin: Mary Waugh Thomas, Rachel Williams.
    Administrators: Joseph Baxter, Thomas Jones, Baruch Williams.

Thomas Booth   117.412   CE   £49.12.10   May 9 1774
    List of debts.
    Administrators: Mary Booth, Jonathon Booth.

Uncle Uncles   117.413   FR   £444.6.9   Apr 15 1774
    List of debts.
    Executors: John Uncles, William Uncles.

Richard Swan Edwards   117.413   SM   £45.16.1   Apr 18 1774
    List of debts.
    Executrix: Martha, wife of Richard Armstrong.

Thomas Williams   117.415   PG   ----   May 13 1774
    List of debts.
    Executor: Thomas Williams.

William Jones   117.419   CE   £3.9.1   Mar 9 1774
    List of debts.
    Administratrix: Rebecca Jones.

Thomas Booth   117.420   CE   £4.4.6   May 9 1774
     List of debts.
     Administrators: Mary Booth, Jonathon Booth.

Jonathon Owden   117.420   PG   £119.14.0   May 9 1774
     List of debts.
     Administratrix: Elisabeth Owden.

Ignatius Compton   117.421   PG   £9.4.3   Nov 25 1773
     List of debts.
     Administratrix: Dorothea Compton.

Col. James Baxter   117.421   CE   £433.9.11   May 24 1774
     List of debts.
     Administrator: Joseph Baxter.
     Executor: William Baxter (deceased).

John Waples   117.423   WO   £361.5.9   Apr 2 1771   Nov 2 1774
     Appraisers: Simon Kollock, John Darby.
     Creditors: Abraham Weglan, William Holland.
     Next of kin: Paul Waples, Peter Waples.
     Executors: Mary Waples, William Waples.

Joshua Jones   117.426   WO   £222.10.8   Jul 19 1773   Dec 2 1774
     Appraisers: John Purnell Robins, John Duncan.
     Creditors: Mary Sturgis, Hammond Reynolds.
     Next of kin: Thomas Sturgis, Jesse Jones, George Jones.
     Executrix: Comfort Jones.

Ambrous Nicholson   117.429   WO   £23.12.6   Aug 10 1773   Oct 21 1774
     Appraisers: Leonard Johnson, Levin Hopkins.
     Creditors: Rachel Trilt, Bigest Co., McKimmey Smock and his wife Betty.
     Next of kin: Thomas Willett, Ruth Slovium.
     Administrator: James Linzey.

George Benson   117.430   WO   £65.0.0   1773   Oct 19 1774
     Appraisers: Peter Dolbie, Jonathon Bell.
     Creditors: John Selfridge, John Mitchell.
     Next of kin: William Benson, Elisabeth Benson.
     Executrix: Rachel Benson.

Michael Milbourn   117.432   WO   £0.8.6   Sep 23 1774
     Appraisers: Thomas Merrill, James Patterson.
     Administrator/Executor: Caleb Milbourn.

Oliver Hastings   117.432   KE   £62.10.0   Dec 10 1773   Sep 22 1774
     Appraisers: William Appley, Kinovin Wroth.
     Creditors: Thomas Smyth, J. Bolton.
     Next of kin: Mary Yardley, Isaac Hastings.
     Administrator/Executor: Sarah (Hastings), wife of Henry Price.

Thomas Canby   117.435   KE   £424.7.11   Apr 4 1774   Sep 21 1774
     Appraisers: James Pearce, Alexander Bims.
     Next of kin: Thomas Canby, Benjamin Canby.
     Administrators: George Browning (Quaker), William Corbett (Quaker).

Thomas King   117.442   PG   £133.0.10   May 9 1774   Sep 30 1774
     Appraisers: Benjamin Brookes, Thomas Clagett.
     Creditors: Richard Brooke, Hugh Lyon.
     Next of kin: Henry Brookes, William Moodie.
     Administratrix: Elisabeth King.

John Jarden   117.444   BA   £3.11.0   Nov 20 1772   Apr 11 1774
     Appraisers: Samuel Ricketts.
     Creditors: Mary Coten.
     Administrator: Benjamin Debruler.

Philemon Smith   117.445   CA   £1509.10.8   Dec 16 1772   Mar 2 1774
     Appraisers: Edward Gantt, Patrick Sim Smith.
     Creditors: Charles Grahame, James Wams (son of David).
     Next of kin: Alexander Ham Smith, Gavin Ham Smith.
     Administratrix: Betty Smith.

John Lowe   117.450   PG   £181.14.3   Jul 12 1774   Nov 27 1774
     Appraisers: Robert Wade, W. Norton.
     Creditors: Michael Lowe, Ignatius Digges.
     Next of kin: John Lowe, John Hawkins Lowe.
     Administrator: Henry Lowe.

Henry Lowe   117.452   PG   £391.0.10   Jul 12 1774   Nov 27 1774
    Appraisers: Robert Wade, W. Norton.
    Creditors: John Contee, Ignatius Digges.
    Next of kin: John Lowe, John Hawkins Lowe.
    Executor: Henry Lowe.

Philip Hodgkins   117.454   PG   £181.2.3   Jun 9 1774
    Appraisers: Henry Brookes, Thomas Clagett.
    Creditors: David Crauford, Thomas Contee for Mr. William Molleson.
    Next of kin: Thomas Hodgkins.
    Administratrix: Rachel Hodgkins.

George Elliott   117.455   QA   £154.3.5   Apr 6 1774   Aug 25 1774
    Appraisers: Richard Mason, William Connar.
    Creditors: Thomas Ringgold, William Robertson.
    Next of kin: Sarah Elliott, Joseph Elliott.
    Administratrix: Margaret Elliott.

Nathan Lane   117.458   QA   £88.12.4   Apr 8 1774   Aug 4 1774
    Appraisers: John Costen, James Chetham.
    Creditors: Christopher Cross Routh, Richard Earle & Co.
    Next of kin: Sarah Lane, Rebecca Lane.
    Administratrix: Elisabeth Lane.

James Reed   117.461   CR   £73.15.4   Jan 9 1775
    Bond.
    Mentions: John Ireland.
    Administratrix: Rachel Reed.

John Donally   117.461   BA   £46.9.5   Apr 18 1774   Sep 1 1774
    Appraisers: Jesse Bussey, Michael Jenkins.
    Creditors: Thomas Bleany, Abraham Jarrett.
    Administratrix: Catharine Donally.

John Pye   117.463   CH   £533.2.6   Nov 16 1772   Dec 2 1774
    Appraisers: Peter Dent, R. B. Mitchell.
    Creditors: Robert Mundell for John Glassford & Co., Jenifer & Hobb.
    Next of kin: Ann Neale, Raphaele Neale.
    Executrix: Henerita Pye, Walter Pye.

Thomas Atkinson   117.467   QA   £188.16.0   Jun 23 1774   Aug 4 1774
    Appraisers: E. Wright, Thomas Hackett.
    Creditors: Samuel Wallis, Aaron Atkinson.
    Next of kin: Aaron Atkinson, Elisabeth Harwood.
    Administratrix: Mary Atkinson.

Unity Hatton   117.470   BA   £139.8.8   Jun 23 1774   Sep 10 1774
    Appraisers: Nathaniel Nicholson, Joseph Crook.
    Creditors: John Skinner for James Russell & Co.
    Next of kin: Chaney Hatton, Nancy Leage.
    Executor: Thomas Baily.

Morgan Brown   117.473   QA   £438.13.0   Jul 2 1773   Aug 11 1774
    Appraisers: James O'Bryon, Edward Chetham.
    Creditors: James Hollyday, John R. Emory.
    Next of kin: John Brown, Catharine Brown.
    Administratrix: Wealthy Brown.

Henry Lamberson   117.475   WO   £14.2.1   Sep 29 1773   Aug 25 1774
    Appraisers: James Patterson, Benjamin Aydelott.
    Creditors: John Carey, James Cherve.
    Next of kin: Ann Roberson, Rachel Lamberson.
    Administrator: Zorabable Hill.

John Ford   117.477   FR   £233.10.5   Oct 18 1774   Nov 16 1774
    Appraisers: Clement Beall, Aaron Lanham.
    Creditors: Robert Ferguson for John Glassford & Co., John Ferguson for Cunningham
        Findley & Co.
    Next of kin: Ann Ford, Ann Johnston.
    Administrator: Joseph Benton, Jr.

John Creagh   117.479   BA   £16.12.0   Oct 25 1774
    Appraisers: William Richardson, Jacob Rubent.
    Creditors: John Boyd, Stenhouse & Gray.
    Administrator: James Holliday.

Thomas Linch/Lynch   117.481   QA   £192.19.1   Aug 20 1774   Sep 8 1774
    Appraisers: Richard Heathers, Andrew Graham.
    Creditors: Gilpin & Jurey, Alletha Ireland.
    Next of kin: Rebecak Lynch, Sanwills Lynch.
    Executor: Edmond Lynch.

Thomas Tennant   117.483   TA   £1.2.6   Nov 3 1774
      Appraisers: Jonathon Nicols, Henry Banning.
      Administratrix: Mable Tennant.

John Sherwood   117.484   TA   £349.5.9   Mar 7 1774   Nov 6 1774
      Appraisers: James Edmondson (dec'd by Nov 6 1774), Daniel Dickerson (Quaker).
      Creditors: Richard Bannaley, William Haywood.
      Next of kin: Alice Sherwood, Hugh Sherwood.
      Administrator: James Lloyd Chamberlaine.

James Denny   117.488   TA   £711.12.2   Jul 5 1774
      Appraisers: Henry Banning, Thomas Harrison.
      Creditors: Joseph Brutt, Jeremiah Banning.
      Mentions: Benjamin Denny, T. Denny.
      Administratrix: Mary Denny.

Jacob Comerford   117.494   TA   £21.15.9   May 31 1774 Aug 5 1774
      Appraisers: Joseph Bewley, J. Baker.
      Creditors: Daniel Kernon, James Lloyd Chamberlaine.
      Next of kin: Elisabeth Barrott, Mary Comerford.
      Administrator: Benjamin Benny.

Henry Harris   117.495   TA   £272.7.3   Aug 12 1774 Aug 16 1774
      Appraisers: Christopher Birckhead, Thomas Jenkins.
      Creditors: Richard Macmaham, Samuel Dickinson.
      Next of kin: Elisabeth Harris, Rachel West.
      Administrators: Henry Harris, William Harris.

Daniel Clark   117.499   TA   £124.7.9   Aug 27 1773 Nov 10 1774
      Appraisers: Richard Johns, Aaron Parratt.
      Creditors: John Clark, Mathew George, Elisabeth Rue.
      Next of kin: Joshua Clark.
      Administratrix: Jean, wife of Parrat Roe (Quakers).

James Barnett   117.501   TA   £133.19.0   Sep 20 1774 Nov 3 1774
      Appraisers: John Stevens, Charles Butten.
      Mentions: Richard Barnett.
      Administratrix: Jean Barnett.

John West   118.1   DO   £71.13.4   Aug 3 1774   Aug 29 1774
      Appraisers: Joseph Ennalls, Francis Hayward.
      Creditors: Thomas Ennalls 3rd, Joseph Ennalls Ferry.
      Next of kin: Frances Langfitt, Ann West.
      Administratrix: Mary West.

Robert Woolford   118.3   DO   £186.3.10   Mar 25 1774 Sep 2 1774
      Appraisers: Thomas Ennalls, Benjamin Woodard.
      Creditors: William Macky, Murray & Sulivane.
      Next of kin: William Woolford, John Woolford.
      Executor: Levin Woolford.

Phillemon Brannock   118.6   DO   £261.3.5   Apr 25 1774 Aug 28 1774
      Appraisers: William Jones, Thomas Vickars.
      Creditors: Joseph Baron, Landan Ball.
      Next of kin: Phillemon Brannock, Edmund Brannock.
      Executor: Nehemiah Brannock.

Cornelius Kollock   118.10   --   £146.17.3   Dec 16 1773
      List of debts.
      Appraisers: William Waples, John Waples.
      Administrator/Executor: Simon Kollock.

Joshua Hitch   118.12   SO   £30.14.2   Apr 12 1774
      List of debts.
      Administratrix: Sarah Hitch.

Jonathon Hayes   118.13   DO   £333.10.12 Mar 31 1774 Aug 22 1774
      Appraisers: Hooper Hodson, John Darby.
      Creditors: R. Stevens, John Hatton.
      Next of kin: William Trippe, Thomas Jones.
      Administrator: Morgan Jones.

Andrew Gootee   118.16   DO   £51.0.1   Feb 25 1774 May 13 1774
      Appraisers: Naboth Hart, James Edger.
      Creditors: George Booze Smear.
      Next of kin: John Wingate, William Billings.
      Executor: Andrew Gootee, Jr.

Joseph Thompson   118.18   DO   £596.0.2   Aug 16 1774
    Appraisers: Levin Kirkman, Edwards Thompson.
    Creditors: James Kirkman, John Hopkins.
    Next of kin: John Vickels Thompson, Samuel Thompson.
    Administrator: Benjamin Thompson.

Thomas Andrew, Jr.   118.22   DO   £195.0.0   May 19 1774   Aug 22 1774
    Appraisers: Henry Dickinson, Peter Richardson.
    Next of kin: Betty Brown, Rebeccah Brown, Joseph Andrew, Isaiah Gray.
    Administrator: Elisabeth Andrew.

Mason Shoehawn/Shehawn   118.23   DO   £135.5.0   Dec 9 1773   Aug 5 1774
    Appraisers: William Jones, Benjamin Woodard.
    Creditors: Joseph Shenton, Thomas Colston.
    Next of kin: Elisabeth Colson, Thomas Colson.
    Administrator: Joseph Shehawn.

George Middleton   118.25   DO   £46.12.8   Mar 10 1774   Aug 10 1774
    Appraisers: Joseph Richardson, Henry Ennalls.
    Creditors: Hugh Eccleston, H. Ennalls.
    Next of kin: Levin Bestpitch, William W. White.
    Administrator: Charles Eccleston.

William Cassety   118.27   DO   £192.9.8   1774   Jul 19 1774
    Appraisers: John Darby, Stevenson Whittington.
    Creditors: Thomas Ennalls 3rd, R. Stevens.
    Next of kin: Sarah Williams, Philip Williams.
    Administrator: Joseph Ennalls, Jr.

James Jones   118.31   DO   £19.1.1   May 25 1774   Jul 5 1774
    Appraisers: Henry Lake, James Edgar.
    Creditors: Henry Hicks, Benjamin Todd.
    Next of kin: Richard Woodland, John Woodland.
    Administrator: George Macomb.

Levi Jones   118.33   DO   £4.15.10   Jun 6 1774

William Smith   118.34   DO   £336.7.3   Apr 20 1774   Jul 14 1774
    Appraisers: T. Hodson, John Darby.
    Creditors: Hugh McBryde, James Gordon.
    Next of kin: William Trippe, Thomas McKeel.
    Administrator: Thomas Smith.

Daniel Tull   118.36   DO   £83.0.0   Jul 14 1774
    Appraisers: Thomas Jones, Stevens Woolford.
    Creditors: Landan Ball, Thomas West.
    Next of kin: Anthony Tull, Nancy Martin.
    Administratrix: Susanna Tull.

James Green   118.39   DO   £15.17.2   Feb 13 1774   Jun 13 1774
    Appraisers: Robert Dixon, Vincent Dehorty.
    Creditors: John Brown, Wilam Hubanks.
    Next of kin: Elisabeth Brown, William Ellet.
    Administrator: Edmund Green.

William Mills   118.41   DO   £96.19.0   Mar 1 1774   May 10 1774
    Appraisers: Thomas Vickars, Jr., Levin Wall.
    Creditors: H. Murray, Thomas Barnes.
    Next of kin: Edward Mills, Susanna Mills.
    Administrator: Weight Mills.

George Cole   118.44   DO   £9.7.0   Jun 6 1774   Jun 13 1774
    Appraisers: Henry Lake, Naboth Hart.
    Creditors: Benjamin Todd, Abraham Safford.
    Next of kin: Rachel Cole, George Scacom (?Slacom).
    Administratrix: Mary Cole.

John Cole   118.46   DO   £25.13.11   May 16 1774   Jun 4 1774
    Appraisers: Henry Lake, Naboth Hart.
    Creditors: John Rooter, John Bennett.
    Next of kin: Rachel Cole, Dyany Cole.
    Administratrix: Dianna Cole.

Mary Boxwell   118.47   DO   £71.16.0   Apr 30 1773   Apr 11 1774
    Appraisers: Roger Ashcom Hooper, Willis Newton.
    Creditors: James Sulivane, John Cranford.
    Next of kin: Mary Bramble, Elisabeth Hubbart.
    Executor: Jeremiah McCollister.

James Breeding   118.49   DO   £25.9.0   Nov 23 1772   May 30 1774
      Appraisers: Nathaniel Botters, Nicolas Fountain.
      Creditors: Nicols & Chamberlaine, Thomas Baynard.
      Next of kin: John Breeding, Robert Bishop.
      Administratrix: Margaret Breeding.

John Greenfield   118.50   DO   £31.13.5   Jan 15 1774   May 30 1774
      Appraisers: Jonathon Patridge, Henry Stewart.
      Creditors: Hugh Eccleston, Edward Staplefort.
      Next of kin: John Bryerwood, Thomas Kune.
      Administratrix: Mary Greenfield.

John Byus   118.53   DO   £33.11.6   Dec 8 1773   May 25 1774
      Appraisers: Benjamin Woodard, James Busick.
      Creditors: Edward Staplefort, W. Byus.
      Next of kin: W. Byus, James Byus.
      Administrator: Landan Ball.

Richard Dawson   118.54   DO   £25.7.5   Nov 13 1773   May 2 1774
      Appraisers: William Jones, Thomas White.
      Creditors: John Dawson, John Anderton, Richard Newton.
      Next of kin: William Dawson, Elisabeth Dawson.
      Administratrix: Mary Dawson.

Mary Bestpitch   118.56   DO   £124.19.9   Apr 11 1774
      Appraisers: B. Ennalls, Hugh Eccleston.
      Creditors: Daniel Sulivane, Jr., representatives of Jonathon Bestpitch (deceased)
         which are minors.
      Next of kin: Mary Bestpitch, Leah Bestpitch.
      Executor: William Harper.

Andrew Collins/Collings   118.59   WO   £734.13.5   Mar 25 1774
      Appraisers: John Laws, Jr., Charles Polk, Jr.
      Creditors: Jonathon Thomas, Jonathon Boyce.
      Next of kin: John Collins, Samuel Truitt.
      Executors: Andrew Collings, John Collings.

Solomon Townsend   118.64   WO   £466.11.4   Apr 12 1774   Sep 2 1774
      Appraisers: William Allen, J. B. Schoolfield.
      Creditors: John Fleming, Stephen Townsend.
      Next of kin: Samuel Townsend, James Townsend.
      Executors: William Townsend, Solomon Townsend.

John Teague   118.69   WO   £199.8.4   Dec 15 1772   Jun 3 1774
      Appraisers: George Spence, William Purnell.
      Creditors: George Martin, Jabez Fisher.
      Next of kin: William Teague, George Teague.
      Administratrix: Mary Teague.

Ebenezar Collings   118.71   WO   £136.4.3   Apr 25 1774   May 6 1774
      Appraisers: John Marshall, John Purnell.
      Creditors: Kendal Collier, Ellis & Purnell.
      Next of kin: Mary Smith, Solomon Collins.
      Administrator: John Smith.

Charles Nicholson   118.73   WO   £92.8.7   Jun 15 1774   Aug 3 1774
      Appraisers: William Holland, Thomas Batson.
      Creditors: Ananias Hudson, Joshua Tull.
      Next of kin: John Parker, George Parker.
      Administratrix: Mary Nicholson.

Matthew Roger   118.75   WO   £141.17.1   May 13 1772   May 6 1774
      Appraisers: William Tingle, Thomas Batson.
      Creditors: Joshua Hill, Pelig Walters.
      Next of kin: Jacob Roger, Jesse Roger.
      Administrator: John Roger.

Robert Hill   118.77   WO   £111.12.6   Jun 29 1773   Aug 5 1774
      Appraisers: Isaac Murray, Whittington Bowin.
      Creditors: John Postly, David Evans.
      Next of kin: William Stevens Hill, Johnson Hill.
      Executrix: Leah Hill.

Ebenezar Campbell   118.79   WO   £1387.9.9   Feb 9 1774   Sep 9 1774
      Appraisers: Joseph Mitchell, John Postly.
      Creditors: John Simpson Campbell, Samuel Handy.
      Next of kin: John Simpson Campbell, John Brevard.
      Mentions: Samuel Campbell, William Smith, son Ebenezar Campbell.
      Executrix: Naomi Campbell.

Joseph Gray, Jr.   118.87   WO   £256.17.11   Jun 24 1774   Oct 26 1774
    Appraisers: John Postly, Josiah Mitchell.
    Creditors: William Rownd, James Wilton.
    Next of kin: Jesse Gray, Benjamin Gray.
    Executrix: Elisabeth Gray.

Laurence Howarth   118.90   WO   £184.3.9   Mar 8 1773   Oct 1 1774
    Appraisers: William Selby, Jr., Samuel Wise.
    Creditors: Mary Milbourn, James Christy.
    Next of kin: Mary Milbourn, Mary Evans.
    Executrix: Sarah, wife of Joseph Scott.

James Colston   118.101   TA   £136.12.1   Jan 27 1774   Mar 29 1774
    Appraisers: Henry Banning, Thomas Harrison.
    Creditors: James Lloyd Chamberlaine, Samuel Chamberlaine.
    Next of kin: James Colston, William Colston.
    Executor: Henry Colston.

Peter Comerford   118.105   TA   £951.9.9   May 15 1773   Mar 22 1774
    Appraisers: Solomon Neall, Aaron Parratt.
    Creditors: Matthais Gale, James Lloyd Chamberlaine.
    Next of kin: Sarah Nabb, Elisabeth Burnett.
    Executor: Richard Johns.

Thomas Western   118.111   TA   £66.5.3   Dec 4 1773   Mar 15 1774
    Appraisers: D. Wilson, Abner Broadway.
    Creditors: George Wilson, J. Goldsborough.
    Next of kin: William Bonny, Rebeccah Tennant.
    Administrator: Daniel Christian.

Stephen Chilton   118.113   SM   £13.12.5   Apr 18 1774
    List of debts.
    Executrix: Ann Chilton.

James Loyd/Lloyd   118.114   TA   £2436.18.8   Apr 12 1774
    List of debts.
    Appraisers: James Dickinson, James Berry.
    Administratrix: Elisabeth Lloyd.

Elisabeth Dudley   118.126   TA   £343.13.4   Jan 5 1774   Mar 3 1774
    Appraisers: Aaron Parratt, D. Wilson.
    Creditors: Mr. Lewis Barnett, Sampson Maddin.
    Next of kin: Jane Barnett, Juliana Bowdle.
    Administrator: Tristram Bowdle.

Ignatius Compton   118.130   PG   £99.5.6   Nov 22 1773   Nov 23 1773
    Appraisers: William Pearce, Richard Queene.
    Next of kin: John Compton.
    Administratrix: Dorothy Compton.

Ignatius Head   118.133   SM   £79.8.1   May 21 1774
    Appraisers: John H. Brome, Robert Hammett.
    Creditors: John Somervell, John Mills for James Buchanan & Co.
    Next of kin: Cuthbert Head, David Johnson.
    Administratrix: Mary Ann Biggs.

William Pantree   118.134   SM   £54.10.9   May 13 1774   May 27 1774
    Appraisers: Hanson Briscoe, Thomas Bond.
    Creditors: John Mills for James Buchanan & Co., Matthew Blair for Cunningham
        Findley & Co.
    Administratrix: Mary Pantree.

John Hargerader   118.136   FR   £226.6.2   May 28 1774
    Appraisers: Allen Farquhar, Jr., Henry Cronell.
    Creditors: Martin Baker.
    Next of kin: Conrad Hargerader.
    Executrix: Mary Hargerader.

Richard Watts   118.138   SM   £624.16.8   Mar 9 1774   Apr 18 1774
    Appraisers: Ignatius Combs, Well. Taylor.
    Creditors: John Masson, John Black.
    Executors: Sarah Watts, Robert Watts.

James Pearl   118.142   FR   £582.11.3   Apr 18 1774   May 12 1774
    Appraisers: Arthur Nelson, Alexander Magruder.
    Next of kin: Basil Pearl, Thomas Pearl.
    Administratrix: Elisabeth Pearl.

Adam Krichbaum/Cruchboom   118.145   FR   £136.17.11   Oct 16 1773   May 25 1774
    Appraisers: George Shaver, Jacob Kinshaw.
    Creditors: Caspar Hofman, Henry Stoltz.
    Administrators: Mary Cruchboom, Davis Jones, Jr.

Philip Wetherall   118.149   CE   £556.11.2   Nov 12 1773   Mar 18 1774
(of Talbot County)
        Appraisers: James Hughes, Alexander Williamson.
        Creditors: Robert Richardson, George Gleave.
        Administrator: Thomas Place of Baltimore County.

Philip Wetherall   118.153   TA   £717.7.11   Jan 13 1774   Mar 13 1774
        Appraisers: Henry Banning, Thomas Harrison.
        Creditors: Robert Richardson, George Gleave.
        Administrator: Thomas Place of Baltimore County.

James Kennedy   118.167   PG   £48.14.1   Sep 28 1773   Jun 7 1774
        Appraisers: John Fend Beall, John Pearre.
        Creditors: Robert Fendlay, Jr. for Cunningham Findley & Co., William Sydebotham.
        Next of kin: John Kennedy, Thomas Kennedy.
        Administrator: Andrew Beall.

Samuel Wheeler   118.169   PG   £151.19.6   Jan 15 1774
        Appraisers: Thomas Macgill, John Macgill.
        Creditors: Jacob Green, Thomas Belt for Brown Perkins & Buchanan.
        Next of kin: Robert Wheeler, William Wheeler.
        Administratrix: Elisabeth Wheeler.

Alexander Walters   118.171   QA   £596.11.9   May 10 1773
        Appraisers: Tobias Willis, Arthur Emory.
        Creditors: John & James Barnes, John Barnes & Co.
        Next of kin: Benjamin Walters, John Walters.
        Executor: Robert Walters.

Moses Orme, Sr.   118.174   PG   £490.9.4   Nov 20 1773   Nov 25 1773
        Appraisers: Thomas Sansbeary, Jr., Sabritt Scott.
        Next of kin: Moses Orme, Ellen Orme.
        Executrix: Ann Orme.

Robert Hardcastle   118.176   QA   £70.15.5   Mar 9 1774   Mar 10 1774
        Appraisers: William Banning, Jeremiah Colston.
        Executor: Thomas Hardcastle.

Peter Holt   118.176   TA   £3.15.6   Mar 23 1772   Mar 22 1774
        Appraisers: Charles Bullen, John Mullikin.
        Mentions: John Holt.
        Administrator: Thomas Jenkins.

James Brown   118.177   TA   £4.6.7   Oct 15 1773   Apr 5 1774
        Appraisers: Charles Bullen, Mr. Lewis Barnett.
        Creditors: John Stevens.
        Next of kin: William Brown, Sarah Brown.
        Administratrix: Cassandra, wife of William Chaplain.

Hemsey Sparrow   118.177   FR   £14.4.9   Jun 6 1772   Jun 7 1774
        Appraisers: John Locker, James Shehan.
        Next of kin: Thomas Sparrow, Jonathon Sparrow.
        Administrator: Adam Steuart.

Matthew Bryan   118.178   QA   £137.17.8   Nov 25 1772   May 5 1774
        Appraisers: Samuel Walters, Jacob Smith (dec'd by Jul 13 1773).
        Executor: John Sayer Blake.

Michael Bence/Bounce   118.179   PG   £240.13.5   Jun 2 1774   Jun 17 1774
        Appraisers: William Deakin, John Beall.
        Creditors: James Miller for Cunningham Findley & Co., Jacob Wirt.
        Next of kin: Catharine Primmer, Vibila Hickel.
        Executor: George Bounce.

Benjamin Meredith   118.182   QA   £223.19.5   Sep 9 1773   Feb 22 1774
        Appraisers: Richard Mason, Richard Costin.
        Creditors: Thomas Ringgold, William Price.
        Next of kin: Mary Green, Thomas Meredith.
        Administratrix: Elisabeth Meredith.

Thomas Booth   118.184   CE   £169.11.9   May 9 1774
        Appraisers: Richard Bond, Samuel Gilpin.
        Creditors: William Passmore, Joseph Ellen.
        Next of kin: Jonathon Booth, Ebenezar Booth.
        Administrators: Mary Booth, Thomas Booth.

John McDuff   118.187   CE   £187.3.7   Oct 9 1772   Mar 1774
        Appraisers: Perig Ward, James Coppin.
        Creditors: John Veazey, Sr., John Veazey, Jr.
        Mentions: Alexander Williamson for Amos Struttell, Mr. Turner for Clayton & Chew.
        Administrator: James Hughes.

Thomas Crouch   118.189   CE   £137.13.6   Apr 2 1774
     Appraisers: Robert Hart, John Hankey.
     Creditors: Thomas Huggins, Tobias Rudulph.
     Administrator: William Crouch.

Thomas Howard   118.192   QA   £72.4.0   May 8 1773   Feb 4 1774
     Appraisers: John Dames, William Carradine.
     Creditors: Robert Browne, Francis Baker.
     Next of kin: brother Baker Howard, sister Elisabeth Stone.
     Administrator: Samuel Nicolls.

Mr. John Money   118.193   CE   £1115.3.10   Mar 9 1774   Mar 11 1774
     Appraisers: John Ward Veazey, John Ward.
     Creditors: Sturgis & Shields, William Ward.
     Next of kin: Ann Money, Richard Money.
     Executors: John Money, Samuel Money.

Philip Weathrall   118.198   TA   £1939.2.1   Mar 13 1774
     List of debts.
     Administrator: Thomas Place of Baltimore County.

William Williams   118.205   FR   ----   Jan 17 1774
     List of debts.
     Executors: Barbarah Williams, Thomas Williams.

David Arnold   118.208   CA   £1897.0.5   Apr 15 1774
     List of debts.
     Executrix: Rebecca Arnold.

David Arnold   118.214   CA   ----   Apr 15 1774
     List of debts.
     Executrix: Rebecca Arnold.

Stephen Lucas   118.219   SM   £236.11.5   May 14 1774   Nov 29 1774
     Appraisers: John Reeder, Benjamin Bean.
     Creditors: William Taylor, Jonathon Armstrong.
     Next of kin: Richard Sparks, Rachel Sparks.
     Administrator: Michael Lucas.

John Baptist Greenwell   118.221   SM   £117.19.9   Feb 15 1774   Nov 29 1774
     Appraisers: Ignatius Abell, John Booth.
     Creditors: John Abell Younger, Archibald Campbell for John Glassford & Co.
     Next of kin: Archibald Greenwell, Elisabeth Greenwell.
     Administratrix: Susannah Greenwell.

Ignatius Bailey   118.222   SM   £22.11.9   Mar 14 1774
     Appraisers: Seneca Nelson, John Graves, Jr.
     Creditors: Jeremiah Jordan, John Somervell.
     Next of kin: Elender Bailey, Elisabeth Bailey.
     Administrator: William Hambleton/Hamilton.

James Corum   118.223   SM   £235.7.9   May 12 1774   Nov 29 1774
     Appraisers: Robert Watts, Samuel Jenifer.
     Creditors: George Plater, John Masson for Cunningham Findley & Co.
     Administrator: Hugh Hopewell.

George Newbolt   118.225   SM   £160.3.11   Jun 2 1774   Nov 29 1774
     Appraisers: Matthew Wise, Sr., Robert Watts.
     Creditors: Edmund Abell, Jr., Ignatius Combs.
     Administratrix: Sarah Newbolt.

James Walker   118.226   SM   £5.2.9   Nov 20 1774
     List of debts.
     Administratrix: Susannah Walker.

John Tarlton   118.227   SM   £70.16.9   Apr 18 1774
     List of debts.
     Executrix: Ann Tarlton.

James Walker   118.227   SM   £11.2.3   Nov 10 1770
     List of debts.
     Administratrix: Susannah Walker.

George Fenwick   118.228   SM   £8.17.1
     List of debts.
     Executrix: Jane Fenwick.

Solomon Smith   118.228   WO   £48.18.0   Jul 8 1774   Nov 2 1774
     Appraisers: Daniel Fookes, William Farlone.
     Creditors: Archibald Smith, Jr., Sarah Davis.
     Next of kin: Archibald Smith, Samuel Smith.
     Administratrix: Sarah Smith.

John Shockly   118.229   WO   £256.12.7   Oct 28 1773   Oct 18 1774
     Appraisers: Stephen Roach, John Richardson.
     Creditors: William McBride, Samuel Killum.
     Next of kin: Benjamin Shockly, Richard Shockly.
     Executrix: Catharine, wife of George Smith.

John Nairn   118.231   WO   £1169.0.5   Jan 1 1772   Nov 11 1774
     Appraisers: Dixon Quinton, Jacob Addams.
     Next of kin: Esme Marshall, S. Whittington.
     Executor: Thomas Marshall.

Joseph Ireland   118.237   KE   £393.14.7   Dec 17 1773   Sep 27 1774
     Appraisers: Ebenezar Reyner, James Black.
     Creditors: John Money, John Wallis.
     Administratrix: Althea Ireland.

Mr. Joseph Man   118.247   KE   £523.4.11   Aug 5 1774   Sep 15 1774
     Appraisers: John Eccleston, Ebenezar Reyner.
     Creditors: Joseph Gilpin, Wiliamhar Beson.
     Next of kin: George Mann, Ann Smith.
     Executrix: Ann Man.

Thomas Crouch   118.249   KE   £329.19.9   Jun 21 1774   Sep 10 1774
     Appraisers: Jacob Glenn, Richard Miller.
     Creditors: J. Page, Thomas Ringgold.
     Next of kin: Rachel Clark.
     Administratrix: Mary Crouch.

Cocker Hammond   118.252   KE   £34.0.11   Jun 15 1774   Nov 1 1774
     Appraisers: A. Calder, Joseph Ringgold.
     Creditors: J. Bolton, Morgan & Stubey.
     Next of kin: Sarah Hammond, John Hammond.
     Administratrix: Hannah Hammond.

Capt. John Carvil   118.252   KE   £22.0.5   Aug 29 1774   Oct 18 1774
     Appraisers: John Wickes, James Dunn.
     Creditors: Morgan & Stubey, Thomas Ringgold.
     Administratrix: Ann Carvil.

Richard Norton   118.252   KE   £2.7.6   Sep 24 1774
     List of debts.
     Administrator: William Merrill.

John Carvell   118.253   KE   £2.0.0   Oct 18 1774
     List of debts.
     Administratrix: Ann Carvell.

Sarah Tilden   118.253   KE   £367.9.0   --- 31 1774   Nov 1 1774
     Appraisers: Charles Groome, Lake Griffith.
     Creditors: Morgan & Stubey, Thomas Ringgold.
     Next of kin: Martha Loram, Tabitha Tilden.
     Executor: Charles Tilden.

John Hepburn, Jr.   118.256   PG   £1039.17.1   Aug 29 1774   Sep 1 1774
     Appraisers: Edward Sprigg, W. Beanes.
     Creditors: David Crauford, John Read Magruder.
     Next of kin: John Hepburn, Frank Luke.
     Executor: Samuel Chew Hepburn.

John Summers, Jr.   118.264   PG   £38.18.8   Sep 10 1774   Oct 24 1774
     Appraisers: Osborn Sprigg, John Osborn.
     Creditors: John Dawcey, R. Contee.
     Next of kin: John Summers, Nathaniel Summers.
     Administratrix: Dorcas Summers.

Mr. William Thorn   118.265   PG   £67.5.1   Aug 30 1774   Nov 8 1774
     Appraisers: Charles Burgess, David Clarke.
     Creditors: Ralph Foster, Edward Parkinson for Gate Feason & Co.
     Next of kin: Abraham Thorn, Peregrine Thorn.
     Executor: Barton Thorn.

William Cooksey, Sr.   118.267   CH   £261.16.7   Jun 19 1773   Sep 12 1773
     Appraisers: Michael Dent, John Dent.
     Mentions: Elisabeth Corry, Edward Edelsen.
     Mentions: Testimean Cooksey, Thomas Richard Cooksey.
     Executors: Barbara Cooksey, Jesse Cooksey.

Benjamin Duke   118.268   CA   £1326.2.10   May 6 1773   Jul 26 1774
     Appraisers: John Bond, William Allnut.
     Creditors: Thomas Reynolds, Charles Graham.
     Next of kin: Samuel Parran, Richard Parran.
     Administrator: Moses Parran Duke.

Thomas Hencock/Handcock   118.270   CH   £182.7.0   Jul 13 1773   Sep 12 1773
    Appraisers: William McPherson, Sr., Raphael Boarman, Sr.
    Creditors: Bennett Perrin.
    Next of kin: William Handcock, Mary Ann Handcock, Mary Ann Boarman.
    Executrix: Ann Handcock.

Jacob Wirt   118.272   PG   £412.3.5   Oct 27 1774   Nov 27 1774
    Appraisers: Abraham Boyd, Jaspar Mauduit.
    Creditors: David Ross, John Steuart.
    Next of kin: Katharine Whetstone.
    Executors: Henrietta Wirt, Jaspar Wirt.

Humphrey Cleave   118.277   QA   £7.6.10   Mar 30 1774   Aug 25 1774
    Appraisers: George Tempel, John Lambdin.
    Creditors: Joseph Sudler, Daniel Cunningham.
    Next of kin: Nathan Cleave, Catharine Cleave.
    Administrator: Richard Cleave.

Solomon Burns   118.277   QA   £40.4.6   Jul 23 1774   Aug 26 1774
    Appraisers: John Serdon, William Carradine.
    Mentions: William Burras, Thomas Burras.
    Next of kin: William Richardson, James Davison.
    Administrator: George Burns.

Benjamin Meads   118.278   BA   £300.19.6   Apr 25 1774   Sep 10 1774
    Appraisers: John Owings, Nathan Nicholson.
    Creditors: John Skinner for James Russel & Co., Thomas Bailey.
    Next of kin: Benjamin Buck, William Foster.
    Administratrix: Martha Meads.

Edward Round   118.281   WO   £1690.12.10   May 10 1773   Jul 30 1774
    Appraisers: Adam Spence, Samuel Handy.
    Creditors: James Wilson, John Bell.
    Next of kin: William Morris, John Round.
    Executrix: Ann, wife of Henry Stevenson.

Roberson Lingo   118.291   WO   £52.7.2   Nov 25 1773   May 12 1774
    Appraisers: Edward Melmes, George Parsons, Jr.
    Creditors: Smith Lingo.
    Next of kin: John Lingo.
    Executor: John Lingo.

Mr. Chirstopher Haw   118.292   CH   £704.0.5   Oct 14 1774
    Appraisers: Edward Edelen, Thomas Richard Cooksey.
    Creditors: Meverell Lock, Sm. Briscoe.
    Next of kin: Philip Briscoe, Sm. Briscoe.
    Executrix: Sarah (late Sarah Haw), wife of Semmes Price.

John Downes   118.297   QA   £1166.16.7   Feb 1774   Jul 21 1774
    Appraisers: John Kerr, John Serdey.
    Creditors: Solomon Wright, Clement Sewell.
    Next of kin: Charles Downes, Jr., Vachel Downes.
    Administratrix: Sophia Downes.

John Green   118.301   QA   £84.11.0   Aug 30 1774   Aug 26 1774
    Appraisers: John Seeders, Richard Tucker.
    Creditors: William McLead, Richard Lloyd for Mr. James Anderson.
    Next of kin: Philemon Green, Sarah Wilson.
    Administratrix: Hester Green.

Thomas Butler   118.304   WO   £62.12.9   Mar 15 1773   Aug 3 1774
    Appraisers: Edmund Northin Nelms, George Parsons.
    Creditors: Joseph Dashun, Smith Lingo.
    Next of kin: Smith Lingo, Thomas Lingo.
    Administratrix: Sarah Butler.

John Drummond   118.306   WO   £29.10.6   Feb 18 1774
    Appraisers: Thomas Sturgis, John Ball.
    Creditors: Leah Drummond, George Reed.
    Next of kin: Leah Drummond, Mary Drummond.
    Administrator: Richard Taylor.

David Richardson   118.307   WO   £325.9.3   Nov 23 1772   Apr 29 1774
    Appraisers: Leonard Johnson, Samuel Scarborough.
    Creditors: Polly Smith, Fisher Walton.
    Next of kin: William Richardson, William Richardson.
    Executor: Thomas Martin.

Ann Tull   118.309   WO   £116.3.10   Nov 9 1773   Jun 6 1774
    Appraisers: Thomas Batson, John Cox.
    Next of kin: Marget Hatfield, Amy Conner, Zeporah Collings.
    Executrix: Ann Collings.

Jonathon Noble   118.311   WO   £12.1.9   Mar 27 1773   Jun 7 1774
    Appraisers: Samuel Dreaden, John Jones.
    Creditors: James Nobel, Solomon Shockley.
    Next of kin: Naomi Diks, Levi Noble.
    Administrator: Benjamin Shockley.

Thomas Canner   118.313   TA   £19.11.4   Jun 1 1774   Nov 2 1774
    Appraisers: Philip Mackey, William Foster.
    Creditors: Archibald Patison for Speirs & French & Co., William Stevens.
    Next of kin: George Canner, Elisabeth Canner.
    Administratrix: Elisabeth Canner.

James Sheepherd   118.314   TA   £20.11.0   Jul 16 1774   Aug 5 1774
    Appraisers: Thomas Martin, Henry Martin.
    Creditors: William Stevens, John Winstanley.
    Next of kin: William Harrison, Sarah Cliff.
    Administratrix: Mary Sheephard.

John Higgins   118.315   TA   £5.19.9   Aug 3 1774   Aug 5 1774
    Appraisers: John Stevens, Thomas Jenkins.
    Administratrix: Bridget Higgins.

Elisabeth Haddaway   118.316   TA   £8.8.6   Aug 13 1774   Nov 5 1774
    Appraisers: Henry Banning, John Denny.
    Next of kin: George Haddaway, William Haddaway.
    Administrator: Joseph Harrison.

Cassandra Saunders   118.316   TA   £316.15.0   Nov 4 1774
    Appraisers: Nicholas Goldsborough, Samuel Dickinson.
    Creditors: Thomas Jenkins.
    Mentions: Cassandra Chaplin, William Stevens.
    Administratrix: Mary, wife of William Parrat.

Thomas Hilsby   118.321   TA   £175.11.4   Jun 16 1774   Aug 8 1774
    Appraisers: John Stevens, Mr. Lewis Barnett.
    Creditors: Samuel Dickinson, Chamberlaine & Co.
    Next of kin: John Hilsby, James Hilsby.
    Administratrix: Ann Hilsby.

William Willis   118.325   TA   £73.9.5   Nov 19 1773   Jun 21 1774
    Appraisers: Thomas Dawson, Thomas Barrow.
    Creditors: Sharp & Dawson, Levin Milliss.
    Next of kin: Rebekah Forster, Robberd Willis.
    Administrator: William Rose.

Grundy Parrott   118.327   TA   £17.8.6   Sep 20 1773   Nov 3 1774
    Appraisers: John Stevens, Mr. Lewis Barnett.
    Administrator: Robert Kemp.

Mr. William Besswick/Beswick   118.328   TA   £798.6.2   Jun 3 1773   Jul 5 1774
    Appraisers: Francis Baker, James Strainer.
    Creditors: Abner Turner, James Lloyd Chamberlaine.
    Next of kin: Richard Besswick, John Blackwell.
    Administrator: Denny Beswick.

Grundy Parrott   118.331   TA   £166.18.11   Jan 25 1773   Aug 6 1774
    Appraisers: John Stevens, William Sharp (dec'd by Aug 6 1774).
    Creditors: Charles Crookshanks for Speirs & French & Co.
    Next of kin: James Parratt, John Parratt.
    Administrator/Executor: Robert Kemp (Quaker).

William Beswick   118.334   TA   £161.9.8   Aug 23 1774   Aug 26 1774
    Appraisers: F. Baker, John Thomas.
    Creditors: Abner Turner, James Lloyd Chamberlaine.
    Next of kin: Richard Besswicke, John Blackwill.
    Administrator: Denny Beswick.

George Dudly   118.334   TA   £439.12.4   Jun 2 1773   Nov 24 1774
    Appraisers: Aaron Parratt, D. Wilson.
    Creditors: Lyddia Dudbly, Matthais Gale.
    Next of kin: Sarah Dudly, H. Clift.
    Administrator: Tristram Bowdle.

Tristram Thomas   118.339   TA   £1699.17.6   Dec 13 1769   Nov 3 1774
    Appraisers: Daniel Sherwood, William Sharp.
    Creditors: Lodm. Elbeart, Richard Barnaby.
    Next of kin: Nic. Thomas, William Thomas.
    Executor: Thomas Martin, Jr.

Jonathon Nicols   118.347   TA   £1729.3.7   Jun 3 1774   Aug 2 1774
    Appraisers: T. Sherwood, Henry Banning.
    Creditors: James Nicols, Henrietta Maria Nicols (executrix of William Nicols).
    Next of kin: Margaret Nicols, John Nicols.
    Executor: Henry Nicols.

Ferdinando Callaghane   118.357   TA   £131.6.1   Sep 6 1773   Nov 4 1774
    Appraisers: Joseph Bewley, James Gibson.
    Creditors: Daniel Dolvin, Sarah Dolvin.
    Next of kin: John Callaghane, Catharine Callaghane.
    Administratrix: Ann Hynson Callaghane.

William Wilson   118.359   TA   £567.4.8   May 6 1774   Nov 2 1774
    Appraisers: Aaron Parratt, Solomon Neill.
    Creditors: Matthais Gale, Samuel Thomas.
    Next of kin: Thomas Wilson, Esther Register.
    Administratrix: Ann Wilson (Quaker).

Mrs. Mary Bond   118.364   CA   £952.1.6   Dec 11 1772   Jun 18 1774
    Appraisers: Joseph Kent, William Dare, Sr.
    Creditors: E. Johnson, Thomas Daniel Claggett.
    Next of kin: Barbara Blake, Mary Beckett.
    Executor: George Gant.

Francis Duling   118.369   TA   £112.6.1   Apr 1 1774   Sep 13 1774
    Appraisers: John Gregory, D. Wilson.
    Creditors: Robert Wilson, William Marsh Catniss.
    Next of kin: Nathan Dueley, Elisabeth Dueley.
    Administrator: Elijah Duling.

Elisha Hobbs   118.372   DO   £20.17.3   Oct 31 1774
    List of debts.
    Administratrix: Tabitha Hobbs.

Levin Robinson   118.373   DO   £1.4.0   Nov 1 1774
    List of debts.
    Executrix: Nancy, Robinson.

Daniel Adams   118.373   DO   £13.1.5   Dec 12 1774
    List of debts.
    Administrator: McNamara Adams.

Winlock Russum   118.374   DO   £66.19.0   Nov 10 1774
    Balances.
    Executrix: Esther Ann Russum.

Levin Ward   118.376   DO   £49.18.10   Apr 5 1774   Nov 28 1774
    Appraisers: Hooper Hodson, Stevenson Whittington.
    Creditors: John Tootell, H. Hodson.
    Next of kin: Ann Ward, Sumars Ward.
    Executor: Jesse Rue.

Winlock Russum   118.377   DO   £990.14.5   Nov 10 1774
    Appraisers: Charles Eccleston, Henry Ennalls.
    Creditors: Jonathon Kollock, James Murray.
    Next of kin: James Russum, Edward Russum.
    Executrix: Esther Ann Russum.

John Ward   118.382   DO   £106.16.1   Apr 7 1774   Nov 21 1774
    Appraisers: Joseph Ennalls, Francis Hayward.
    Creditors: Thomas Ennalls 3rd, Harrison & Sprigg.
    Next of kin: Summers Ward, Ann Ward.
    Administratrix: Lucy Ward.

Elisha Hobbs   118.385   DO   £45.13.6   Jan 6 1774   Oct 31 1774
    Appraisers: Nathaniel Potter, John A. Hooper.
    Creditors: Zabdiel Potter, John Richardson, Jr. for Nicols & Chamberlaine.
    Next of kin: Joy Hobbs, William Hobbs.
    Administratrix: Tabitha Hobbs.

Sarah Wright   118.386   DO   £152.4.6   Apr 11 1774   Nov 16 1774
    Appraisers: John Trice, James Hooper.
    Creditors: Richardson Stevens, Ledya Tickle.
    Next of kin: William Noble, John Noble.
    Administrator: James Wright.

John Harper   118.390   DO   £167.11.9   Nov 25 1774
    Appraisers: Joseph Richardson, Charles Eccleston.
    Creditors: James Sulivane, Thomas Logan for James Kirkpatrick.
    Next of kin: David Harper, Cratcher Lord.
    Executor: John Harper.

Thomas Ball   118.394   DO   £894.16.1   Jan 10 1774   Dec 6 1774
    Appraisers: James Muir, Ralph Green.
    Creditors: Samuel Davidson for Speirs & French & Co., Henry Hooper 2nd.
    Next of kin: Levin Ball, Benjamin Ball.
    Administratrix: Priscilla Ball.

Thomas Wheeler   118.399   DO   £255.11.2   Jul 25 1774   Nov 10 1774
    Appraisers: Roger A. Hooper, Willis Newton.
    Creditors: John Tootell, James Giflin.
    Next of kin: Charles Wheeler, Henry Wheeler.
    Administrator: James Ross.

Thomas Braugham   118.403   DO   £380.3.10   Dec 13 1774
    Appraisers: John Pitt Airey, Henry Ennalls.
    Creditors: Henry Steele, Samuel Kirkpatrick.
    Next of kin: Margaret Harper, William Harper.
    Executors: Patrick Braugham, James Kirkman.

William Walker   118.407   DO   £297.19.1   Dec 13 1774
    Appraisers: Stevenson Whittington, John Darby.
    Creditors: Thomas F. Eccleston, Morgin Jones.
    Next of kin: Pearson Wall, Levin Hives.
    Administratrix: Margaret, wife of William Willoughby.

Jonathon Morain/Moreign   118.410   DO   £176.17.3   Aug 6 1774
    Appraisers: Edward Stephens, John Scott.
    Creditors: Thomas Muse, Harrison & Sprigg.
    Next of kin: Thomas Moreign, Moses Moreign.
    Administratrix: Mary Moreign.

Jane Harris/Harrison   118.413   DO   £485.5.1   Jun 2 1774   Nov 24 1774
    Appraisers: Edward Stephens, Jonathon Bestpitch.
    Creditors: John Scott, William Mackey.
    Next of kin: Elisabeth Hodson, Nicholas Harrison.
    Administratrix: Amy Harrison.

John Trippe, Jr.   118.417   DO   £760.2.2   Apr 5 1774   Nov 7 1774
    Appraisers: John Darby, Stevenson Whittington.
    Creditors: Henry Steele, William Ennalls.
    Next of kin: Elisabeth Langfitt, William Trippe.
    Executrix: Ann Trippe.

Perry Harrison   118.421   DO   £435.6.4   Jun 18 1770   Nov 24 1774
    Appraisers: Hugh Eccleston, Edward Stephens.
    Creditors: John Scott, Moses Brodess.
    Next of kin: Jonathon harrison, James Harrison.
    Administrator: Perry Harrison.

John Brooke/Brooks   118.425   DO   £377.0.5   Jul 29 1774   Nov 7 1774
    Appraisers: John Darby, William Trippe.
    Creditors: John Henry, Thomas Ennalls.
    Next of kin: Daniel James Brooks.
    Note: Deceased children are minors.
    Administratrix: Sarah Brooks.

William Jarvis   118.428   SO   £28.9.11   Jul 16 1774   Jan 10 1775
    Appraisers: William Venables, Joshua Hitch.
    Next of kin: Elisabeth Jarvis, Ann Jarvis.
    Administrator: John Noble.

Nancy Jones   118.429   SO   £35.15.3   May 25 1774   Dec 29 1774
    Appraisers: Levin Ballard, John Jones.
    Creditors: Levin Ballard, John Shureff.
    Next of kin: George Wilson, George Waggaman.
    Administrator: Isaiah Dorman.

John Huffington, Jr.   118.430   SO   £49.16.9   May 22 1772   Dec 6 1774
    Appraisers: George Gilliss, Joseph Venables.
    Creditors: Charles Dashiell, ------.
    Next of kin: Gilbert Huffington, Joshua Huffington.
    Executor: Jonathon Huffington.

Thomas Mersey/Mercer, Jr.   118.432   CE   £42.19.1   Nov 1 1774
    Appraisers: John Ward Veazey, John Beedle.
    Creditors: Sturgis & Shields.
    Next of kin: Thomas Marcer.
    Administrator: William Walmsley, Jr.

Alen
  Tomsoline 31
Alexander
  Amos 61
  Mark 12, 24, 79, 84, 87
Alford
  Edward 18
  Joseph 18, 68
  Maccabeus 18, 33, 66, 68
  Mary 68
  Moses 73, 74, 77
  William 68
Alison
  Robert 90
Alkin
  Ellin 78
All
  Benjamin 84
Allein
  William 44
Allen
  Archibald 31
  Moses 18, 42, 64
  Rachel 54
  Thomas 54
  William 30, 51, 76, 101
Allender
  William 19
Allford
  Mary 25
  William 25
Allin
  William 91
Allison
  Mary 53
Allnut
  William 105
Allston
  Thomas 38
Alnutt
  William 43
Altend
  Methe 88
Alvey
  Thomas Green 38
Amery
  Robert 83
Amoos
  William 7
Amos
  Joshua 75
  Mordecai 55
Amoss
  Benjamin 55
Anderson
  Benjamin 37
  Catharine 55
  Isaac 41
  Isabella 37
  James 5, 8, 9, 12, 14,
    16, 26, 27, 40, 41,
    45, 46, 48, 50, 57,
    58, 67, 73, 74, 106
  John 15, 37, 41, 55, 86
  Marget 40
  Robert 22, 40, 71, 73,
    77
  Sarah 40, 86
  William 5, 37, 55
Anderton
  John 68, 81, 101
Andrew
  Abraham 37, 55
  Elisabeth 66, 68, 100
  John 81
  Joseph 100
  Rebecah Brannock 66
  Thomas 66, 68, 100
  William 55
Andrews
  Eleanor 62
  John 62

Moses 13
Ankragh
  James 58
Ankrim
  Archibald 39
  George 39
Appley
  William 97
Apsley
  William 22
Archer
  John 79
  Thomas 6
Armstrong
  Benjamin 84
  Edward 23, 77
  Elisabeth 13, 14, 19
  James 7
  John 23
  Jonathon 104
  Martha 96
  Mary 23
  Rebecca 23
  Richard 96
  Robert 4, 80
Arnold
  David 20, 104
  Rebecca 53, 104
  William 75
Arrington
  William 2, 65
Ashburner
  John 13
Ashcom
  Nathaniel 3
  Samuel 3
Ashcomp
  Charles 3
  Margaret 3
Ashford
  Martha 77
Ashley
  Edward 77
  John 52
  Sophia 77
  William 52, 77
  Zachariah 52
Ashmer
  George 84
Ashpaw
  George 6
  Henry 6
  John 6
Aspenall
  John 25
Atkinson
  Aaron 19, 42, 69, 98
  Isaac 86
  J. 25
  John 12, 17, 27, 35, 49,
    50, 93
  Joshua 35
  M. J. 36
  Mary 98
  Sarah 35
  Sophia 35
  Thomas 98
Attix
  Aquilla 77
Attox
  Aquilla 73
Attwell
  Yonell 81
Atwell
  Benjamin 52
  Joseph 52
Auld
  John 29
  Philemon 29
Austen
  James 67
Austin

Ann 63
Henry 63
James 67
Richard 63
Solomon 83
Thomas 63
William 63
Avan
  Archibald 55
  Magdalin 55
Aydelord
  William 35
Aydelott
  Benjamin 98
  James 36
  John 35, 36
  Joseph 35
  Mary 35, 36
  Samuel 35, 36
  William 35, 36, 49, 91
Aydlott
  Mary 50
Ayres
  John 93

Backer
  Elisabeth 37
  John 37
  Peter 37
Bacon
  John 12
Badly
  William 15
Baggs
  Isaac 47
  James 69
  John 47
  Rebecca 47
  Thomas 28, 46
  Tibbels 47
Bailey
  John 64, 84
  Samuel 84
Bailiss
  Benjamin 71
  Samuel 71
Baily
  John 64
  Thomas 19, 37, 98
Baird
  Alexander 57
  Thomas 61
Baker
  Ann 46
  Evet. 37
  Francis 23
  J. 99
  James 2
  John 37, 42, 54, 95
  Jonathon 46
  Martin 102
  Nathaniel 90, 96
  Sarah 19
  Thomas 41, 91
  William 95
Balding
  Caleb 70
Ball
  John 73, 88
  Landan 99, 100, 101
  Landon 15, 66, 86
  Levin 82
Ballard
  Javis 16
  Levin 62
Banister
  Charles 16
Banks
  Henry 63
  Josiah 61
  Robert 61

Thomas 61, 63
Bannaley
  Richard 99
Bannard
  Wealthyam 28
Banning
  Benoni 18
  Henry 63, 90, 99, 102,
    103
  Jeremiah 99
Bannister
  Thomas 46
Barker
  John 94
  William 33
Barnes
  David 30
  Edmund 25
  J. 6
  James 30, 103
  John 30, 103
  Mary 20
  Richard 3, 53, 89
  Thomas 15, 20, 30, 45,
    48, 100
Barnet
  Lewis 42
Barnett
  James 42, 94, 99
  Jane 102
  Jean 42, 99
  John 29
  Lewis 63, 102
  Matthew Lewis 64
  Rebecca 12
  Richard 42, 99
Barnhouse
  Ann 4
  Elisabeth 4
  James 4
  Richard 4
Barnwell
  James 63
Barnwill
  James 41
Baron
  Joseph 1, 99
Barratt
  Thomas 4
Barrington
  John 72
Barrish
  Catharine 55
  Peter 55
Barrott
  Elisabeth 99
Barrow
  James 64
  Thomas 64, 94
Barry
  Cornelius 79
Bartlett
  Thomas 46
Baruck
  Benjamin 86
Bate
  James 38
Batson
  Ann 70, 78
  Thomas 92, 101
Battson
  Richard Able 66
Bauck
  Hannah 73
Baud
  Alexander 14
Bavington
  John 19, 20
  William 16, 19, 20
Baward
  Henry 34
Baxter

Benjamin 26
Edmund 26
James 96, 97
Joseph 71, 96, 97
Rachel 26
William 96, 97
Bayard
  Samuel 20
Bayles
  Jonas 71
  Nathaniel 71
  Samuel 71
Bayley
  Clemence 49
  Clement 68
  Esme 31
Bayly
  Esme 51, 52, 70
  Thomas 38
Baynard
  Peter 84
  Samuel 84
  Sophia 46
  Thomas 11, 12, 82, 101
  William 46
Baynes
  John 30
Bays
  Isaac 26, 28
Beadle
  John 76
Beakins
  William 63
Beale
  Bennett 60
  Eleanor 90
  Elisabeth 90
Beall
  Andrew 103
  Brooke 29
  Clement 98
  Elisabeth 95
  John Fend 103
  Patrick 60
  Samuel 15
  Walter 95
Beans
  William 8
Beard
  John 44
  Lewis 61
  Rachel 44
  Richard 44, 78
  Thomas 37, 61
Beargupil
  Catorn 56
Beath
  Thomas 95
Beatty
  C. 34
Beaty
  Archibald 56
  Jane 56
Beauchamp
  Fountain 51
  Handy 9
  Levin 9
  Mary 9
Beaumont
  Elisabeth 37
  Joseph 37
Beavens
  Richard 90
  Rowland 27
  Sarah 27
  William 27
Beazy
  John 72
Beck
  Edward 83
  Elijah 7
  John 14

Mary 7, 83
Mathew 7
Samuel 7
Beckett
  Rachel 94
Beding
  Nathaniel 71
Beech
  Jonathon 48
Beedle
  Augustine 19, 20, 23, 57
  John 39
  Thomas 72
Bell
  Jacob 32
  John 15
  Jonathon 88, 89, 92, 93,
    97
  William 47, 59, 69
Belsner
  John 75
Belt
  Jel. 31
  Thomas 60, 103
Belton
  Samuel Dyne 12
Bennett
  George 52, 86
  John 82, 100
  Lauranna 68
  Robert 80
  William 18, 68
Benny
  Benjamin 99
  William 41
Benson
  Ann 29
  Betty 88
  Elisabeth 97
  George 97
  James 42, 88
  Rachel 97
  Sarah 48
  William 97
Benston
  George 27
  John 16
  Rebeckah 16
  William 16
Benton
  Joseph 98
Berg
  Johannes 55
  Wilhelm 55
Bergenboyle
  Andrew 56
  William 56
Bergh
  Peter 55
Bergupile
  Andrew 56
Berkley
  Henry 59
Berry
  Ann 3
  Hezekiah 3
  Humphrey 3
  James 102
  Joseph 3
Besswick
  Denny 23
  Richard 23
  William 23
Bestpitch
  Jonathon 67, 101
  Leah 101
  Levin 100
  Mary 101
Beswick
  Denny 23
  Rachel 23
  William 41, 54

Bettel
  Thomas 85
Betts
  Hezekiah 45
Betty
  Charles 55
Bevans
  William 27
Bewley
  Joseph 3, 10, 23, 41,
    42, 54, 63, 64, 99
Biddel
  Elisabeth 28
  Thomas 28
Biddle
  Augustine 39, 72, 73, 77
  Dom. 23
  Dominick 39, 77
  Elisabeth 23
  Jesse 72, 73
  John 72, 73
  Noble 23, 77
  Richard 39, 77
  Thomas 23, 28, 72, 77
Biggs
  Mary Ann 102
Bigsby
  Joseph 36
Billings
  William 99
Billingslea
  Francis 56
  Walter 56
Billingsley
  James 56
  Ruth 56
Bims
  Alexander 97
Bin
  Hugh 11
Birckhead
  Christopher 65, 99
Bird
  Joseph 44
  Solomon 85
Birkhead
  Christopher 11
  John 6
  Samuel 6
Biscoe
  George 38
Bishop
  Charles 89
  Elisabeth 89
  Henry 27
  J. 35
  Joseph 89
  Robert 12, 13, 101
Bitting
  Anthony 8
Black
  Ebenezar 57
  James 8, 14, 16, 57, 83
  John 102
Blackburn
  David 15
  Elenor 15
  John 15
  William 15
Blackdock
  Charity 6
  Edward 6
Blackiston
  Ann 14, 43
  Benjamin 73
  Ebenezar 9, 14, 22
  George 77
  Henrietta 9, 14
  James 43
  John 16, 17, 43
  Joseph 14
  Michael 9

Stephen 9
  William 12, 73
Blackmore
  Ann 34
  James 34
  Samuel 34
Blackstone
  Elijah 56
Blade
  James 20
Blades
  Dorothy 63
  Edmund 63
  Elisabeth 41, 63
  Hezekiah 32
  John 41, 63, 88
  Samuel 88
Blair
  Charles 25, 66, 67
  Mathais 94
  Mathew 90
  Matthew 81, 102
Blake
  Charles 59
  Elisabeth 59
  Henrietta Maria 59
  John Sayer 5
  Sarah 59
Blakiston
  George 43
Bleany
  Thomas 98
Blear
  Charles 1
Block
  John 80
Blue
  Richard 55
Blunt
  Benjamin 48
  James R. 46, 48
  James Robert 9, 10
  Samuel 45, 48
  Sarah 48
Blyth
  John 42
  Sophia 42
Boardley
  Sarah 57
Boarman
  Edward 62
  Francis 38
  Henry 34
  Leonard 23, 86
  Raphael 23, 86, 90
  Richard 3, 38
Bolden
  James 16, 57
  Jesse 76
Boldin
  Elijah 28, 76
  James 28
  Jesse 28, 39, 61
  Mary 28
  Nathan 28
Bolten
  John 14
Bolthrop
  Ann 3
  Boles 3
Bolton
  ------ 77
  Henry 45
  J. 97
  John 57, 58
Bond
  Ann 30
  Elisabeth 76
  Garard 94
  Gerard 38, 53, 80
  Girard 45
  John 13, 76, 80, 83

Jos. 13
  Richard 60
  Robert 20
  Thomas 30, 45, 75, 76,
    84, 102
  William 13, 80
  Zachariah 75, 80
Bonny
  William 102
Boon
  Joseph 47
  William 5, 48
Boone
  Burle 78
  Hannah 12
  Jacob 12
  Samuel 95
Booth
  Jonathon 96, 97
  Mary 96, 97
  Thomas 96, 97
Boots
  Isaac 8, 17
  Joseph 17
  Rebecca 8, 17
  William 17
Bordely
  James 69
Bordley
  Anthony 9
  Arthur 9
  Henry 9
  J. 69
  John 45
  Joseph 23
  Sarah 39
  Stephen 9
  William 3, 9, 11, 23, 83
Borman
  Francis 4
  Richard 8
Boston
  Sarah 28
Boswell
  John 19
  Joseph 19
  Sarah 19
  William 19
Boteler
  Thomas 59
Botters
  Nathaniel 101
Bouchell
  J. G. 23
Boughman
  Sarah 77
Bouldin
  James 23, 76, 77
  Jesse 13, 61
  Thomas 13, 84
Bounds
  James 41, 48, 70
  Jones 70
Bourne
  Betsy 21
  Ester 53
  Esther 21
  Jacob 21, 53
  Susannah 53
Bowan
  Thomas 22
Boward
  Ann 34
  Henry 34
Bowdle
  Elisabeth 1
  Henry 1, 42
  John 1
  Joseph 1
  Juliana 102
  Tristram 64, 102
  William 72

Bowen
  Benjamin 6
  Isaac 85
  Jehu 12
  Josias 6
  Mary 6, 12
  Nathan 12
  Solomon 6
Bower
  Temperance 73
Bowers
  Bordley 9
  Pearce 9
  Temperance 67
  Thomas 9, 14
  William 9
Bowie
  Allen 5, 30, 55, 70
Bowin
  Jethro 88
  Luke 88
  Martha 49
  Whittington 101
Bowling
  Thomas 13
Bowman
  Ann 41, 42
  Samuel 41
Boxwell
  Mary 100
Boyce
  Andrew 13
  Jonathon 26, 101
  William 49
Boyd
  Abraham 30, 54
  John 24, 75, 98
Boyer
  Augustine 14, 20, 57, 83
  Elisabeth 83
  John 35
  Mary 71
  Nathaniel 14, 71, 83
  Nathel 40
  Paul 35
  Richard 71
  Stephen 71
  Thomas 14, 20, 40, 57,
    71, 83
Boyle
  James 20
Boyles
  James 16, 76
Boyne
  William 94
Bracco
  John 63, 64
Bradford
  Levin 49
Bradley
  Charles 47
  Isaac 32
  Nathaniel 47
  Thompson 47
Brady
  James 74
  Jonathon 25
Braishway
  Emmanuel 34
Bramble
  Mary 100
Brandiller
  Emmanuel 34
Brandt
  Charles 3
Braner
  William 8
Brannock
  Edmund 99
  Nehemiah 99
  Phillemon 99
Branson

Benjamin 86
Hewyean 86
John 86
Michael 86
Bratton
  Joshua 27
Braughan
  Patrick 67
Braughton
  John 50
  William 50
Bravard
  Adam 35, 36, 50
  Benjamin 23, 28, 57, 72,
    77, 84
  Thomas 57
Bready
  Jonathon 33, 82, 92
Breeding
  James 12, 101
  John 12, 101
  Margaret 12, 101
Brevard
  Adam 49, 89, 93
  John 92, 101
Brian
  Susannah 71
Brice
  Frances 15
  James 48
  John 15, 17, 43, 52, 78
  Judah 8
  Judith 21
  Richard 8, 83
  Robert 15
  Sarah 48, 79
Brickhead
  Christopher 64
Bright
  William 8
Briley
  Isabel 66
  John 66
  Samuel 66
Brinsfield
  Elisabeth 81
Briscoe
  Hanson 102
  James Sotheron 81
  Jane 21
  John 75, 80
  Judah 24
  Philip 33
  Richard 24
  Samuel 33
  Sarah 67
Brison
  Thomas 76
Brite
  Benjamin 95
Britten
  Abraham 37
  William 19
Brittingham
  Belitha 50
  Jeremiah 91
  John 48
  Mary 50
  Nathaniel 91
  Patience 91
  Samuel 88
  Solomon 50
  William 27, 50
Britton
  Abraham 75
Broadaway
  Abner 65
  Mary 65
Broadway
  Abner 102
Brodwatters
  James 36

Brody
  James 28
  Margaret 28
  Robert 28
  William 28
Brogdin
  William 52
Brohawn
  Patrick 68, 82
Brome
  John 14, 15
  John H. 102
  Thomas 15
Bromw
  John Hooper 38
Brook
  Catharine 19
  Clement 95
  Leonard 19
  Rachel 8
  Richard 19, 95
Brooke
  Ann 13, 14
  Baker 13
  Barbara 30
  Basil 14, 53
  Boyer 14
  C. 13
  Dorothy 14
  Elisabeth 14
  John 14
  Leonard 13
  Richard 31, 70, 97
  Roger 14
  Sarah 14
Brookes
  Benjamin 55, 97
  Henry 97, 98
Broom
  John Hooper 94
Broome
  Ann 15
  Henry 15
Broughton
  John 50
Brown
  Anderton 68
  Betty 66, 100
  Cassandra 63
  Catharine 98
  Charles 25, 28, 59, 68,
    82
  Curtis 25
  David 57
  Edward 48, 72, 88
  Elisabeth 52, 72, 100
  Elisha 59
  Esther 14
  Ezekiel 68
  Francis 68
  G. R. 62, 86
  George 34
  James 48, 55, 63, 66
  John 5, 7, 29, 52, 59,
    98, 100
  Joseph 44, 71
  Josias 26
  Marget 52
  Morgan 48, 98
  Nathan 59
  Nicholas 57
  Priscilla 28
  Rebeccah 100
  Robert 5, 12, 50, 56,
    57, 61
  Sarah 52, 63
  Susannah 57
  Thomas 61, 71
  Tilghman 25
  Wealthy 98
  William 50, 51, 63, 71
Browne

Priscilla 45
Robert 45, 46, 48
Browning
George 97
Thomas 16, 73
Bruce
Normand 34
William 3
Bruff
Joseph 23
Mary 23
Susannah 23
Thomas 23
Bruffett
Garner 18
Brull
Normand 45
Brumfield
William 20
Brumwell
Abraham 41
Edward 2
Mary 2
Robert 2
Brutt
Joseph 99
Bryan
Charles 79
Ignatius 94
James 20
John 45, 94
Mary 20
Philip 94
Susannah 71
Tabitha 45
Bryarly
Robert 55
Bryerwood
John 101
Bryon
Arthur 5
Hannah 11
John 5
Matthew 5
Stephen 11
Buchanan
Andrew 26, 28, 55, 60,
86
Ann 60
Archibald 37, 75, 87
George 28, 60, 86
Gilbert 91
John 6, 24, 52, 55
Robert 9, 58, 61
Buck
Jonathon 51
Buckley
James 94
Thomas 94
Budd
John 16, 25
Bull
Edmund 24, 56
William 7
Bullay
John 92
Bullen
Charles 2, 42, 63
Bullidge
John 55
Burbage
John 27
Mary 27
Burgess
Ann 63
Benjamin 79
Charles 21, 55
George 42, 64, 94
Jane 79
Richard 15
Samuel 79
Burgin

James 39
Jesse 73
Joshua 39, 73
Philip 39, 73
Burk
Hannah 74
Burkard
Christopher 34
Burke
Michael 11
Tobias 17
Burkham
John 42
Rebekah 42
Burn
Elisabeth 67
Thomas 67
William 67
Burnett
Elisabeth 102
William 38
Burnitt
James 28
Burnside
John 71
Burroughes
Valentine 46
Burroughs
Elijah 59
Frances 59
George 90
Nal. 12
Vallentine 59
Burrus
Rebecca 59
Burtles
William 23
Burton
Benjamin 91
Jacob 91
Molly 91
William 91
Bush
Elisabeth 45
George 45
William 45
Busick
James 101
Solomon 1
Bussey
Jesse 98
Jessey 7
Butler
Jane 12
Joseph E. 29, 84
Peter 12
Butten
Charles 99
Joseph 7
Sarah 7
Buttler
Joseph 56
Button
Richard 37
Byrd
Benjamin 51
Joshua 51, 70
Thomas 51, 70
Byrn
Ignatius 33
James 20
John 11, 68
Mary 20
Byus
James 101
John 101
W. 101
William 65

Cadobel
Weud 34

Cadwalader
John 9
Caffey
Charles 82
William 82
Cagan
Milt 64
Cain
Elisabeth 9
Cake
Rachel 18
Calder
A. 14, 22, 105
Caldwell
John 52
Calhoun
James 34, 79
Callaghane
Ann Hynson 108
Catharine 108
Ferdinando 108
John 108
Callender
William 76, 77
Callerton
Michael 53
Calyea
Stephel 24
Cammill
Isaac 74
Campbell
Archibald 4, 38, 54, 80,
81, 104
Ebenezar 15, 22, 36, 61,
101
John 6, 7, 15, 22, 30,
36, 78, 79, 92
John Simpson 101
Mary 61
Naomi 101
Peter 3, 8, 53, 54, 86,
94
Robert 5, 10
Samuel 101
Campbile
Colin 44
Campble
Peter 93
Camper
John 65
Philadelphia 65
Solomon 65
Camplin
Hanary 17
Camull
Isaac 57
Canby
Benjamin 97
Thomas 97
Cann
Frances 58
Jane 58
Cannel
Isaac 58
Jeremiah 58
Cannell
Abraham 9, 22
Isaac 22, 58, 83
Jerom 22
Monica 22
Canner
Elisabeth 107
George 107
Thomas 107
Cannon
Absolom 32
Benjamin 82
Constantine 82
Curtis 81
Elijah 35
Joseph 27, 32
Mary 18, 33

Sarah 32, 82
Thomas 32
William 18, 33, 69
Cantwell
Mary 18
Caradine
James 12
Carey
James 82
John 98
Thomas 92
Carman
William 10, 46
Carmichael
Duncan 26
Carmon
William 57
Carnan
Christopher 19
Elisabeth 19
George 19
Carpenter
Thomas Smith 17
William 17
Carradine
Samuel 12
William 48, 59, 104, 106
Carroll
Charles 63
Mary 63
Carse
Barney 77
Carslake
Henrietta 23
John 23
Carteel
Cassandre 54
Charity 54
Edward 54
Machash 54
Carter
Bridget 85
Henry 11, 48
Jacob 46
Rebecca 12, 78
William 78
Cartwright
John 38, 94
Carvell
Ann 105
John 105
Carvil
Ann 58, 105
John 58, 105
Carvill
Ann 27, 74
John 27, 74
Cary
Edward 50
James 82
Cassety
William 100
Casson
Henry 4, 5, 11, 26, 28,
    44, 45, 46, 47, 59,
    69, 70
John 5, 10, 26, 69
Robert 69, 70
Sarah 69
Cathell
Daniel 50
David 26
James 26, 50
John 26
Jonathon 23, 31, 48, 50
Cather
Elebeth 76
John 13
William 76
Catniss
William Marsh 108
Catogs

John 2
Catrop
John 65, 94
Lemmon John 94
Ruth 65, 94
Cattely
John 13
Catterton
Michael 30, 43
Caudry
John 93
Caulk
Ann 28
Asenah 67
John 67, 71, 72, 73
Mary 65
Richard 67, 73
Cauther
Robert 76
William 76
Cavendar
James 82
Cavender
James 32
Cawlk
Samuel 93
Cazier
Jesse 67
Richard 20
Chaille
Peter 26, 35, 93
Chaird
Hewerm 40
Chaires
Henrietta 69
Sarah 45
William 69
Chairs
John 28
Chalmers
James 15
William 15
Chamber
Rebecca 94
Chamberlain
James Loyd 64
Samuel 11
Chamberlaine
James Lloyd 2, 41, 42,
    64, 94, 99, 102, 107
Samuel 63, 102
Thomas 64
Chamberlaing
James Hays 63
Chambers
Alice 70
John 40, 70
John Campbell 61
Michael 40, 71
Robert 70
Sarah 70
Chance
Absolom 5, 48
Batchelder 5, 48
Boon 5, 48
Peter 48
Rachel 5
Richard 5
Chandler
John 33
Michael 9, 57
Nathaniel 9, 57, 58
Stephen 33
Tahpenah 57
Tahponah 9
Thomas 9, 57, 58
Chaplain
Cassandra 103
William 103
Chaplin
Cassandra 107
Elisabeth 64

Francis 64
Joseph 64
Mary 64
Chapline
Joseph 15
Josiah 15
Moses 15
Chapman
James 10
Jeremiah 78
Chauncy
George 55
Chears
Thomas 69
William 69
Cheezum
John 81
Samuel 81
Chenoweth
Peter 88
Cherve
James 98
Chetham
Edward 59, 98
James 5, 19, 45, 46, 47,
    98
Chew
Cassandra 96
Phineas 96
Richard 6
Samuel 6
Chezum
Daniel 81
John 18
Rebakah 81
Chick
Joseph 13
Mary 13, 85
Rebecca 13
Chiffin
William 17
Chiffins
Christian 73
James 73, 77
Chilcoate
Humphrey 13
John 13
Child
Henry 29
Samuel 29
William 29
Zachariah 29
Chilicate
Humprey 12
James 13
John 13
Sarah 13
Chilton
Ann 54, 102
George 54
Matthew 26, 46
Stephen 54, 102
Chrisfield
Benjamin 23
Christian
Daniel 102
Christy
James 102
Chun
Henry 53
Chunn
Joseph 53
Lancelot 53
Zack 62
Cigel
Ann 52
Cimmey
Sarah 48
Cinnamon
Mary 59
Cladgett
Mary 30

Clagett
    Alexander 95
    Charles 30
    Posthumous 15
    Richard 53
    Thomas 31, 60, 70, 94,
        97, 98
Clagget
    Thomas 60
Claggett
    Thomas Daniel 108
Claland
    Thomas 28
Clapham
    John 52
Clare
    Isaac 14, 15, 20, 30,
        53, 56
    John 30
Claridge
    Henry 87
Clark
    Abraham 18
    Alexander 23, 84, 85
    Caleb 42, 64, 65
    Daniel 99
    David 16
    Edward 29, 64
    Elisabeth 29
    Henry 2, 42
    Jean 42
    John 26, 82, 99
    Joshua 4, 26, 42, 46,
        64, 99
    Mathew 29
    Philip 38
    Rachel 105
    Rebekah 64
    Richard 13, 26, 65, 66
    Samuel 24, 75
    Thomas 16
    William 16, 17, 24, 25,
        26, 65, 82
Clarke
    Alexander 76
    David 105
Clarkson
    Abraham 87
    Barzillai 81
    Binniah 81
    Edward 7, 8
    Joseph 82
    Mary 82
    Richard 87
    Robert 1, 17, 25, 32,
        33, 57
    Thomas 81
    William 87
Clarrage
    Elisabeth 87
    Henry 87
    John 87
Clayland
    Susannah 69
Claypool
    James 24
Claypoole
    James 14, 72, 83
Clayton
    Charles 3, 5, 45, 46, 96
    Edward 5
    Elisabeth 45
    Hannah 19, 44, 59
    Mary 5, 45
    Solomon 5
Cleave
    Catharine 106
    Humphrey 106
    Nathan 106
    Richard 106
Cleaver
    Ann 9

Benjamin 9
    Mary 9
    William 9
Clegg
    John 84
Cleland
    Robert 69
Clements
    Caleb 46
    Christiana 62
    Elisabeth 23, 24
    Fra. 62
    Francis 24
    George 24, 62
    Henry 62
    John 24, 62
    Rebecah 69
    Thomas 24, 62
Cliff
    Sarah 107
Clift
    H. 107
Clinkscales
    Adam 28
    Frances 28
    John 28
    Mary 28
Clinton
    Francis 10
Clopper
    Cornelius 71
Clough
    Chaney 12
Cluck
    Joseph 20
    Mary 20, 57
Coale
    James 75
    Sarah 59
    William 22, 79, 90
Cobey
    John 53
    Mary 53
    Ralph 53
Cobourn
    William 64
Coburn
    Anne 64
    Solomon 64
    William 64
Cockayne
    Samuel 2
Cod
    John 4, 36
Coe
    Daniel 16
    John 50, 93
Cole
    Dennis Garret 80, 83
    Dianna 100
    Dyany 100
    Fs. Sinah 73
    George 100
    Hennery 83
    Henry 80
    James 75
    Jane 73, 75
    John 100
    Martha 73
    Mary 100
    Mordecai 80
    Rachel 100
    Robert 4
    Thomas 80, 83
Coles
    Mordecai 83
Coley
    Edward 83
    John 83
Coller
    Nathan 92
Collier

John 22
    Kendal 101
    Kendall 22
    Robert 86
    Tabitha 22
    William 91
Collings
    Andrew 101
    Ann 106
    Belitha 49
    Ebenezar 101
    John 33, 35, 88, 101
    Mary 50
    William 4, 46
    Zeporah 106
Collins
    Abraham 33, 81
    Andrew 101
    Elisabeth 4
    Elisha 49
    John 35, 49, 89, 101
    Mary 27
    Mathew 4
    Solomon 101
Collis
    Richard 81
Collison
    Richard 81
Colliss
    Elisabeth 81
    Richard 81
Colson
    Elisabeth 100
    Thomas 100
Colston
    Henry 102
    James 102
    Jeremiah 11, 26, 45, 46,
        59, 103
    John 45
    Thomas 100
    William 102
Comb
    Elisabeth 69
Combs
    Ignatius 102, 104
Comegys
    A. 9
    Edward 71
    John 14
    Nathaniel 14
    Sarah 4, 71
    William 77
Comerford
    Jacob 99
    L. 18
    Mary 99
    P. 42
    Peter 102
    Robert 41
Compton
    Dorothea 97
    Dorothy 102
    Ignatius 97, 102
    John 102
    Stephen 3, 8, 53
    William 62
Conant
    John 70
Conaway
    Vachel 43
Conely
    Michael 80
Conerly
    Elisabeth 10
    Patrick 10
Conestable
    Thomas 37
Coney
    Richard 66
    Robert 17
Connar

William 98
Connaway
    Jane 25
    Rachel 43
Connelly
    Jeremiah 10
    Terry 10
Conner
    Amy 106
    Rackclif 49
Connoway
    George 43
    John 49
Contee
    John 98
    R. 105
    Thomas 23, 28, 98
Conway
    John Span 40, 51
Conwill
    John 20
Cook
    Ambrose 95
    John 95
    Mary 95
Cooke
    Edward 87
Cooksey
    Barbara 105
    Jesse 105
    Justinian 53
    Samuel 53
    Testimean 105
    Thomas Richard 33, 53,
        62, 105, 106
    William 105
Cooledge
    Judson 70
Coolidge
    Judsan 55
Cooper
    Ann 45, 65
    Benjamin 17
    George 45
    Hezekiah 57, 74
    Isaac 49, 70
    John 17, 25
    Joseph 25
    Rebecca 10
    Richard 45
    Samuel 48
    Sharpless 17
    Thomas 17, 48, 67
Cop
    Elisabeth 73
Copes
    Robert 17
Coppen
    James 61
Copper
    Charles 9
    William 40
Coppin
    James 39, 103
Corbett
    William 97
Corbin
    Salley 36
Cord
    Isaac 55
    John Robins 93
    Rhoda 93
    Thomas 13
Corden
    Jesse 16
Corey
    Mathew 17
Corhe
    John 83
Cornell
    Benjamin 7
    jacob 7

Richard 7
Smith 7
William 7
Corry
    Benjamin Lesly 27
    Elisabeth 55, 105
    John 27, 55
    Margaretta 55
    Mary 55
Corse
    Barney 73
Corum
    James 104
Cosden
    Alphonso 73
    Elisabeth 73
    James 20, 39, 73
    Jesse 20, 71
    Thomas 73
Costen
    John 98
Costin
    James 19
    John 44, 45, 47
    Richard 96, 103
Coston
    Isaac 48
Coten
    Mary 97
Cotman
    Benjamin 51
Cottingham
    Daniel 27
    Elisha 91
    William 85
Cottman
    Benjamin 48, 50, 61
Cottrell
    James 28
Couden
    Richard 79
    Robert 15, 43, 44, 77
Coudry
    John 35
Coulbourn
    Elijah 70, 85
Coun
    James 13
Counce
    Henry 34
Countis
    Peter 46
Countiss
    James 17, 46
    Peter 46
    Sarah 46
Coursey
    William 45
Court
    Robert Hendley 33
Courtenay
    H. 37
Cowarden
    William 40, 57
Cowden
    Robert 90
Cowman
    Joseph 6
Cowt
    Onchil 95
Cox
    Ann 7, 94
    Elisabeth 30
    Isaac 96
    James 59, 84
    John 7, 8, 29, 49, 91,
        93, 94, 106
    John Davis 91
    Martha 52, 91
    Nathaniel 29
    Priscilla 18
    Rachel 18

Samuel 33, 52
Sarah 7, 8
Walter B. 7
Cozden
    Alphonso 73
Crabb
    Jeremiah 29
Crabbin
    Martha 71
    William 71
Craddock
    John 27
    Thomas 27
Craig
    Andrew 52
    John 19, 55, 60, 90
Craigh
    John 8, 13
Craik
    James 3, 8, 34, 90
Crane
    Martha 48
Cranford
    John 100
Cranner
    Moses 25
Crapper
    Levin 33, 57, 93
    Mathew 88
    Molton 92
    Noble 93
Crauford
    David 98, 105
Craw
    John 62
Crawford
    David 31
    John 5, 10, 18, 40, 71
Crawley
    Richard 75
Craycroft
    Jane 74
Creager
    Valentine 55
Creagh
    John 98
Creaton
    Thomas 16, 17, 32, 65,
        66, 87
Crew
    Andrew 77
    Mary 22
    Thomas 83
    William 17
Crexall
    R. 34
Crickmore
    Elisabeth 78
    Francis 78
Crider
    Barbara 29
    John 29
Crock
    Joseph 7
Crockett
    Elisabeth 26
    Gilbert 79, 80
    John 26
    Richard 26, 35
    Samuel 80
    William 26
    Wurder 26
Crompton
    Ann 30
Cromwell
    Comfort 44
    Elisabeth 87
    John 29, 44
    Joshua 44
    Nathan 84
    Oneal 44
    Sarah 52

Cronell
  Henry 102
Crook
  Joseph 98
Crookshanks
  Charles 2, 29, 64, 65,
    94, 107
  John 96
Croome
  Thomas 40
Crosby
  Joseph 30
  Mary 30
  Richard 30
Crouch
  Mary 105
  Thomas 104, 105
  William 104
Crow
  Thomas 57
Croxall
  Charles 95
Cruchboom
  Adam 102
  Mary 102
Cruckshank
  R. 74
Cruisanks
  Edward 56
Cudge
  Elisabeth 52
Culbreth
  John 47
Cullen
  Edward 51
  Elisabeth 42
  John 42
  Mary 51
Cullin
  David 42
  John 42
Cullingham
  Elisha 89
Culpepper
  John 20
  Michael 20
Cummings
  Agnes 20
Cunningham
  Daniel 106
  George 16, 76
  Sarah 16, 76
Currer
  William 44, 73, 96
Curtis
  Daniel 37
Cutler
  Jacob 52
  Rachel 35

Daher
  Morrilis 24
Dailey
  Cornelius 2
Dale
  Christopher 24
  James 89
  John 13, 22, 25, 36, 89,
    92
  Josiah 36, 92
Dallam
  Richard 24
Dames
  John 104
Daney
  Martha 36
Darby
  Curtis 15
  Custis 81
  John 68, 87, 97, 99,
    100, 109

Dare
  Nathaniel 30
  Samuel 15, 20, 30
  Thomas Cleverly 43
  William 30, 43, 108
Darnal
  Henry 91
Darnall
  Bennett 29
  Henry 6, 52, 54
  Thomas 86
Darnell
  Henry 79
Darrack
  Charlotte 16, 77, 83
  James 16
  John 16, 77, 83
  Thomas 16, 77, 83
Darrah
  John 73
Darrumple
  Elisabeth 15
Darsy
  Samuel C. 96
Dashiel
  Ann 61
  Levin 62
Dashiell
  ----- 51, 52
  Ann 50
  Anna 51
  Arthur 51, 70, 91
  Charles 109
  G. 32
  George 31, 40, 41, 51,
    86
  Jane 70
  Jesse 51
  Joseph 22, 52, 91, 92
  Levin 70
  Louther 51
  Matthais 50
  Richard 50
  Robert 40
  Thomas 70
  W. 86
Dashun
  Joseph 106
Daughaday
  John 55, 56
Daugharty
  John 32
Daughterte
  Mary 58
David
  John 89
Davidford
  James 59
Davidge
  John 78
Davidson
  James 69, 91
  John 6, 15
  Samuel 67, 87, 109
Davis
  Aaron 38
  Ann 38, 89
  Beauchamp 9
  Daniel 88
  Edward 89
  Enoch 95
  Esther 17
  Fulda 95
  James 22, 39, 40
  John 21, 29, 43, 78, 89,
    92
  John Briscoe 80
  Lawson 80
  Mary 80
  Philip 72
  Rachel Wood 80
  Richard 34

  Robert 15, 89
  Robert Pain 15
  Samuel 22, 26, 83, 88
  Sarah 15, 104
  Thomas 19, 89
  William 75, 89
  Zaccheus 3
Davison
  James 106
Daviss
  Catharine 6
  Samuel 6
Dawcey
  John 105
Dawel
  Thomas 53
Daws
  Benjamin 40
  Margaret 40
Dawson
  Ailce 29
  Ann 54
  Anthony 68
  Danes 54
  Elisabeth 101
  John 54, 68, 101
  Mary 41, 101
  Obediah 68
  Richard 33, 101
  Sarah 33
  Thomas 33, 41, 54, 65,
    107
  William 29, 101
Day
  Edward 7, 19, 36
  Francis 67
  John 7, 36
Dayson
  Philip 88
Deakin
  William 103
Deakins
  William 30, 45, 63
Deal
  Christian 55
  Elias 9
  Richard 20
  Sarah 20
Deale
  Jacob 20
  Thomas 6, 44, 79
Dealins
  William 54
Deall
  James 52
  John 20
Dean
  Edward 86
  John 40, 59, 69
  Rachel 81
  William 86
Debrular
  Micajah 37
  William 37, 38
Debruler
  Benjamin 97
  William 7
Debrunler
  William 83
Decker
  Frederick 24
Deford
  Thomas 96
Dehorty
  John 11, 82, 87
  Vincent 100
Delahay
  Sarah 2
Delehay
  James 91
  Prichard 11
  Pritchett 91

Richard 91
Dell
  Frederick 91
Denness
  Lyded 64
Denning
  Issebella 58
  John 58
Denny
  Benjamin 27, 99
  J. 94
  James 99
  John 29, 41, 107
  Mary 99
  P. 94
  Peter 10, 64
  Richard 2
  T. 99
Denson
  Isaac 92
  Philip 92
  Sarah 92
  Saul 92
Dent
  Hatch 53
  John 105
  Michael 105
  Peter 3, 53, 86, 98
  Thomas 30, 31, 54
  Warren 62
Deny
  Peter 64
Derickson
  Levin 92
Derochburne
  Joseph 45
  Lewis 45
  Margaret 45
Derrick
  Edward 28
  John 28
Devanns
  James 59
  Mice 59
  Michael 59
Dick
  J. 24
  James 6, 78
  Robert 59
Dickenson
  Esther 48
  John 68
Dickerson
  Daniel 99
  Isaac 62
  James 62
  Joshua 62
  Lewis 49
  Sarah 62
Dickeson
  Isaac 49
  James 49
  Joshua 49
  Levi 49
Dickinson
  Charles 10, 66, 67
  Henry 1, 66, 100
  James 102
  John 32
  Lydia 2
  Samuel 40, 64, 99, 107
  William 10
Digges
  Ignatius 63, 97, 98
Dikes
  Arthur 88
  Daniel 88
  Stephen 88
Diks
  Naomi 107
Dill
  Solomon 28

Dintson
  John 53
Dirickson
  Joseph 92
  Levin 36, 91
Dirk
  Robert 5, 54
Dirrikson
  Levin 49
Disharoon
  Francis 40, 70
  George 40
  Obediah 40, 51
  Thomas 40
Disheroon
  Constant 91
  Frances 91
  John 91
  Joseph 91
Divers
  Ananias 19
  Christopher 19
  Frances 19
  Mary 19
Dixe
  Daniel 61
Dixon
  David 6, 49
  Robert 100
Dobbe
  Peter 49
Dobie
  Ann 55
Dobson
  Isaac 2
  James 2
  John 2
  Jonathon 94
Dodson
  Henrietta 34
  Jacob 34
  John 34
  Thomas 41
  Walter 34
Doherty
  Barnaby 10
  John 10
Dolbee
  Peter 27
Dolbie
  Jonathon 49
  Peter 93, 97
Dolvin
  Daniel 108
  James 59
  Margaret 59
  Richard 59
  Sarah 108
Domagan
  William 28
Donaldson
  John 16
Donally
  Catharine 98
  John 98
Donnock
  William 81
Dorman
  Isaiah 109
Dorsett
  W. 70
  William 70
Dorsey
  Ann 79
  Greenberry 80, 95
  Greenbury 24, 36, 56
  John 21, 79
  Joseph 6
  Joshua 79
  Nicholas 79
  Samuel 90
  Sarah 79

Thomas 79
Dossey
  Levin 1
  Philip 30
Dots
  Barton 59
Dotts
  Baston 54
Dougerty
  Barnaby 41
Dougherty
  Barnaby 41, 64
  Edward 73, 96
  John 41, 52, 58, 64, 91
  Samuel 60, 61
Douglass
  Benjamin 28
  William 1, 33
Dowell
  John 30
  Mary 30
  Phillip 30
  Susannah 30
Downes
  Ann 10
  C. 5
  Charles 46, 106
  Elbert 47
  Henry 26, 70
  Hester 47
  Jacob 15
  John 5, 106
  Littleton 35
  Mary 3, 23
  Phil. 5, 26
  Philemon 12
  Philip 45, 46, 48
  Rachel 57
  Rebeca 64
  Sophia 106
  Vachel 12, 47, 96, 106
Downey
  John 59
  Tabitha 59
  Thomas 59
Downs
  Vachel 59
Dowson
  Robert 16
Doxey
  James 38
  William 38
Doy
  Joshua 86
Doyl
  John 88
  Jonathon 88
  Richard 88
Doyle
  Elisabeth 88
  John 88
Drane
  Cansande 29
  James 31
  Susannah 29
  Thomas 29
Dreaden
  Samuel 89, 107
Drummond
  John 106
  Leah 106
  Mary 106
Dubberly
  Ezekiel 35, 91
  Jemima 35, 91
Duberly
  John 35
Dubsby
  Esther 49
Duckett
  Thomas 43
Dudbly

Lyddia 107
Dudley
    Abner 45, 46, 47, 59
    Elisabeth 102
    George 2, 18, 23, 29,
       41, 64, 94
    Mary 64
Dudly
    George 107
    Sarah 107
Dueley
    Elisabeth 108
    Nathan 108
Duer
    Joshua 36
Duffee
    Mary 14
Duke
    Benjamin 105
    Moses Parran 105
Dukes
    Parker 88
Duling
    Elijah 108
    Francis 108
Duncan
    John 15, 92, 97
    Thomas 92
Dundass
    James 44
Dunlop
    William 81
Dunn
    Frances 72, 74
    Hezekiah 8, 9
    James 14, 27, 58, 67,
      71, 72, 73, 74, 105
    Richard 52
    Thomas 52
Durbin
    Mary 34, 35
    Samuel 34
    Thomas 34
    William 34, 35
Durham
    Mordecai 7
Dutton
    Notly 27
Duvall
    Samuel 6
Duyer
    John 9, 58
Dwiggens
    Nancy 4
Dwiggins
    John 10
Dyer
    Edward 47, 59
    John 57
    Nathaniel 47
    Sarah 47
Dylaney
    James Bracco 94
Dymock
    Edward 22, 49, 50, 92
Dymoke
    Edward 88
Dyson
    Bennett 62
    Gerard 62
Dyus
    John 63

Eagles
    Elisabeth 46
    Mary 46
    Mary Dyre 46
Eaglestone
    A. 88
Ealey
    Elisabeth 10

Eareckson
    Ann 18
    Charles 46
    Elisabeth 46
    Johnson 15
    William 46
Earle
    ------ 77
    John 58
    Mary 58
    Robert J. 59
Eason
    Abraham 12
Eaton
    Anderton 1, 67
    Richard 2
Eberle
    John 15
Eccleston
    Charles 66, 81, 87, 100,
      108
    Hugh 87, 90, 100, 101,
      109
    James 66, 68
    John 14, 16, 67, 74, 77,
      83, 105
    Joseph 66
    Thomas F. 109
    Thomas Firmin 1, 67
    William 66, 68, 81
Edelen
    Edward 55, 106
    Josaph 55
Edelin
    Christopher 34, 63
    Edward 19, 33, 34
Edelon
    Edward 90
Edelsen
    Edward 105
Eden
    James 81
Edgar
    Henry 100
Edgell
    Abraham 33
    Elisabeth 33
    James 33
    John 33
Edger
    James 99
Edmondson
    James 99
    Peter 1, 18, 33, 65, 66
    Pollard 64, 94
    Rachel 64
    Sophya 94
    William 1
Edwards
    James 71, 84
    Richard Swan 96
    William 71
Eichelberger
    Frederick 19
    Martin 19
Elbeart
    Lodm. 107
Elbert
    H. 17
    Henry 64
    Lodman 3, 64
    Macklin 3
    Mary 3
Elborn
    William 14
Elderig
    Rachel 82
Eliason
    Abraham 84
    Andrew 76
    Cornelius 76, 84
    Elias 76, 84

John 19, 20, 76
Mary 76
Ellegood
    John 26, 27, 49
Ellen
    Joseph 103
Ellet
    James 7
    William 100
Elliott
    George 98
    Henry 4
    John 46, 59
    Joseph 98
    Margaret 98
    Richard 6
    Sarah 98
    Thomas 11, 64
Ellis
    Joseph 32
    Josiah 32
    Levin 32
    Stephen 32
Elliss
    Josiah 32
Ellsbury
    Frederick 19, 20
    Rebecca 19, 20
Elston
    William 41
Elzey
    Elisabeth 51
    John 51, 85
    Robert 51, 61
Emerson
    Elisabeth 64
Emory
    Ann 69
    Arthur 15, 45, 47, 48,
      59, 103
    Charles 69
    Gideon 10, 47, 96
    James 69
    John 96
    John R. 59, 98
    Sarah 96
    Sophia 96
    Thomas 96
    William 96
Englis
    James 51
English
    James 48, 85
Ennalls
    B. 33, 101
    Elisabeth 33
    H. 100
    Henrietta 25
    Henry 25, 100, 108, 109
    Joseph 99, 100, 108
    Margaret 87
    Mary 25
    Thomas 25, 32, 67, 81,
      90, 99, 100, 108, 109
    William 33, 65, 109
Ennis
    Henny 80
    Jesse 88, 89
    Joseph 89, 91
    Leah 88
    Luke 88
    Mary 80
    Nathaniel 88, 89, 92
    Samuel 89, 92
    William 80
Enson
    Abraham 87
    Elisabeth 87
    John 87
Ensor
    Darby 12
    Elisabeth 12

George 12
John 12, 19
Joseph 12
Ensot
Joseph 20
Eokin
James 20
Esenberg
Gabriel 95
Etherington
Buthew 13
Eubanks
George 2
John 2
Rebeca 2
Rebecca 2
Evans
Ann 27, 59
David 92, 93, 101
Evans 92
Isaac 26, 35, 36
James 94
John 31, 59
Mary 94, 102
Philip 59
Walter 30
William 10, 94
Evelin
Richard 54
Everett
Joseph 46
St. Leger 67
Evertt
St. Leger 9
Ewing
Patrick 61
Thomas 71
Eych
Johannes 95

Fairbank
David 41
Fairbrother
Elisabeth 64
Francis 79
Mary 64
Richard 64
Falconar
Gilbert 40
Falconer
Hannah 2
John 2
Falkner
Hannah 96
Fallin
Shadrack 88, 93
Faly
Shadrack 89
Fares
Mary 76
Farguson
James 10, 11
Rosannah 10, 11
Farlone
William 104
Farlow
William 89
Farquhar
Allen 102
Thomas 95
Thomas Allen 95
William 95
Farrel
Daniel 9
Farrell
Daniel 73
Fassett
David 26
Fassitt
John 50
Mary 50, 92

William 15, 22, 50
Faulkner
Asa 1
John 2
Jonathon 2
Nathan 1
Salathiel 1
Thomas 1
Fead
William 95
Featherston
Esther 69
William 69
Feddeman
Bartholomew 26
Phillip 45
Feddey
Henry 82
Fedey
Debro 82
Fenia
Andrew 10
Fenwick
Benjamin 4
Bennett 38, 39
E. 4
Enoch 4, 38, 54
George 4, 104
Ignatius 4
James 4
Jane 104
Richard 38, 39
Robert 4
Ferguson
Andrew 26
Elisabeth 26
John 35, 45, 98
Joseph 26
Robert 30, 98
Ferriss
Nathan 25
Ferry
Joseph Ennalls 99
Field
James 72
Joseph 72
Fields
Christopher 40
James 40
Joseph 40
Filbeg
Elisabeth 89
Findal
Phil. 23
Findlay
Robert 103
Findley
John 16
Finney
Catron 20
Daniel 20, 85
Eleanor 85
Elisabeth 20
John 20
Fisher
Abraham 78
Henry 96
Jabez 93, 101
John 4, 11, 12, 25, 44,
    46, 47, 59, 69, 96
William 70, 75, 78
Fitch
Henry 84
Fitzgerald
James 62
Flanagan
Bartholomew 62
Timothy 62
Flannagin
Timothy 62
Fleet
James 96

Lyttleton 96
Rebecca 96
Fleharty
Stephen 25
Fleming
Elisabeth 57
John 35, 88, 91, 93, 101
Sarah 52
William 16, 32, 48, 86
Flemming
William 61
Fletcher
George 75
Levin 85
Flint
Betty 22
David 8
Nancy 22
Sarah 22
Thomas 22
Flowers
Charles 91
John 91
Lambert 91
Rebecca 91
Floyad
Milka 44
Fookes
Daniel 104
Fooks
Daniel 92
Jesse 92
John 92
Thomas 92
William 92
Forbes
James 90
Ford
Allanson 3
Ann 98
Athanasius 4
Charles Allison 3, 62
Constrany 3
Edward 3
Elisabeth 3, 62
George 84
John 54, 84, 85, 98
Mary 17, 84
Nathaniel 54
Richard 3, 84
Richard Boulden 84
Sarah 59
Thomas 46
Zadock 95
Foreman
Hezekiah 21, 29, 43
Hezekius 44
Joseph 43
Mary 43
Rachel 43
Forey
Rachel 3
Forman
Hannah 22
Robert 50
Forrest
Thomas 4
Zachariah 4
Forry
Jacob 3
Forster
Rebekah 107
Foster
Ralph 105
William 20, 106, 107
Fountain
Major 66, 68
Marcy 11, 87
Mary 82
Mary Ann 81
Nicholas 12, 81
Nicolas 101

William 66, 68
Fourney
 David 44
Fowke
 Gerard 62
Fowler
 Arthur 92
 Jesse 92, 93
 Mary 92
Frames
 John 19, 87
 Mary 87
Frampton
 Ann 65
Franklin
 Eleanor 26
 Henry 26
 Jacob 6, 52
 John 52
 Thomas 83
Fraser
 William 80
Frasier
 Elisabeth 4
 William 4
Frazier
 Ann 9
 Hugh 79
 James 79
 John 9
 Ruth 79
 William 3
Freeland
 Frisby 53
Freeman
 Abraham 57, 58
 Ann 67
 Avarilla 58
 Dennis 56
 Isaac 58, 67, 73, 74
 Mary 58, 67
 Moses 36
 Thomas 7, 15
 William 67
French
 Ignatius 4, 38
 James 4, 6, 38
 John 4, 38
 Martin 38
 Philip 67
 William Hynson 40, 71
Friency
 John 91
Frisby
 A. 83
 Peregrine 14, 67
 Richard 16, 58, 71
 William 21, 25
Fuller
 Henry 78
 Sarah 78
Fulton
 Alexander 61
 Ann 60, 61
 Francis 60, 61
 Samuel 61
 William 77
Furness
 William 51
Furnie
 David 44
Furniss
 William 16, 86
Furroner
 Edward 20
 Elisabeth 20
Furry
 Jacob 62
 Rachel 62
Fury
 Jacob 62
Fyfe

James 55

Gachen
 William N. 90
Gafford
 Joseph 4
 Richard 4
 Sarah 4
Gaither
 Benjamin 6
 Edward 7, 22, 70
 Ephraim 15
Gale
 Henry 52, 70
 Mathais 94
 Matthais 2, 18, 29, 42,
  63, 64, 65, 67, 81,
  93, 94, 102, 107, 108
 Phebe 58
 Rassin 58
Gallion
 Jacob 95
 James 95
 Nathan 95
 William 95
Galloway
 Moses 37, 55
Galt
 James 24
Galwith
 Elisabeth 21
 John 21
 Jonas 21
 Sarah 21
Gambell
 Gideon 66
Gambrill
 A. 52
 Benjamin 44
 W. 43
 William 44
Gance
 John 34
Gant
 Edward 20
 George 108
Gantt
 Edward 76, 97
Gaose
 James 94
Gardiner
 Henry 62
 William 62
Gardner
 Edward 90
 Hugh 28
 John 56, 90
 Kinsly 56
 Philip 90
 Robert 56
Garey
 John 29
 Mary Ann 29, 64
 William 29
Garland
 Henry 55
 James 9
 John 9
 Rebecca 9
Garnbull
 Augustine 21
Garnder
 Hugh 19
Garner
 Alice 11
 Charles 62
 Hezekiah 90
 James 11
 Jean 90
 John 62
 Joseph 11, 62

Parrish 11
Garnet
 George 42, 48
Garnett
 C. 12
Garret
 Amos 29
Garrett
 Amos 24, 37, 75
Garrettson
 Edward 56
 Sarah 56
Garyble
 Phillip 19
Gash
 Thomas 26
Gassaway
 Henry 78
 Mary 78
 Michael 7
 Thomas 7, 15, 70, 78
Gates
 Theophilus 86
Gatrall
 John 43
Gatton
 Azariah 60
 Benjamin 55
Gaulsbery
 William 38
Gault
 Anjaletta 92
 Ann 36
 David 92
 John Turvill 92
 Obediah 36
 William 36, 92
George
 Mathew 99
 Nicholas 61, 85
Germant
 Robert M. 96
Ghow
 John 66
Gibb
 Andrew 25
 Isabel 25
Gibbins
 George 27, 93
 John 4, 50, 91
Gibbons
 John 49
Gibson
 Ann 85
 Elisabeth 85
 Frances 63
 Jacob 85
 James 63, 108
 John 2, 53
 Jonathon 63
 William 2
Giels
 William 51
Giflin
 James 109
Gilbert
 Charles 71, 75
 John Henry 84
 Thomas 75
Gilchrist
 Robert 15, 21
 William 15
Giles
 Eunice 85
 Isaac 85
 Jacob 85
 William 70, 85
Gill
 Stephen 80
Gillen
 James 55
Gillett

Agnes 23
Jarman 23
Gillispie
Samuel 61
Gilliss
Ezekiel 62
George 15, 16, 31, 32, 109
Levin 32, 50
Mary 32
Sarah 32, 50
Gilmer
Robert 87
Gilmor
Robert 18, 66, 67
Gilpin
Joseph 60, 105
Samuel 20, 60, 103
Ginners
Elisabeth 52
Gist
Mordecai 12, 37
Gladden
Howell 28
Glanvil
Rachel 83
Glasgow
James 13, 14, 19, 76
Glass
Gartruge 4
John 4
Margaret 4
Rebecca 4
Glassford
Elisabeth 57
Gleave
George 90, 103
Glenn
Jacob 105
James 71
Godfrey
Ann 91
Joseph 49
Godwin
Joseph 33, 82
Goldsborough
Charles 5, 10, 17, 45, 59, 96
J. 102
John 69
Nicholas 63, 64, 107
Robert 41, 42, 64
Goldsmith
Ann 80
John 80
Lilly 13
Thomas 13
William Copeland 13
Golott
George 94
Good
Jacob 34
William 15
Gooden
Robert 93
Goodhand
Mary Ann 47
Goodman
Marmaduke 11
Richard 11
Goodwin
William 21
Goote
George 19
Gootee
Andrew 99
Gordon
James 1, 100
John 23, 63
Goslen
Ambros 81
Goslin

Ambros 87
Gott
Ann 91
Ezekiel 91
John 91
Walter 91
Gough
H. D. 19
John 84
Prudence 19
Gould
B. 4, 12, 17, 59, 96
Benjamin 17, 44, 45, 46, 69
Maremy 72
Richard 4
William Thomas 77
Govane
William 90
Gover
Elisabeth 27
Ephraim 27
Jane 54
Gow
William 66
Gowe
Mary 66
Grace
William 41
Grach
Conrad 95
Graham
Andrew 59, 72, 98
Charles 20, 105
Ezekiel 16
James 72
John 22, 48
Mary 16
Philip 51
Rebecca 72
Richard 14, 22
William 11
Grahame
Charles 8, 30, 43, 76, 97
Christopher 24
Grainger
John 82
Grandee
Mary Roberts 70
Rensher Roberts 70
Granlee
James 68
Grason
Richard 29
Graves
Elinor 81
John 81, 104
Joshua 4, 38
Gray
Benjamin 3, 102
Bridget 49
Dannas 92
Elisabeth 102
Elisha 49
George 3
Isaiah 100
James 3, 49
Jeremiah 3
Jesse 102
John 3, 23, 39, 52, 78, 92
John Nelson 43
Joseph 102
Joshua 52, 78
Nicholas 92
Samuel 14, 21, 30, 44, 53, 56
Sophiah 3
Thomas 81
William 51, 81, 92
Grear

William 76
Green
Abraham 88
Benedict 8, 55
Edmund 100
Elijah 7, 78
Elisabeth 1, 8
Emelia 66
Francis 8
Henne 19
Hester 106
Jacob 103
James 100
John 14, 19, 106
Leonard 62
Mary 103
Michael 19
Moses 88
Philemon 26, 106
Phillemon 59
Ralph 87, 109
Richard 52, 78
Samuel 8
Sarah 19
Solomon 88
William 1
Greene
Job 13
Greenfield
James 36
John 101
Mary 36, 77, 101
Micajah 36
Truman 80
Greenlee
Robert 77
Samuel 77, 82
William 77, 82
Greenwell
Archibald 104
Elisabeth 104
John Baptist 104
Susannah 104
Greenwood
George 9
Gideon 9
John 67
Greer
David 51
Jane 51
William 51
Gregory
John 108
Greig
Margaret 92
Griest
Isaac 75, 76
Griffith
Arsennah 73
B. 21
Benjamin 43, 84
Charles 52
Comfort 78
Coter 40
Elisabeth 11, 69
Henry 95
John 46, 52, 78, 82, 93
Joshua 21
Lake 105
Luke 58, 71, 73, 77
Mary 19, 69
Matthew 46
Nathan 12, 19, 87
Nathaniel 12
Rachel 43
Robert 82
Ruth 46
Samuel 24, 32, 56, 80, 82, 83, 95
Thomas 11
William 46, 52
William Eliot 46

Grimes
  Ann 16
  Elisabeth 82
  Henry 16
  Mary 56
  Peter 82
Groome
  Charles 9, 22, 57, 58,
    67, 71, 73, 77, 105
Grosh
  Conrad 55
  Conrod 54
Ground
  Samuel 71
Guishard
  Mark 75
  Sarah 75
Gun
  Levin 62
Gunby
  John 70
Gurts
  Charles 88
Guyther
  George 6
  Grace 54
  William 6
Guyton
  Benjamin 7
  Underwood 55
Gwin
  James 69
Gwinn
  Hannah 69
  Susannah 27
Gwynn
  Joseph 90

Hackett
  James 4, 5, 47, 69
  Thomas 98
  William 47
Haddaway
  Elisabeth 107
  George 94, 107
  Susannah 94
  Thomas 94
  William 107
Hadder
  Ann 91
  Elisabeth 26
  John 26
  Warran 26
  Warren 26
Hagan
  Henry 13
  John 13
  Joseph 13
  William 13
Hage
  John 43
Haill
  Nicholas 12
Hale
  William Jordain 49
Haley
  Charles 83
  William 10
Hall
  Adam 10
  Aquila 24, 37
  Christopher 9, 39, 72,
    73, 83
  Edward 15, 20, 30
  Elisabeth 9
  Francis 5
  Isaac 6, 29, 52, 79, 91
  John 6, 9, 15, 45, 64
  Joseph 6
  Joseph Corole 29
  Joshua 50, 93

Leonard 55
Margaret 94
Martha 9
Robert 47
Thomas Henry 7
William 93
William Ford 92
Halley
  Elisabeth 93
  John 93
  Samuel 93
Hambleton
  Margret 10
  Nancy 42
  Patrick 89
  William 81, 89, 104
Hamenley
  William 3
Hamersley
  Basil 8
  Francis 8
  Henrietta 8
  William 8, 80, 81
Hamilton
  A. 24
  Alexander 62
  Charles 96
  James 89, 90
  James H. 96
  Jane 96
  John 96
  Kerenhappuk 84
  Patrick 90
  Pattrick 90
  Samuel 90
  Thomas 7, 31
  William 104
Hamlin
  William 83
Hammett
  McKlore 80
  Robert 94, 102
Hammitt
  William 80
Hammond
  Cocker 105
  Corker 22
  Edward 49, 88
  Hannah 22, 105
  John 5, 49, 59, 69, 105
  Leah 49
  Mordecai 19
  N. 29, 52
  Na. 21, 22, 78, 79
  Nathaniel 79
  Philip 6, 22, 43, 44
  Sarah 105
  Thomas 52
  William 49, 87
Hamon
  Ann 22
Hance
  Benjamin 30
  Betty 53
  Christopher 30
  James 30
Hancock
  Mary 64
Handcock
  Ann 106
  John 49
  Mary Ann 106
  Thomas 106
  William 106
Handly
  Sarah 20
Hands
  Thomas Bedingfield 14
  Thomas Bendly 58
Handy
  Ann 40
  Betty 51

Esther 61
George 26, 32, 40, 51,
    61, 70
Isaac 40, 61
Isaak 61
Joseph 40
Robert 53
Samuel 16, 26, 35, 50,
    88, 89, 101, 106
Thomas 51
William 51, 61
Hanest
  Hannah 54
Hankey
  John 61, 104
Hannarloud
  Susey 96
Hansbury
  Joseph 79
Hanson
  Benjamin 95
  Contee 55
  Frederick 22, 82
  Gustavius 22
  J. C. 72, 74
  John 8, 19, 34, 90
  Mary 22
  Robert 11
  S. 13
  Samuel 13
  Theodore 53
  Theophilus 28
  William 2
Harbert
  Charles 16
Harbin
  James 95
Hard
  Jesse M. 43
  Mary M. 48
Hardcastle
  Robert 103
  Thomas 103
Harden
  Alice 72
  Reuben 72
Hardey
  Anthony 31
  George 31
  Henry 31
Hardie
  Levin 15
Hardin
  Ealce 77
  Rhubin 77
Harding
  Alice 72
  Charles 34
  Elias 34
  Rebecca 72
  Reuben 72
Hardshorn
  Jonathon 76
Hardy
  George 30, 31
  Henry 31
Hargadine
  Jamme 45
Hargerader
  Conrad 102
  John 102
  Mary 102
Harmersley
  Henrietta 55
Harnen
  Adam 95
Harney
  Thomas 22
Harper
  Catharine 36
  David 108
  Edward 36

Elisabeth 84
John 36, 108
Joseph 81
Margaret 109
Martha 84
Priscila 81
Rachel 81
William 67, 101, 109
Harrington
Abel 55
Anthony 4, 11, 46, 47,
    69, 96
Elisabeth 82
Henry 47
Nathan 47, 55
Temperance 55
William 47, 55
Harris
Benjamin 47
Benton 26, 35
Betty 35
Charles 47
Edward 26, 75
Elisabeth 12, 99
Henry 99
James 28
Jane 109
John 70
Rebecca 28
T. 3, 8, 53, 60, 62
Thomas 12, 28, 75
William 12, 43, 47, 99
Harrison
Amy 109
Anthony 59
Benjamin 25
Henry 53
James 109
Jane 109
John 2
Jonathon 109
Joseph 107
Kenelm 4
Mary 80
Nicholas 109
Perry 109
Rachel 42
Robert 25
Samuel 53
T. 3
Thomas 29, 63, 90, 94,
    99, 102, 103
William 2, 107
Harriss
Edward 75
Nathan 5
Nathaniel 5
Thomas 5
Zachariah 5
Hart
Ann 61, 85
Anna 85
Augustin 45
Henrietta 45
James 45, 61, 85
John 12
Mary 38
Naboth 11, 99, 100
Patrick 45
Robert 61, 85, 104
Hartley
Thomas 19
Hartshorn
Jonathon 13, 14, 44
Harvin
Thomas 86
Harwood
Elisabeth 98
Mary 10, 17
Peter 10, 17
Robert 2
Thomas 6, 15, 21, 43,

44, 52, 56, 78
Haskins
William 25, 33
Haslett
Moses 44
Hasselback
Catharine 24
Nicholas 24
Hastings
Isaac 97
Oliver 97
Sarah 97
Hatchem
John 71
Hates
Roger 58
Hatfield
Elijah 1
Elisabeth 1
John 1
Jonathon 1
Marget 106
William 1
Hath
William 51, 91
Hatton
Catharine 38
Chaney 98
John 99
Thomas 38
Unity 98
Haw
Christopher 33, 106
Sarah 106
Sarah Price 33
Hawes
Mary 70
Hawkings
J. 93
Hawkins
Henry Smith 33
John 72, 90
Haycraft
William 44
Hayden
Bazil 4
Clement 4
Haye
Meriam 6
Hayes
James 76
John 6, 76
Jonathon 99
Sarah 76
Hayman
Ann 50
Charles 50
David 48
James 48
John 48
John Harris 48
Margaret 48
Racel 89
Haynes
Abraham 58
Haynie
James 52
Judith 52
Samuel 52
Hays
John 76
Jonathon 34
Hayter
Abraham 24, 34
Hayward
Adday 67
Betty 18
Francis 18, 99, 108
John 49, 67
Mary 18
Sarah 18, 68
Thomas 18, 50, 67, 68

William 2, 64
Haywood
George 35
William 99
Hazel
William 9, 73, 77
Head
Cuthbert 102
Ignatius 102
Hearsey
Solomon 84
Heath
Charles 61
Daniel Charles 73
William 69
Heather
Isaac 27
Rachel 27
Richard 46
Heathers
Richard 59, 98
Hebner
Michael 29
Hedler
John 95
Hedon
John 87
Hegen
Jonathon 95
Heine
Benjamin 82
Helly
James 56
Helsby
John 65
Mary 65
Vincent 65
Hembrey
John 82, 83
Hemmons
Elisabeth 36
John 36
Hencock
Thomas 106
Henderson
Charles 91
Elisabeth 52
Ephraim 88
Mary 91
Richard 63, 95
Robert 34
Samuel 28
Thomas Frisby 57, 61, 85
Hendrickson
Augustine 13
Henry 13
John 13, 24
Henry
John 56, 66, 87, 109
Mary 56
William 67, 71, 72
Hepburn
John 105
Samuel Chew 105
Hernson
Priscilla 53
Hertnegel
George 95
Hetherington
Bat. 20
Heugh
Andrew 5, 6, 35, 43
Hewitt
John 79
Morgan 21
Thomas 43
William 79
Hey
C. T. 90
Heyes
Jonathon 34
Hickel

Hubanks
Wilam 100
Hubbard
Leving 87
Nehemiah 87
Hubbart
Elisabeth 100
Hubbert
Peter 32, 49
Huckens
Benedick 64
Hudson
Ananias 101
Annanias 22
David 49
Esther 49
John 63
Lot 49
Samuel 88
Sarah 63
Huett
Morgan 83
Huff
Sarah 24, 74
Huffington
Gilbert 109
John 109
Joshua 48, 109
Huffinton
Joshua 48
Huggins
Thomas 57, 104
Hughes
Hannah 12
Israel 83
James 103
Hughs
John 34
Levi 34
Sophia 37
Thomas 46
Hughson
Sarah 63
Hughston
William 83
Hull
James 9
Hulse
Randall 7
Humfrey
Henry 6
Humphrey
Frances 54
Henry 90
Martha 54
Humphreys
Francis 41
Martha 41
Humphries
Joseph 51
Joshua 31
Hun
Samuel 15
Hungerford
Jane 27
Thomas 23, 62
Hunt
George 2, 41
James 52
Mary 2
Hunter
Ezekiel 47
Samuel 46
Hurley
Daniel 54
John 81
Mark 81
Hurlock
Jonathon 81, 82
Mary 69
Hurly
Constantine 81

Darby 15
Elijah 81
John 15
Mary 15
Matthew 19
Roger 19
Hurrd
Kole 89
Husband
William 7
Hust
John 93
Josiah 93
William 93
Hutcheson
John 83
Nathan 21, 67, 73
Nathaniel 83
Rachel 83
Hutchings
Benedict 42
Grace 6
James 11
Thomas Elliott 47, 48
William 6
Hutchins
Benedict 23
Hutchison
Joseph 67
Hutten
Aquilla 7
Catharine 7
Choney 7
Sarah 67
Thomas 7
Hutton
George 66
Mary 66
William 66
Hyde
Thomas 43, 44, 56, 78,
79
Hyland
Isaac 84
Lambert 51
Nicholas 84
Samuel 85
Hynson
Charles 9, 14, 25
J. C. 27
Mary 71
Richard 27, 58, 74
Thoams 58
Hyple
Christian 34

Ijams
George 44
William 44
Ingersoll
Samuel 92
Ingram
Job 35
John 29
Inloes
Abraham 37
Inneurs
Samuel 25
Inote
George 87
Ireland
Alletha 98
Althea 105
John 4, 30, 98
Joseph 16, 30, 105
William 53
Ironshire
Joseph 22, 25, 26, 36,
93
Irving
John 85

Joseph 86
Thomas 40, 86
Irwin
William 79

Jackson
Alexander 60
Benjamin 83
Caleb 9
Henry 24, 85
Julius Aug. 18
Mary 83
Mary Ann 69
Samuel 47
Thomas 24, 75
Jacob
Jesse 21
Jacobs
Abraham 36
Curtis 33
Eliphalet 91
John 33
Jonathon 36
Joseph 78
Kendall 33
Richards 78
Sarah 33
William 33
Jacobson
Richard 78
Jacques
Denton 44
Lancelot 44, 78
James
Jarvis 9, 25
Jervis 25
John 21
Sarah 25
Thomas 62
Jameson
James 19
John 19
Janney
Enoch 28
Isaac 28
Thomas 28
Janvier
Jeme 16
Jarden
John 97
Jarrett
Abraham 98
Jarvis
Ann 109
Elisabeth 109
William 109
Jasterett
C. 84
Jay
Joshua 60
Jefferson
Richard 93
Jemmison
James 8, 13
John 8, 13
Jenbil
Crist---orbor 56
Jenifer
Daniel 4
Elisabeth 38
John Read 38
Michael 38
Michael Parker 4
Samuel 38, 104
Jenkins
Ann 64
George 28
Henry 2
Jane 8
John 8
Lurana 2

Matthew 42, 94
Matthew Lewis 2
Michael 98
Philip 8
Thomas 2, 8, 42, 63, 64,
    99, 103, 107
William 55
Zachariah 6
Zadock 90
Jenkinson
    John 47
Jenness
    James 54
Jernigham
    Catharine 81
Jerningham
    Frances Henrietta 80
    Henry 80
    Katharine 80
Jerrum
    Thomas 14
Jevens
    John 43
Jewell
    Bety 95
    Moses 95
Jinner
    Elisabeth 52
Jobson
    Michael 58
Johns
    Richard 2, 42, 52, 64,
        93, 94, 99, 102
    Thomas 45
Johnson
    Aaron 78
    Affradozi 61
    Ann 93
    Atkadozi 50
    Barnet 24
    Barnett 56
    Bartholomew 35
    Christian 93
    David 102
    E. 53, 108
    Edward 13
    Eleazer 89
    Elisabeth 68
    Esther 19
    Ezekiel 32, 68, 82, 87
    George 96
    Greenberry 78
    Heather 24
    Henry Blare 93
    Hester 56
    Jacob 12, 37, 56
    James 81
    Jeremiah 56, 79
    John 52, 56
    Joseph 6
    Leonard 91, 97, 106
    Liddia 15
    Robert 68
    Sothy 49
    Thomas 24, 34, 56, 95
    William 24, 68
    Wittington 93
Johnston
    Ann 98
    John 41
Jonas
    Samuel 86
Jones
    Abraham 31, 94
    Alleydenor 20
    Ann 94
    Caleb 62, 85
    Comfort 97
    David 102
    Edward 94
    Elisha 23, 35, 48, 49,
        88, 91

Elishe 28
George 70, 85, 92, 97
Gideon 36
Henry 94
Jacob 37, 72
James 42, 67, 100
Jesse 92, 97
John 35, 46, 47, 55, 85,
    107, 109
Joshua 97
Leah 42
Levi 100
Maclemmy 92
Matthais 38
Mordecai 53
Morgan 99
Morgin 109
Nancy 109
Nelly 51
Rebecca 76, 96
Richard 24, 37
Roger 1, 66
Samuel 55
Thomas 12, 41, 54, 71,
    88, 96, 99, 100
William 1, 11, 24, 32,
    37, 50, 51, 76, 85,
    96, 99, 100, 101
Jordan
    Dorothea 56
    James 4, 45, 53, 60, 62,
        75, 80, 81, 94
    Jeremiah 81, 104
    John Morton 56
    Robert 88
    W. 94
    William 74, 80
Joseph
    Clement 38
    Justinan 81
    William 38
Joy
    Joseph 27
Joyce
    Joseph 78, 79
Joyse
    Elisabeth 6
Jump
    Abraham 45
    Isabella 45
    Leavin 45
    Thomas 45

Kay
    Robert 37
Keech
    George 8, 33, 86
Keen
    Benjamin 17, 81
    Henry 17, 65
    John 17
Keene
    Benjamin 12, 32, 65, 67,
        68
    Charles 66
    Ezekiel 65, 87
    Henry 11, 12, 32, 65
    John 12, 32, 65, 67, 68
    Mary 65
    Matthew 65
    Richard 11
    Zebulon 11
Keir
    John 10
Kellam
    Isaac 93
    John 35
    Tabitha 35
    Thomas 35
    William 35
Kelly

Alexander 14
Daniel 27
Hannah 14
James 75
John 27
Thomas 37, 38
Kemp
    James 2, 10, 42
    Robert 107
    William 2
Kennard
    Ann 40, 72
    Daniel 40, 74
    John 40, 72
    Mary 77
    Sarah 8
    Stephen 40
    Thomas 8
Kenned
    Hugh 26
Kennedy
    Arania 12
    David 16, 73
    James 103
    John 103
    Murdock 84
    Patrick 12
    Thomas 103
Kennett
    Kendal 22
    Presgrave 22
    Turvile 22, 36
Kent
    Daniel 79
    Edmund 78
    James 5, 47
    Joseph 20, 30, 108
Kenton
    Solomon 26
    Thomas 26
Kerbuy
    Joseph 66
Kernon
    Daniel 99
Kerr
    Adam 34
    John 48, 69, 90, 91, 106
    Martin 34
Kersey
    Prewell 85
Key
    Ann Arnold 77
    Ann Ormd. 34
    Francis 34, 77
    Philip 21
    Phillip 45
    Susanna Gardiner 45
    Susannah Gardiner 21
    Theodosia 45
    Thomas 21
Keyser
    William 34
Kibble
    George 48
Kilgour
    William 80
Killum
    Daniel 41
    David 41
    Samuel 105
King
    Benjamin 30, 53
    Charles 53
    Eleanor 53
    Elisabeth 97
    Ephraim 91
    Frances 30
    Francis 30, 31, 62
    James 38
    John 53, 68, 87
    Joshua 91
    Leonard 53

Margaret 30
Margrett 53
Mitchell 91
Robert 91
Solomon 47
Thomas 53, 97
William 60, 61
Kinlnmont
Sarah 63
Kinnard
Daniel 58
Mary 58
Kinnemont
Francis 29
Kinshaw
Jacob 102
Kinsler
James 30
Kirby
Mary 36
Sarah 36
Kirchner
Caspar 27
Christian 27
Kirk
Susannah 71
Kirkham
William 10
Kirkman
James 100, 109
Levin 67, 100
Sarah 25
Kirkpatrick
James 20, 90, 108
John 90
Samuel 109
William 13
Kirshaw
Francis 14
Kirwan
Judah 10
Matthew 10
Peter 19
Klein
Frietrich 34
Johann Heinrich 34
Knight
Elisabeth 31
James 31
Jonathon 31
Nehemiah 31
Knock
Nathaniel 25
Knott
Frances 60
James 60
Sarah 60, 80
Kollock
Cornelius 99
Jonathon 108
Simon 27, 50, 91, 92,
    93, 97, 99
Kremer
Keiser 15
Krichbaum
Adam 102
Kune
Thomas 101

Ladelar
Elisabeth 86
John 86
Lahill
Hannah 40
Thomas 40
Laing
Alexander 32
Laived
Julyanna 17
Lake
Henry 10, 11, 17, 19,

65, 66, 81, 100
Lamb
George 58
John 83
Joshua 74, 83
Lambden
John 17
Lambdin
John 106
Robert 94
Lamberson
Henry 98
Rachel 98
Lamberton
George 2
Lancaster
John 60
Joseph 60
Raphael 38, 62
Tocesia 62
Lane
Bretanna 66
Elisabeth 98
John 66
Lucy 66
Nathan 98
Rachel 63
Rebecca 98
Samuel 6, 44
Sarah 98
Thomas 21
Valentine 95
William 66, 89
Laney
John 34
Magdalene 34
Margaret 34
Matthew 34
Langfitt
Elisabeth 109
Frances 99
Langley
William 80
Langlin
Peter 37
Langrell
William 11
Lanham
Aaron 98
Edward 6, 90
Winefred 6
Winiford 90
Lank
Francis 18
Lankford
David 9
Ezekiel 61
Killiam 52
Killiard 91
Lazarus 70
Thomas 61
Latcham
Dinah 4
Latham
Elisabeth 20
John 20
Laughinghouse
William 50
Laurence
Elebath 92
Elijha 92
Elisabeth 2
George 2
Henry 92
John 92
Mary 92
Laurenson
Andrew 20
Lavell
William 3
Lavery
Agness 26

Lawrence
Elisabeth 41
Lawrenson
Andrew 28
Laws
Alexander 33, 82
Anne 33
Elijh 89
John 101
William 82
Lawson
John 75
Lazarus
Henry 54
Lead
William M. 45
Leage
Nancy 98
League
Betty 17
Leany
Matthew 34
Leatherbury
Charles 44, 69
John 40
Jonathon 24
Mary 24
Pen. 44
Peregrine 24
Thomas 44, 69
Leavens
William 90
Lecompt
John 18
Moses 65
Lecompte
John 67
Philemon 33
William 65
Lee
Edward 78
Richard 53
Samuel 53, 80
Thomas 53
William 2
Leeds
William 59
William M. 69
Leek
Frank 31
Leer
Richard 8
Legate
Ann 37, 38
John 37, 38
Legg
James 47
John 47
Sarah 47
Leggitt
Joseph 37
Legitt
Sutten 37
Leider
Henry 96
Leigh
George 38, 53
Joseph 4
Massey 38, 53
William 8
Leighter
Melchar 96
Leith
Alexander 47
John 47
Sarah 47
Leman
Rachel 3
Lenan
Francis 72
Lendrum
Andrew 24

Lucundra 24
Mary 24
Robert Burgess 24
Lennan
Francis 72
Leslie
Cornelius 23
Lewis
Clement 12, 13
George 20
Joseph 12, 13
Sarah 20
Leybourn
George 83
Leyburn
George 25
Patrick 66
Leybury
Patrick 87
Liden
Richard 32
Sarah 32
Lighter
John 96
Lilly
Richard 29
Linch
Hannah 36
Levi 36
Reubin 50
Thomas 98
Lindell
John 36
Lindenberger
George 27, 75, 79
Lindsey
David 69
Lingo
John 22, 52, 106
Leah 52
Priscilla 22
Roberson 106
Robinson 22
Smith 22, 52, 106
Thomas 106
William 52
Linsey
Samuel 93
Linthicum
Hezekiah 7
John 7
Thomas 18, 66, 82
Linzey
James 97
Lisby
Samuel 90
Littel
Adam 57
George 57
Mary 57
Little
Adam 21
George 21, 57, 71, 77
Mary 16, 21, 77
Michael 34
Peter 34
Livers
Anthony 29
Lizard
Mary 41
Lloyd
Edward 11, 18, 26, 29,
    82
Elisabeth 102
H. 42
James 102
Richard 9, 16, 22, 40,
    58, 106
Robert 96
Thomas 87
Lloyed
Richard 57

Loble
Wilhelm 27
Lock
Meverell 106
Locker
John 103
Lockerman
John 69
Lockett
Thomas 86
Lockwood
Benjamin 93
John 93
Mary 93
Samuel 93
Loe
Davis 69
Loeble
Wilhelm 27
Logan
Thomas 108
Logwood
Mary 89
Samuel 89
Loker
Elisabeth Parrot 4
Loluwry
Ellenor 26
Long
Comfort 22
Daniel 15
David 51
Jesse 15
John 15, 17
Solomon 22, 51
Thomas 26
Longue
Betty 65
Look
Meverell 33
Lorain
Mary 16, 73
Thomas 73
Loram
Martha 105
Lord
Cratcher 108
Love
Henry 60
John 79
Samuel 33, 62, 90
Loveday
Ann 29
John 29
Sally 29
Sarah 29
Thomas 29
Low
Pagiby 90
Lowe
Henry 97, 98
James 60
John 54, 59, 60, 97, 98
John Hawkins 97, 98
Michael 97
Thomas 60
Verlinda 60
Lowes
William 26
Lowman
Samuel 14
Lownds
Christian 34
Lowry
Margaret 26, 27
Loyd
Elisabeth 64
James 102
Thomas 70
Lucas
Ann 4
Eleanor 4

Elisabeth 4
John Baptie 4
Michael 104
Stephen 104
Luke
Frank 105
Lull
Stephen 83
Lunch
William 8
Lusby
Robert 20
Samuel 6
Lux
William 12, 24
Lycan
Jacob 73
Lydebotham
William 59
Lyles
William 30
Lynch
Edmond 98
Rebecak 98
Reubin 36
Sanwills 98
Thomas 98
Lynn
David 6, 29
Lyon
Hugh 97

Maawell
H. 57
J. 21
Maccubbin
Nicholas 43, 52, 78
Maccwill
Robert 40
Mace
Ann 87
Edmund 1, 66, 86, 87
John 66
Josias 87
Nicholas 66
Thomas 66
Macgill
John 103
Thomas 103
Machinkinnon
Peter 84
Mackall
Benjamin 76
James 44
James John 44
John 44
Thomas 44
Mackay
James 70
Mackey
James 39
John 70
Philip 64, 107
Robert 39
William 109
Mackie
Ebenezar 10
Henrietta 70
Mackiston
James 22
Mackubin
Richard 79
Macky
William 99
Macmaham
Richard 99
Macomb
George 100
Maddin
Sampson 102
Maddox

John 8
Samuel 80
Maddux
Bable 85
Bell 85
Lazarus 85
Marrel 92
Paul 85
Madkin
John 86
Madkins
Sarah 82
William 86
Magee
David 88
Maglamary
Isaac 88
Maglamore
Ann 88
Isaac 88
Magoffin
Joseph 37
Magruder
Alexander 43, 102
Alexander Howard 59
Basil 31
Edward 54, 59
Hezekiah 55
James 55
Jeremiah 94
John Read 21, 31, 60,
70, 105
Mary 55
Nathaniel 21, 31, 35,
43, 55
Samuel 55
Zadok 5
Maison
James 93
William 93
Makey
Robert 13
Makin
William 77
Mallard
William 85
Man
Ann 105
Joseph 105
Mankin
Charles 19
Manley
Ann 53
Thomas 53
Manlove
Betty 33, 57, 68
Boaz 57
Jonathon 57
Manuel 1, 17, 57
Robert 68
Mann
George 105
Joseph 72
Manner
P. 52
Portland 6, 54
Manning
Anthony 87
Elisabeth 77
Nathan 77
Mannon
P. 79
Manor
Elisabeth 46
Mansfield
Ann 57
Mary 57
Samuel 57
Thomas 64
Manship
Charles 10, 67
Nathan 67

Mantz
Caspar 34
Marbury
Joseph 8
Luke 31
Marcer
Thomas 109
Marchant
Anane 26
George 24
Sarah 28
Mare
Cathern 71
Mariny
John 37
Markey
James 13
Markland
John 2
Orpah 87
Marky
David 13
Robert 13
William 13
Marly
Rebecah 71
Robert 71
Marriott
John 21, 43, 52, 79
Marsh
Catharine 69
Marshall
Esme 105
Isaac 51
John 8, 23, 50, 60, 68,
86, 88, 89, 92, 101
Mary 8
Thomas 50, 53, 105
Thomas John 68
Marthezn
Georg 56
Martin
Bettey 70
Etheldar 3
George 26, 35, 85, 89,
93, 101
Henry 107
John 2, 3, 82
Levinia 3
Lisabeth 85
Martha 37, 38
Mary 37
Nancy 100
Nanny 35
Solomon 94
Thomas 29, 106, 107
Thomas Green 53
William 38, 80, 85
Zadock 48
Martindale
Samuel 28
Maslin
James 83
John 32
Mason
John 21
Mary 20
Richard 5, 17, 28, 46,
47, 48, 59, 69, 96,
98, 103
Solomon 69
William 93
William Winchester 17,
26, 28, 46, 47, 48
Massay
Zerobabel 71
Masse
John 26
Massey
Alexander 26
Daniel 14, 57, 83
Jonathon 27

Joseph 22
Peter 57, 71, 83
Masson
John 80, 102, 104
Massy
Elijah 71
Elisabeth 71
Peter 72
Mather
John 64
Mathew
Oliver 56, 79
Mathews
Elijah 62
Matkin
Solomon 32
Matkins
Sarah 86
Theador 86
Matterford
John 47
Matthes
Thomas 26
Matthews
Elisabeth 51
Hugh 16, 23, 57, 72
Jesse 55
Mary Ann 69
Matting
Ann 54
Mattingley
Leonard 60
Mattingly
Ann 81
Clement 81
James 54
John 54
Robert 4, 54
Ruth 81
Thomas 81
Mauduit
Jaspar 106
Mauldin
Benjamin 61, 85
Maw
Edmund 78, 79
Elinor 79
Elisabeth 78, 79
James 79
John 79
Maxwell
H. 57
Henry 58
James 7
John 14, 16
Robert 58, 67, 71, 73
William 74, 83
Maynadier
Daniel 2, 94
Mary 87
William 63
Mayner
John 75
Mayo
Thomas 79
McAdow
John 84
McAllister
John 7, 24
Robert 88
McBride
William 105
McBryde
Hugh 62, 100
William 23, 52, 61, 70,
85, 89, 91, 92
McCallister
Andrew 87
James 87
Mary 87
McClain
Alexander 14

James 14
McClare
  William 6
McClary
  William 34
McClaster
  Sarah 16
McClayland
  Fenley 2
  Samuel 2
  Thomas 2
McClean
  Alexander 21
  James 9, 24, 25, 73
  Mary 73
McClelan
  John 37
McCleland
  Thomas 3
McClellan
  David 37
McClemming
  William 88
McClure
  William 14, 44
McCollister
  Jeremiah 100
McComas
  Aquila 24
  Sarah 24
  William 75
McComb
  Eleazer 59
McConchie
  William 3, 89
McCoy
  Benjamin 28
  Eleanor 84
  James 84
  John 28
  Mary 28
  Sarah 84
McCraikin
  Nancy 68
  Thomas 68
McCrakin
  Nancy 68
  Thomas 68
McCreary
  James 90
McCubbin
  Zachariah 87
McCuddy
  William 89
McCulloch
  David 84
McDaniel
  Ann 3
  Miles 3
McDearmott
  Daniel 74
McDermot
  Daniel 74
  Helen 74
McDonald
  Alexander 3, 86
  Ann 86
  Deborah 86
  John 44, 77
  Miles 3
  Virlinder 86
  Zachariah 3
McDuff
  John 103
McFerson
  Samuel 7
McGavin
  Catharine 16
  John 16
McGhee
  Andrew 67
McGinis

John 72
McGinnis
  John 40, 72
McGonegill
  Jacob 12
McGowan
  John 14
  Robert 90
McGowin
  John 14
McHand
  Joseph 9
McHard
  Mary 20
  Samuel 20
McIntosh
  Daniel 55
  James 55
McKay
  John 6
McKeel
  Thomas 100
McKenny
  Hugh 26, 27
McKorkle
  John 7
McLane
  James 73
  Mary 73
McLaran
  James 30
McLaughlin
  Alexander 51
McLauglin
  Alexander 70
McLead
  William 106
McLean
  John 53, 76
McLeod
  William 69
McMullen
  Neil 35
McMullin
  Neil 26
McNabb
  John 71
McNamara
  John 82
McNee
  William 26
McPherson
  Alexander 62, 90
  Benjamin 55
  Daniel 23, 24, 54, 62,
    90
  John 38
  Rachel 38
  Thomas 23, 24, 62, 90
  William 106
McVeigh
  Joseph 48
McWeyilet
  Judith 16
McWilliams
  Kenelm 53
Mead
  Benjamin 7
Meads
  Benjamin 106
  Martha 106
  Rachel 10
Medcaff
  Elisabeth 54
  John 54
Medford
  Macal 67
  Macall 58, 67, 73, 82
  Macaul 82
  Marmaduke 58
Medith
  Frances 77

Medley
  Bennet 38
Meedes
  Thomas 26
Meeds
  John 26, 46
  Lida 46
  Rachel 26, 46
  Thomas 26, 46
Meek
  Christopher 52
  Jane 52
  Samuel 52
Meeke
  Samuel 52
Meekins
  Abraham 66
  Mark 87
  Mary 87
Meeks
  Ann 9
  Francis 40
  Mary 9, 40, 82
  Robert 9, 82
  Susannah 9
Megay
  Robert 95
Meglauglin
  Peter 29
Mekins
  Benjamin 87
Melmes
  Edward 106
Melson
  Joseph 48, 50
Melton
  Elisabeth 28
  Richard 4
Menering
  Nathan 9
Mennor
  Peter 91
Meraday
  Absalam 69
Mercer
  Ann 28
  Frances 28
  John 57
  Robert 28
  Thomas 109
Merchant
  George 28
  John 63
Meredith
  Benjamin 103
  Elisabeth 103
  John 5, 47
  Margaret 5, 47
  Mary 47
  Sarah 5
  Simon 30
  Thomas 5, 47, 103
Merodeth
  William 96
Meroshaw
  David 43
Merrick
  Andrew 42
  David 42
  Elisabeth 42
  John 42
Merriken
  John 79, 90
Merrill
  Jesse 82
  Joseph 36
  Joshua 75
  Thomas 28, 97
  William 105
Merritt
  William 57, 67
Merriwether

Reuben 56
Merryman
  John 12, 13, 56, 79
  Nicholas 12, 71
  Samuel 71
Mersey
  Thomas 109
Messersmith
  Samuel 37
Messex
  Obedia 35
Messick
  Comfort 35
  George 35, 50
  Obediah 35
Metcalf
  Francis 94
Meullan
  James 71
Meyers
  Balser 84
Mezick
  Benjamin 52
  Margaret 91
Michel
  Jane 13
Middleton
  Ann 78
  George 100
  Gilbert 78
  Ignatius 8, 24
  Joseph 78
Miel
  Francis 56
Miers
  Elijah 48
  John 48
Mifflin
  Warner 47
Milbourn
  Ann 22
  Caleb 28, 97
  Jonathon 28
  Mary 102
  Michael 28, 30, 97
  Thomas 22
Milbourne
  A. 38
  James 38
Miles
  Bettey 85
  Eleanor 86
  Hannah 17, 27
  Henry 85, 86
  John 86
  Matthais 16, 51
  Nathaniel 27
  Sarah 86
  Stacy 85
  William 16, 51, 85, 86,
    88, 89
Miller
  Andrew 72, 77
  Elisabeth 55
  Griffin 9
  Isabela 36
  James 26, 103
  Jenny 6
  John 49, 75
  Joseph 55
  Nathaniel 43, 83
  Nehemiah 6
  Richard 22, 43, 82, 105
  Samuel 13
  Sarah 36
  William 23
Milles
  Levin 42
Millington
  George 63
  Hannah 63
  Isaac 63

Milliss
  Levin 107
Mills
  Andrew 75
  Charles 75
  Edward 100
  Eleanor 86
  James 75, 80
  John 80, 81, 82, 102
  Joshua 13
  Mary 2
  Samuel 50
  Susanna 80, 100
  Weight 100
  William 23, 38, 100
Milstead
  Edward 28
Milton
  Abraham 16, 17
  John 16
  Joseph 16
  Mary 16
Minner
  Edward 66
  Richard 66
  William 66
Minor
  William 45, 69
Mitchell
  Abraham 84
  Benjamin Nuttly 90
  David 79
  Edward 20
  Elisabeth 20, 90
  Isaac 51
  Jane 13
  John 25, 73, 97
  John Pope 92
  Joseph 101
  Josiah 36, 102
  Kent 75
  R. 25
  R. B. 98
  Rebecca 51
  Stephen 32
  William 51
Mithell
  John 32
Mlten
  Alexander 79
Moffett
  John 83
Mohler
  Elisabeth 75
  Jacob 75
Mokes
  Rachel 34
Moleston
  William 5
Molleson
  William 30, 63, 76, 98
Molleston
  William 69, 70
Mollison
  William 14, 30, 44
Molliston
  William M. 47
Molson
  Samuel 54
Money
  Ann 104
  John 13, 28, 77, 104,
    105
  Richard 104
  Samuel 104
Montgomery
  John 19, 20
  Lydia 19, 20
  Nelly 32
  William 32
Moodie
  William 31, 97

Moody
  Robert 24
Moor
  Isaac 85
  James 85
  Thomas 85
Moore
  ------ 41
  David 63
  Elisabeth 81
  Isaac 85
  James 54, 87
  Jemima 85
  John 63, 85
  John Leonard 84
  Julian 85
  Peregrine 85
  R. 67
  Risdon 1, 17, 18, 87
  Rudolph 77
  Rudulph 72
  Thomas 85, 87
  William 40, 41, 81, 87
Morain
  Jonathon 109
More
  Ealie 14
  John 81
  Rudulph 14
  Sarah 36
Moreign
  Jonathon 109
  Joseph 90
  Mary 109
  Moses 109
  Thomas 90, 109
Morgan
  Amy 22
  Avery 22
  Edmund 56
  Edward 7
  Grace 41
  Hannah 22
  Jonathon 82
Morningdoler
  John 8
Morres
  Mary 40
Morris
  Dennis 93
  Edward 88
  Elijah 49
  Elisabeth 88
  Elisha 88
  John 35
  Jonathon 35
  Joseph 46, 93
  Joshua 41, 93
  Martin 54
  Mary 35
  Samuel 35
  William 89, 93, 106
Morrison
  Samuel 72, 77, 85
Morten
  Thomas 7
Morton
  Alexander 25
  Thomas 78
Mossman
  Archibald 37
  Christian 37
Mountiell
  Prudence 47
Mourningdoler
  John 8
Mudd
  Ann 23, 86
  Jonathon 23, 86
Muir
  Charles 87
  James 109

Sarah 66
Thomas 33
Mulliken
  John 2
Mullikin
  John 65, 103
Mumford
  Comfort 27
  Rachel 28
  William 28
Mundale
  Robert 13
Mundel
  Robert 55
Mundell
  Robert 3, 28, 33, 53,
    62, 86, 89, 90, 98
Murdock
  William 31
Murphey
  Daniel 62
Murphy
  Dorothy 25
  James 25
  Joseph 25
  Susanna 53
  Thomas 25
Murray
  Ann 91
  Benjamin 67
  Christopher 84
  David 91
  Gavin 72
  H. 100
  Henry 87
  Isaac 26, 92, 101
  James 10, 18, 33, 66,
    81, 87, 91, 108
  Josephus 84
  Margaret 67
  Nathaniel Hopkins 26
  Richard 91
  Ruth 84
  Shadrack 84
Murrein
  James 90
  Joseph 90
  Moses 90
Muse
  Thomas 32, 87, 109
Musgrove
  Abraham 13
  Anthony 7
  John 13
  Samuel 7
Mussin
  John 4
Mustitle
  Catharine 34
  Simon 34
Mydith
  Joseph 77
Myers
  Balser 84
  Catharine 54
  Frederick 84
  John 54
  Margaret 84
Mynck
  Mary 70

Nabb
  Sarah 102
Nairn
  John 105
Nash
  Ann 62
  Thomas 62
Nattison
  Aaron 71
Navey

Henry 65
Mary 65
Naylor
  Elisabeth 23
Neal
  Edward 94
  Gerrard 53
  Robert 94
  Solomon 63
Neale
  Ann 53, 60, 98
  Bennett 60
  Francis 6
  Gerard 60
  Gerrard 53
  James 62
  John 53
  Joseph 60
  Raphael 8
  Raphaele 3, 53, 89, 98
  Richard 60
  Robert 41
  Solomon 41
Neall
  Elisabeth 65
  Solomon 2, 42, 64, 65,
    94, 102
Neally
  Solomon 93
Nedels
  Ann 18, 42
  Edward 18, 42
Nedles
  Edward 42
  John 42
Needham
  ------ 46
Needles
  Ann 64
  Edward 18
  Nancy 18
Needs
  Easter 96
Neele
  Richard 60
Neighbrough
  Luranna 88
  Thomas 88
Neighenbrough
  John 88
Neill
  Francis 7
  Solomon 108
Neille
  John 35
Nelms
  Edmund Northen 92
  Edmund Northin 106
  Edward Northen 22, 26
  John 22, 92
Nelson
  Arthur 102
  Elisabeth 8
  John 86
  Joseph 8
  Michael 66
  Seneca 4, 81, 104
  William 8
Nevitt
  John Rider 66
  Sarah Ennalls 66
New
  Joseph 54
Newbolt
  George 104
  Sarah 104
Newcomb
  George Vansant 20
  George Vincent 73
  Mary 20
  Thomas 20
  William Salisbury 20

Newell
  Margaret 95
  Nicholas 95
Newman
  Daniel 69
  Elisabeth 69
  John 48
  Joseph 63
  Nathaniel 69
  William 69
Newton
  Mary 4
  Richard 91, 101
  Susannah 54
  Thomas 54
  William 54, 88
  Willis 18, 66, 67, 100,
    109
Nice
  Hugh 18
Nicholls
  Thomas 81
Nichols
  James 2
Nicholson
  Ambrous 97
  Benjamin 84
  Charles 16, 101
  J. 47
  John 93
  Joseph 69, 93
  Mary 101
  Nathan 19, 106
  Nathaniel 37, 98
  Richard 50
  Samuel 16
  Tabitha 16
Nickols
  William 31
Nicolls
  Isaac 81
  Samuel 104
Nicols
  Daniel 1
  Deborah 2
  Henrietta Maria 108
  Henry 108
  Isaac 25
  James 4, 108
  John 108
  Jonathon 18, 63, 99, 108
  Margaret 108
  William 2, 41, 64, 108
Nighenburgh
  John 88
Nobel
  James 107
Noble
  John 108, 109
  Jonathon 107
  Levi 107
  Mary Ann 17
  William 17, 108
Noel
  Thomas 33, 66, 67
Noele
  Thomas 1
Nok
  William 78
Noke
  William 44, 52
Noohes
  John 16
Norman
  Nicholas 43
Norris
  Abram 24, 79, 84
  Benjamin 24, 79, 84
  John 24
  Joseph 24, 79, 84
  Mary 84
  Susanna 24

Thomas 52
William 34, 52
Norriss
Benjamin 79
Prisilah 2
North
George 1
Gilbert 18
Katharine 37
Rebecca 1
Norton
Nathan 61
Richard 105
Thomas 61
W. 97, 98
Norwood
Edward 21, 90, 95
Ruth 21
Samuel 21, 95
Susannah 12
Nowland
Benjamin 76
Silvt. 76
Sylvester 57
Nus
Mathis 34
Nuton
Rachel 91
Nutrel
Ann 70
Nathan 70
William 70
Nutter
Christopher 32, 33
David 1, 25, 33
William 70
Nutters
David 1

O'Bryan
James 45, 59
O'Bryon
James 4, 10, 69, 98
Patrick 69
O'Meill
Felix 56
Oard
Eleanor 81
Jesse 81
Thomas 81
William 81
Obryon
James 19
Oden
Elisabeth 31
Jonathon 31
Susanna 31
Vincent 31, 90
Offutt
Alexander 29
Elisabeth 35
Hannah 35
Hezekiah 35
Mordecai 35
Samuel 43
Ogg
Alexander 30
Benjamin 7
George 7
Hellen 7
William 7
Ogle
Benjamin 34
James 29
Thomas 29
William 29
Oldfield
Henry 5
Oldson
Abraham 45
Thomas 45

Oneale
Charles 6
Orme
Ann 103
Archibald 29, 45
Ebenezar Edn. 45
Ellen 103
James 29, 43, 45
John 43, 45
Lucy 43, 45
Moses 8, 103
Orndorstz
Christian 29
Orrel
Francis 10
Orrick
Carroline 12
John 12
Nicholas 7
Orruck
Richard 7
Osborn
Elisabeth 31
James 36
John 105
William 31
Osbourn
James 55
Oteley
James 91
Otly
Coventon 91
Covington 91
Ottey
Ann 87, 88
William 87
Ottwell
James 88
Otty
William 88
Otwell
William 92
Outen
Obed 81
Outten
Mathew 35, 89
Matthew 26
Purnell 51, 61, 62, 85
Owden
Elisabeth 97
Jonathon 97
Owen
Edward 95
Lawrence 5
Robert 43, 95
Ruth 95
Sarah 5
Thomas 95
Owens
Dority 8
William 92
Owings
Bale 6, 29
Christopher 7
John 106
Samuel 19, 71, 95
Ozment
Richard 33

Paca
John 37
Pacol
Stephen 77
Paddison
Margaret 94
Pagan
William 29
Page
Acquilla 74
J. 105
John 8, 9, 14, 21, 22,

67, 73, 82, 83
Mary 74, 76
Pahlar
Jantzan 27
Pain
John 49
Joseph 49
Moses 49
Tabitha 49
Pamphilon
Nicholas 64
Pantree
Mary 102
William 102
Pardo
John 53
Paremore
John 16
Parker
Elisha 23
George 23, 101
Jacob 23, 88
John 23, 57, 85, 101
Richard 13
Schoolfield 89, 91
Parkinson
Edward 64, 66, 105
Elisha 48
Parks
Kesiah 55
Parode
John 53
Parran
John 30
Moses 30
Richard 30, 53, 105
Samuel 105
Young 21, 30
Parrat
Mary 107
William 107
Parratt
Aaron 64, 93, 94, 99,
    102, 107, 108
Aron 2
Benjamin 2, 93
Hannah 94
James 41, 107
John 107
Joseph 41
Mary 41, 93
Perry 41
Richard 41
Susannah 42
William 46, 93
Parrish
William 37
Parrot
Perry 64
Parrott
Aaron 42
George 42
Grundy 107
Peter 29, 64
Parsons
George 22, 26, 48, 88,
    92, 106
Pasan
William 94
Passmore
William 103
Paterson
Jacob 40
James 28
Patison
Archibald 87, 91, 107
Patrick
Tabitha 27
Patridge
Ann 8
Dobner Buckler 8
Jonathon 32, 67, 101

William 8
Patterson
  James 48, 97, 98
  Sarah 94
  Vincent 94
  Vinson 94
Pattison
  Archibald 1
  Jacob 32
  Jeremiah 32
  John 11
  Mary 11
  Richard 32
  Sarah 32
Patty
  Powell 22
Paul
  George 19
Paulus
  Nicholas 15
Pavat
  John 80
Payn
  William 28
Payne
  Basil 28
  Jacob 49
  John 60
  Joseph 18
  William 28
Peacock
  Susanna 80
Pearce
  Andrew 23
  Cassandra 23, 39, 57
  Daniel 23
  Henry W. 57
  James 16, 24, 57, 97
  John 95
  Margaret 95
  Rachel 23, 57
  Richard 39
  Thomas 95
  William 83, 95, 102
Pearl
  Basil 102
  Elisabeth 102
  James 102
  Thomas 102
Pearre
  John 60, 103
Pearse
  James 74
Pearson
  Henry 24, 75
Peaters
  Agnes 46
Peirry
  Eleanor 67
  Thomas 67
Penington
  Henry 67
  Mary 67
Penney
  Robert 90
Pennington
  Charles 21
  Eleanor 44
  Henry 39
  John 44
  Mary 39, 67
  Thomas 17
  William 21, 44
Pepper
  Levi 36
Perdue
  John 22
  Sabra 22
Perkins
  Frederick 67
  Isaac 14, 67, 73, 74, 77
  Mary 2

Philip 2
Solomon 2
Thomas 58, 74
Pernam
  Thomas 17
Perrin
  Bennett 106
Perry
  James 29
  Martha 29
  Rebecca 29
  William 81
Peters
  Agnes 46
  James 45
  John 45, 46
  Jonathon 45, 46
  William 45, 46
Pettebone
  Ann 79
  Charles 79
Pharoutish
  Daniel 55
Phillips
  Bedder 54
  Benjamin 50
  Francis 71
  John 32, 50, 70, 85
  William 44, 65
Phillipshill
  Charles 39, 76
Philpot
  John 60
  Thomas 31, 43
Philpott
  Benjamin 86
  David 60
Pickarring
  Charles 2, 94
Pickering
  Richard 64
  Robert 3, 10, 23, 26
Pickerson
  John 26
Pierce
  James 73
Pike
  Grace 66
  John 66
  Sarah 66
Pilchard
  Mary 36
Piles
  Elisabeth 70
  Francis 70
  Leonard 70
  Linny 70
Pindell
  Ann 6
  Elisabeth 6
  John 6
  Philip 6
Pinder
  Edward 4
  William 4
Piner
  Ann 57, 67
  Barten 58
  James 9, 57, 67
  Sarah 24
  Susannah 67, 74
Piper
  James 83
  John 40, 41, 61, 86
Pitt
  Thomas 68, 87, 91
Pitts
  Mary 88
  William 88
Place
  Thomas 90, 103, 104
Plara

David 30
Plater
  George 104
Plowden
  George 74
Plowman
  Johnathon 56
  Jonathon 12, 37, 56, 79,
    83, 87
Plummer
  Abiezer 29
  James 2
  John 21
Polk
  Benjamin 70
  Betty 17
  Charles 93, 101
  Daniel 1, 11, 18, 33, 65
  David 82
  Eleanor 32, 33
  Gillis 52
  John 1, 33
  Joshua 92
  Robert 11, 17, 18, 65
  William 32, 33, 50, 51,
    61, 91
Pollit
  John 50
  William 51
Pollock
  David 33
  John 33
  Joseph 33
  Priscilla 32
Pollot
  Nancy 51
Porter
  Ann 42
  David 6
  Elisabeth 42
  Ezekiel 89, 92
  Hugh 16, 52
  James 39, 61
  John 89
  Layronce 42
  William 90
Posey
  Ann 33
  Elisabeth 33, 86
  Francis 90
  Richard 33
  Thomas 33
Possey
  Elisabeth 86
Postly
  Ann 93
  John 22, 25, 26, 36, 49,
    92, 93, 101, 102
Posy
  Joshua 90
Potter
  Nathaniel 12, 25, 33,
    66, 81, 108
  Zabdiel 66, 81, 108
Potters
  Nathaniel 32
Pousonby
  Richard 60
Povey
  Ann 86
Powell
  Cakziah 49
  Elisabeth 2
  Howell 2, 64
  Thomas 2
  William Howell 94
Powles
  Jacob 15
  Susannah 15
Powling
  T. 86
Pratt

Charrity 71
Elisabeth 5
Henry Wright 47
John 5
Nathan 47
Solomon 47
Thomas 71
Pratter
Rignal 34
Presbury
Cordelia 7, 37
John 36
Thomas 75
William 7, 75
William Robertson 75
William Robinson 7
Price
Ann 41
Aquila 56, 79
Benjamin 56, 76, 79
Charles 59
Henry 97
Hugh 41
John 3, 47, 56, 76, 79,
80, 83, 93
Margaret 46
Mordecai 12, 56, 79
Nicholas 5, 46
Samuel 12
Sarah 97, 106
Semmes 106
Thomas 55, 74, 84, 96
Thomas Archer 46
Vincent 64
William 19, 76, 103
Prichard
John 11
Priestly
David 94
Perry 94
William 94
Primmer
Catharine 103
Prior
Randal 62
Pristman
George 37
Pritchard
John 11
Richard 11
Pritchell
Henry 11
Pritchett
Ezekiel 32
Jane 11
William 43
Zebulon 11
Pryce
Benjamin 39, 72, 76
Ephraim 39
Pryor
Esther 62
Thomas 62
William 17, 44, 69
Pue
M. 90
Pullitt
Thomas 51
Pumphrey
Greenbury 43
Rezin 43
Walter 43
Purnall
John 49
Purnell
Benjamin 89
Jeptha 89
John 101
Mary 89
Thomas 93
William 91, 101
Wolton 26

Zadock 35, 88
Pusey
John 93
Puzey
Isaac 93
John 92, 93
Lankford 93
Pye
Henerita 98
John 98
Sarah 55
Walter 98

Queen
Marsham 19
Queene
Richard 102
Quillin
Joseph 17
Quineley
Priscilla 82
Rebecca 82
Quinelle
Priscilla 11
Quinley
Stephen 82
Quinnelle
Rebecca 11
Quinnerly
Stephen 11, 87
Quinton
Dixon 88, 105
Philip 35, 89
Quynn
Allen 15

Rackliff
Charles 22, 89
Rackliffe
Charles 93
Rag
Thomas 64
Ragling
David 40
Rais
Christopher 84
Ramsay
William 71
Ramsey
Elisabeth 7
Joseph 34
Nathaniel 35
Sarah 7, 35
William 7, 37
Ran--gn
Stephan 95
Randall
Christopher 15
William 29
Ranton
Solomon 4
Rapour
Richard James 3
William 3
Rasin
Abraham 58, 72, 74
John 58
Joseph 9, 57, 58
Philip 58
Sarah 72
Thomas 58, 72
William 72
Ratcliff
Hannah 3
Ignatius 33
Stephen 3
Raven
Abraham 87
Luke 24
Rawlings

Ann 78
Rawlins
John 78
Ray
Benjamin 54, 95
John 95
Thomas 42, 94
Read
Andrew 96
Ann 38
John 71
Reccords
Thomas 31
Records
Alexander 31
Lamee 31
Sarah 31
Redgrave
Joseph 39, 73
Redman
Sarah 38, 80
Thomas 38, 80
Reed
Abraham 45
Amos 83
Eleanor 43
George 83, 106
Hannah 17, 83
Isaac 45
Jacob 89
James 43, 45, 98
John 17
Joseph 9, 83
Marget 40, 71
Martha 89
Mary 9
Michael 9, 58
Rachel 45, 98
Samuel 17
Thomas 45
William 9, 43, 58, 73
Reeder
John 4, 104
Thomas 38
Reeves
Mary 28, 62
Samuel 62
Thomas 62
Register
Esther 108
Francis 2
Hannah 2
James 2
Samuel 63
Reid
Araminta 83
John 83
Joseph 83
Reider
Thomas 3
Reith
Robert 79
Rennols
Robert 96
Resteau
Abraham 87
Sarah 87
William 87
Reston
Robert 86
Revel
Esther 48
Samuel 48
Revell
William 48
Reyland
John 20
Reyner
Ebenezar 40, 58, 105
Reynolds
Hammond 97
James 34

John 30
Mary 34
Robert 96
Samuel 44
Thomas 30, 105
William 34
Ricards
Archibald 68
Charles 68
Joshua 68
Rice
Ann 42
Hugh 29, 42
Mary 29
Richard
John 1
Richards
Daniel 63
Deligance 93
James 91
William 49
Richardson
David 106
John 105, 108
Joseph 1, 100, 108
Meriam 6
Peter 66, 67, 81, 91, 100
Richard 18, 34, 52, 78, 91
Robert 103
Thomas 4
William 1, 18, 37, 66, 67, 79, 98, 106
Richey
Daniel 91
Rickets
William 95
Ricketts
Benjamin 60
John 58, 60
N. 22, 57
Samuel 36, 97
Thomas 60
William 44
Rickords
William 21
Ricords
Joseph 68
Riddle
Ann 79
George 13
James 54, 79
Jennett 13
John 13
Lucy 54
Samuel 13, 54
Ridenour
Adam 95
Ridgaway
Samuel 17
William 17
Ridgeley
Charles 95
William 95
Ridgely
Charles 84
William 6
Ridgley
Mary 44
Ridgly
Joshua 79
Rigg
Susanna 60
Thomas 60
Riggen
Benton 48
Charles 92
Darby 93
Hannah 50
James 92
Joshua 92

Teague 92
Riggin
Ann 89
Clear 89
Darby 89
Elisabeth 88
Hannah 48
James 88
John 48
Pierce 89
Teague 48, 86, 88
Riggon
Teague 51
Right
Charles 51
Rigon
Thomas Baker 56
Riley
Benjamin 24, 74
Nicholas 24, 74
William 24
Ringgold
Charles 71
Joseph 22, 105
Sarah 71
Thomas 4, 5, 6, 14, 16, 17, 27, 28, 43, 47, 57, 58, 67, 71, 72, 74, 98, 103, 105
William 9, 17, 48, 57
Risteace
George 29
Ristead
George 6
Ritchey
Daniel 91
Delilah 91
Ritchie
Archibald 91
Ritter
Abraham 15
Conrad 15
John 15
Marget 15
Rittlemeyer
George Michael 84
Roach
James 4
Stephen 22, 26, 35, 40, 48, 50, 51, 70, 88, 105
Thomas 71
Robards
Sarah 70
Robart
Sarah 20
Roberson
Ann 98
Roberts Grandee
Mary 70
Rensher 70
Roberts
Edward 32
Elisabeth 92
Francis 32
James 45, 47
John 3, 28, 85
William 32, 92
Robertson
Alexander 96
Ester 92
James 50, 51, 61, 62
John 96
Joseph 92
Joshua 92
Margaret 96
Patrick 96
Thomas 2
William 15, 17, 69, 98
Robeson
Elijah 43
Robins

Bowdoin 36, 49, 50
John Purnell 36, 50, 88, 97
Josiah 93
Mary 93
Robinson
Betty 92
Charles 7
George 89
James 42
John 92
Joseph 82, 92
Lambert 42
Leeth 82
Levin 82, 108
Nancy 82, 108
Richard 7
William 7
Robosson
Elijah 43, 78
Robson
Joseph 11
Robsson
Joseph 25
Robwith
Thomas 76
Rochester
John 47
Mary 71
Rockhold
Clark 43, 78
Rodgers
Melicent 57
Roe
Davis 69
Hannah 69
James 46
Jean 99
Parrat 99
Thomas 69
Roger
Jacob 101
Jesse 101
John 101
Matthew 101
Rogers
Benjamin 56
Cornelius 27
Elisabeth 34
Jacob 16
John 29
Mary 21
Nathaniel 6
Philip 71, 79
Solomon 92
William 16, 24, 39, 57, 72, 74
Rohrer
James 34
Rolle
Fiddeman 42
Romer
Michael 54
Rond
Richard 61
Rooter
John 100
Rose
William 107
Roser
Henry 95
Ross
Ann 82
Catrun 67
David 30, 106
Elisabeth 65
George 30
James 109
Thomas 63
Rotemfer
David 94
Rothwill

Mary 76
Round
  Edward 106
  John 106
Rourk
  Ezekiel 89
Routh
  Christopher Cross 19,
    45, 46, 59, 69, 96,
    98
Rownd
  James 22, 50, 88
  William 102
Rownds
  James 26
Ruark
  John 89
  Mary 89
Rubent
  Jacob 98
Rudolph
  Tobias 23
Rudulph
  Tobias 60, 61, 84, 104
Rue
  Elisabeth 99
  Jesse 108
Ruke
  John 89
  Sehive 89
Rumbly
  Edgar 11, 82, 87
  Jacob 25
Rumsey
  Benjamin 96
  Charles 96
  William 20, 23, 76, 84
Runnell
  Hammond 88
Runney
  Elisabeth 59
Rupe
  Jacob 24
Russam
  Winlock 81
Russell
  Alexander 26
  Henry 21
  James 8
  John 53
  Josiah 26
  Price 26
  Solomon 26
Russum
  Edward 108
  Esther Ann 108
  James 108
  Winlock 66, 108
Ruth
  James 19, 69
  Robert 56
Rutledge
  Abraham 55
  John 55
Rutter
  Hannah 13, 88
  Joseph 13
  Thomas 13, 88
Ryland
  Aldridge 76
  Alldridge 76
  Fredies 76
  Jehu 76
  Silvester 39
  Stephen 76
Ryley
  Nicholas 74
  William 74
Ryner
  Ebenezar 74
Ryon
  Ignatius 62

Safford
  Abraham 100
  James 18
  Mary 18
Sailes
  Gabriel 29
Sails
  Clemane 29
  Clement 29
Sanders
  Andrew 89
  Charity 89
  Charles 25
  George 25
  Joseph 25
  Joshua 13, 19, 62
  Nathaniel 89
  Richard 18
  Sarah 89
  William 25, 73
Sands
  Benjamin 10
  John 79
Sansbeary
  Thomas 103
Sappington
  Benjamin 39, 76, 85
  Hartley 39
  Hartly 85
  Richard 39
Saterfield
  John 46
Satterfield
  Hinson 46
  James 59
  John 46
  Margaret 59
  Neriah 47
  Solomon 46
Saulsbury
  James 25
  John 25
  Olive 25
Saunders
  Cassandra 107
  Lilley 91
  William 25, 91
Savin
  Thomas 20
Savon
  Thomas 84
Sayer
  John 59
  Marah 59
Scacom
  George 100
Scarborough
  Samuel 89, 106
Scarse
  Catharine 54
  Shadrack 54
Scearse
  David 54
  Nathaniel 54
Schneider
  John 43
Schoolfied
  J. B. 36
Schoolfield
  Betty 27
  Henry 49
  J. B. 35, 89, 91, 101
  John 27
  Robert 27
  Sophiah 48
  Thomas 27
Schoot
  Keziah 51
Scot
  Jeane 2
  Windom 51
Scott

Benjamin 91
Catharine 89
Daniel 24
David 83
Edward 4
Elisabeth 89
George Day 51, 86
Jesse 89
John 83, 109
Joseph 35, 102
Mary 83
Mitchell 51
Moses 16
Sabritt 103
Sarah 102
Sary 51
Windom 51
Zachariah 54
Scrivener
  Charles 47
  Francis 6
  Juliana 47
  Mary 6
  Robert 47
  William 6
Scrogin
  John 27
  Joseph 23, 52
Sebby
  Jemima 7
Seeden
  John 69
Seeders
  John 5, 45, 46, 106
Seegar
  Elisabeth 83
  Samuel 83
Selby
  Benjamin 78
  John 35, 89
  Mathew 50, 89
  Parker 22, 36, 50, 89,
    91, 92
  William 35, 89, 93, 102
  Zadock 89
Selfridge
  John 97
Sellers
  Thomas 84
Selman
  Jonathon 78
Semans
  Solomon 40
Semmes
  Edward 86
  Hennerutter 90
  Henrietta 86
  Marmaduke 86, 90
  Thomas 3, 8, 90
Semmon
  Alexis 56
Senan
  Francis 40
Seraghim
  Joseph 70
Seragin
  Robert 70
  Samuel 70
Serdey
  John 106
Serdon
  John 106
Serogin
  John 70
  Joseph 70
Seth
  Jacob 3, 5, 28, 69, 91
  James 2
  John 69
  Mary 69
Severson
  Rebecca 28

Sewall
   Nicholas Lewis 4
Seward
   Daniel 21
Sewell
   Clement 45, 106
   Henry 54
   Vachel 15
Shanks
   John 21, 45, 53, 74
Shannahan
   Elisabeth 41
   John 41
Shardith
   Susannah 53
Share
   Josias 54
Sharf
   Lydia 73
Sharp
   Birckhead 63
   Birkhead 2
   Catharine 63
   Elisabeth 63
   Lydia 63
   Margaret 63
   Mary 63
   Nancy 63
   Peter 64
   Samuel 63, 65, 94
   William 2, 64, 107
Shaver
   George 102
Shaw
   Arminta 56
   Edward 29
   James 18, 87
   John 43, 78
   Mary 18
   Samuel 56
   Sarah 29
Shawn
   Martha 22
Shearman
   Jacob 24
Shearswood
   William 73
Sheel
   John 56
   Mary 56
Sheepherd
   James 107
   Mary 107
Sheerer
   Archibald 30
Sheerswood
   William 73
Sheets
   Barbara 95
   Frederick 95
Shehan
   James 103
Shehawn
   Dennis 58
   Joseph 100
   Mason 100
Shenton
   Charles 66
   Joseph 66, 100
Sheredine
   Upton 63
Sheriff
   J. 32
   John 85
Sherreff
   John 51
Sherriff
   John 51
Sherwood
   Alice 99
   Catharine 5, 17
   D. 94

Daniel 10, 11, 18, 29,
   63, 64, 107
   Hugh 99
   John 5, 17, 94, 99
   Jonathon 5
   T. 2, 63, 108
   William Cowper 5
Shield
   John 56
Shields
   David 71
   John 75
Shiles
   John 86
   Sarah 86
   Thomas 86
Shinwood
   Stephen 58
Shireff
   John 61, 70
Shiriff
   John 48
Shirreff
   John 32, 51
Shits
   Peter 75
Shockley
   Benjamin 107
   Solomon 107
Shockly
   Benjamin 105
   John 105
   Richard 105
Shoehawn
   Mason 100
Shores
   Luke 16
Short
   Phillip 50
Showell
   John 24
Shridt
   Phillip 34
Shriver
   David 29, 34
Shryock
   Henry 34
Shureff
   John 109
Shuttleworth
   John 6
Silden
   Charles 16
Sim
   Isaac 81
Simmes
   Thomas 33
Simmonds
   Bridget 18
   Elisabeth 44, 69
   Thomas 1
   William 44
Simmons
   Abigail 52
   Abraham 52
   Bridget 1
   Elisabeth 38
   Jeremiah Chapman 70
   John 38
   Peggay 1
   Richard 52
   Roseannah 1
   Thomas 1, 18
   William 52, 70, 78
Simms
   Thomas 89
Simpson
   Ann 4, 79, 88, 94
   Gaither 79
Sims
   Mark 62
   Pha Delmno 62

Sinnet
   Robert 28
Sinnett
   Samuel 22
Sipley
   William 17, 40
Sirman
   Joshua 22
Siste
   Richard 28
Siverson
   Ezekiel 23
   Mary 23
   Rebecca 23
   Thomas 23
Skinner
   Andrew 41, 42
   Benjamin 30
   Daniel 42
   John 37, 98, 106
   Richard 29, 42
   Thomas 10, 42
Slade
   Joseph 83
Slay
   Edward 17
   Sophia 17
Slipper
   Thomas 8, 71
Sloane
   James 75
   Jane 75
Sloss
   Samuel Shelton 35
Slovium
   Ruth 97
Slubey
   William 21, 57
Sluyter
   Henry 84
   Peter 84
Sly
   Clare 74
   George 74
Slye
   George 74
Slyter
   Peter 84
Small
   Conrad 13
   Richard 70
Smallwood
   Thomas 3
Smear
   George Booze 99
Smith
   Alexander Ham 97
   Andrew 22, 96
   Ann 17, 105
   Archibald 104
   Basel 81
   Betty 97
   Buchanan 56
   Buckanna 7
   Catharine 105
   Charles 16
   Daniel 6, 43, 58
   David 44
   Edward 25, 51, 86
   Elisabeth Wheland 87
   Gavin Ham 97
   George 105
   Hollady 18
   Huldah 7
   Jacob 103
   James 12, 16, 17, 22,
     23, 40, 51, 58, 71
   Jean 7
   John 4, 7, 19, 21, 22,
     27, 37, 39, 44, 49,
     57, 61, 75, 76, 80,
     84, 86, 101

John Christian 95
John Green 46
John Hamilton 30, 43
Jonathon Green 5
Joseph 29, 30, 49, 60
Josias 83
Margaret 44, 86, 95
Mary 4, 8, 16, 19, 39,
    49, 61, 76, 101
Mordecai 30, 54
Nathaniel 79
Obediah 27
Oliver 9, 39
Patrick Sim 76, 97
Philemon 97
Philip 57, 71, 95
Polly 106
Purnel Fletcher 22
Ralph 7
Rebekah 33
Richard 5, 47
Rizden 90
Robert 12, 56
Samuel 27, 83, 84, 104
Samuel Messer 37
Sarah 18, 22, 49, 104
Solomon 1, 18, 104
Susanna 5
Thomas 7, 10, 18, 19,
    71, 73, 81, 87, 90,
    100
William 5, 25, 40, 46,
    66, 71, 75, 78, 86,
    90, 95, 100, 101
Smithson
    Thomas 79
Smock
    Betty 97
    Edward 60
    Hinve 50
    John 50
    Kendale 92
    Leah 49
    Lemuel 92
    Makemmey 92
    Mary 50
    McKimmy 97
    William 27, 50, 92
Smook
    William 15
Smoot
    Edward 3
    George 62
    George Clk. 3, 23, 86
Smyly
    Samuel 27, 50, 89, 91,
    92
Smyth
    F. 86
    John 9, 10
    Richard 5, 46
    T. 57
    Thomas 9, 14, 24, 25,
    60, 71, 83, 97
    William 9, 10
Snead
    John 93
Snowden
    Elisabeth 22
    Henry 22
    James 30
    Richard 22
    Thomas 22
Soale
    Leonard 81
Somervell
    Alexander 30, 44, 56
    James 20, 21, 30
    John 94, 102, 104
Somerville
    Alexander 75
    John 75

Sootton
    James 17
    Lydia 17
    Richard 17
Soward
    Charles 18, 66
    Daniel 44
    Edward 18
    John 18, 66
    Mary 18
    Richard 66
    Sarah 66
Spangler
    Ann 95
    John 95
Sparks
    Rachel 104
    Richard 104
Sparrow
    Hemsey 103
    Jonathon 103
    Thomas 103
Spavold
    James 29, 75
Speake
    Richard 53
Spear
    James 23
Spearman
    John 40
Spedden
    John 18, 66, 82
Spedding
    Hugh 68
Spence
    Adam 26, 50, 93, 106
    George 101
Spencer
    Isaac 20, 39, 40, 47,
    71, 82
    John 40
    Richard 72
    Thomas 14
    William 13
    Wolman 83
Speney
    George 93
Spong
    Elisabeth 33
    Francis 33
Sprigg
    Edward 31, 105
    J. 31, 94
    John 29
    Osborn 105
    Thomas 6
Spry
    Abraham 47
    Humphrey 47
    Jehu 47
    Mary 47
    Ruth 69
Spuron
    Sarah 41
Srectrer
    George 96
St. Clair
    William 40
St. Tee
    James 59
    Phillemon 59
Stack
    Ann 67
    Patrick 67
    Thomas 67
Stainson
    Benson 11
Stainton
    Benson 46
Stall
    John 29
Stamper

Josiah 1
Stanford
    Richard 66
    Thomas 50, 51, 70
Stanhouse
    Alexander 84
Stansbury
    Dix 83
    Mary 37
Stanwer
    Johannes 37
Staplefort
    Edward 87, 101
Steel
    Thomas 37
Steele
    Henry 10, 68, 109
Steiger
    Jordan 78
Stenhouse
    A. 84
Stephens
    Edward 109
    William 73
Stephenson
    Ann 84
    John 84
    Robert 84
Sterling
    Aaron 52
    Littleton 85
Sterrett
    Samuel 40
Steuart
    Adam 103
    Benjamin 76
    Frances 73
    Henry 67
    John 106
    Thomas 76, 87
    William 86
Stevens
    Charles 21
    Ephraim 50
    Francis 73
    Hester 73
    John 21, 33, 41, 42, 63,
    64, 65, 66, 84, 99,
    103, 107
    Joseph 21
    Peter 11, 64
    R. 99, 100
    Richardson 108
    Sarah 64
    Vachel 21, 52
    William 2, 15, 42, 63,
    64, 65, 94, 107
Stevenson
    Ann 106
    Edward 85
    H. 21, 55, 56, 79
    Henry 12, 37, 75, 106
    James 49
    John 19, 37, 78, 88
    Joseph 23
    Katharine 24
    Margaret 24
    Robert 84
    Sarah 23
    William 24
Steward
    Charles 58, 73
    John 16, 58
    Sarah 58, 73
    Stephen 6, 52
Stewart
    David 71
    Elisabeth 11
    George 56
    Henry 101
    James 11
    John 36, 55, 56, 73

Jonathon 33
Joseph 11
Mary 89
Thomas 11, 76
William 16, 31, 51, 70,
  91
Stimptson
  Solomon 95
Stinchcombe
  Nathaniel 79
  Thomas 79
Stockett
  Lewis 43
  Thomas N. 43
Stockley
  Sophiah 48
Stockton
  John 67, 76
  Richard 34
Stoddert
  Kenhelm 53
  Marget 53
  Walter Trueman 53
Stoler
  John 13, 84
Stoltz
  Henry 102
Stone
  Betty Ann 89
  Catharine 24
  David 89
  Elisabeth 89, 104
  John 55
  John Haskins 89
  Mary 27
  Thomas 89
Stoner
  John 55
Stonestreet
  Basil W. 7
  Edward 7, 8
  Eleanor 8
  John 7, 8
  Thomas 7
Stoops
  John 67, 76
Strainer
  James 107
Stratford
  Teresa 3
Strawbridge
  John 60, 61
Strieper
  ------ 24
Striker
  George 15
Stringer
  Richard 22, 90
Strong
  Michael 9, 57
Struttell
  Amos 103
Stuart
  Alexander 23, 76
  Benjamin 76
  William 76, 83
Stull
  John 44
Stump
  John 23
Sturgis
  Joshua 35, 89, 92
  Mary 92, 97
  Outten 50
  Richard 93
  Stephen 93
  Thomas 88, 93, 97, 106
  William 93
Sub
  Adam 95
Sudler
  Elisabeth 46

Emory 9, 11, 15
James 46
Joseph 17, 44, 47, 69,
  106
Thomas 17
Sulivane
  D. 82
  Daniel 1, 15, 32, 33,
    65, 66, 81, 101
  James 66, 67, 81, 87,
    100, 108
  Martha 83
  Patience 81
Sullivane
  James 25
Summers
  Dorcas 105
  John 105
  Nathaniel 105
Sunderland
  Benjamin 30, 43
  Josias 43
  Lydia 30
  Stockett 30
  Thomas 30, 43
Surman
  Edward 40
  Isaac 40
  Joseph 40
  Joshua 40
  Leah 86
  Mary 86
Sutton
  Jeremiah 76
  John 4, 58
  Rebecca 22
Swain
  Ann 49
  Anne 49
  John 49
  William 49
Swan
  Rebecca 81
Swift
  James 26
  Moses 26
Sydebotham
  William 31, 103
Sylvester
  Als 59
  Benjamin 69
  Deborah 47
  James 47
  Thomas 47, 59

Talbot
  Belinda 37
  John 43
  Joseph 43
  Philip 43
  Thomas 12, 37, 43
Talbott
  Belinda 83
  Benjamin 37
  Edmund 83
  James 55
  John 37
  Sophia 37
  Thomas 37, 83
Taney
  Elisabeth 4
  John Francis 4
  Michael 14
Tannehill
  William 95
Tarbutton
  Rachel 59
Targyhill
  John 54
Tarlton
  Ann 104

John 104
Stephen 81
Thomas 54, 80
Tarr
  Elenor 92
Tasker
  A. 24
Tate
  Robert 90
Taubman
  Julyanna 17
Tayler
  James 36
  Joshua 88
Taylor
  Christian 8
  Dennis 51
  Elias 51
  Elisabeth 47
  Ignatius 38
  Jenifer 38
  Jeremiah 23, 57, 85
  John 8, 15, 54, 79
  Loillen 51
  Martha 47
  Richard 47, 106
  Samuel 49
  Sarah 15, 25, 51, 89
  Solomon 89
  Thomas 15, 25, 47, 89
  Well. 102
  William 15, 25, 28, 89,
    104
Teague
  George 101
  John 15, 27, 50, 101
  Mary 101
  William 101
Tempel
  George 106
Temple
  George 4
Tenant
  Moses 74
  Thomas 63
Tenley
  Philip 94
Tennally
  John 94
  William 94
Tennant
  Elisabeth 74
  James 41, 63
  John 74
  Mable 63, 99
  Moses 74
  Rebeccah 102
  Thomas 63, 99
  William 74
Tennelly
  Hannah 94
Tennely
  Philip 94
Tenneson
  Jesse 38
  Thomas 38
Tennison
  Matthew 81
Terray
  Sarah 17
Tharp
  Eunice 48
  Michael 48
  Ruth 76
Thawley
  Mary 26
Theobalds
  Samuel 80
Thisby
  Peter Harrout 28
Thomas
  Elisabeth 87

James 74
John 6, 107
Jonathon 101
Joseph 8
Mary Waugh 96
Nic. 107
Philip 34, 55
Samuel 17, 41, 42, 73, 108
Sarah 81, 82
Tristram 107
William 18, 107
Thompson
　Ann 50
　Benjamin 100
　Catharine 5
　Edwards 100
　Ephraim 20, 45
　George 27
　Henrietta 8
　Hester 5
　James 27, 50, 78
　Jesse 27
　John 5, 22, 38, 50
　John Vickels 100
　Joseph 100
　Richard 76, 84
　Robert 28, 45, 81, 85
　Samuel 5, 47, 100
　Sarah 12
　W. 28
　William 50
Thorn
　Abraham 105
　Barton 105
　Peregrine 105
　William 105
Thoroughgood
　Paul 35
Tibbol
　Thomas 10
Tickle
　Ledya 108
　William 66
Tigue
　John 49
Tilden
　Charles 25, 105
　Marmaduke 21, 25
　Sarah 105
　Tabitha 105
Tilghman
　C. 46, 47
　Isaiah 51
　James 10
　Mathew 29
　Matthew 42, 94
　Nehemiah 35
　Peregrine 96
　Richard 17
Tilghmand
　Edward 5
Tillard
　Ann 70
　Edward 70, 78
　Martha 78
　Thomas 78, 79
　William 70, 78
Tillotson
　John 45
　Sarah 45
Timmons
　Joseph 25, 36
　Rebeckah 36
　Rebecke 25
　Samuel 36
　Sarah 93
　Solomon 25, 36
Tindall
　Benjamin 53
Tingle
　Caleb 92

William 50, 101
Tiplin
　William 83
Tippet
　Butler 80
　Dennis 80
　James 80
　Joseph 80
　Margaret 80
　Notley 80
Tippett
　Dennis 80
　John 80
　Sarah 81
　William 80
Tipton
　William 13, 80
Toadvine
　Thomas 51
Todd
　Benjamin 1, 10, 11, 19, 100
　Charles 78
　Joseph 1
　Mary 29
　Rachell 78
　Rezin 29
　Sarah 29
Todvine
　Arnold 51
　Dixen 51
　Dixon 51
　Henry 51
　Stephen 51
　Thomas 51
Tolson
　Benjamin 46, 59
　John 59
　Mary 59
Tongue
　Robert 6
Tool
　James 44
　Sarah 44
　Timothy 44
Toomey
　Sarah 13
Tootell
　James 32
　John 66, 108, 109
　Richard 78, 79, 90
Touchstone
　John 23
Towgood
　Joseph 52
Towler
　Mary 7
Towney
　John 52
Townsend
　Barkley 61, 70
　Comfort 88
　James 10, 35, 91, 101
　John 35, 50
　Joshua 88
　Levin 35
　Linsey Joshua 93
　Luke 50
　Major 35, 89
　Mary 50
　Nathaniel 88
　Nehemiah 88
　Samuel 91, 101
　Solomon 27, 91, 101
　Stephen 91, 101
　William 91, 101
Towson
　Dinah 19, 37
　Ezekiel 19, 37, 87
　William 19, 37, 38
Traup
　John 64

Travers
　Levin 18, 25
　Mathew 11
　William Hicks 16
Traverse
　Ann 16
　John Hicks 16
　Priscilla 16
　William 16
　William Hicks 16
Trice
　John 1, 108
Trilley
　Richard 40
Trilt
　Rachel 97
Trippe
　Ann 109
　Edward 2, 23, 33, 39, 41, 42
　Elisabeth 33
　Henry 32
　John 18, 109
　Margaret 33, 39
　William 10, 42, 87, 99, 100, 109
Trivitt
　Mary 90
Troth
　Henry 42, 63, 64, 65, 94
　William 41
Trotwill
　Adam 81
Troutner
　Michael 95
True
　John 1, 10, 66, 67
Truitt
　Ede 93
　George 49
　Mary 27, 49
　Nehemiah 49, 93
　Samuel 101
　William 27
Tubman
　George 3, 86
　John 66
　Richard 3, 19
　Samuel 28
Tucker
　Richard 106
Tull
　Ann 106
　Anthony 100
　Daniel 100
　John 28, 36, 49, 50, 91
　Joshua 101
　Stephen 28
　Susanna 100
Tunnell
　William 93
Turbull
　Elisabeth 64
Turbut
　Ann 10
　Richard 64
　Sarah 64
Turbutt
　Richard 41
　Sarah 65
Turnbull
　John 63
Turner
　Abner 2, 42, 107
　Hannah 5, 12, 42
　Isaac 5, 12
　James 5
　Jonathon 58, 67, 72, 73, 74
　Joseph 42
　Lam 62
　Mary 27, 90

Mr. 103
Rhoda 27
Samuel 34
Sarah 5, 27
Zephaniah 3, 53, 90
Turpin
  Beauchamp 18
  Mary 18
  William 61
Twiford
  Barthol 33
Twilley
  Eloner 51
  John 51
Twilly
  John 51
Twonsend
  Tabitha 35
Tylor
  Elijah 64
  John 64
  Thomas 64

Uch
  Abraham 95
Umsted
  Nicholas 95
Unckles
  Unckle 95
Uncles
  John 95, 96
  Uncle 96
  William 95, 96
Underhill
  Thomas 14
Upton
  John 60
  Martha 60
  Thomas 60
Urquhar
  Peter 80
Usher
  Andrew 16
  Hannah 16

Valliant
  John 1, 65, 81
Van Bibber
  Alm. 96
  Isaac 96
Vance
  Adam 76, 84
Vandegrift
  Peregrine 20
Vanes
  Gracy 84
Vanhorn
  Barnet 23, 76, 84
Vansandt
  Benjamin 76
  Rachel 76
Vansant
  George 73
Vaughan
  Betty 61, 70
  Charles 51
  Ephraim 61, 70
  Jethro 70
  Joseph 26
  Levin 35, 70
  Sarah 51
Veach
  William 87
Veale
  Wilfred 21
Vearet
  Rebecca 36
Veazey
  Edward 72
  John 77, 96, 103

John Ward 23, 39, 73,
  104, 109
  Samuel 20
  Thomas B. 72
Venables
  Benjamin 32, 51
  Joseph 15, 16, 31, 32,
    48, 50, 51, 109
  Richard 32
  Wil. 32
  William 109
Venles
  Cyrus 81
Vickars
  Thomas 1, 18, 65, 99,
    100
Vineyard
  James 8, 33
Vinsand
  Benjamin 76
Vinson
  Ann 49
  Benjamin 49
  Betty 18
  George 49, 92
  James 18
  John 18
  Prisse 49
Voorhees
  John 24, 58, 72, 74, 83
Voorhey
  John 67

Wade
  Josiah 54, 59
  Robert 7, 8, 97, 98
  Zachariah 93
Waggaman
  George 109
  Mary 85
Waggoner
  Michael 30
Wailes
  George 51, 61, 62, 70,
    85
  John 51, 85
Wakefield
  Benjamin 94
  John 96
Waland
  William 40
Wales
  John 83
Walker
  Ann 3
  Charles 33
  Elisabeth 25
  Henry 80
  James 62, 80, 104
  John 19, 59
  Joseph W. 53
  Mark 62
  Mary 80
  Priscillah 33
  Sarah 19
  Sophia 62
  Susanna 80
  Susannah 104
  Thomas 62
  William 109
Wall
  Levin 100
  Pearson 109
Wallace
  Andrew 13
  Ann 67, 68, 76
  Charles 67, 68
  David 60
  George 68
  James 32, 65
  John 14, 28, 58, 60, 69

Joseph 13, 61, 67, 68
Michael 60
Richard 67, 68, 76
Sarah 60
Thomas 84
Waller
  Ebenezar 85
  Elisabeth 94
  John 48
  Joseph 48
  Nathaniel 48
  Richard 52, 62
  William 70
Walles
  George 32
Wallis
  Francis 14
  Hannah 14
  Henrietta 14
  Henry 14, 21, 57, 74
  Hugh 93
  John 14, 57, 105
  Samuel 16, 21, 47, 57,
    98
  Sarah 67
Wallon
  Nathaniel 94
Walls
  George 15
Wallston
  Rorly 62
Walmsley
  James 39
  Nicholas 39, 73
  William 39, 109
Walsh
  Rebecca 78
  Robert 79
Walten
  John 45
Walter
  Daniel 15
  George 95
  Peleg 16
  Polig 49
Walters
  Alexander 103
  Ann 46
  Benjamin 103
  Jacob 78
  John 36, 103
  Pelig 101
  Robert 46, 103
  Samuel 10, 90, 103
  Stephen 36
  Susannah 46
Waltham
  Margaret 71
Walton
  Fisher 36, 50, 106
  Mary 50
Wams
  David 97
  James 97
Wamsley
  Alethia 77
  Nicholas 77
  Robert 77
  William 13, 77
Waples
  John 35, 36, 49, 97, 99
  Mary 97
  Paul 97
  Peter 97
  William 97, 99
Ward
  Ann 85, 108
  Bridget 49
  Cornelius 32
  James 30
  Jesse 32
  John 30, 72, 73, 76, 85,

90, 104, 108
Joseph 32, 85, 86
Levin 108
Lucy 108
Mary 30, 85
Matthew 32
Nathaniel 72
Peregrine 67
Perig 103
Richard 30
Samuel 30, 49
Sarah 20, 32
Saul 16
Stephen 85
Sumars 108
Summers 108
William 72, 73, 104
Ware
  Francis 13, 28
Warebrum
  Henry 56
Warfield
  Alexander 7, 44
  Basil 4, 5, 10, 19, 28,
    45, 47, 59, 69
Warington
  Margaret 23
Warran
  Richard 36
  Thomas 36
  William 36
Warren
  Edward 27
  Orson 42
  William 42
Warrin
  Edward 90
Warrington
  Benjamin 61, 62
  Charity 61, 62
  Esther 61
  Sarah 61
Waters
  G. 1
  George 10, 32, 33, 50,
    81, 87, 91
  John 7, 42
  Joseph 94
  Mary 94
  Peter 48
  Samuel 5
  Sarah 42
  Thomas 94
  William 90, 95
Watkins
  Bennett 62
  Gassaway 78
  John 21
  Rachel 15
  Thomas 15, 17, 43
Watson
  Charles 49
  Elisabeth 49
  James 24
  John 59
  Jonathon 49
  Nathan 49
  Robert 49
Watt
  Isabella 21
Watts
  ------ 43, 52, 79
  Hugh 84
  Margaret 84
  Richard 102
  Robert 6, 102, 104
  Sarah 102
Wavolen
  Thomas 38
Weaklin
  Richard 38
Wealthy

Andrew 24
Weatherall
  Henry 7
Weathrak
  Philip 63
Weathrall
  Philip 90, 104
Weavers
  John 24
Webb
  Ann 4
  Edgar 4
  James 10
  Mary 4, 10
  Samuel 56, 80
  William 10, 56, 79, 80
Webster
  John 33
  John Lee 24, 29, 37
  Philip 62, 90
  Richard 33
  Solomon 33
Weedon
  Richard 90
Weems
  James 43, 96
  John 96
Weglan
  Abraham 97
Weil
  George 95
  Johann 95
Weir
  John 9
  Robert 15
Wekmer
  Nathan 56
Welch
  John 15
Wellman
  Elisabeth 80
  Michael 80
Wells
  Alexander 84
  Charles 71
  Hester 96
  John 67, 68
  Mary 8
  Nathaniel 96
  Thomas 8, 49, 96
  Tobias 46, 47
  William 7, 8
Welsch
  Jacob 37
Welsh
  Andrew 73, 76, 77
  Elisabeth 76, 77
  John 21
  Mary 90
  Thomas 42
Welter
  Andrew 24
Wersler
  Morrice 84
West
  Ann 99
  John 47, 99
  Mary 99
  Rachel 99
  Raphael 7
  Samuel 9, 17, 58, 73
  Stephen 22, 54, 90, 95
  Thomas 50, 100
  William 36
Western
  Thomas 102
Wetherall
  Henry 36, 37, 83
  Philip 103
Wewler
  Morie 27
Wharton

Charles 28
David 22
Sarah 28
Wheatley
  Marsey 25
Wheatly
  Elisabeth 80
  John 80
  Richard 38
Wheeler
  Basil 6, 43
  Bennett 53
  Charles 11, 65, 109
  Edward 5
  Elisabeth 103
  George 57
  Henry 109
  Ignatius 8, 30, 53, 60
  Jane 53
  John 57, 65
  Mary 11, 65
  Nansey 65
  Rebecca 6
  Rebeccah 43
  Richard 56
  Robert 103
  Ruth 56
  Samuel 103
  Thomas 11, 109
  William 56, 103
Wheland
  James 87
  William 1, 32, 87
Wheller
  Roger 96
Whelsh
  John 21
Whetstone
  Katharine 106
Whichcote
  Martha 16, 58
  Paul 16, 58
Whiett
  Stephen 22
Whitaker
  Alexander 31
  Henry 31
  Robert 31
  Susanna 31
Whitby
  William 23
White
  Edward 18, 48
  Elisabeth 79
  Henry 87
  John 40, 48, 51, 79, 81
  Mary 52
  Richard 39
  Samuel 29, 40, 94
  Stephen 22
  Thomas 11, 82, 101
  William 70, 87, 90
  William W. 100
Whiteford
  Hugh 37
Whitely
  Arthur 15, 32, 33, 65
Whitesides
  Rebecca 20
  Robert 20
Whittington
  Isaac 70
  John 52, 71
  Mary 93
  Mary King 35
  S. 91, 105
  Southey 70
  Southing 70
  Stevenson 100, 108, 109
  William 35
Whorton
  Henmon 92

Wickes
   John 27, 58, 72, 74, 105
   Sarah 74
Wickham
   Henry 34
   Samuel 34
Wicks
   Samuel 72
Wiesenthal
   Charles 6
   Christoph 27
Wilcoxon
   Thomas 59, 60
Wilder
   John 3, 53
Wilkens
   Bartin 25
Wilkins
   Bartens 57
   Honour 78
   John 26
   Joseph 78
   Samuel 85
   Thomas 22, 57
   William 43
Wilkinson
   Alexander 39
   William 8, 26
Willcox
   Michael 87
Willet
   William 31
Willett
   Charles 60
   Edward 31
   Isaac 60
   Mary 31
   Ninian 21, 31, 60
   Thomas 21, 97
   William 31
Williams
   Aaron 30, 59
   Barbarah 104
   Barbry 95
   Baruch 96
   Basil 34
   Benjamin 39, 78
   Elie 30
   Elisabeth Owen 5
   Elisha Owen 5
   Ezekiel 93
   Henry 78
   James 36
   John 67, 78, 82, 95
   Joshua 78
   Oth. Hold. 30
   Philip 100
   Planner 9, 40, 41, 85,
     91
   Rachel 96
   Sarah 46, 53, 100
   Thomas 96, 104
   Towen 5
   William 5, 104
Williamson
   Alexander 76, 103
   Jean 58
   John 6, 17
   Meliscent 84
Willin
   George 86
   Mary 86
   Thomas 86
Willing
   Thomas 86
Willis
   John 87
   Joshua 81
   Nathaniel 88
   Rachel 87
   Richard 14, 77, 87
   Robberd 107

Tobias 103
   William 107
Williss
   Richard 16, 58
Willoughby
   John 2
   Margaret 109
   Rachel 2
   William 109
Willson
   Christopher 30
   James 92
   John 5, 29, 96
   Rebeccah 47
   Richard 5, 12, 48
   Susanna 30
   Thomas 30
   William 33, 47
Wilmer
   James 67
   John Lambert 57
Wilmore
   Simon 57
Wilpper
   Benjamin 71
   Mary 71
Wilson
   Abraham 73
   Ann 108
   Benkid 75
   Betty 51
   Cordelia 36
   Cordelia William 83
   D. 18, 42, 102, 107, 108
   Daniel 2
   George 57, 65, 102, 109
   Henry 56
   J. 74
   James 23, 26, 36, 72,
     88, 89, 106
   John 10, 31, 36, 37, 47,
     48, 59, 71, 72, 73,
     74, 91
   Joseph 15, 53
   Mary 57
   Rachel 72
   Richard 46, 73
   Robert 108
   Samuel 7, 73
   Sarah 72, 106
   Sinha 38
   Thomas 36, 108
   William 37, 71, 95, 108
Wilton
   James 102
Wimsatt
   John 54
   Robert 54
Wimson
   George 59
Winchester
   Isaac 48
Winder
   John 85
   William 26, 48, 50, 61,
     70, 91
Windser
   James 35
Wing
   James 25, 67
Wingate
   John 50, 91, 99
Winser
   James 49
Winstanley
   John 107
Winter
   John 23
   William 62
Winwright
   Nowry 51
Wirckworth

Sarah 6
   William 6
Wirt
   Henrietta 106
   Jacob 103, 106
   Jaspar 106
Wise
   Bridget 14, 16
   Matthew 104
   Samuel 102
   William 54
Wist
   Stephen 45
Witchol
   Joseph 55
Witherow
   William 34
Wolf
   Paulish 55
Wood
   Ann 41
   Benjamin 53
   Edward 53, 96
   Elisabeth 53
   John 36
   Joseph 34
   Leah 40, 41
   Leonard 90, 96
   Levi 40, 41
   Martha 40, 41
   William 40, 41
Woodard
   Benjamin 65, 87, 99,
     100, 101
Woodeson
   Elisabeth 73
Woodgate
   John 82
Woodland
   Abraham 16
   Blackledge 36
   Cassandra 27
   Elisabeth 36
   John 100
   Jonathon 27, 36, 37
   Richard 100
Woodshier
   John 73
Woodward
   Benjamin 11, 18
   Elisabeth 38
   John 13
   Priscilla 44, 79
   Thomas 44
   William 7, 15, 44, 79
Woolf
   Frances 53
Woolford
   Charles 62
   David Peterkin 66
   James 32
   John 32, 99
   L. 85
   Levin 32, 62, 99
   Mary Ann 62
   Robert 32, 99
   Roger 86
   Stevens 66, 100
   Thomas 32
   William 32, 99
Woolsey
   George 71
Wooters
   Hannah 59
Woott
   U. 21
Wootten
   Benjamin 88
Wootters
   Shadrack 59
Wootton
   T. Spricht 29

T. Sprigg 35
Work
  Thomas 94
Worman
  Hannah 96
Worrel
  Simon 22
Worrell
  Priscilla 22, 77
  Priscillah 40
  Simon 22, 77
  William 22
Worten
  Thomas 21
Worth
  Jonathon 74
Worthington
  Brice B. 79
  Catharine 52
  Charles 7
  Elisabeth 52
  John 7, 15
  Nicholas 44, 52
  Samuel 7, 84
  Thomas 24, 79, 84
  Vachel 7
  William 21
Wotters
  Jonathon 59
  Shaderick 59
Wright
  Amos 63
  Archibald 39, 57, 74
  E. 98
  Edmund 10
  Edward 18
  Gowen 85
  Henry 11
  Jacob 10, 65, 66
  James 1, 67, 81, 108
  John 12
  Joseph 10, 37, 63
  Levin 10
  Mary 59
  Philip 63
  Rebecca 63
  Roger 1
  Sarah 1, 65, 108
  Sarrah 92
  Solomon 106
  Sophia 37, 59
  Sophiah 92
  Turbutt 42, 48
  William 1, 10, 37, 65,
    92
Wrightstone
  James 10
Wroth
  James 23, 57, 77, 83
  Kinovin 97
  Kinvin 77
  Kinwin 40
Wyatt
  Anne 49
  Caleb 4, 36, 49
  Jehu 4
  William 4
Wye
  Catharine 95
  John 95
Wynn
  John 31
Wyvill
  Marmaduke 79

Yardley
  Mary 97
Yates
  Donaldson 9
  Theophilus 8, 23
Yeates

Donaldson 57, 58, 67, 73
Yieldhale
  William 52
Young
  Daniel 28
  Elender 5
  Jacob 34
  John 23, 64
  Joseph 69
  Notley 63
  Peter 21, 31, 60
  Rebecca 3
  Robert 3, 13, 30
  Thomas 5
  William 56, 84
Younger
  John 8
  John Abell 54, 104
  Joseph 8

Zegen
  Dewalt 95

Heritage Books by Vernon L. Skinner, Jr.:

Abstracts of the Administration Accounts of the Prerogative Court of Maryland, 1718–1724, Libers 1–5

Abstracts of the Administration Accounts of the Prerogative Court of Maryland, 1724–1731: Libers 6–10

Abstracts of the Administration Accounts of the Prerogative Court of Maryland, 1731–1737: Libers 11–15

Abstracts of the Administration Accounts of the Prerogative Court of Maryland, 1737–1744: Libers 16–20

Abstracts of the Administration Accounts of the Prerogative Court of Maryland, 1744–1750: Libers 21–28

Abstracts of the Administration Accounts of the Prerogative Court of Maryland, 1750–1754: Libers 29–36

Abstracts of the Administration Accounts of the Prerogative Court of Maryland, 1754–1760: Libers 37–45

Abstracts of the Administration Accounts of the Prerogative Court of Maryland, 1760–1764, Libers 46–51

Abstracts of the Administration Accounts of the Prerogative Court of Maryland, 1764–1768, Libers 52–58

Abstracts of the Administration Accounts of the Prerogative Court of Maryland, 1768–1771, Libers 59–66

Abstracts of the Administration Accounts of the Prerogative Court of Maryland, 1771–1777, Libers 67–74

Abstracts of the Balance Books of the Prerogative Court of Maryland: Libers 2 and 3, 1755–1763

Abstracts of the Balance Books of the Prerogative Court of Maryland: Libers 4 and 5, 1763–1770

Abstracts of the Balance Books of the Prerogative Court of Maryland: Libers 6 and 7, 1770–1777

Abstracts of the Inventories and Accounts of the Prerogative Court of Maryland, 1674–1678, 1699–1703

Abstracts of the Inventories and Accounts of the Prerogative Court of Maryland, 1679–1686

Abstracts of the Inventories and Accounts of the Prerogative Court of Maryland, 1685–1701

Abstracts of the Inventories and Accounts of the Prerogative Court of Maryland, 1688–1698

Abstracts of the Inventories and Accounts of the Prerogative Court of Maryland, 1697–1700: Libers 16, 17, 18, 19, 19½A, 19½B

Abstracts of the Inventories and Accounts of the Prerogative Court of Maryland, 1699–1704: Libers 20–24

Abstracts of the Inventories and Accounts of the Prerogative Court of Maryland, 1708–1711: Libers 29, 30, 31, 32A, 32B

Abstracts of the Inventories and Accounts of the Prerogative Court of Maryland, 1711–1713: Libers 32C, 33A, 33B, 34

Abstracts of the Inventories and Accounts of the Prerogative Court of Maryland, 1712–1716: Libers 35A, 35B, 36A, 36B, 36C

Abstracts of the Inventories and Accounts of the Prerogative Court of Maryland, 1715–1718: Libers 37A, 37B, 37C, 38A, 38B, 39A, 39B, 39C

Abstracts of the Inventories and Accounts of the Prerogative Court of Maryland, 1699–1708: Libers 25–28

Abstracts of the Inventories of the Prerogative Court of Maryland, 1718–1720

Abstracts of the Inventories of the Prerogative Court of Maryland, 1720–1724

Abstracts of the Inventories of the Prerogative Court of Maryland, 1724–1727

Abstracts of the Inventories of the Prerogative Court of Maryland, 1726–1729

Abstracts of the Inventories of the Prerogative Court of Maryland, 1728–1734

Abstracts of the Inventories of the Prerogative Court of Maryland, 1733–1738

Abstracts of the Inventories of the Prerogative Court of Maryland, 1738–1744

Abstracts of the Inventories of the Prerogative Court of Maryland, 1744–1748

Abstracts of the Inventories of the Prerogative Court of Maryland, 1748–1751

Abstracts of the Inventories of the Prerogative Court of Maryland, 1751–1756

Abstracts of the Inventories of the Prerogative Court of Maryland, 1755–1760

Abstracts of the Inventories of the Prerogative Court of Maryland, 1760–1763

Abstracts of the Inventories of the Prerogative Court of Maryland, 1763–1766

Abstracts of the Inventories of the Prerogative Court of Maryland, 1766–1769

Abstracts of the Inventories of the Prerogative Court of Maryland, 1769–1772

Abstracts of the Inventories of the Prerogative Court of Maryland, 1772–1774

Abstracts of the Inventories of the Prerogative Court of Maryland, 1774–1777

Abstracts of the Proceedings of the Orphans' Court of Sussex County, Delaware:
Libers 1, 2, 3, 4, A (1708–1709, 1728–1777)

Abstracts of the Proprietary Records of the Provincial Court of Maryland, 1637–1658

Abstracts, Worcester County, Maryland Estate Docket, 1742–1820

Colonial Families of the Eastern Shore of Maryland,
Vernon L. Skinner, Jr. and F. Edward Wright
Volumes: 10, 18, 20 and *22*
Other Wills in the Prerogative Court for Somerset and Worcester Counties, 1664–1775

Provincial Families of Maryland, Volume 1

Somerset County Will Books, 1750–1772

Somerset County Wills, 1667–1748: Liber EB9

Somerset County Wills, 1770–1777 and 1675–1710: Liber EB5

Supplement Abstracts Inventories and Accounts, Prerogative Court, 1691–1706

Worcester County Inventories and Accounts, 1694–1742: Inventory Book JW15

Worcester County Wills: Will Book MH3, 1666–1742